ENGLISH METRISTS

ENGLISH METRISTS

BEING A SKETCH OF ENGLISH PROSODICAL
CRITICISM FROM ELIZABETHAN TIMES
TO THE PRESENT DAY

BY

T. S. OMOND

Phaeton Press
New York
1968

Library Of Congress Catalogue Card Number 68-15694

PUBLISHED BY PHAETON PRESS 1968

PREFACE

I HAVE long wished to recast into one volume the two original parts of my *English Metrists*, bringing also the record down to date, and I owe the present opportunity of doing so to the good offices of the Oxford University Press Delegates.

I believe I may still claim that this book is the only one which examines in detail the attempts of those who have sought to explain the nature of English metre, and traces the progress of sounder views about our verse-structure ; nor do I know of any book dealing similarly with the prosodists of any European nation.

The survey is carried down to the end of 1920. Temporary ill-health has prevented my acquainting myself so fully as before with the periodical literature of this country and of America, and I can only hope that no contribution of outstanding importance has escaped my attention.

If this result has been attained, it is due in part to the kindness of correspondents who have supplied me with information, and among these I must this time mention particularly Professor James Wilson Bright of Baltimore, U.S.A., himself a distinguished metrist, who has aided me with guidance through regions which he knows so well.

It is hardly necessary now to repeat my advice to American and other ' out-landish ' authors to send copies of their works to the British Museum Library, since most of such books at present have London publishers ; but the advice, given on grounds of international comity, may be not wasted upon writers in the periodical press.

The price of this volume has been kept as low as is possible in these disastrous days for book-production, with intent to bring it within the purchasing power of students, for whose use it is primarily intended. I trust that its labour of love may prove of assistance to those interested in the problems with which it deals.

T. S. OMOND.

CONTENTS

CHAPTER I

CHAPTER II

CHAPTER III

CHAPTER IV

CHAPTER V

CHAPTER I

FAINT BEGINNINGS

(1500–1700)

ENGLISH metrical criticism practically begins with the
Elizabethans. Nothing before that date needs notice here.
Aldhelm and Bede wrote on Latin verse, nor during the long
Centuries when our language was making need we expect to
find self-conscious analysis. Creation must precede criticism,
since the critic does not invent rules, only infers them from
practice. Even the work of Chaucer and his followers originated no school of grammarians. The earliest separate
treatise on English verse seems to have been the little tract of
George Gascoigne (1575).[1] Books on the subject-matter of
poetry—figures, tropes, and the like—were not wanting prior
to this date, but I do not know any of these which contains an
actual reference to verse-structure.

Even before Gascoigne wrote, however, a movement had
arisen which threatened to revolutionize our verse entirely.
A serious attempt was made to substitute for native measures
the " quantitative " structures of ancient Greece and Rome.[2]
The beginnings of our metrical analysis synchronized with and
were powerfully affected by this attempt. Nearly every subsequent writer on English prosody has referred to its history,
and has spent much time comparing English with Classical
verse in respect of form. Convenience, therefore, as well as
chronological accuracy, requires us to deal with this movement first. It will be possible to trace it to its early conclusion
before returning to begin with George Gascoigne the more
familiar and orthodox developments of regular prosody.

A reference in the *Scholemaster* (Arber's Reprint, p. 144) of
Roger Ascham (1515–68) shows us, some forty years before
Gascoigne wrote, a band of young students at St. John's

[1] For particulars of this and all books mentioned later see chronological lists in Appendices. Wherever possible, my references are to
the cheap and handy volumes known as " *Arber's Reprints* ", which can
be obtained from Constable & Co., Westminster.

[2] For these see (besides many other sources) my *Study of Metre*,
Chap. III.

College, Cambridge, prominent among them Ascham himself
and Cheke (who later " taught Cambridge, and King Edward,
Greek "), discussing the possibility of remodelling English
metre. These men were scholars, but not pedants. Cheke
discarded traditional pronunciation of ancient Greek, substituting that convenient if barbarous vocalization which still
parts us from Continental Hellenists. And he and his com-
peers were equally ready to abandon " rude beggarly ryming,
brought first into Italie by Goths and Huns," and devise other
forms of verse.[1]

Ascham recalls longingly his " sweet time spent at Cambridge," and talks with such men as Cheke and " mine old
friend Mr. Watson " (Thomas Watson, not the Elizabethan
poet of same name, but the prelate who took active part in the
ecclesiastical troubles of his day, and was probably at the time
this was written a prisoner in the Tower), and quotes a couplet
by the latter which may rank as the earliest specimen of
English " hexameter " verse known to us—

All travelers do gladly report great praise of Ulysses,

For that he knew many men's manners, and saw many cities.[2]

No doubt Cheke and Ascham taught orally to their pupils the
expediency of adopting quantitative measures. Their teaching
spread, and became fashionable. By the end of the Sixteenth
Century's third quarter, a society calling itself " Areopagus "
—of which Sidney, Dyer, and Drant [3] were leaders, Spenser
and Abraham Fraunce pupils—was making an earnest attempt
in this direction, and the *Arcadia* of Sidney (probably written
about 1580) contains many pieces framed on Classic models.[4]

[1] Sir Thos. More is said to have favoured the movement, and
Cheke's friend Sir Thos. Smith probably help d. About the same
time Ronsard and others made a similar attempt in France, while the
work of Trissino in Italy was a little earlier, and may have inspired
the others. At any rate, the idea was afoot, and scholars in all nations
soon caught it up.

[2] *Ibid*, p. 73. The symbols of quantity are supplied by me, here and
elsewhere.

[3] Neither Dyer nor Drant left anything to quote in the present connection. The others will be referred to again later.

[4] The late Dr. Whewell (Macmillan's Magazine, August, 1882) speaks
of the " great mass of elegiacs " written by *Surrey*. Is not this a slip
for *Sidney* ?

What was the aim and meaning of this attempt ? We read
lines like Watson's with a smile at their halting accents, and
probably condemn them as doggerel. But this is to prejudge
matters. The halting accents were part of the scheme, or at
least not inconsistent with it. The scheme itself was no
ignoble one. Enthusiastic over the lately rediscovered Greek
literature, these men found it recorded that the Romans,
already possessing metres of their own, threw them aside on
becoming acquainted with Greek verse, and adopted the
rhythms and measures of the latter. Why should not England
do likewise ? Our language was still rude, chaotic, formless.
The glories so soon to be revealed were hidden. It was not
unnatural to suppose that for us, too, salvation lay in following
Greek guidance. Chaucer was our Livius Andronicus ; might
not our Lucretius, Catullus, Virgil come with the new measures ?
If a dream, it was greatly conceived ; a magnificent ideal,
however impossible to realise. We must comprehend its intention before criticising its methods.

Essentially, however, it was a scholars' movement. Pride
of caste reinforced love of letters. Inception and execution
alike rested with them ; they alone had the keys of the new
knowledge. Any ignorant person can " easily reckon up
fourteen syllables, and easily stumble on every ryme " ; but
only the learned can " search out true quantity in every foot
and syllable ".[1] This was the weakness as well as strength of
their position. Sometimes, indeed, they go further, and seem
to claim not merely to discover but actually to create quantity,
as if it depended on a master's *ipse dixit*. But, rightly understood, the task of inquiring whether our language might be
capable of receiving rules of quantity like the Classic was an
enterprise not unworthy to be attempted. There perhaps was
no *a priori* reason to assume its impossibility. We can be
wise after the event, but it is not so clear that they should
have seen the issue beforehand. At any rate they thought the
attempt worth making, and some of the best minds in England
agreed with them.

It does not seem to have been noticed that no less a critic
than Ben Jonson, quite late in life, upheld this view. His
English Grammar (1640), written in old age, and published
after his death, contains a passage so clear and pertinent that

[1] *Scholemaster*, p. 146.

it may be quoted in full. I transcribe *verbatim et literatim*, which was needless with Ascham, whose spelling is quite erratic. " Here order would require to speake of the *Quantitie* of *Syllabes* [syllables], their special *Prerogative* among the *Latines* and *Greekes :* whereof so much as is constant, and derived from *Nature*, hath beene handled already. The other which growes by *Position*, and placing of letters, as yet (not through *default* of our *Tongue*, being able enough to receive it, but our owne *carelessnesse*, being negligent to give it) is ruled by no Art. The principall cause whereof seemeth to be this ; because our *Verses* and *Rythmes* [rhymes] (as it is almost with all other people, whose *Language* is spoken at this day) are *naturall*, and such whereof Aristotle speaketh, ἐκ τῶν αὐτοσχεδιασματῶν, that is, made of a *naturall*, and *voluntarie* composition, without regard to the *Quantitie* of *Syllabes*.

" This would ask a larger time and field, then [than] is here given, for the examination : but since I am assigned to this Province ; that it is the *lot* of my *age*, after thirty yeares conversation with men, to be *elementarius Senex* [an old man teaching rudiments] : I will promise, and obtaine so much of my selfe, as to give, in the heele of the booke, some spurre and incitement to that which I so reasonably seeke." Not, however, that he wishes to abolish " the *vulgar* and *practis'd* way of making, ... but, to the end our *Tongue* may be made equall to those of the renowned Countries, *Italy* and *Greece*, touching this particular ". (Chap. VI.) [1]

The promise thus given was not fulfilled. But its giving proves, both that Jonson intended writing on prosody—which his namesake the Lexicographer blames him for not doing—and that he was prepared to discuss the principles of English quantity. It indicates acceptance of the " Classical " view-point, and suggests a rational and plausible explanation of the phenomena. Wherein was the explanation defective ? Why, in other words, did the attempt in question fail ? That it did fail is evident. English poets would have none of it. Spenser, Greene, and Campion dallied with it in their youth,

---

[1] In his lively verses, " A fit of rhyme against rhyme,' Jonson pours scorn on

> Vulgar languages that want
> Words, and sweetness, *and be scant*
> *Of true measure. (Underwoods.)*

but soon threw it aside. The course of our literature was not diverted into this channel. To realise the causes of this want of success is essential to a due appreciation of the attempt.

These causes have been examined by several writers, particularly by the late W. J. Stone in a pamphlet (1898) to which I shall have cause to refer again, most of whose criticism is as sound as it is brilliant.[1] But in one respect he and others seem to go astray. They do not realise the vast changes which have passed over our pronunciation. Stone judges each syllable by his own ear, and fearlessly proclaims " false quantities " where this test finds fault.[2] Such judgement is somewhat hasty. The rules which Sidney and Drant prepared for the " Areopagus " have not come down to us ; with others, which have survived, Stone seems to have been unacquainted. On many points they differ from his own rules, and so far invalidate his too confident censure. It need not be contended that they are correct in themselves, or even always self-consistent ; but they do appeal to sound, not to spelling, and they show that many words were sounded differently then to what they are now. It will not do, therefore, to judge these verses wholly by our ears.

The causes of failure I should myself say were three—two technical, one general. The first was their too lax view of quantity, especially that depending on vowel-sound. They believed and asserted, as do many English grammarians, that most of our vowels are vague and indeterminate, and treated the syllables formed by these as " common "—long in one line, short in the next. But such a view is fatal to quantitative verse. A few exceptions are permissible, but the great majority of syllables must be known and settled if the reader is to follow the metre. When words like *squeak, vain, coy,* are made short, what possibility is there of an intelligible system ? Nor were they better advised as regards consonants. Phono-

---

[1] Stone's principles have been developed by Mr. Bridges in various productions, for a list of which see Appendix A.

[2] Thus Stone finds fault with *my* being accounted short, forgetting that alternative vocalization which survives in the barrister's " My Lud ". Similarly, the two last syllables of *testify, prophesy,* &c., are usually short with the Elizabethans, and so old people sometimes pronounce them. Had this verse taken root, our quantities would have become stereotyped, and perhaps *love* would have still rhymed with *prove ;* the vowel in *love* and *loving* was clearly a long one to Elizabethan ears.

graphy was more to them than phonetics. The " doubled
consonant fallacy " [1] for the most part held them fast, though
there were protests even then. Their unsettled spelling let
them play tricks to the eye, which carried no conviction to
the ear, the only true judge. The attempt was thus ruined at
the outset by faults of execution. Making every allowance
for changes of pronunciation, it is still obvious that they had
no proper feeling for, no real sense of, the quantity they
professed to observe.

The second technical reason relates to " halting accents ".
It was open to them to treat English accent in two ways,
either making it coincide with quantity, or frankly opposing
the two. Stone holds they should have done the latter. He
maintains—as Spedding and others before him—that such
opposition was essential to Latin verse, and that no metre not
reproducing this can claim to follow Classic type. Leaving
this point for scholars to settle, we may at least say that
choice was imperative. They were bound to make the
principle of their measure clear. This they failed to do. We
never know what was their ideal, whether the accents in
particular lines are merely " halting " or designedly " combative ". One writer is credited with studying reconciliation,
another with delighting in bold opposition. These opinions
of critics show how tentative was the whole undertaking.
And, in so artificial an attempt, uncertainty was ruinous.
A native verse might have been left to work out its own
methods ; an exotic like this must have them defined *ab extra*.
Imagine the Romans ignorant of the true nature of Greek
quantity and Greek verse-structure ; what success would have
attended their enterprise ? The Elizabethans courted defeat
by uncertainty of aim.

These two causes—which will be illustrated presently by
examples—were sufficient themselves to ensure failure. But
a third more general and more unavoidable one remains. In
stating this I differ *toto caelo* from Stone. The verse which he
recommends I hold impossible in English.. It proceeds on
a radically false assumption that syllables constitute the
whole basis of our verse, that strict feet—whether framed by
accent or by quantity is immaterial—explain the secret of our
metre. No true English poetry has been written on these

[1] Stone's pamphlet, p. 29.

assumptions. " Which feet ", says an old writer truly, " we have not, nor as yet never went about to frame, the nature of our language and words not permitting it." [1] When our poets are run away with by false theories—when, like Sidney and Spenser at this time or Coleridge and Southey later, they write by rule instead of ear, counting syllables and constructing " feet " instead of singing as their souls bid them—then their magic ceases, and they write verses no better than those of the critic and the poetaster. Apart from this, any attempt to separate accent, quantity, and metrical stress habitually in English is unlikely to succeed. Our ears are trained to combine them, and accent is so all-powerful in English speech that it does not easily assume a subordinate position. But the Elizabethan attempt was foredoomed to failure, apart from such secondary matters and in spite of the nobility of its aim, by the fact that it sinned against the genius of English poetry. It took no account of pause, no account of time underlying syllable-structure. An artificial and derived verse might possibly have superseded our native measures, had it been based on principles which appealed to us and could be verified by our ears. Quantity must have so appealed to the Latin ear. This pseudo-Classic attempt was based on principles foreign to our speech and music, and deserved, not indeed ignorant scorn, but the rejection which it unhesitatingly received.

In the light of these principles, it should now be possible to judge any sample of quantitative verse we may come across. As no complete account [2] has ever been given of this curious side-eddy in our literary history, it seems desirable to enumerate the writers who figured in it, carrying down the tale to its ending before going back to other work of the Elizabethan age. Beyond a few specimen verses, the exhumation of these venerable curiosities may be left to inquisitive students, there being little beyond historical interest in their dry and withered limbs or lineaments.

---

[1] *Puttenham* (1589), *Arber's Reprint*, p. 222.
[2] The fullest known to me is that of Prof. Elze in his tract *Der englische Hexameter* (Dessau, 1867), the ablest that of Mr. Stone, not the least valuable by Mr. McKerrow in the *Modern Language Quarterly* for December 1901 and April 1902, the latest known to me by Dr. Konrad Wölk in *Normannia* (Berlin, 1909).

The *Toxophilus* (1545) of Ascham contains several lines and parts of lines, the earliest specimens of this "new verse" which have reached us, except Watson's already quoted. Most are translations, and those from Greek iambics read smoothly enough, e.g.

> It is my wont alwaies my bow with me to bear.

(I scan as seems intended, *my* being pronounced short). His hexameters are scarcely so good. Observance of Classic rule makes him shorten two long vowels in

> Quite through a door flew a shaft with a brass head ;

but why is *I* short twice in

> Eight good shafts have I shot sith I came, each one with a fork head ?

A better line is this from Callimachus—

> Both merie songs and good shooting delighteth Apollo,

allowing the grammar to pass muster ; but if

> Stop the beginnings

be meant for a dactyl and spondee, the last word is hopeless. He contends himself that our language "doth not well receive the nature of Heroic [*i.e.* hexameter] verse", because it "doth rather stumble than stand upon monosyllables", and therefore, "*Carmen Exametrum* [note the spelling, and compare our common *Eureka*] doth rather trot and hobble than run smoothly in our English tongue" (*Scholemaster*, pp. 145–6). Here he voices a complaint which has been repeated to our own day, though other writers find the dactyl natural and indigenous in English.[1] Something, perhaps, is due to the practitioner ; Ascham's attempts at ordinary triple-time verse are not very happy. In hexameters, at all events, he was a pioneer, and it would be unreasonable to expect any great smoothness or success. What does seem extraordinary, and from any point of view unfortunate, is that in these initial experiments by a respected teacher the basis of English quantity was not clearly laid down and illustrated for future use.

---

[1] *e. g.* Puttenham, *ut supra*, p. 137 ; Stanihurst, and others.

From Ascham to Sir Philip Sidney, is to pass from school-master to poet. By far the larger part of the verses scattered throughout *Arcadia* is in ordinary metres. But the Classic attempts are numerous, and comprise hexameters, elegiacs, sapphics, phaleuciacs, asclepiads. The last-mentioned is a pretty piece, beginning—

‾ ‾ | ‾ ‿ ‿ | ‾ | ‾ ‿ ‿ | ‾ ‿ |
O sweet woods, the delight of solitarinesse !

In this line the *a* of " solitarinesse " must have had natural length. But in other pieces we have such startling solecisms as *Hēraclītus, shăll Ĭ sĕe* (dactyl), *tĕll mĕ thў* (dactyl), *shīnīng in harness, būt Oh*, etc., while *bĕ, bў, dŏ*, and the like meet us continually. *Ērrand, păllace* [sic], *pĭttie, pŏssible*, explain themselves, but what can be said to justify *hŏnour* and *dēsert ?* These last come from " Dorus and Zelmane," the longest piece in *Arcadia*. Sidney was naturally a singer, and some of his Classic verses are not unpleasing, especially the " rhyming iambics " of the " Hymn to Apollo," which reads naturally as English metre—

" Apollo great, whose beams the greater world do light,
And in our little world do clear our inward sight."

But to show how for the most part his lines " halt ill on Roman feet," I will quote one translated quatrain from " Certaine Sonnets ", asking the reader to notice how the first syllable of *woman* is short in the first line and long in the third, while the second syllable of the same word is mis-scanned in the first line ; other apparent false quantities are explained by Latin rules, but if *untō* is long, why is *dŏ* short ?

‾ ‿ ‿ | ‾ ‿ | ‾ ‿ | ‾ ‿ ‿ | ‾ ‿ | ‾ |
Unto nobody, my woman saith, she'd rather a wife be

Than to myself, not though Jove grew a suitor of hers.

‾ ‿ ‿ | ‾ ‿ | ‾ | ‾ ‿ ‿ | ‾ ‿ ‿ | ‾ ‿ |
These be her words ; but a woman's words to a love that is eager

‾ ‾ | ‾ ‿ ‿ | ‾ ‿ | ‾ ‿ ‿ | ‾ ‿ |
In wind's or water's stream do require to be writ.

The rhythm of this is surely as halting as the metre is faulty ; yet this is no unfair specimen of what seems to have satisfied the Areopagite ear.[1]

An early follower on these lines was one James Sandford, a specimen of whose work will be found in Appendix A. As

[1] Sidney's ' *Defence of Poesie* ' will be noticed later among prosodies.

nothing is known of this writer except as author of one book, we may pass him by at present and turn to a more notable name.[1]

Gabriel Harvey was some ten years older than Sidney. He stood aloof from the Penshurst school, vaunting his independence, and actually claiming to be the " inventor of the English hexameter " (*Four Letters*, 1592 ; third letter).[2] A Cambridge graduate of considerable parts and much self-conceit, he was evidently looked up to by his fellow-Cantab Spenser, to whom he was senior by six or seven years. Some letters which passed between them in the year 1580 [3] show Harvey assuming quite a magisterial pose. He talks of Sidney and Dyer helping " our new famous enterprise ", believes " mine own rules and precepts " not greatly repugnant to theirs, asks Spenser to " commend me to good Mr. Sidney's judgement ". He thinks nothing can be done till they have got a settled orthography. When Spenser complains that accent " yawneth and gapeth ill-favouredly ", and quaintly compares the word *carpenter*, with mid-syllable lengthened, to " a lame gosling that draweth one leg after her ", while *Heaven*, in one syllable, is " like a lame dog that holds up one leg "— Harvey is ready with his answer. We must not blindly follow Classic precedent. " The Latin is no rule for us." " The vulgar and natural mother Prosody alone maketh quantity . . . . position neither maketh short nor long in our tongue, but as far as we can get her good leave." That is, he confounded accent with quantity. We must not " devise any counterfeit fantastical accent of our own." He will not allow *carpēnter*, nor such words as *majēsty, royălty, sciēnces, facŭlties, suddēnly, certāinly, merchāndise*. But this is to cut away the roots of

---

[1] The prosodic discussions in *The Mirror for Magistrates* (1577) are carefully analysed by Prof. Saintsbury in his *History of English Prosody*, Vol. II, pp. 189 seq., but there seems little available for our purpose. One of the authors, Thomas Blenerhasset, is believed the first critic to call our most common type of verse *iambic*.

[2] See Appendix A, 1580. Recent critics generally identify Harvey with the Penshurst school : I know not on what authority. Attempts have also been made to prove that he did not actually claim to have " invented " the hexameter in English, but his words seem to me to bear no other construction. Mr. Spingarn (Appendix A, 1899) in his study of this epoch places Harvey outside the Areopagus.

[3] Accepted now as genuine, though Nash hinted doubts ! Spenser is " Signor Immerito " ; compare *Shepherd's Calendar* (preface).

quantitative verse. If his contention be right, it is fatal to the system he seeks to establish. The Sidneian school was at least consistent—or tried to be—though consistency led to untenable positions. Harvey's boastful superiority issued in mere *ignoratio elenchi*. Accentuation and quantitative structure are clearly not the same things, though he may be right in protesting against their separation. His confusion between them shows how indefinite and unreasoned were his ideas. So far as he followed a path of his own, it led him up a blind alley.

Spenser's attempts survive only in this correspondence, as he did not reprint them with his poems. His "*Iambicum Trimetrum*" is certainly not better than others of the kind, the very first word, *Unhăppie*, containing a clear false quantity. Of his elegiacs one couplet may suffice—

> See yee the blind-folded pretie God, that feathered Archer,
>
> Of lovers' miseries which maketh his bloodie game ?

Prĕttў is good, if he had not thought it necessary to write it with one *t*; but to spell *ye* with two vowels, and then sound it short, is truly grotesque. Was the first syllable of *feathered* pronounced long, the first of *maketh* short, as in Scotch? For *lōvers* see before. Spenser undoubtedly took these attempts seriously, if the letters are genuine; but we may rejoice that he soon abandoned them, and went back to his "old use of toying with rhymes." As to Harvey's own contributions, they are as incorrect as Spenser's, and much less interesting. What an atrocious line is

> Not the like Trinitie again, save only the Trinitie above all.

Besides crude elision, we have *lĭke*, *Trīnitie*, surely indefensible. In another piece the diphthong *æ* is first long, then short, in the same line. His best known attempt begins—

> What might I call this Tree? *A Laurell?* O bonny Laurell:
>
> Needs to thy boughs will I bow this knee, and vayle my bonetto.

The wits made great fun of this *bonetto*, as ridiculous as it is incorrect in scansion. He drew a hornets' nest upon him by attacking Greene, and his critics grasped at any opportunity to sting. There must have been good in the man, since Spenser valued his friendship, and addressed him much later in a well-known sonnet. But neither his verse nor his prose writings reveal any thing admirable, and his incompetence seems to us equal to his pretentiousness. His claim to father the hexameter is but of a piece with the rest of his braggart vaunts.[1]

Another writer of the same time, who might with more justice have posed as patentee of English hexameters, was Richard Stanihurst or Stanyhurst, a Roman Catholic Anglo-Irishman of good family, resident in the Netherlands, who published at Leyden in 1582 a translation of the first four books of Virgil's *Aeneid,* with a few other pieces, forming by far the most considerable contribution yet made to the new school of verse. Harvey claims him as a pupil, but in his preface he speaks of Ascham as the inspirer of his attempt, and of his own work as a maiden book. He had, however, read Harvey's letters, and borrows from them their unfortunate confusion of accent with quantity, considering that " position " cannot " suffice against the natural dialect of English ", so that while we say *bŭckler* we must also say *swashbŭckler.* But most of Stanihurst's qualities are emphatically his own. His translation is one of the most extraordinary pieces of English ever penned. " A foul lumbering boisterous wallowing measure " Nash calls it, and this description is faint beside the reality. Rabelaisian wealth of words, piled up with apparently no sense of incongruity, is made more wonderful by magnificently eccentric spelling. He tries to show quantity by letters, writing *hobble* when long and *hobel* when short, *forrest* and *forest, flee* and *fle* [!], and so forth. This, however, does not explain why he always spells *the* as *thee, to* as *too* or *toe,* whatever their quantity. His book is a treasure-house of old English ; from it Browning perhaps pilfered some of his quaint phrases like " put case " and " dandiprat ".[2] There is vigour enough in it, but extravagance beyond words. Nash's parody is hardly a caricature—

Then did he make heaven's vault to rebound, with rounce robel hobble

Of ruffe raffe roaring, with thwick thwack thurlery bouncing.

---

[1] Some think that Sir Fulke Greville (later Lord Brooke) was an Areopagite, and Prof. Saintsbury (*History of Prosody,* Vol. II, p. 91) thinks some lines of his were meant for ' sapphics '. If they were, they are quite unrecognizable, and are certainly not quantitative.

[2] These, however, are not peculiar to Stanihurst.

Indeed much of this comes verbatim from a fragment of *Aeneid*, Book VIII, which is quite as funny. Such an attempt could not bring much credit to the cause. It is difficult to believe it serious, which however it undoubtedly was. Its madness has method. But for Harvey's misleading, Stanihurst would probably have exemplified the combative accent more thoroughly, for he not seldom does it with boldness. However uncouth the garb, there is stuff in this translation, not mere verbal padding. But the garb is too irresistibly comic to produce any effect save one of motley.

An important part of his book is the " private precepts " concerning quantity. He explains that he does not wish to " chalk out " rules for others—his prose style is as racy as his verse—but must explain certain points, else " some grammatical pullet, hacht [hatched] in Dispater his sachel, would stand clocking agaynst mee, as though hee had found an horse nest ". Accordingly he gives a list of words which he makes " common ", including *sky, sea ; mouth, your ;* all words ending in *o* ; and a host of others. He professes to write phonetically, and " would not wish thee quantitie of syllables to depend so much upon thee gaze of the eye, as thee censure of thee eare ". I infer that he meant spelling to represent sound, so that *passadge* is to be pronounced differently to *passage*, and when he writes *oaten* as *oten* we are to sound a short vowel. The wild license of his quantities, therefore, may be mainly covered by his rules ; but this only shows the absurdity of rules which actually allow such a dactyl as *the snow white* (" thee snoa whit ") ! Such monstrosities would be fatal to any verse, and perhaps in any measure Stanihurst would have been as wild.

He used hexameter mostly, though the " other Poetical Devices " appended to his volume contain a few attempts in other metres. Unlike most of his contemporaries, he held that " The Iambical quantitye relisheth soomwhat unsavourlye in oure language ", and that most other measures " sown [sound] not al so pleasinglie to the eare " as hexameter and elegiac. The first six lines of his fragment from *Aeneid* VIII give a fair idea alike of his erratic quantities and his extraordinary manner, and will show how impossible it was that such a production should recommend any new metre.[1]

[1] The book was printed abroad, and the publisher apologises for

Tw'ard Sicil is seated, toe the welken loftelye peaking,

A soil, ycleapt Liparen, from whence, with flownce furye slinging,

Stoans, and burlye bulets, lyke tamponds [?] mainlie be towring.

Under is a kennel, wheare chymneys fyrye be scorching

Of Cyclopan tosters, with rent rocks chamferye [channel-wise N.E.D.]
    sharded,

Lowd dub a dub tabering with frapping rip rap of Aetna.

'Very different was William Webbe, author of *A Discourse of English Poetrie* (1586), whose modest preface and epilogue go far to disarm criticism of the specimen verses appended to it, comprising versions of Virgil's First and Second Eclogues, a translation from Spenser, and one or two fragments. To the *Discourse* itself we shall return again. At present we need only note that Webbe, a Cambridge graduate, favoured quantitative verse, but perceived that there was no definite agreement as to the value of syllables, and appealed to the " famous and learned Laureate Masters of England " to lay down rules (preface). He sees that Latin rules may not always hold good in English (Arber's edition, pp. 68–70), but in his own experiments strives to follow them, even to elision of vowels (*me out, thou art, ye O, yea I*, etc., are thus compressed into one syllable). He is driven, however, to make " most of our monosyllables "short (p. 70), for convenience in versifying; and he notes that the pronoun *I* is always short in such verses, while the second syllable of words like *goodlie* is long.[1] We must be prepared, therefore, for such scansions, for quantities like *hĕ, shĕ, sŏ, gŏ, mў, thў, pŏssess* (duplicated consonant), *wĭllow*, etc. The result is chaotic; we find " doo " short in one line, long in the next, and must guess at the length of every monosyllable. And what can excuse *bŭsy, stŏny, lĭzard, crēdit, ēver, Amphĭon?* For the rest, his verse is painfully

possible misprints due to compositors ignorant of our language. The second edition, printed in England, differs a good deal in "ortographie", and was not revised by the author.

[1] Yet he is better than his principles in making " pretty " (*pretie* or *prettie*) a dibrach, even before mute and liquid; see second quotation following.

prosaic. Cicalas become " grasshops mournfully squeaking ".
Neither his hexameters after Virgil—

    Tityrus, happily thou lyste tumbling under a beech-tree—

nor his tradition of Spenser into " such homely Sapphic as
I could "—

    O ye Nymphs most fine who resort to this brook,
    For to bathe there your pretie breasts at all times—

ever reminds us we are reading poetry. Accent is seldom
violated, an almost unique instance being *sĕcŏnd* as an iamb.
Spelling is equally seldom distorted on purpose ; *ahlas* yields
one amusing case. With better rules of quantity, Webbe would
doubtless have written correcter verses, but they could never
have been more than a scholar's byplay. His brief excursion
into "numbers" did nothing to help the cause he had at
heart.

A more persevering experimenter comes next. Abraham
Fraunce was a cadet of the Penshurst School, and attached in
some capacity to Mary, Countess of Pembroke—" Sidney's
sister, Pembroke's mother "—to whom he dedicates his poems.
While one piece appeared in his *Lawyer's Logic* (1588), and
his *Arcadian Rhetoric* (same date) shows him a keen student
of poetry in many languages, his verse is practically contained
in two volumes, the *Lamentations of Amintas* (1587) and *The
Countess of Pembroke's Ivychurch* (1591). The first is a translation from a Latin pastoral of Thos. Watson's (*ante*, p. 2),
and Dr. Grosart accuses Fraunce of concealing this fact. But
the authorship must have been well known, and Watson's
annoyance was probably only at Fraunce's forwardness in
undertaking the work of translation. *Ivychurch* is a curious
medley, containing more pastorals, a rendering of Virgil's
Second Eclogue, a translation from Heliodorus, poems on the
Nativity, etc., of Christ, and versions of a few psalms. All
(or next to all) of these are in hexameter verse. " Abram
Fraunce was a fool with his hexameters ", remarked Ben
Jonson to Drummond of Hawthornden ; meaning, it would
seem, not that the design was foolish, but that the execution was faulty. With this verdict one is forced to concur.
There is little swing, little original music, in his lines.

His first attempts read like school exercises, beginning
thus—

Silly shepherd Corydon lov'd hartyly fayre lad Alexis.

With practice he improved, and a couplet from the dedication
of *Christ's Nativity* may illustrate his later style—

Mary the best Mother sends her best babe to a Mary,
Lord to a ladies sight, and Christ to a Christian hearing.

His pastorals sometimes run pleasantly, but there is nothing
in them to create a taste or an audience. It was the misfortune
of the " new verse " that no capable singer took it up ; this
fact alone perhaps condemns its theory. Fraunce at any rate
was not the man to force a hearing. Of rules he says nothing,
probably accepting the Areopagite tradition. Its laxness
appears in his quantities ; on the first page of the *Lamentations*
occur -*ĭng* and * īng* (both before vowels), *dĕsert*, and the usual
hĕ, bȳ, etc. On the whole, Fraunce does not seem to have
contributed much to either the theory or the practice of
"reformed" verse, sheer mediocrity being the distinctive mark
of his poems.

George Chapman, the poet, in his hymn " Ad Cynthiam "
(1594) thus scoffingly refers to quantitative verse :

> . . . as sweet poesie
> Will not be clad in her supremacie
> With those strange garments (Rome's Hexameters),
> As she is English : but in right prefers
> Our native robes (put on with skillful hands
> English heroics) to those antic garlands,
> Accounting it no meede, but mockerie,
> When her steep brows alreadie prop the skie,
> To put on start-ups, and yet let it fall.

Hexameters were now becoming not uncommon. Robert
Greene, a young poet of eminence, introduced them into
several of his works, particularly his *Mourning Garment*
(1590 ?), which among but a few verses contains two hexameter pieces. His friend Thos. Nash, championing his
memory against Harvey, included the latter and his verse in
common condemnation. Though the hexameter, he says in
Strange News (1592), be " a gentleman of an ancient house,
. . . . yet this clime of ours he cannot thrive in ; our speech is
too craggy for him to set his plough in ". Yet both Greene

and Nash could play this tune when they chose, and one
suspects Nash of the authorship of a capital line which he
professes to quote at second-hand about

> that good Gabriel Harvey
> Known to the world for a fool, and clapt i' the Fleet for a rymer.

The voluminous works of both poets may contain more such
isolated lines ; Greene's occur mostly in *Mamillia*, Part II. ;
Farewell to Folly; and the *Mourning Garment*.[1] While spirited
enough, they are lax in quantity (*ēbon, ēvery, āmorous,
Ŏ, thē*), and contribute no new element to the discussion.   As
for the bellicose productions of the Harvey-Nash controversy,
the reader who wades through these will find more to amuse
than edify—certainly as regards questions of verse-structure—
and will probably be most impressed with each champion's
limitless command of abusive Billingsgate.

The fashion spread, and some lesser lights come next under
review.   Richard Barnfield, in his *Affectionate Shepherd* (1594),
has a piece called " Helen's Rape ", of about seventy-five
hexameter lines.   Barnfield is a writer of some name, disputing
with Shakespeare himself the authorship of one famous sonnet.
But his hexameters are simply detestable !   Reckless quantities (*ādultrous, Pāris, Jŭpiter, Pēloponessus, rēconciled, Ŏn Idā*
immediately followed by *Thăt ŏn Idā*—all in the first few
lines) combine with unblushing repetition to make such lines as

> Only a Lasse, so loved a Lasse, and (alas) such a loving
> Lasse, for a while (but a while) was none such a sweet bonny Love-Lasse
> As Helen, Maenelâus loving, lov'd, lovelie a love-lasse.

(*Bŏnny* must be counted for righteousness, but *Maenelaus* as
an anapaest is truly prodigious !)   The worst Elizabethan
conceits, coupled with atrocious versification, make Barnfield's
single almost a record among many unfortunate
experiments.   Some comic lines in Peele's *Old Wives Tale*,
however, two lines of which are quoted in Appendix A, may
be said to run him pretty close.

---

[1] In the preface to Greene's *Menaphon* (1589) Nash thus renders a
well-known line—

> He that appal'd [made pallid] with lust would sail in haste to Corinthum.

The author of *Pans Pipe* (1595)—not to be confused with
Pan his Syrinx or Pipe, a prose work by William Warner
(1584)—is known to us only as " F.S." [1] He claims indulgence
as a " young beginner," and in truth needs it sorely. The
poem consists of " Three Pastorall Eglogues," introduced by
snatches of ordinary verse, to which latter the name " Pan's
Pipe " specially applies. The " Eglogues " are in pseudo-
Classic verse, hexameters, elegiacs, and what seems meant
for choriambics, of which last this is a sample—

> Winter | now wore away | cold with his hoa | ry frost.

The quantities are astounding ; *mine, great, stable, frameth,
equal, vary*, etc. One hexameter actually begins " Faustus,
infaustus," as if he did not know even Latin rules. And here
is an attempted pentameter—

> Forewarn that death is ready to strike daylie.

A set of " Sapphics " is almost worse. " F.S.'s " unfortunate
attempt must rank little above Barnfield's from any impartial
standpoint.

Less open to censure, but not in any way distinguished, is
the work of John Dickenson. His *Shepherd's Complaint*
(1596 ?), *Arisbas*, and other pieces, are in prose, with verses
interspersed, a few only in " stile Heroicall " or other Classic
metre. For the most part these are fairly correct. Quantity
is still vague (*I, the, lament, Cupid*), and accent only casually
contrasted, as in this couplet—

> What shal I doe ? shal I sue to the pow'r whom Cyprus adoreth,
>
> Love's love-worthy Mother, though not a friend to Cupid ?

He claims to have followed Sidney, Dyer, and Watson, and
speaks of his work as the " fruit of an unripe wit, done *sub-
secivis horis*." Slight as his attempts are, and without salient
points, they show how widely this form of verse had found
acceptance, and how easily young writers could have adopted
its principles had these been sound and self-consistent.

Noting as we pass that Joseph Hall, afterwards a Bishop,
in his *Virgidemiarum* (1597), Satire VI, echoes Nash's ridicule

---

[1] I believe these initials denote Francis Sabie, of whom otherwise
nothing is known. Compare note in Appendix A.

of "headstrong dactyls" and "drawling spondees", we come
next to a singular anonymous book called *The Preservation of
King Henry VII.* (1599). The unknown author of this book
was an admirer of Fraunce and Stanihurst. In a long curious
preface, where prose alternates with verse, while remarking
that Fraunce "observed a better Prosodia", he keeps special
praise for Stanihurst, who "being but an Irish man" had
translated Virgil in his own measure. He would have him,
indeed, "refile" his lines ; but

> If the poet Stanihurst yet live and feedeth on ay-er,
> I doe the man reverence, as a fine, as an exquisit Author.

Treading in his steps, he aspires to write "five books, in
rhythming [1] Hexameters," on his historical subject. Only
the first and part of the second appear to have been finished ;
they are followed by a few short pieces, while the hexameter
interpolations in the preface, the "praiers," dedications, and
addresses of various kind, considerably increase his tale of
verses. He gives his rules, too, evidently based on Stanihurst's, and sanctioning the same fatal laxity ; and alters
spelling like him, as in this line—

> My life is but a blast, I feel death woful aproching.

Ordinary verse he describes as "lines of prose, with a rythme
at the end ;" and to this "rythme-prose" or "prose-
rythme" he much prefers his

> new rythmary verses
> Lately become metricall, which are right verses of Antike,
> . . . in heroical English
> Rythmical Hexameters.

Though he admits that his "simpel" verses have their faults,
he ends with *Iamque opus exegi*—

> Here is a book that I made which pagan Jove in his anger,
> Nor steele shall outweare, nor time authentical, ever.

---

[1] *Rhythming* or rhyming is applied by this and other writers to lines
ending in mere unaccented assonance (e.g. *printer, alter ; observe,
conserve*) as well as to lines which rhyme in our sense of the term.

(Why is *ēver* long ?) The book is verse, not poetry, and the four lines to his printer illustrate the style of it so appropriately that I cannot resist quoting them.

> Print with a good letter, this booke, and carefuly Printer :
> Print each word legibill, not a word nor a sillabil alter :
> Keep points, and commas, periodes, the parenthesis observe ;
> My credit and thy reporte to defend, both safely to conserve.

It will be seen that he has some idea of opposing accent to quantity.

Two more writers belong to the Elizabethan period. A collection of poems called the *Poetical Rhapsody* (1602) contains some quantitative verses, apparently by " J. W.," which is supposed to be a pseudonym of the chief editor, Francis Davidson. They are not remarkable, except as showing how widespread was the fashion ; and they are as loose as others in quantity, e. g.

> Or love the Muses, like wantons, oft to be changing ?

Quantity and accent seem rather prettily contrasted in the following couplet, addressed to Sir Philip Sidney—

> Cambridge, worthy Philip, by this verse builds thee an altar,
> 'Gainst time and tempest, strong to abide for ever.

Some " phaleuciackes " are less satisfactory.

The last of the Elizabethans to attempt quantitative measures seriously was Thomas Campion. Long lost sight of as a poet, he is now again recognised as one of the sweetest singers of his wonderful time. To find him " Classicising " is therefore of high interest. One single piece of " sapphics " in his *First Book of Airs* (1601) is, I think, his sole actual attempt to copy Classic metres.[1] It is the last piece in that book, a sacred piece, beginning—

> Come, let us sound with melody the praises
> Of the king's King, th' omnipotent Creator ;

---

[1] Compare, however, a doubtful piece mentioned in Appendix A under his name.

and is neither better nor worse than others that have been
quoted. But in his *Observations on the Art of English Poesie*
he goes minutely into the question, and arrives at independent
results. He considers that the dactyl is " altogether against
the nature of our language", and that " passing pitiful
success " has therefore rewarded hexametrists. He thinks
iamb and trochee alone suitable, and from these constructs
eight different measures. Thus, for the sapphic measure he
would substitute stanzas like this—

> Lo, they sound ; the knights, in order armèd,
> Ent'ring threat the list, addressed to combat
> For their courtly loves ; he, he's the wonder
> Whom Eliza graceth.

Another metre, which he calls the " English March ", runs
thus—

> Greatest in thy wars,
> Greater in thy peace,
> Dread Elizabeth !

while instead of elegiacs he proposes a curious couplet alter-
nating thus—

> Constant to none, but ever false to me,
> Traitor still to love, through thy faint desires.

(The reader must scan these himself, if he thinks it necessary
and possible.) A more irregular piece of " trochaics " may be
quoted for its intrinsic merit :

> Rose-cheek'd Laura, come ;
> Sing thou smoothly with thy beauty's
> Silent music, either other
> Sweetly gracing.

This is different melody to that of the metre-mongers we have
been considering. It is poetical verse, destitute of rhyme, and
moving to strange measures, but still capable of being read
as ordinary English verse. The secret of this success is of
course his sedulous observance of accent. We read his lines
by accent, not by quantity, the latter only contributing
smoothness to their structure. How little rules of quantity
have to do with the effect may be seen by comparing any of
his poems written without observance of these rules, e.g.—

> Never weather-beaten sail more willing bent to shore,
> Never tired pilgrim's limbs affected slumber more.

To most ears the difference between this and the preceding extracts—regarded as verse, not as poetry—lies simply in length of lines, and final rhyme ; other questions of structure practically do not exist.

In his tenth chapter Campion goes minutely into rules of quantity. Admitting that quantity must be looser in English than in Latin, owing to our many monosyllables, he still professes to scan by sound—" we must esteem our syllables as we speak, not as we write "—[1] instancing words like *perfect, love-sick, ransome*, which he says are pronounced *perfet, love-sik, raunsum*. He recognises the character of doubled consonants, and makes such words " common, but more naturally short, because in their pronunciation we touch but one of those double letters, as *atend, apear, opose* ". So too when " silent and melting consonants " come together, as *adrest, oprest, retriv'd*. All this is a great advance, and puts him far before any contemporary. But he couples this with the extraordinary assertion that accent " is diligently to be observed, for chiefly by the accent in any langüage [sic] the true value of any syllable is to be measured." Nevertheless he admits length by position, giving *Trumpīngton* as an example. The inconsistency here shown runs through all his exposition. Thus, he makes the first syllables of *glory* and *spirit* equally long, because of their accentuation ; the first syllable of *holy* short, the first syllable of *diligent* long. This is surely to abandon phonetics altogether. Vowel before vowel is short, therefore *dўing, gŏing*, etc. ; yet the middle syllable of *denying* is long, because " the accent alters it ". Elision is recognised and allowed. It would be tedious to examine his rules in detail, or criticise such abnormal scansions as *fūr, wĕ, nŏ, dŏ, virtŭe, follŏw, hāving, glŏrying*. Campion's recognition of the supreme importance of accent was undoubtedly creditable to him as an English poet, but it ruined his sense of quantity. He deserted his own principles, so well expressed in the twice repeated rejection of the doubled consonant fallacy. Had he followed phonetics faithfully, he would probably have given us verses in which accent and quantity invariably coincided. To a great extent, this is the effect now produced by his verses, on ears not trained to

[1] My quotations are from Dr. Bullen's edition (1889) with its slightly modernised spelling. Of the poetical works there are several editions.

observe minute differences of sound. But the careful critic must confess that even Campion, though he came nearer than any of his predecessors to writing successful " reformed " verse, failed in the task which he had set himself by not having a true and accurate sense of phonetic quantity.

With Campion the movement practically ends. His verses were hardly distinguishable from ordinary English metre except as being unrhymed. On this point he laid special stress ; [1] on this his critics fastened and joined issue. Rhyme carried the day, and " numerous verse " suffered because it was rhymeless. During the whole remainder of the Seventeenth Century it became virtually extinct. Critical research has unearthed two or three minute exceptions to this absolute rule. A book called *Sorrow's Joy*, printed at Cambridge [2] in 1603, contains among other verses twelve hexameters by an unknown " L. G.," beginning thus—

Turn to the Lord, proud Pope, by thy bulls nought setteth a good king.

Curse though thou dost, yet shall we be blest, for God is on our side.

Quantity is here loose as ever, and remains so in the instances which follow. Robert Chamberlain or Chamberlayne in a book called *Nocturnal Lucubrations* (1638) has one epigram of ten hexameter lines on " Death's Impartiality," beginning—

High-minded Pyrrhus, brave Hector, stout Agamemnon.

And one John Hockenhull contributed to the second edition of *Barker's Book of Angling* (1657) other ten lines, of which the first will be more than sufficient specimen—

Trout, carp, perch, pike, roach, dace, eel, tench, bleke, gudgeon, barbell.

A reference here and there may also, no doubt, be traced. John Taylor, the " water-poet ", in *The Beggar* (1621) ridiculed hexameter verse, comparing it to a certain creeping insect possessed of six feet. Ben Jonson's already noted advocacy found belated and fruitless utterance in 1640. But with

[1] Hostility to rhyme was common to all the Classic experimenters, and they often speak as if rhymeless verse of any pattern belonged to the school. Thus Surrey's blank verse is referred to by Webbe and others as pioneering the way for Sidney's hexameters,

[2] At its birthplace this movement would naturally linger longer than elsewhere.

Campion the quantitative crusade may be said to have died. Attempts at revival during the Eighteenth and still more during the Nineteenth Century will be chronicled in due course. The original enterprise has now been traced to its finish, every writer known to me as taking part in it having been enumerated (I shall esteem it a favour to be apprised of any omission [1]). The singularity of this whole movement, its aloofness from the main current of our verse, seemed to justify treating it by itself. Now the time has come to leave it, and go back to trace the main course of our metrical criticism, beginning with the work of Gascoigne.

George Gascoigne, our oldest metrical critic, was a poet of some note at the outset of the Elizabethan era. His tragedies in blank verse, his comedies and lyrics, gained him encomiums as " the very chief of our late rymers ".[2] Nash, in his preface to Greene's *Menaphon*, says that Gascoigne " first beat the path to that perfection which our best poets have aspired to since his departure." Other critics echo this praise. The tract with which alone we have to do, " Certayne notes of instruction in English verse ", appeared first as the introduction to his *Posies* (1575), and was afterwards reprinted in his collected works. It does not go very deep, nor is learning the writer's strong point. He speaks of " crambe bis positum," and is more familiar with Chaucer than Horace. But native wit, pithiness, and humour make his little book pleasant reading. He is full of quaint phrases like " a tale of a tub " or " this poetical license is a shrewd fellow ", and introduces us to " riding rhyme " and " Poulters' Measure ". He gives excellent advice on the choice of a subject, and on " holding just measure ". As regards technique, he puts accent first and foremost, identifying it with " emphasis or sound ". And he asserts that it " maketh that syllable long whereupon it is placed " (§ 4). Beyond this there is little to notice. The only pauses he recognises are " Ceasures " (§ 13), and they are optional ; the only foot acknowledged by him is the iamb.

[1] Prof. Arber (*Webbe*, introduction, p. 9) credits Phaer with translating the *Aeneid* into hexameters. Perhaps the word " heroical ", used by both Webbe and Puttenham in speaking of Phaer, caused the slip. Phaer and Twine's version is of course in fourteen-syllable verse, the metre most used of any, according to Gascoigne.

[2] This phrase is quoted by Webbe (p. 33) as occurring in E.K.'s notes on Spenser's Ninth Eclogue, but I cannot find it in those notes.

Yet he points out that older poets had more freedom, that "our father Chaucer" balanced dissyllables against trisyllables in lines which seemed equal in length ; and he "can lament" that this variety of rhythm has been lost (§ 4). On the whole, one cannot feel that Gascoigne had given much thought to his subject, and the identification of accent with quantity was disastrous indeed ; but the pleasant style, the unpedantic and sensible tenor, of these lively Notes secure our interest, and make us glad to hail in their writer the *doyen* of English prosodists.

Sidney's well-known *Defence of Poesie* (1581 ?) deals with the matter rather than the form of imaginative composition, prose as well as verse being expressly included, and makes no direct reference to his own metrical experiments. But toward the end (Arber, pp. 70–71) he has a few weighty words on the difference between ancient and modern verse, "number" and "accent" being made the basis of the latter, and rhyme its "chief life". The English language he pronounces capable of either, and notes that in our native verse both accent and caesura are observed "very precisely". No examples are given, and the treatise makes no other reference to prosody unless in the phrase "that numbrous kind of writing which is called verse" (p. 28). But Sidney, like Gascoigne, shows that from the very beginning *accent* was seen to be a distinctive feature of our verse, holding in it a place other than it held in ancient, or contemporary modern, literature.

James VI. of Scotland, at the age of eighteen, in his *Essays of a prentice* (1584) published "ane short treatise" dealing with rules of verse. Like Gascoigne, he recognises but one legitimate type, the so-called "iambic". (Neither writer uses this word, however.) He divides syllables into *short, long, indifferent*, without saying what makes them so ; "your ear must be the only judge and discerner" (c. 2). In common verse short and long syllables alternate, which causes "flowing" or rhythm ; but in "tumbling verse", fit only for *flyting*, two short alternate with one long (c. 3, end). "Proper Verse" has an even number of such alternations, but "broken verse, daily invented by divers poets" (c. 2), has uneven. From four to fourteen feet [syllables ?] make a usual line (*ibid.*). Each line must have its *section* [caesura], at which point a long syllable is desirable (*ibid.*). He enumerates eight varieties of [iambic] metre (c. 8), adding one of "tumbling" verse, and curiously anticipates modern stylists by speaking of rhymes as "just colours" (c. 1, first words). For a boy of eighteen, the small tract is able enough ; but it makes singularly slight contribution to prosody. Like Gascoigne, its royal author evidently identifies accent with quantity. In the word *Arabia*, he remarks, the second syllable "eats up" the last (c. 1). This is vigorous description, but hardly scientific analysis. Time is never mentioned by him ; Gascoigne had some notion of it when he spoke about Chaucer, but did not follow up the idea. Thus early was English prosody led to consider syllables apart from time, in imaginary and impossible isolation. King James's "flowing" is but the "syllabic foot" of a later generation of critics.

Webbe's *Discourse* (1586) has been already mentioned. It differs from its predecessors in containing (besides a preface) a regular historical introduction, of great interest when he comes to recent verse. He knows "no memorable work written by any poet in our English speech, until twenty years past," Gower and Lydgate, and even Chaucer, being evidently thought antiquated. Recent writers are rapidly run through, notably high praise being given to the *Shepherd's Calendar*, though Harvey is bracketed with Spenser for promise if not for performance. This occupies the first section of his *Discourse*, while the second and part of the third discuss the subject-matter of poetry. Finally (p. 56 *seq.* of Arber's edition) he takes up "the form and manner of our English verse". First he deals, in somewhat languid and half-hearted fashion, with that "rude kind" of measure which constitutes English verse properly so called ; then (p. 67) he proceeds to expound his recipe for "reformed" metre, and continues on this to the end. Some ten or eleven pages, therefore, exhaust what he says on English verse proper, and most of this naturally deals with length of lines and the like, the line of fourteen syllables being again spoken of as "the most accustomed of all other". He does, however, define metre (p. 57) as correspondence "in equal number of feet or syllables, or proportionable to the time whereby it is to be read or measured".[1] He speaks of "a natural force or quantity in each word" (p. 62 ; *cf.* p. 57,

---

[1] *Cf.* (p. 37) "measurable speech, framed in words containing number or proportion of just syllables".

" the true quantity thereof "), but his illustration shows that
" quantity " here means simply accentuation. He claims
iambic character for our common metres—" the natural
course of most English verses seemeth to run upon the old
Iambic stroke " (p. 62)—borrowing from contemporary
grammar this unhappy and misleading comparison. He
points out (p. 61) that much of our verse is written to music,
and evidently thinks that such can hardly be said to have
metre of its own. Apart from his " Classical " heresy, Webbe
is scholarly and sensible as well as modest, and the " summer
evenings " (see preface) which gave birth to this book were
worthily employed. But we cannot expect more than side-
lights on English verse-structure from a critic whose pet wish
was to " reform it altogether ".

These were all comparatively slight productions. The first
extensive and systematic manual of prosody in our tongue
was *The Art of English Poesie*, published anonymously in
1589, but known to be by George Puttenham, who wrote it
for the delectation of Queen Elizabeth and her Court (see
dedication to Lord Cecil, and several references in body of
work). This full and erudite treatise is divided into three
books, of which the first is general and historical, while the
third—longer than the other two put together—deals with
figures of speech. None of these touches on verse-structure,
though in Book I. chap. 2 he denies that our native verse
consists of *feet*, and in chap. 5 claims for rhyme greater anti-
quity than belonged to Classic measure. It is in Book II.,
whose subject is " Proportion ", that Puttenham propounds
his theories of metre, and very startling they are. Our ordinary verse he scans entirely by numeration of syllables (c. 3),
and devotes many chapters to varieties of line and stanza,
even to those most artificial compositions which took a shape
of lozenge or triangle or pillar. Neglecting these, we find that
he compares English verse-structure with Classical, and gives
a most erroneous account of the latter, confounding syllables
with times (c. 3) ; that he measures time by " motion or
stir " (*ibid.*), the latter word being identified with accent
(c. 7) ; that he fails to distinguish between metrical and
rhetorical pauses (c. 5, " Of Cesure ") ; that he regards
rhyme or " concord " as practically the sole distinctive mark
of our verse (c. 8–11) ; that like Webbe he thinks Classical

feet might be " reduced " into our verse (end of c. 12, and succeeding chapters), but that this is to be done by treating every accented syllable as necessarily long, while in other respects obeying Latin rules of position, even to regarding the doubled consonant as two consonants and eliding consonants as well as vowels before a following vowel (c. 13).

Into this question of "Classicising" we need not enter again. Puttenham was undoubtedly right in perceiving the importance of accent. But his remarks reveal a misconception so fatal that it fundamentally vitiates his whole analysis. He has no idea of quantity apart from accent. Why a vowel followed by two consonants should be accounted long he does not explain ; of inherent length in vowels he has never dreamed. He actually thinks (c. 13) that the first syllable of " Penelope " is long in Latin, the first of " cano " short, simply because the first poet chose to make it so. " It stands upon bare tradition " (*ibid.*), and is due merely to " pre-election " (*ibid.*). A misconception so radical makes not only Latin verse unreal to him ; English verse also becomes mere rhymed prose. Of anything beyond syllable-counting and rhyme-relation he seems absolutely unconscious. Apart from this terrible want, his notions and methods are accurate, his points well and pleasantly put. He intersperses his teaching with plentiful anecdote, sometimes of that remarkably broad type which Elizabethan humour thought suitable for drawing-rooms. To each figure of speech he gives an English name, so that *irony* becomes " the dry mock ", *hyperbole* " the loud liar ", and so on (III., c. 18). In all questions of history, or external form, Puttenham is valuable authority, and most of his long book is excellent reading. But as regards verse-structure he is entirely useless, whether in expounding Classic metre or analysing English.[1]

By these books, of which Puttenham's is far the most important for our purpose, English prosody was fairly set

---

[1] Critics differ much about Puttenham. Mr. Stone is contemptuous, a feeling amusingly reflected by the compiler of his index (in the posthumous edition), who enters without qualification " Puttenham, his foolish book ! " Mr. McKerrow, on the other hand, calls him " the one really clear-headed man among all the Elizabethan critics " (second paper, p. 9). It must be remembered that his inability to realise vowel quantity was apparently shared by all the " Classicisers " of his day. Prof. Saintsbury's verdict hovers between the two.

agoing. It will be seen under what conditions it began. No reasoned attempt had been made to determine the basis of our metre. Obsessed by Classic analogies, and owing much to contemporary Italian art, our critics assumed likenesses which did not exist. Historically, modern English verse is a compromise between the freedom of Old English (" Anglo-Saxon "), with its loose syllable-structure punctuated by alliteration, and that greater strictness of syllabic numeration which Romance languages favoured. The former element was wholly lost sight of ; the latter became an influence ever increasing in force. At the very time when Shakespeare and others were writing blank verse of great variety and mobility, our critics were preaching that such lines consisted of ten syllables and no more, with regular succession of accents. " Numbers " came to mean simply arithmetic applied to syllables ; " rhythmus " (from which word they believed *rhyme* to be derived) became merely alternation of stronger and weaker accents. This mechanical view of metre, founded on no sufficient induction of instances, spread and flourished without challenge. Either it reacted on our verse, or—more probably—the same influences which produced the theory produced also the practice. French succeeded Italian as the literature most affecting ours, and brought in still greater rigidity of pattern. It is long indeed before we come to any expositor who conceives of verse as other than a definite arrangement of syllables in prescribed order, of prosody as more than the counting and classifying of those syllables.

The four books named had no immediate successor. Criticism as well as creation rose to great height, and treatises on poetry were not wanting. But they deal with matter, not with form. Harrington's " Apologie of poetrie," prefixed to his translation of the *Orlando Furioso* (1591), refers approvingly to Puttenham, but contributes nothing itself. When Campion (*ante*, p. 20) is not riding his quantitative hobby, he produces excellent laws like this : " As in Musick we do not say a straine of so many notes, but so many sem' briefes, . . . so in a verse the numeration of the sillables is not so much to be observed, as their waite [weight] and due proportion." The *Palladis Tamia* of Meres (1598) criticises authors merely. Daniel's well-known *Defence of Rhyme* (1603 ?), in reply to Campion, has some general observations pertinent to our subject. "All verse is but a frame of words confined within certain measure." This frame is "Rithmus or Metrum, Number or Measure ". "As Greek and Latin verse consists of the number and quantity of syllables, so doth the English verse of measure and accent." Measure he identifies with number, accent with harmony ; yet harmony *is* number ! Though English verse "doth not strictly observe long and short syllables, yet it most religiously respects the accent," and possesses number, measure, and harmony in the best proportion of music.[1] He scoffs at Campion's quantities, calling him the would-be "Rhadamanthus of verse," while his so-styled *iambic* line is "just the plain ancient verse consisting of ten syllables or five feet, which hath ever been used amongst us, time without mind ".[2] His vindication of rhyme is excellent, and he has some good observations on the proper management of that auxiliary ; blank verse he thinks most suitable to tragedy.[3] In fact, so far as criticism goes he is thoroughly sound, but as an exponent of verse-structure leaves much to be desired. No coherent or sufficient analysis can be extracted from the above-quoted random sentences, which give his only attempt at a definite statement of theory.

During the remainder of the Seventeenth Century there is very little to note. Bolton in his *Hypercritica* (1610 *seq.*) and Peacham in his *Compleat Gentleman* (1622) have Sections on poetry, but nothing about metre. Ben Jonson mentions it only in the one passage already cited. D'Avenant's preface to *Gondibert* (1651), with the remarks by Hobbes that follow, have interest in themselves, but touch on our subject only when Hobbes speaks of "recompensing neglect of quantity with the diligence of rhyme " (p. 55). Cowley's voluminous prefaces ignore it entirely ; Milton has only the ungrateful rejection of rhyme in his preface to *Paradise Lost.* Grammars of the day may refer to verse-structure, but the only instance I have come across is in *Grammatica linguae Anglicanae* (1653) by the well-known John Wallis, whose "cap. 15 de poesi " notices briefly the pseudo-Classical movement. Prosody seems to have been nearly a dead art through the greater part of this Century. As it nears its end, we find revived interest in poetics. The new school of elegance and "correctness " had

---

[1] Grosart's edition of Daniel's *Works*, Vol. IV. pp. 38–39.
[2] *Ibid.*, pp. 57–58.   [3] *Ibid.*, p. 65.

come in. Denham and Waller had led the way ; Dryden was now following gloriously in their wake. From 1675 onwards, in the critical writings of the day—in Dryden's own prefaces, in the treatises of Rymer and Dennis, in the verse of Beaumont and Suckling, in the versified " Essays " of Roscommon, Buckingham, Samuel Wesley, and others—we find much analysis of poetry, little of verse.[1] What of the latter there is goes into no debateable questions, merely specifying with Dryden—

> pauses, cadence, and well-vowell'd words,[2]

or with Wesley bidding us mind our " pauses and accents ".[3] The transformation of English poetry was accomplished. Elizabethan freedom was replaced by mechanical exactness ; the syllable-counters had triumphed. While the metamorphosis proceeded, metrical criticism had remained all but silent. Now its lips were opened again, with every encouragement to be precise and formal and rigorous.

Eighteenth-Century poetical criticism was rarely marked by diffidence. Dryden, and still more Pope, were proclaimed supreme masters ; theirs was the Augustan age of English literature. Metrology shared this confidence. Bysshe's *Art of English Poetry* (1702) may be taken as the first *modern* book of its kind, the first to formulate the familiar doctrines which still form the text of our grammars.[4] He has no doubt about the matter. English verse consists of syllables, arranged with undeviating regularity of accentuation ; a misplaced accent

---

[1] It should be noted that Dryden, toward the end of the " Dedication " prefixed to his translation of the *Aeneid*, says : " I have long had by me the materials of an English Prosodia, containing all the mechanical rules of versification, wherein I have treated with some exactness of the feet, the quantities, and the pauses." As in the previous case of Ben Jonson, one feels regret that this project was not executed. Still more must it be regretted that Milton left no record of the principles which guided him. We should at least have known how these great poets viewed the subject-matter of their art. As it is, we are told only what critics think, until, toward the end of our survey, we find prosody discussed by singers such as Poe, Patmore, and Lanier.

[2] Commendatory verses to Roscommon's *Essay on translated verse* (1684). Roscommon himself speaks of " accents regularly placed ".

[3] *An epistle to a friend concerning poetry* (1700).

[4] Prof. Saintsbury questions this assertion, and asks where the doctrines are to be found. I reply, in the precepts of poets and critics from James I. and VI. onward.

is like a false quantity in Greek or Latin (Chap. I, Section 1). We have here the creed of Johnson and Lindley Murray in all its bareness. No qualification is made, no reference to the practice of Shakespeare or Milton. Caesural pause is laid down as of equal necessity. Bysshe's exposition is short, most of the book being taken up with (1) a rhyming dictionary, (2) a collection of passages quoted from our poets. But his book is important, since it formed the basis of most which followed. Nearly every manual of prosody for the next hundred years builds more or less on Bysshe. His theory is demonstrably false when tested even by the poetry he admired ; Pope would be condemned by it again and again. Instead of judging from practice, he sets up an imaginary and ridiculous ideal calling on our poets to conform to it. They, fortunately, had too much good sense to do anything of the kind. Glover, author of *Leonidas* (1737), is the only writer of whom it is told that he aimed at perfect regularity of accent. Only in an artificial age could such a doctrine have been promulgated, but not even that artificial age was able to carry it into effect.

From what immediate sources Bysshe derived his doctrine does not appear. Probably he repeated the current teaching of the schools. For it will be noticed that his theory carries out and makes more definite what the Elizabethan grammarians had asserted. Number and stress of syllables were the points emphasised by them. While our poets were taking time-periods as their basis—manifestly in their lyric verse, and as I maintain not less really in their most regular measures —their critics paid attention only to syllables. They read the music by its *notes*, ignoring *rests*. Hence the divorce between theory and practice, which has made our prosody so unreal and unsatisfactory. Its artificial character becomes more marked than ever during the period next to be reviewed.

Pope's *Essay on Criticism* (1711), Addison's papers on Milton in the *Spectator* (1711), Swift's *Proposal for correcting the English tongue* (1711–12), rightly protesting against our love of unmusical contractions such as *fought'st* for *foughtest*, may be dismissed with bare mention. Pope has some general remarks towards the end, and one well-known passage (337 *seq.*) beginning—

But most by numbers judge a poet's song.

He does not, however, really analyse verse-structure.[1] Addison, even while praising Milton's verse, does not grapple with the question of his method. Nor, later, in Bentley's notes on Milton (1732), and Swift's fierce animadversions on the same, is this discussed. Even Milton's admirers, at this time, seem to claim merely that he was a great irregular genius, whose metrical eccentricities must be pardoned and tolerated. To Shakespeare the same measure is applied. That these old-fashioned writers had command of harmonies unknown to their successors it would have been thought altogether absurd to maintain.

The small critics are more interesting than the great. Brightland's *English Grammar* (1711), though a mere school-book, questions some of Bysshe's views—unless the criticism be a later addition to the issue (1759) which alone I have seen. Dilworth and Dyche's *Guides to the English Tongue* (dates uncertain), immortalized by a line in the *Anti-Jacobin*—

> Dilworth and Dyche are both mad at thy quantities—

are both mere school-books, dealing mainly with spelling and pronunciation. Dyche has no Section on prosody ; Dilworth has a single page on it (Part III, Chap. 2), from which I take the following choice excerpt :

> " What is an accent ?
> " A tone or accent denoteth the raising [*sic*] or falling of the voïce on a syllable, according to the quantity thereof.
> " How many accents are there ?
> " There are three accents ; the long, the short, and the common."

Long and short are exemplified by *mīnd* and *lŏt* ; then—

> " The common accent hath no regard to the grammatical quantity of a syllable, but being placed over a vowel denotes the tone or stress of the voice to be upon that syllable ; as, *plénty*."

This extraordinary confusion between two very different things is by no means confined to Dilworth, and may warn us to expect some loose writing. Both men were London school-masters, Dilworth at Wapping, and wrote other books of an educational nature ; but that reference in the *Anti-Jacobin* now alone rescues them from oblivion.

---

[1] A letter of Pope's, dealing with versification, is given by Prof. Saintsbury in his *History of Prosody*, Vol. II, p. 471, foot-note.

Some short strictures of an ordinary kind by William Coward (1709) will be found mentioned in Appendix B. But Charles Gildon, in his *Complete Art of Poetry* (1718) and *Laws of Poetry explained and illustrated* (1721), does undoubtedly occupy new ground, and raises for the first time (to my knowledge) a question which was to employ our critics for many a day, *viz.*, what was the exact nature of that " accent " which from the earliest age of our literature had been felt and acknowledged a leading feature of verse. This question, like so much else in our prosody, came from the Classics. A controversy had raged among scholars—it is not wholly determined to this day—whether Greek should or should not be pronounced according to its accent-marks ; whether, that is to say, stress should be laid on the syllables which bear an acute accent. Gildon states very clearly the view which is now considered orthodox. Greek accent, he says, was probably a mere rising and falling of the voice, without regard to quantity ; a musical variation, not existing in Latin, and which had been lost by the time of Quintilian. Our accent, on the other hand, consists in the " force and emphasis which we put upon one syllable more than another", and which give length to that syllable (*Laws of Poetry*, pp. 315–16).

The sting of this proposition lies in its last words. Does accent create quantity ? This question was debated at inordinate length by learned and unlearned. A fashion began of printing Greek without accent-marks ; if they were not to be observed, they should not be written. And no treatise on English verse was complete without a discussion of the nature of accent. Naturally, those who regarded accent as the sole regulative principle of metre were deeply concerned to establish its true function. Yet the main subject of their debate seems one incapable of argument. How can it possibly be maintained that stress lengthens the first syllable of words like *rapid, level, limit, comic, bury*—let us add, of words like *banner, letter, little, bonnet, butter ?* Take the word *hegemony*. We may accentuate either the second or the third syllable of this word, but do we in either case necessarily prolong the vowel ? That there is a natural tendency to do so may be frankly conceded ; our habitual inclination in English is to make quantity follow accent. But to exalt this inclination into a universal law of speech is manifestly absurd ; and this these controversialists did without scruple. It was roundly asserted, and indeed usually admitted on both sides, that you could nɔt accentuate the third syllable of such a Greek word as ουλομενην without lengthening the vowel. We have here to do only with the influence of this extraordinary delusion on English prosody. Confusion of accent with quantity has been seen to be characteristic of it from the first. This confusion now wears a scientific mask, and will be found to pervade and vitiate nearly all Eighteenth Century criticism.

Before proceeding to treat of the mass of scholarly writing which, especially during the latter part of the Eighteenth Century, dealt with English verse and with metre generally, I may, for the sake of completeness, add here a short notice of some few attempts at writing quantitative verse made subsequently to the date of those last cited.

Dr. Watts, in the first book of his *Poems chiefly of the lyric kind* (1709) has one ode "attempted in English Sapphics". Its terrible subject ("The day of Judgement") and unshrinking realism make the bulk of it unquotable ; but the first two stanzas are at once unobjectionable and a fair sample of his metre.

> When the fierce north wind with his airy forces
> Rears up the Baltic to a foaming fury ;
> And the red lightning with a storm of hail comes
>   Rushing amain down ;
> How the poor sailors stand amazed and tremble !
> While the hoarse thunder, like a bloody trumpet,
> Roars a loud onset to the gaping waters
>   Quick to devour them.

It will be seen that false quantities here are plentiful as ever. Why is *the* made long in the second line after being short in the first ?—why is the second syllable of *foaming* short ? What can justify *rūshing, stănd, līke, dĕvour ?* Dr. Watts does not state his rules, but they may be presumed to be the usual ones, and pronunciation cannot have changed materially since he wrote. It is clear that he had no ear for phonetic quantity. Accent is evidently meant to follow quantity, but usually

rebels in the fifth syllable of each longer line, where the difficulty of getting three consecutive strongly stressed syllables
makes itself felt. The remaining stanzas are no better than
their predecessors. Among other lapses I notice *thĕse, ărch-
angel, marblē, rĕpose, hōrrōr and, whĭle, līving, prĕy, hŏw,
gloomȳ, fancȳ ăll.* A schoolboy showing up Latin verses with
such blunders would be heavily sat upon ; what shall we say
to an English poet who perpetrates such atrocities ?

Hexameters, after more than a century's neglect, were
revived by the anonymous author of a very curious book
entitled *An Introduction of the Ancient Greek and Latin
Measures into British Poetry* (1737), with " a preface in vindication of the attempt". Translations of Virgil's First and
Fourth Eclogues, and an original poem on Jacob and Rachel,
are offered as specimens, all in hexameters. The preface is
interesting. He thinks Sidney (to whom alone he refers) failed
because our language was still too harsh, but that we can
" make music of " his lines quite as easily. as of Chaucer's.
The Latin poets did not succeed all at once ; Ennius is less
musical than Virgil. Why should

> In Syrian Pastures, on a flow'ry Bank,

be held more melodious than

> ‾ ᴗ ᴗ ‾ ‾ ᴗ ᴗ ‾ ‾ ᴗ ᴗ ‾ ‾
> In Syrian Pastures, on a flowery bank by a Fountain ?

It is a question of taste, perhaps of fashion. " The ear after
all must decide the dispute." Should his specimen verses be
approved, he will leave " the eminent genius's of the Age " to
perfect what he has begun.

A postscript gives his rules, which in many ways are excellent. Elision is wholly forbidden. A syllable remains short
" where the same Consonant is immediately repeated, as in
approaching ;" and also " where one Consonant is followed
by another very near akin to it," e. g. *bp, cg, dt.* Accent is
not to be wrenched, as " the Greek poets, and for aught I know
the Latin ones too," did at pleasure. Less commendable are
his treatment of initial *y* as a vowel (*sevĕn years*), and of *sh* as
two consonants. But these are as nothing to his repetition of
the old fatal blunder that English has no fixed vowels. He
has made the quantities of syllables long or short as the verse
required, " they having never yet been ascertained in our

language", except where position constitutes length. "Diphthongs and triphthongs" are long when sounded as such, but when sounded as single vowels may be short. Of single vowels which are long or short *per se* he has no conception.

Verse written on such principles could not prosper. Occasionally, when quantities happen to be approximately correct, we get such not unpleasing lines as—

> While from tall Mountains shades huger fall to the Valleys—

(yet *Valleys* transgresses his own rule), or

> Thence from a steep precipice shall Wood-men sing to the Breezes.

But more often the result is an abomination like—

> A Deity gave us this Leisure, O Meliboeus ;
> For he shall a Deity by me be for ever accounted,

which simply bristles with error. It were waste of time to quote further. I notice *blŏssoming,* yet *rēdden ;* and hosts of words like *wĕighty, dīvine, stŭpified, căpable, ūnŭsŭal.* Accents are frequently distorted, in spite of the preface. In fact, this later attempt repeats all the faults of its predecessors, and falls over the same obstacles. It seems to have attracted little or no attention, and remains a mere curiosity of literature.

In the year 1763 Goldsmith, in a paper on " Versification " now included in his *Miscellaneous Essays*, defended pseudo-Classic measures, and asserted that Sidney's failure was due to ignorance on the part of his public. He also mentions that he has seen " several late specimens of English hexameters and sapphics" which he found " as melodious and agreeable to the ear as the works of Virgil and Anacreon, or Horace." I know of no published verses to which these remarks can apply, other than the two last quoted. But it is of course possible, and perhaps probable, that Goldsmith referred to verses that he had seen in manuscript. At any rate two books published in 1773 contained, one some remarkable hexameters, the other some hexameters and sapphics of a peculiar type ; and it seems not unlikely that Goldsmith may have had a private perusal of these long before they were published.

The former of these books is *Vocal Sounds*, by " Edward Search " (a pseudonym for the well-known Abraham Tucker).

This bright little volume contains excellent remarks on phonetics, and recognises—perhaps for the first time in this connection—inherent and unalterable length of vowels. He is therefore able to draw up proper tables of quantity, and his hexameters are based on these, accent being deliberately set aside. It is true that his rules admit considerable licence. He thinks that " most of our little particles, the vowel immediately preceding an accent, the final *y*," and a long vowel immediately followed by another vowel, may all be accounted " common " (p. 69 *seq.*) ; while " and " may be reckoned short, since the final *d* is hardly heard. He is also unsound about the double consonant, writing *dĭffuses, āllotted*, and yet elsewhere *whŏlly, countlĕss abundance.* Nor does this practice always square with his rules, else why *lŭcid, dīvine, celestĭal* ? Yet the blots of execution are few in lines like the following.

A spirit internal penetrates through earth, sky, and ocean,

Mounts to the moon's lucid orb, and stars in countless abundance ;

One soul all matter invigorates, gives life to the system,

O'er each particular member diffuses alertness.

* * * * *

Thence men and all animals sprang forth, beasts and feathered fowl,

And whatever monsters swarm through the watery kingdom.

On general questions " Edward Search " is vigorous and sensible. The letter *h* he makes a consonant when sounded, a nullity when not. Accent is to be opposed to quantity, but not too violently ; such an ending as

from gross matter exempt

seems to himself too harsh, more suitable for prose. Taken as a whole, this book makes an immense advance on anything earlier, and if Goldsmith knew Tucker he may well have been struck by his examples. Had the Elizabethans worked on principles like these, their attempt might possibly have been longer-lived.

The other volume is interesting from its limitations. *The Elements of Speech*, by John Herries, frankly abandons quantity. Classic quantity the author does not profess to understand ; the " harmony of Greek and Latin verse " seems to him due entirely to their accents (p. 184 *seq*.). Naturally, therefore, he sees no reason why these should not be reproduced in English. Numbering the accents in two familiar lines thus—

> [1]Te, [2]dulcis [3]conjux, [4]te [5]solo [6]in litore [7]secum
> [1]Te, [2]veniente [3]die, [4]te [5]decedente [6]canebat—

he suggests the following as an equivalent—

> [1]Thee, [2]lovely [3]partner, [4]thee [5]only he [6]constantly [7]chanted,
> [1]Thee, at the [2]dawn of [3]morning, [4]thee thro' the [5]shades of the [6]evening.

Similarly, his notion of Sapphic structure is this—

> [1]Place me in [2]regions of [3]eternal [4]winter
> [1]Where not a [2]blossom to the [3]breeze can [4]open,
> [1]But dark'ning [2]tempests [3]closing all [4]around me,
> [1]Chill the [2]creation.

His English syllables are meant to correspond with the Latin in number and (as he read them) in accentuation of syllables ; and this seems to him sufficient. It is needless to dwell on the futility of this view ; but it is important to note that here for the first time we have accent deliberately proposed as a substitute for quantity in what professed to be an imitation of Classic structure. Here, therefore, is struck the first preluding note of what was soon to sound forth in a noisy (some would say, barbaric) orchestra.

Readers will know to what this last remark refers. Klopstock and Voss in Germany, followed by Goethe and Schiller and a host of imitators, invented " hexameters " which discarded quantity, and were framed upon a supposed accentual basis. Taylor of Norwich (see Appendix B, 1796) introduced these to English readers, Coleridge and Southey took up the idea, and many subsequent writers have applied it to that and other forms of Classic measure. Into these multitudinous developments we need not now enter. I have elsewhere contended that they have no claim to be accounted *simulacra* of Classic verse, and owe what success they obtain to their accidentally coinciding with native verse-forms. Thus the

" hexameter" of Southey, Longfellow, Clough, Kingsley, and
others is in no sense an equivalent of the ancient hexameter ;
but it is a perfectly legitimate form of ordinary English verse,
and should be written as such. Passing by all lines composed
on this model, it remains only to notice that—partly, perhaps,
as a protest against the shapeless and lumbering awkwardness
of the " accentual hexameter" as too commonly written—
a reaction in favour of quantitative verse was essayed by a
few writers, including Clough (" essays in Classical Metres"),
James Spedding, Tennyson (" experiments in quantity"),
Charles Bagot Cayley, Professor Robinson Ellis, William
Johnson Stone, and (most conspicuously of all) Mr. Robert
Bridges. These again divide into two classes. Clough and
Spedding aimed at contrasting accent with quantity, Cayley
followed suit, Stone and Mr. Bridges insist on this as essential.
Tennyson, on the other hand, except in his satirical " elegiacs", sought to unite accent and quantity on the same
syllable, and was followed in this surpassingly difficult task
by Professor Ellis with his hypersubtle renderings from
Catullus. To myself either school seems doomed to failure
as attempting the impossible ; nor can I esteem success
desirable. Be this how it may, previous pages are believed
to mention most writers of note who have produced or criticised
quantitative verse in English. Accentual verse-writers, it
need hardly be said, transcend enumeration ; a few chief ones
are cited in my Appendices. Of real attempts to imitate
Classic metre in our tongue I trust that the foregoing will be
found a practically exhaustive list.

CHAPTER II

THE OLD ORTHODOXY

1700–1750

ONLY during the last two Centuries has there been any systematic study of English prosody. We have examined the faint beginnings of English prosodical criticism which preceded the opening years of the Eighteenth Century, and have made an endeavour (the first so far as my knowledge goes) to compile a bibliography of the subject. The following survey is confined to works written in the English language ; to go farther would have immensely increased a labour already arduous, perhaps without satisfactory result. At any rate, this volume deals only with criticism of English verse by English-speaking authors ; and I believe that all which is of consequence in that criticism occurs during the period now to be surveyed.

It may be well to summarize results already reached. We have seen that, naturally enough, English verse as we know it was written long before any discussion arose about its nature or methods (with its origin and historical derivation we are not concerned) ; that when such discussion did arise it began without proper preliminaries, without inquiry into the actualities of English speech-sounds ; that our first critics were wholly possessed by Classic precedent, and sought to interpret English metre in terms of Latin and Greek ; and that contemporaneously with them a deliberate attempt was made to revolutionize our verse by substituting rules of Classic 'quantity' for native measures. This ill-starred attempt was followed to its foregone conclusion ; a few *addenda* are mentioned in Appendix A. Thereafter were examined the scant records of English metrical study during the Sixteenth and Seventeenth Centuries, ending with Charles Gildon (1718). From that date, early in the Century before last, the tale is now to be resumed ; all that is vital to the science of English prosody, as well as much that is quite other, still lying before us.

Most of the work which falls first to be examined is occupied by discussions of accent and quantity. Echoes of dreary controversy are roused by these words. Arguments about them seem as arid and as hopeless of solution as arguments about free will or the origin of matter. Nor can it be said that the writers we are about to take note of deal helpfully with the questions at issue. Their method is pre-scientific ; they talk round and about their subject rather than really investigate it. We seldom find any thing like true analysis. Can we, then, before plunging into this dusty arena, get some clear ideas for ourselves as to the matters in dispute, to prevent entire confusion and bewilderment ?

' Quantity ' presents no great difficulty. I have already stated the meaning of the word in Greek and Latin verse, and need now only repeat that it referred solely to the time syllables took to pronounce ; and that this was held to depend either on vowel-duration or on retardation by separately pronounced consonants. A long syllable was accounted equal to two short, and carried two time-beats as against the one apiece of the short syllables. In English we have nothing analogous to this fixed rule. Our ears are presumably not different from those of old Greeks and Romans, but our habits of speech are different. We have a powerful stress-accent, which reduces quantitative distinction to low and fluctuating values ; they, apparently, had a very slight one. Were our language more like theirs—did it contain a large proportion of vowels, rarely separated by more than two or at most three consonants, and were it devoid of strong accentuation—we, too, might have made quantity the basis of our verse-structure. As it is, any attempt to write English quantitative verse seems vain and meaningless. Bearing in mind, then, that quantity refers solely to length of syllables, let us go on to consider what can be determined about accent.

Three elements must be distinguished in every spoken sound—pitch, force, and duration. I purposely use the least ambiguous terms. Pitch is synonymous with height of tone, force with loudness ; duration represents what we have just called ' quantity '. These three elements are distinct and different, separable always in thought, separated often in

practice. No analysis can be accurate which confuses them.[1]
In the books before us accent is defined sometimes as one of
these (each in turn by different writers !), sometimes as any
two of them, occasionally as all three together. At present it
is usually defined as consisting of force. The question which
most exercised our metrists—the only question of consequence
for the measuring of verse—is, does or does not accent also
imply duration, does emphasizing a syllable necessarily
prolong its utterance ?

There is certainly a well-marked tendency this way. The
typical Scot inclines to say *leemit, releegion, trayvel* and
trayveller, abohminable. That is, he likes to prolong the
accented vowel. The same tendency prevails farther south.
When we shift stress from the first to the second syllable of
doctrinal, we also lengthen that second syllable. We change
the quality, and therewith the ' quantity ', of its vowel.
Countless instances of this tendency might be cited. But it is,
after all, only a tendency. Other influences create other
tendencies, as when hurry leads us to scamp words, to reduce
fore-head to *forred, cheer up* to *chirrup, don't know* to *dunno.*
This influence will in most cases overpower the other. Careless
talk may be to blame for it, but we must take facts as they
are. It seems impossible to argue that, in our ordinary speech,
accentuation necessarily implies prolongation.

I submit that, as a matter of fact, ' accent ' (or, to be very
exact, let us say accentuation) with us does not necessarily
imply either elevation of pitch, or increase of loudness, or
prolongation of time. Normally we like to unite all three on
one syllable, and this is probably our commonest type of
accent. But it is possible to accentuate a syllable by lowering
the voice instead of raising, by uttering it more softly instead
of more loudly, by shortening instead of prolonging its duration. Any device which thus distinguishes a syllable from its
fellows makes it conspicuous, and this conspicuousness is what
we really mean by ' accent '. This rendering conspicuous of
some syllables more than others is highly characteristic of
our speech. Compare, for instance, the ideal of French
speaking. There no syllable must predominate rudely over

---

[1] This account is not put forward as complete. Other qualities,
especially *timbre* or tone-quality, play their part. But the first necessity
is to distinguish clearly between the three factors above named.

its neighbours, and in French regular metre every syllable is accounted of the same value. With us it is quite the reverse. In common talk, as in oratory or verse, every second or third syllable is usually rendered conspicuous in some way, and a dead level of pronunciation is repulsive to us.

We carry this habit of speech into other languages. We read Greek and Latin verse as we do our own, and imagine that when we make ' long ' syllables conspicuous we are reading by quantity. Conversely, we believe that in English verse a conspicuous syllable is necessarily protracted. Many will refuse to admit that the first syllable of words like *very, limit, busy, banner, muscle, cockle, patter, petty* is as short as the second. (Spelling is of course no guide.) To a musician this will seem incomprehensible. He knows that three crotchets with an accent on the first is not the same thing as a minim followed by two crotchets. Till we can similarly distinguish accentuation from quantity, conspicuousness from duration, the problems presented by English verse must remain insoluble. In what precise manner accent operates is a question for the philologer rather than the metrist. The one point of importance for prosody is to feel sure that accentuation does not by itself involve any change of duration.

If the definition of ours as a " force-accent " be meant to exclude other elements, it is certainly too narrow. Nine times out of ten, I venture to say, raising of pitch accompanies increase of loudness in our speech. The very term " accent ", common to our earliest observers, properly means elevation of tone. Names do not always describe facts ; yet the using of this one is significant. The words ' stress ' and ' stress-accent ', on the other hand, are conveniently vague, since any thing which gives importance to a syllable may be said to lay stress on it. In any case, those who make accent synonymous with force cannot claim that it necessarily implies prolongation, since the length of a syllable and its loudness are clearly two different things.

The writers we are to deal with took for the most part no such broad view of their question. Each brought with him his own preconception. To one accent is pitch, and he will not admit any other element. To another it is length, and no short syllable can ever be accented. Yet a third makes it loudness, and finds in English verse such music only as attends

the beats of a drum. Each view is partial, one-sided ; built
on *a priori* argument rather than induction of instances. In
one point, however, they all agree. Unanimously they assert
that accentuation plays in our verse the part that quantity
did in Greek and Latin. Even this, surely, is but a half-truth.
How can accentuation form a basis of metre ? It is an intensive,
not an extensive factor. The phrase "accentual foot"
involves a misconception. The essential quality of a ' foot '
is duration, and this is not created by accent. Without
doubt, accentuation is the most salient feature of our verse, as
' quantity ' of Classic verse. But to presume identity between
their functions is illogical. The one records time, the other
only illustrates it. With us, accent is mainly a signalizing
element. It calls attention to periods, but does not and cannot
create these. So far as it makes the voice linger on a syllable,
it becomes a constitutive element in verse ; but its main
function is to emphasize recurrence. The old confusion
between accent and time is perceptible again here, and turns
the "half-truth" into "wholly a lie". Accent and quantity
are incommensurate, and to draw elaborate parallels between
them as in the same plane can only mislead.

The conclusions sketched in these last paragraphs are,
I believe, in accord with modern phonetic science. They may
at least serve as a clue through the mazes of prosodic controversy, among which the unwary reader, without some
guidance, will inevitably find himself entangled.

Resuming chronological order, I must add a word more
about Gildon, with whom we left off. Though he says very
little about metre, what he does say is to the point. In his
Complete Art of Poetry (1718) but ten pages (293–302) are
given to versification. He maintains against Bysshe that
we have real "numbers" [a great word at this time to denote
verse-structure], denies that they are formed merely by
accentuation, represents feet by musical notes, distinguishes
high, loud, and *long* as qualities of sound, and contends that
Sidney's attempt failed through accidental causes. He thinks
pronunciation might be noted by something like the "prick'd
notes of Musick", and represents whole passages of verse by
minims and crotchets. But "our Business is the Art of
Poetry, not of Versifying". All this in these ten pages ; the
rest of the book does not concern us. *The Laws of Poetry . . .*

explained and illustrated (1721) consists mainly of criticisms on Buckingham, Roscommon, and another from a general point of view, but in one place (p. 62 *seq.*) he touches on " numbers and rhime ", and protests against too great uniformity of cadence.   Milton and Dryden are styled " the greatest masters of English versification ", Shakespeare a " great but very irregular genius ", Ben Jonson " of the most consummate comic genius that ever appeared in the world, ancient or modern " (p. 33).   Slight and sketchy as are his remarks, they show independent judgement ; but " complete " is not the word one would think of applying to either book.

Pope and Addison, Bentley and Swift, were briefly referred to in my previous Chapter, which also noted *An Introduction of the Ancient Greek and Latin Measures into British Poetry* (1737).   To these may now be added *Letters concerning Poetical Translations, and Virgil and Milton's Art of Verse*, published anonymously, but ascribed to one William Benson.   The edition I have seen is dated 1739, but I believe an earlier appeared in 1713.   There is little to report on in these Letters.   Their " art of verse " means merely management of rhetorical pauses.   Milton's " bottomless pit " cadence is said to be introduced for variety's sake, as any one might be glad to do after writing thousands of regular verses (p. 50).   Scansion (Letter VIII) is of the crudest kind, *e. g.*—

$$\breve{\text{Arms}} \; \bar{\text{and}} \; \text{the} \; \breve{\text{man}} \; \bar{\text{I}} \; \breve{\text{sing}}.$$

We have here the " old orthodoxy " untouched by doubt.

These were followed by a group of able though unprofessional prosodists—Pemberton, Manwaring, Harris, Say, and Mason. Henry Pemberton, M.D., Professor of Physics at Gresham College, was author of several medical and scientific treatises, and in the " Advertisement " to his *Observations on Poetry* (1738) apologises for leaving " employments of a quite different nature " to play the critic.   Most of his book deals with the substance of epic poems, and contains such excellent remarks as :   " The essence of poetry consists so much in making a due impression upon the imagination, that a single word productive of that effect . . . shall give a poetic turn to the plainest thought " (Sect. V, p. 83).   His sixth Section or Chapter is headed " Of Versification ", and alone concerns

us. With a fair show of learning, and much eulogy of " the
power of numbers ", that is, of " a just and harmonious
measure of verse " (p. 106), he nevertheless lays down rules
of the very narrowest kind. Like the other members of his
group, he refers much to music. " All verse intended for
rehearsal [recitation] consists of those species of measures
which are directly divisible into a musical movement " (p. 112).
He sees that we have in our ordinary English metres no
quantitative structure, and notes that we read Sapphic
measure to dactylic times, thus—

$$- \cup \cup \mid -- \mid \cup \cup \cup \cup \mid -- \text{(p. 107).}$$

Salinas divided this measure into quintuple feet, which is
" a division wholly unknown to the modern music " (p. 109 ;
this is no longer true). Instead of quantity, we have only
" such a rangement of the words whereby the syllables follow
one another with a free and easy cadence " (p. 106). This
free and easy cadence [the adjectives have been wickedly
misused since his time] he afterwards calls *rhythmus* [*rhythm*
was hardly yet an English word], and thus defines it : " rhythmus in speech is every orderly succession of long and short
syllables, which will pass agreeably over the ear ; but metre
and verse is [*sic*] such rhythmus confined within a short compass, and successively repeated " (p. 123). What makes syllables
long and short he does not say, and complains that " the
measures [*sic*] or rhythmus of our verse has not been so much
considered by writers on this subject, as it might have been "
(p. 125) ; but he evidently identifies accentuation with length.
Our accent " is constantly attended with an emphasis which
implies greater length in the syllable " (p. 126). And his one
demand is that every alternate syllable in our " iambic "
verse should be accented (p. 130). " Two syllables placed
together in the same foot, which must both of necessity be
pronounced short, will certainly destroy the harmony of the
verse." So he proceeds to suggest how several of Milton's lines
could be made to run more smoothly, and censures that poet
for ending lines with a syllable which is not " firm and stable "
(p. 134). Even Pope's initial trochee violates his rule, for
though " any error in the measure of the verse is least offensive
toward the beginning of it ", yet the error is greater when
the second syllable cannot be lengthened (pp. 130–1). In

fact, the critic's whole conception of verse is that it should be absolutely and regularly monotonous ; the slightest variation of accenting is to him a positive blemish.

We have seen already, when dealing with Bysshe (1702), that this was the fashionable creed of the day. But I cannot refrain from pointing out that Pemberton exemplifies a very common failing of metrists, who are prone to think that any line which violates their rules must be bad. They forget that these rules are and can be drawn only from the prevailing practice of poets, and must be faulty if at variance with this. Modestly as Pemberton puts his criticism, he has evidently no doubt whatever that he is right and Milton wrong. His book originated in an examination of Glover's *Leonidas*, the versification of which is monotonously regular, and therefore— on Pemberton's showing—superior to Milton's. We can see that this position is absurd, because we have outgrown this particular view. But how often are similar mistakes made even now ! How often are individual lines pronounced defective or unmetrical because they transgress some fancied canon ! I do not claim that poets are infallible, that they never write bad lines. But the presumption certainly is that a great poet understands his business better than any critic. The burden of proof rests with the latter. Milton mingles ' iambic ' and ' trochaic ' beginnings in his young poems, ' iambic ' and ' trochaic ' cadences in *Paradise Lost*. This fact should have been made the starting-point of an inquiry which would have shown how and for what reasons English verse differs from Greek. Ample illustration awaits us of how critics persisted in arguing from supposed *a priori* laws, instead of by patient search ascertaining the facts of English prosody ; it were well if we could believe this to be altogether a thing of the past. Dr. Pemberton at any rate had the courage of his convictions—convictions shared by very many among his contemporaries and successors.

Of Edward Manwaring, or Mainwaring, D.D., I know only that he was author of several books on Classic verse, one entitled *Stichology* [science of lines]. His treatise on *Harmony and Numbers* (1744) is dedicated to Pepusch the musician, who had introduced him to the writings of Mersennus on ancient poetry. Fired by these, and convinced that " modern music falls infinitely short of antient harmony ", he turns to our verse, and finds that " English poetry is from the same principles of harmony as the Greek and Latin iambic metre " (Chap. V, beginning). His definition must be given *verbatim*. " Our Pentametre, or English Heroics, is a seventh in Music, which is made up of a Tierce Minor and a fifth. The Tierce Minor is a tone and a half, and the fifth has three tones and a half, equal in all to ten half tones in the Diatonic scale, or, to ten half feet in the Pentametre " (*ibid*.). What precisely this mysterious deliverance means, I must leave musical scansionists to tell. I gather that he thinks our heroic verse should always divide unequally, and note that a Tierce Minor is equivalent to a trochee or iamb, a Tierce Major to a spondee. He is ready to praise or blame Milton, " our incomparable poet ", according as he finds agreement or disagreement with his rules. In an earlier Chapter he illustrates feet not amiss, rightly making *flattery* a tribrach and *slavery* a dactyl (Chap. II) ; but again (Chap. III) he makes *holy* and *blessèd* equally trochees, and the first word in " *let every man* " a long syllable. I do not think Manwaring's pages need detain us, even if musicians pronounce his formulas satisfactory and intelligible.

James Harris, author of *Hermes*, preluded his philological studies by *Three Treatises* (1744) in a lighter vein on the various Arts, including that " most important of them all ", the Art of Happiness ! The second treatise, divided into six Chapters, discusses music, painting, and poetry in a sketchy fashion, dwelling mostly on their mimetic character. *Onomatopoeia* is noticed in Chap. III, where also he points out that music has at least five lengths of sound (semibreve to semiquaver inclusive), which may be infinitely compounded, while " poetry " has but two. Chap. IV deals with imitation by symbol (" sound significant "), and in Chap. V he concludes that " poetry is on the whole much superior to either of the other mimetic arts " since, while equally accurate as they, it takes subjects of a higher kind. In this fifth Chapter (p. 92, *note*) he contends that " there is a chárm in poetry, arising from its numbers only ", and illustrates this by quoting the first six lines of *Paradise Lost*, each of which consists of " ten semi-peds ", while the natural pause or break varies in position from the third to the seventh half-foot. Beyond these not very profound remarks, I notice nothing whatever bearing on verse-structure.

Samuel Say was a fellow-pupil at school with Watts, and dedicated his *Critical Essays* to Richardson the novelist. They came out in his posthumously published volume of Poems, in 1745, but had been written seven years earlier, after reading Pemberton's book, to which he refers without naming it (pp. 140–1). He is all for freedom and variety, for *Paradise Lost* as against *Leonidas*, ridiculing Bentley's contractions and the whole notion that a heroic line must contain only ten syllables. A couplet made up by him in imitation of Chaucerian and Spenserian cadences (quoted in my Bibliography) proved a rare bone of contention to contemporary and subsequent metrists. While thus sound about variations, he is less clear as to what they vary from, and ignores fundamental uniformity. Feet are simply " so many sounds as may be united together in one movement " (p. 102), four being the maximum, and of these he recognises in English six principal ones. Like the others of his group, he represents syllables by musical notes, and he recognises that our pronunciation of Latin substitutes accent for quantity, making two trochees of *miserarum* (p. 107). Still more striking is his description of ordinary English verse as " iambics in accent, yet in real Quantity of Time nearer to spondees " (p. 142). On the whole, Say strikes one as eminently sane and reasonable, while deficient in his conception of what actually constitutes verse. His width of view, and sympathy with Elizabethan liberty, are welcome amid so much that is narrow and perverse, though he omitted to lay any solid foundation on which to erect a definite prosody.

The last member of this group comes nearest to dealing with the actual mechanism of metre. Mason's two *Essays on the Power of Numbers* came out in 1749, but I quote the revised second edition of 1761. Its modest Preface disclaims profound inquiry ; his work is merely practical, for the use of students. The Essay on " Poetic Numbers " comes first. These consist of " times, syllables, feet, measures, verse ", each after the first being made by a combination of several of the preceding (p. 5). This use of " times " is evidently borrowed from Greek prosody, and he recognises that " custom and accent often . . . contract a double Time into a single one, e.g. Th' Infernal Serpent " (p. 7), also that some " Times " are shorter than others, but this makes no " great alteration in

the Harmony of Numbers " (p. 8). Into the pitfall of confusion between accent and quantity he tumbles headlong.
" By Quantity I mean that space of time, whether long or
short, in which any syllable is pronounced ; which in English
numbers is determined almost altogether by the accent "
(p. 9). And so, again—" The proper Accent and Emphasis
then is the chief rule that determines the English quantities "
(p. 11). Acting on this view, he has no doubt that our ordinary
verse is iambic, a short time followed by a long, and scans it
by Greek symbols—

$$\breve{\text{I}}\text{ lift} \mid \text{m}\bar{\text{y}}\text{ heart} \mid \text{t}\breve{\text{o}}\text{ thee.}$$

Nevertheless, when later he comes to analyse the opening
lines of *Paradise Lost*, he admits variations, this being how
he renders the famous first line—

$$\breve{\text{O}}\text{f man's} \mid \text{first dis-} \mid \breve{\text{o}}\text{be-} \mid \text{dience, and} \mid \text{th}\breve{\text{e}}\text{ fruit.}$$

He sees, however, that our ' quantities' often differ from
Latin ones, as when a vowel before another vowel remains long
(p. 10). How entirely his English quantities depend on accent
appears from his making *abominate* a double iamb (*cf.* pp.
17–19). His most interesting Section begins with Chap. VII
(p. 20 *seq.* ; the Chapters are very short), on the musical
proportion of feet. Again following Greek prosody, he classifies
feet according as they divide equally or unequally. Equal
feet (dactyl, anapaest, *etc.*) " are in proportion of the unison
in music ". Iambs and trochees are " in proportion of the
Octave or Diapason, which is the most perfect chord in
music ". Feet of sesquialterate ratio (3 : 2 or 2 : 3) " answer
to the Diapente or fifth in Music, which is the next most
perfect concord ". He lays down quite clearly (p. 22) that
feet in verse correspond to bars in music, and that equal and
unequal times in verse answer to the common and triple times
of music. The musician's " beating time " thus represents
the metrist's " arsis and thesis ", which terms he uses in their
true Greek sense,[1] referring for justification to *Chambers's*

---

[1] In Greek prosody, the *thesis* or down-stroke indicated a strong
syllable, the *arsis* or up-stroke a weak one. Latin grammarians, oddly
enough, inverted the terms. This mistake passed into English use,
and still survives in many grammars, but is being generally discarded.

Cyclopaedia [for the Eighteenth Century, too, had its so-named repertory of knowledge]. By these he scans all lines, holding that a foot must not exceed one arsis and thesis, and that four-syllable feet are impossible in English [why ?]. But he has no objection to trisyllabic feet in heroic verse, approves Say's couplet already referred to, and quotes as a parallel Milton's " many a dolorous groan ". When, however, it comes to that other line of Milton's—

> In their triple degrees, regions to which . . .

his indulgence is exhausted. Like any dryasdust critic, he pronounces this " no verse, much less iambic " (Chap. XIV, p. 58). For the most part, however, he is liberal and reasonable. As against Pemberton, he maintains that trochee followed by iamb is legitimate in our strictest verse, and he recognises dropped syllables in triple-time verse, *e.g.*—

> My time, | O ye Mu- | ses, was hap- | pily spent,

where he has no doubt that the feet are anapaests. *Caesura* (Chap. X) he thinks is as necessary in English heroic as in Latin hexameter verse, " and hath as many variations " ; but he does not explain its rationale in either. Of natural quantity in English words he takes no account whatever ; every accented syllable is long, every unaccented short, but when two long or two short syllables meet in a foot he simply records the fact, and does not offer any explanation of how their meeting is possible.

The second Essay, on " Prosaic Numbers ", contains little that is material. In it he scans many passages of both verse and prose by – and ᴗ, and remarks that our modern verse is as much too strict in its rules as our " antient " verse was too lax (Chap. VII, p. 47). Incidentally he observes that Greek accent-marks were probably intended " to regulate the tone or key of the voice, not the stress or force of it " (Chap. III, p. 25). On the whole, Mason must be credited with recognising, more fully than any other of his group, the close analogy that exists between verse and music ; and he is quite

---

Whenever the terms occur in an English treatise, it is necessary to know whether they are employed in the orthodox Greek or the heterodox Latin sense.

against the Bysshian attempt to reduce all feet to one pattern (*Poetic Numbers*, p. 52, *note*). He wants but a better funda-mental theory of verse-structure to be a sympathetic and intelligent critic. Any theory which, ⋅ like his, starts by assuming that every " unaccented " syllable in English verse is equally " short ", every accented one equally long, is bound to wreck itself against the rocks of plain fact ; and some of Mason's scansions are astounding. Yet, after all deductions, his two Essays (for the third, on " Elocution ", is entirely negligible) stand out above the ruck of common prosodies, and must be remembered as one of the earliest attempts to vindicate for verse its rhythmical basis and relations.[1]

The relative shortness of this Chapter may excite surprise. Virtually, all that has gone before, from the little treatise of Gascoigne onward—setting aside quantitative verse as a thing by itself—may be regarded as belonging to it. Three Centuries of English verse did hardly more than produce the " old orthodoxy " of prosodical criticism, varied latterly by a few faint protests. Serious attempts to analyse that verse all date from after 1750, and will demand, when reached, examination at considerably greater length.

[1] He speaks of " rhythmus ", whence our word " rhime ", now assigned a special meaning of its own, though Milton used it to mean verse of any kind—

        Things unattempted yet in prose or rhime.

Cf. Poetic Numbers, p. 13, *note*, with its Classic references.

˙CHAPTER III

RESISTANCE AND REBELLION

1750–1800

WE now pass into the latter half of the Eighteenth Century, far more fruitful and interesting metrically than the former. It will be remembered that already, by 1750, a new spirit was awakening in English poetry ; life was stirring in the dry bones of Classicism. Gray, Collins, the Wartons, and others were groping, however stiffly and sentimentally, after Romantic motives. Cowper was already writing his "Early Poems", among them a piece of ' sapphics ' which I omitted to mention in its due place, but have now noted among *addenda* (see Appendix A). The way was being prepared for that great outburst and upheaval which is called the Romantic Reaction. In criticism, too, old creeds were being examined, old shibboleths discarded. Criticism, however, as a rule follows rather than precedes creation, and we need not be surprised to find the Bysshe school of prosody still potent for many a day. As a matter of fact, the first book that meets us in the new Half-Century is by one of its most uncompromising supporters, the great Dr. Samuel Johnson.

In my original Bibliography, I erroneously stated that the first volume of Johnson's *Dictionary* appeared in 1747. That was the date when his prospectus was issued ; the work itself, though he had hoped to complete it within three years, came out in two massive folio volumes in 1755. To Vol. I was prefixed a " History of the English language ", and a " Grammar of the English tongue ", the latter ending with a Section on " Prosody ". The Grammar underwent several corrections in subsequent editions, but I have not noticed any material change in the Prosody Section. It is short, clear, straightforward. The first part deals merely with rules of pronunciation, and one sentence alone in it requires note by us : " Pronunciation is just, when ... every syllable has its proper accent, or, which in English versification is the same, its proper quantity." Then he comes to "laws of versification ". Recognising only iambic and trochaic verse—except that anapaestic is mentioned by way of afterthought as a " very quick and lively measure ", in which " a syllable is often retrenched from the first foot "—he makes syllabic uniformity the basis and ideal. " In all these [iambic] measures the accents are to be placed on even syllables [in trochaic on odd] ; and every line considered by itself is more harmonious, as this rule is more strictly observed. The variations necessary to pleasure belong to the art of poetry, not to the rules of grammar." After exemplifying various lengths and combinations of rhymed and unrhymed lines (the latter being represented by one casual reference to Addison's blank verse), he concludes : " Our versification admits of few licenses, except a *synaloepha* or elision of *e* in *the* before a vowel, as *th' eternal* ; and more rarely of *o* in *to*, as *t' accept* ; and a *synaeresis*, by which two short vowels coalesce into one syllable, as *question, special* ; or a word is contracted by the expulsion of a short vowel before a liquid, as *av'rice, temp'rance.*"

That is literally all ! No inquiry into facts, no historical or philosophical treatment, no appeal to either reason or authority. Had this dictator been asked whence his " laws " were derived, what could he have answered ? Not that they were drawn from the practice of our chief writers ; Shakespeare and Milton laugh them to scorn, and it is noteworthy that he neither quotes from nor refers to these poets. Nor from the inherent nature of verse ; no such analysis was even attempted. Probably he would have said that they were rules observed by the " best wits " of his day. To these gentlemen our Elizabethan singers were barbarous and uncouth. Proper verse began with Denham and Waller, made great advance under Dryden, reached its climax in Pope. To us, such a view is almost unthinkable. But even granting its truth, Johnson's rule is still too narrow. It is by no means a fact that Pope's best lines, " considered by themselves," are harmonious in the ratio of their regularity of accentuation ; rather is the contrary true. Johnson's own verse, vigorous and strenuous if not very highly inspired, belies his critical precept. No English poet (unless Glover deserve the name) ever sanctioned by his practice this monstrous canon, which owes its conception and promulgation to grammarians alone. So artificial and unreal had our theoretic prosody become. Divorced from fact, it invented imaginary "laws", which were broken by even our most "correct" verse-writers, and whose observance would have killed all life in our poetry. Since Johnson's ideas probably still sway a good many people's minds, and shape to some extent the teaching of our grammars, it is needful here to protest against them entirely. They are utterly fallacious as a test of good verse, and can produce no vouchers for their pretence of authority. Unfortunately, Johnson was neither the first nor the last critic to substitute assertion for argument and imagination for fact. In any other science such procedure would be scouted ; one does not see why an exception should be made in regard of prosody.

I find nothing else to cite published during the decade 1750–60. But here should be mentioned some notes which may belong to it. When the poet Gray died in 1771, his posthumously published papers included certain fragments entitled " Observations on English metre ". These had been written several years before, to form part of a History of English Poetry projected but abandoned by him, as related in Mason's *Memoir*, Section V. In spite of the title, they contain little which bears on our subject. Gray did, indeed, purpose to give a full historical sketch of our poetry, commencing with the " Scaldic, British, and Saxon " sources which gave rise to a literature whose actual beginning he dated from Chaucer ; and he " made many elaborate disquisitions into the origin of rhyme, and that variety of metre to be found in the writings of our ancient poets ". The fragments which were printed justify this description, and show Gray to have been a careful and sympathetic student of our early verse. But they contain nothing definitely bearing on verse-structure. He enumerates various forms of versification, and declares his inability to understand what is meant by the " riding rhyme " of older critics.[1] He abandoned his task on finding that Warton [*infra*, 1774] was similarly engaged, and

---

[1] This term was applied to ' ten-syllable couplets ' like those of Chaucer's *Canterbury Pilgrims*, as distinguished from statelier quatrains and stanzas. For long such couplets were considered unfit for serious themes—an idea in Gray's time hardly comprehensible, though he himself wisely preferred quatrains for his famous *Elegy*.

made over some of his memoranda to him. Probably, therefore, the bulk of his notes may have been made shortly before
or after the year 1760.

The second decade of the Half-Century, on the other hand,
was marked by several publications important for us, particularly those which appeared in the year 1762. Foremost of
these comes a book in which prosody takes only a secondary
place. ' *Foster on Accent* ' was long reckoned a standard work,
its first edition as above being speedily followed by a much
enlarged edition a year later, while the most useful and
accessible one, that of 1820, contains further additions as well
as Gally's two Dissertations. Dr. Henry Gally, or Galley,
a versatile and accomplished divine, had published in 1754
a *Dissertation* against pronouncing ancient Greek according
to its accent-marks. Dr. John Foster, sometime head master
at Eton, and a good Classical scholar, was at first inclined to
accept Gally's view, but finally dissented, and wrote his *Essay
on the Different Nature of Accent and Quantity* to prove that
Greek should be so pronounced. Gally replied in a second
Dissertation which appeared while Foster's second edition was
passing through the press, but in time to let Foster append
a " Review of some passages in the preceding Essay, in reply
to Dr. G.'s second Dissertation ". " Dr. G." is Foster's usual
way of referring to his opponent, whose Dissertations were
published anonymously after a rather tiresome fashion of the
time, even when the authorship was no secret.[1] The dispute
between the two authors, therefore, referred primarily to
Greek and not to English. Foster contended that it was
theoretically possible to accentuate a short syllable without
lengthening it ; Gally maintained the opposite view. I referred briefly to this controversy before (p. 34), and need not
now dwell on it so far as Greek is concerned. For us the main
thing to notice is how both disputants agreed that in English
speech an acute accent involved prolongation of time. Foster,
indeed, recognises that such an accent may rest on a short
syllable, as in " privy " (1820 edition, p. 25, *note* ; this note
added in second edition) ; but even so he thinks it gives

---

[1] Sometimes no author's name is given on a title-page, though the
Preface or Dedication is subscribed with either initials or full name.
And sometimes, to make matters worse, such a book will be referred to
in other books by the publisher's name instead of the author's.

additional length to that syllable. He only maintains that
it need not have done so in Greek ; that there a short syllable
might have its tone raised without any alteration of " quantity ". He even believes that he can illustrate this in his own
pronunciation of Greek (p. 269). But he entirely agrees with
Gally that, in our ordinary English way of speaking, " *elevation*
doth not commonly subsist . . . without a *prolongation* too "
(p. 140, and *passim*) ; that all accented syllables in English
" sound long to the ear " (Gally, p. 374).

" Accent," according to Foster, means merely elevation or
depression of the voice (p. 3). All through his discussion he
distinguishes between accent and quantity [pitch and dura-
tion]. These are closely united, yet quite distinct (p. 7) ;
and " are equally founded in the very nature of the human
voice, are necessary and inseparable from it " (p. 5). To the
third element, *force*, he makes no reference, except in a passage
toward the end of his first Chapter where he terms it " spirit
or emphasis ", identifies it with aspiration, and adds that it
" is very distinct from accent and quantity, though occasionally joined with them " (p. 10). Our syllabic accent, according
to him, has nothing to do with this last, but is a combination
of higher tone and longer duration. Therefore the first
syllables of *liberty, heavily, honestly, character* are all marked
" long " by him ; the second syllable of *solicit* equally with
the second syllable of *mistaking* ; the first syllable of *folly* is
long, though less so than that of *dowry* (pp. 16–17). While
asserting this of English pronunciation, he finds it different in
Scotch, Welsh, and Irish. The Scot, he declares, accentuates
(and thereby lengthens) the last syllable of *majesty*, while still
prolonging the first syllable ; and similarly deals with the
last syllables of *human, subject, summons, monarchs* (pp. 25
and 35). The Scotch keep or rather increase our quantity, but
alter our accent ; the Irish observe both, but with a greater
degree of " spirit or emphasis " ; the Welsh keep our quantity
and alter the accent, adding a peculiar manner of voice
(pp. 38–9). He stoutly contends (Chap. II) that modern
languages have " natural quantity ", instancing the word
Chrultznitz (p. 28 ; in first edition *Grotzky*) ; yet he says that
the first syllable of *strengthen* " hath as quick and easy a pronunciation as the first syllable of *oozy* " (p. 25). On the whole,
his view seems to be that length, in English syllables, depends

mainly on accent. " Those syllables which I call long receive a peculiar stress of voice from their acute accent. . . . They are elevated ; but they are lengthened too. . . . We English cannot readily elevate a syllable without lengthening it" (*ibid.*). Surprise must be felt that a writer who could so accurately distinguish pitch from duration, and so clearly see that the two were separable, was yet content to mark as alike " long " the first syllable of *private* and the first syllable of *privy*.

Foster's remarks on English verse will be found in his third Chapter (largely added to in second edition). He makes our common verse *iambic*, our heroic line " trimeter brachycatalectic ", boldly scanning thus :

    An honest man's | the noblest work | of God.

But he admits three-syllable feet, making *visible* a dactyl [!], while other combinations of syllables yield tribrachs and anapaests, as " would appear much oftener, with propriety and grace, if abbreviations were more avoided ". He praises the " nervous springiness " of Pope's initial trochee, and in defiance of Johnson asserts that Pope's most regular lines are his weakest in point of versification. The trochee may occur anywhere save in the last foot [Milton would have had something to say to this restriction] ; and he finds one even where his principles would seem to require a pyrrhic, *e.g.*—

    As full, as perfect, in a hair as heart.

The pyrrhic he also recognises, as in the last two syllables of *eternity* or *philosophy* (all the foregoing in pp. 29–31). " The admission of so many different measures into our common verse gives it a variety . . . not to be exceeded, if equalled, in any of the ancient kinds of metre " (p. 32). But the comparative shortness of our heroic line, and the infrequency of dactyls in our language, not to speak of spondees, prevent our verse from reproducing the cadence of ancient hexameter. " For the most part the long and short syllables of our language are alternate " (p. 33). (Gally, on the other hand, thinks that English abounds in dactyls, but " hath no trisyllable that maketh an anapaest " : p. 319.) Singularly enough, Foster thus scans a trisyllabic line (p. 34)—

    With honour | and glory | through trouble | and danger—

where the cadence might equally well be termed dactylic or
anapaestic, and where two short syllables intervene between
each long one. With more consistency he makes (next page)
the following line consist of *cretics*—

Ō thĕ sweēt | coūntry̆ līfe | blēst wĭth heālth | peāce ănd eāse.

But his most remarkable contention (p. 35 *seq.*) is that the
essence of English verse is " founded in quantity alone ", not
upon accent, though the latter " jointly with quantity doth
direct it ". In support of this he quotes the couplet—

> All human things are subject to decay,
> And when fate summons, monarchs must obey—

and makes the extraordinary assertion that, though a Scots-
man should accentuate the final syllables of the words *human,
subject, summons, monarchs,* the metre would still " essentially
subsist ". What metre would remain after such violation of
rhythm I am as unable to imagine as I am to pronounce on
the accuracy of Foster's description of Scottish pronunciation in
his day. It seems to me that the metrical cadence would be
entirely destroyed by such mispronunciation, and that what
" subsists " is only a possibility of restoring that cadence by
proper pronunciation. In what sense " quantity " would be
unaltered, either on Foster's showing or any other, I fail to
see. Yet he goes on to say that while metre depends on
quantity alone, " rhythm is in its nature more complex, and
seems to comprehend accent with quantity " ; justifying this
by saying that an English line needs no caesural division,
because with us " the long times and acute tones coincide ",
so that such a line as—

> Heroes, repel attacks, command success,

is good rhythmically as well as metrically. Even were this
passage less hesitating and vague than it is, I do not think
that any intelligible account of the basis of English verse can
be extracted from it ; nor, perhaps, is it altogether reasonable
to look for one from a writer whose main concern was to teach
the true nature of the ancient Greek accent.

It may be added that Foster freely uses the anglicised word
rhythm, being one of the earliest writers to do so ; and that
Gally speaks several times of *stress,* though not identifying it

with force. Primatt, another writer who joined the fray with
a book called *Accentus Redivivi* (1764), writes the former word
as " rythm ". The further fortunes of the Greek-accent
controversy do not concern us, though we shall find it ob-
truding itself in several later studies of English verse. The
fashion of printing Greek without accent-marks had a very
prolonged existence. After the end of the first quarter of the
Nineteenth Century, it appears in a book by the Public
Orator at Oxford [*vide infra*, 1827], and in publications of the
Galignani press of Paris ; at one time it bid fair to become
universal.[1]

From Scotland came, in the same year 1762, a work of much
larger scope, the first of many attempts to consider scientifically the whole field of artistic labour. Henry Home or
Hume, a judge in Court of Session under the title of Lord
Kames (sometimes spelt Kaims by his contemporaries),
published in 1762 his *Elements of Criticism* in three octavo
volumes. A second edition was called for two years later, and
others followed ; that of 1824, in one volume, can still be
procured. The twenty-five Chapters of which the book
consists are divided into Sections, and the whole arrangement
is admirably clear. Whereas " Bossu, a celebrated French
critic," rests his rules merely on the practice of Homer and
Virgil, supported by the authority of Aristotle, Kames seeks
to discover principles, working upward from facts (*Introduction*). The promise of this beginning is to some extent
fulfilled, as a glance at the chapter-headings will show. The
style may be somewhat stiff and dry, the matter somewhat
verbose and platitudinous ; but the scientific spirit is fairly
awake. In each department the endeavour is to get at facts,
not merely to repeat traditional phrases.

Our particular subject is reached in his Chap. XVIII on
" Beauty of Language ", particularly in its fourth Section on
" Versification ". Noteworthy hints occur in the other three
Sections, as indeed throughout the book ; in the second
Section he assumes that *feet* are pronounced " with a sensible
interval between each " (p. 249 of 1824 edition, to which my
references are made), and the last paragraphs of the third

---

[1] Accent-marks are omitted in Leigh Hunt's *Imagination and Fancy*,
published by Smith, Elder & Co. in 1844. Can a later instance be
quoted ?

Section deal with pronunciation. He distinguishes five qualities of sound, according to which it can be *harsh*, *long*, *high*, *loud*, *quick*, or the opposites. In syllables the first and second are fixed by component elements, the others are at the speaker's option. Such matters, however, belong chiefly to the delivery of verse ; its actual formation is considered in Section 4. Here we find at first somewhat of Johnsonian rigour. The number of syllables in a line is assumed not to vary. Verse and prose alike please by intermixing long and short syllables ; verse differs from prose only in doing this more perfectly, and is " subjected to certain inflexible laws ". Pope's *Rape of the Lock* is held up as being, " in point of versification, the most complete performance in the English language." Five things are said to be of importance in all verse, *viz.* (1) the number of syllables in a line ; (2) their different lengths, *i. e.* " the difference of time taken in pronouncing " each ; (3) the arrangement of these syllables into words ; (4) the " pauses or stops in pronouncing " ; (5) " the pronouncing syllables in a high or low tone." The first three of these are " obviously essential to verse ". Two short syllables are " precisely equal " to one long ; and this rule holds good in all verse. The fourth and fifth " things " he also finds in both ancient and modern verse. Having thus laid his foundation (all this is in the first two or three pages of § 4), he next considers the structure of ancient hexameter verse, rejecting the usual division into feet—which he deems a mere invention of grammarians (p. 276, *note*)—and substituting a constructive canon of his own formulation. Then (p. 282) he comes back to English verse. Our heroic line he treats in the same way. While discarding feet, he demands absolute succession of long and short syllables, condemning such a line as—

> This nymph, to the destruction of mankind,

because *the* is not a long syllable. Structurally considered, he allows only two variations from iambic uniformity : the initial trochee, and the final extra syllable. (*Cf.* p. 276, *note*, last paragraph.) The occasional use of an " Alexandrine " is also pronounced legitimate (p. 282). Variety he would have provided simply by dividing the line at different points, and he enumerates four types of heroic line, according as the " capital pause " comes after the fourth, fifth, sixth, or seventh syllable

(p. 295). But, just as one has concluded that his view is wholly restricted to the Popian couplet, he goes on to blank verse (p. 300), and surprises us by preferring it. Shakespeare's blank verse, indeed, he dismisses as " a sort of measured prose ", " perfectly well adapted to the stage " (p. 301) ; but Milton's contains " the richest melody as well as the sublimest sentiments ", and he exalts it not only above rhyming couplets but in some respects above Greek or Latin hexameter verse. The passage which he quotes, curiously enough, contains two instances of the very fault objected to in Pope ; but these pass unnoticed. It need hardly be said that each of Milton's lines is made to contain ten syllables by writing *th' eastern, temp'rate, etc.* ; yet *aëry* [*sic*] is not altered to *airy*. The " great defect of Milton's versification, otherwise admirable," is said to be a " want of coincidence between the pauses of the sense and sound " (p. 303). A short explanation of the inability of English verse to reproduce " hexameter " melody, and some sensible remarks about rhyme, conclude the Section.

This analysis is certainly too narrow. A view which sees in Shakespeare's lines only " measured prose ", and in Pope's best verse habitual incorrectness, may safely be pronounced faulty. Yet, on the other hand, there is vigour and sense in Kames's criticism, despite its cramping theory. His *obiter dicta* are usually sound. He sees clearly that accent is not a structural but an illuminative element. Identifying it with tone (pp. 271, 275), he notes that " an accent considered with respect to sense is termed *emphasis* " (p. 293, *note*). He feels how vague is our perception of quantity. " Every language has syllables that may be pronounced long or short at pleasure ; but the English above all abounds in syllables of that kind " (p. 282). Even his rigid doctrine of caesural pause and the way it is reinforced by accent (p. 295), while too universally stated, is founded on observation. Our heroic line does naturally tend to break into two sections, less often equal than unequal ; but we have no right to make this a law, for our chief poets often disregard it. So, too, even Pope sometimes neglects the pause or break at the end of a couplet ; this licence, however, Kames does not wholly condemn (pp. 290, 291), while to the running on of sense at the end of a blank verse line he is altogether tolerant (pp. 300–1). Also, though recognising four regular places of capital pause, he admires the boldness with which this rule is disregarded by Milton, and occasionally by Pope (p. 292). He is ready to admit licences " where the sense or expression requires a variation " ; but he regards them as cases where " the melody may justly be sacrificed " (*ibid.*), instead of as instances of a higher melody. English verse he considers decidedly superior to French, through its variety of pause (p. 302), and he censures Boileau for letting sentences end with the first line of a couplet (p. 300, *note*) ; but he admits the greater liveliness of French speech (p. 295, *note*). In one place he strangely professes not to know if our language contains any word of five syllables (p. 283). His prime contention that " a musical pause ought never to be placed where a pause is excluded by the sense " (p. 291) must be pronounced too sweeping, and his condemnation of scores of lines in consequence altogether too dogmatic. With a better theory, Kames would have made a critic of high quality ; but it is only too evident throughout his book that as yet English prosody had never faced the whole facts of verse as exhibited by our best poets.

Ireland vied with Scotland in study of our subject. Sheridan published in 1762 some remarkable theories about accent, but as his chief work on English verse appeared in 1775 I reserve consideration of him till then, asking readers to remember that his influence as writer and teacher was at work during the years which intervened. A fourth book dated 1762, however, also had Hibernian antecedents. Daniel Webb, Irishborn though Cambridge-bred, published his *Remarks on the Beauties of Poetry*, as two years earlier he had published *An Inquiry into the Beauties of Painting*, and as seven years later he published *Observations on the Correspondence between Poetry and Music*. All three were reprinted, with other papers not to our purpose, in a quarto volume entitled *Miscellanies*, by the late Daniel Webb, Esq. (London, 1802 ; my references are to this edition), and may be considered together ; the more so, as the interval between 1762 and 1769 produced no outstanding work on our subject. The first two are in dialogue form, not without dramatic liveliness, especially in the second, which opens with an entirely imaginary reference to "a gentleman who has just left us ". Seven dialogues discuss Painting in the first treatise ; in the second, on Poetry, there are but two. Beginning with a spirited defence of Shakespeare and

Milton, he ridicules the monotony of Pope, and extols the superior variety of blank verse (pp. 103–14). Then, after some censure of sibilants, he goes on to treat of expressiveness in verse ; the remainder of the first dialogue, and the whole of the second, deal either with this or with the more general attractions of verse.

But much more important, in itself and for us, was Webb's volume of 1769. In this Essay—for such is its form—he makes a real attempt to consider verse-structure. Beginning with more general questions, he reaches this subject in pp. 197–222. There must, he thinks, be quantities in verse ; but whether these " are governed by an invariable prosody, or flow from the impression of the sense and accent, the effects will be much the same in all parallel movements ". Therefore English and Greek lines of similar length produce identical effects,[1] even though in our case " the quantities of syllables are but the variations of accent ". Greek verse, like ours, founds on contrasting grave and acute accent ; a dactyl does but repeat the second stroke of a trochee, an anapaest the first of an iamb. Like Kames, he thinks no language is incapable of metre, unless there be one whose syllables are all pronounced in equal times, which some say is the case in Hebrew, but this he does not believe (p. 200). On the contrary, he thinks the root of " natural prosody " is the same in all known languages (p. 203). In English verse (p. 204 *seq.*) he recognises feet, but will not admit a dactyl where such scansion would leave an adjacent foot of one syllable, as in " And | vindicate ". He praises the spirited effect of trochee followed by iamb. " When an enforced or ascending accent strikes on a monosyllable, the vibrations continue, as in the chord of a musical instrument, after the impression or articulation hath ceased ; especially when the stroke is succeeded by a pause." " As our accents are modes of expression, sound is influenced by sense " ; " where accent and structure co-operate," they may give some additional length to a syllable. " It should seem that the mechanism of the Greek verse took its rise, and derived its advantages, from the opposite principle " (p. 205). For this reason monosyllables are not necessarily heavy with us ; " the feeblest and heaviest lines in our language are those

---

[1] Webb's illustrations of this thesis—" I fain would sing of Cadmus," *etc.*—are quoted by almost every subsequent metrist of the Century.

which are overcharged with polysyllables " (*ibid.*). So, later (pp. 212–13), he says that two monosyllables are as good as any dissyllable, and two dissyllables as any quadrisyllable ; we have subdued our polysyllables, in verse, to the tenor of a monosyllabic rhythmus, although music tends to shorten the mid-syllable of a trisyllabic word. Dealing with " imitation of classical rhythmus ", he remarks that with us " the accent governs the measure, while the sense, in conjunction with the laws of musical succession, governs the accent " (p. 209).[1] Before we could write hexameters of Classic type, we must recast our language. Finally, dealing with the " separation of Music from Poetry ", he is puzzled " how their union could have subsisted after the institution of measures founded on artificial quantities " (p. 212). (" The movements of prose hold a middle course, between a total neglect, and an absolute strictness of measure " : *ibid., note.*) All artificial prosody thwarts musical accent. " Modern lyrical poesy is a school for painters, not for musicians " (p. 215). As the spirit of expression declines, a taste for description begins ; this is seen both in verse and music. Imitative description is only good when striking ; *procumbit humi bos* is trivial, Milton's Behemoth sublime. The more syllables we can get into the same time, the greater impression is produced of lightness and rapidity ; but an " Alexandrine " is not lighter or swifter than a " pentameter ".

Webb's ideas seemed upsetting to his contemporaries, and are often animadverted on by later critics. To us they seem amateurish and tentative, yet possessed of a certain freshness and individuality. There is an attempt to look at verse with his own eyes, not through pedantic spectacles ; to recognise that verse and music are akin, and that metre is something more than a mere counting of syllables. He does not define accent, rather takes it for granted, and does not spend time over caesural pauses. It is the actual structure of verse, not merely its delivery, that engages his attention, though he is aware that sound is often regulated by sense. If he does not do much to determine the questions he raises, he at least deserves the credit of raising them for others to settle. He is a pioneer in the search or a more rational prosody than that

[1] " Strong passions . . . were never destined to creep through monotonous parallels ; they call for a more liberal rhythmus " (p. 208).

which made verse be mainly an exercise in arithmetic. The frequent references to his books show that they made their mark on men's minds.

Little of consequence can be cited between 1762 and 1769. Three publications only during this time need be named. Dr. John Brown, Vicar [according to the British Museum Catalogue] of Newcastle-on-Tyne, printed at Dublin in 1763 a small book entitled *A Dissertation on the Rise, Union, and Power, the Progressions, Separations, and Corruptions, of Poetry and Music.* Though this learned treatise begins and ends with a poem by the author, and though its erudition ranges from Greek and Latin writers to Snorro Sturleson and Lafiteau's Iroquois, it is taken up almost entirely with ancient and modern music, and deals very little indeed with verse,[1] though he does speak of " rythm [*sic*] or measure " (p. 29, and elsewhere). In the same year, 1763, the *British Magazine* contained a paper by Oliver Goldsmith, now included among his " Miscellaneous Essays ", on " Versification ", to which I have before referred (p. 37) on account of its allusion to pseudo-Classic metres. Otherwise there is little new or noteworthy either in this Essay or in its neighbours, which merely repeat current ideas, and utter vague phrases like " the words we term *emphatical* are such as by their sound express the sense they are intended to convey " (Essay XV, on " Poetry distinguished from other writing "). In this same Essay he observes that versification is not the sole criterion that distinguishes poetry from prose, another being " its own peculiar expression " ; and in the preceding one (on the " Origin of poetry "), after starting with the doubtful axiom " poetry sprang from ease ", he goes on to draw a vigorous picture of the tribal emotions and acts of worship in which verse almost certainly had its origin, whatever we may say about the origin of " poetry ". But these are commonplaces, as are most of his remarks on *metaphors* and *hyperbole* (Essays XVI and XVII) ; while the short paper on versification (Essay XVIII) contains no outstanding feature. Verse is still " an harmonious arrangement of long and short syllables ", our verse containing feet similar to those of Classic verse ; " to assert that modern poetry has no feet, is a ridiculous absurdity." The real difference is merely that " rhythmus

---

[1] It is, however, very often referred to by subsequent writers.

or number " in ancient verse relates to the feet, and in modern
to the syllables.   So with his remarks on " pause and accent ".
It is all just what others have said, expressed with Goldsmith's
delightful ease and clearness, and without any apparent mis-
giving.   The speculations of heterodox critics have left no
trace on his teaching, which repeats with tranquil assurance
doctrines much more familiar than convincing.

In 1765 was published a treatise by one John Rice, of whom
I know nothing, entitled *An Introduction to the Art of Reading
with Propriety and Elegance* (8vo, London, Tonson).   This
might be supposed a mere elocutionary manual, but several
Sections deal with prosody.   Say, " Kaims ", Mason, Harris,
Sheridan are referred to by name and criticised, the last with
severity, though Rice agrees with him in dissociating accent
from tone.   English verse is discussed in the last three
" Sections " of Chap. II more especially, without any definite
result, except to protest against pedantic rules.   Johnson's
tenet is directly challenged ;   " from. what Principle of
Nature " does it follow that regular alternation is preferable
to irregular (pp. 110–11 ; *cf.* 153) ?   Classic laws of prosody
do not apply in English ;   to measure our verse by dactyls and
spondees reminds him of an Oxford wag " selling strong beer
by the ell " (p. 116).   Milton's harmony is exalted above the
" mechanical form of versification " used by Dryden, Pope,
and Addison (pp. 156–7).   When, however, he passes from
criticism to construction, his teaching is indefinite.   " The
harmony of verse principally consists . . . in the consonance
or affinity which the words of such verse bear to their meaning " (p. 115).   Accent does not determine quantity, yet
quantity is a compound of accent and time (p. 116).   " Accent
and emphasis do not actually give time, but supply the want
of it in the composition of metrical feet " (*ibid.*).   Feet, however, need not be equal, except when accompanied by music
(p. 137).   The mechanism of English verse is a mixture,
" founded on heterogeneous principles " (p. 165) ;   he does
not even think that equal lines are necessary to blank verse
(p. 179), and makes its harmony depend on " the quick succession of a few flowing syllables " (p. 176).   In fact, he ends
by almost denying the necessity of any structural form at all.
These revolutionary ideas seem to have excited less notice
than might have been expected, but the fact of their being

put forward at all is remarkable, and contrasts curiously with Goldsmith's easy conservatism.

The third last decade of the Eighteenth Century was richer far than its predecessors as regards metrical criticism. In passing may be mentioned a *History of the Science and Practice of Music* (5 vols. 4to, 1771), published anonymously after the prevailing fashion, but known to be by Johnson's biographer Sir John Hawkins ; mentioned, merely because its " Preliminary Discourse " is so often referred to (generally without naming the author) by metrical writers when treating of the " principles and power of harmony ". And then we come to a little book on *Vocal Sounds* (1773), written by Abraham Tucker under the pseudonym of " Edward Search ". This I have already mentioned in connection with its author's attempts at quantitative verse. Of ordinary English measures he says little, being content to regard them as mainly " iambic " (pp. 50–2). His merit and originality depend on his clear statement of phonetic principle, that indispensable basis of a true prosody. He is, indeed, bewildered by the false doctrine that a vowel followed by two consonants was sounded long in Latin, and troubles himself about this to no purpose. But he states plainly that we have quantitative difference of vowel-sound in English, instancing *wood* and *wooed*, *have* and *halve*, *Mary* and *merry*, etc. (pp. 9, 21). He reprobates our method of teaching spelling, since *a. n. d.* should stand for *aind*, *g. o. n. e.* for *jony* (p. 11) ; and desires symbols like those since invented. He sees that speaking, not writing, determines quantity, and that a doubled consonant produces no sensation of length in English (p. 65). Later (p. 89 *seq.*) he deals with prose, which also has measure, but in it " the art of periodic measure consists . . . in approaching as near as possible, without falling into, direct verse " (p. 93). Pope's Homer he finds " cloying " (p. 98), and he notes that " we can still make shift to read Chaucer " (p. 115). Further quotation is needless, but Tucker must always be remembered as one of the first, if not the very first, to apply phonetic method to our verse, to point out that verse-structure depends on sound not on spelling, and thus to pave the way for a more adequate and helpful conception of metre.

Very different is another little book, also published in 1773, and also referred to by me before (p. 38). *The Elements of*

Speech, by John Herries, A.M., has an ambitious title, which its 259 pages hardly justify. The first part deals with voice-formation and organs of speech, the second with qualities and " command " of speech. In the third Chapter of this Part II he remarks that " an absurd notion has long prevailed " according to which accented syllables are long and unaccented short (p. 123) ; but the hopes raised by this promising dictum prove illusory. As stated before, he admits that he does not know what ' quantity ' means, either in Latin or English (*ibid.*), and excuses himself from discussing the nature of accents in either tongue (p. 171), his aim being wholly practical. He sees " no reason why the same accents, intervals, pauses, and cadences that occur in any Greek or Latin verse may not be introduced into the English " (p. 185). " Upon the whole, it appears a very easy task to reduce into English the exact measure of every verse or stanza in Homer, Sappho, Anacreon, Horace, or even Pindar, so far as it [*sic*] regards the arrange-ment of the accented syllables " ; but he does not think this " would greatly promote the harmony of our compositions " (p. 187). The purport of quoting these remarks is to show that their author, like most people still, read Latin verse to English measure, his total ignorance of quantity bringing about the same result as their substitution of accent for quantity. It was natural that he should think our triple-time verse represented the flow of ancient hexameter ; but it is extra-ordinary that trained scholars should think so. Otherwise there is nothing noteworthy in this book, and we must pass on to matter of greater importance.

James Burnet, Lord Monboddo (his title derived, like that of his elder colleague Lord Kames, from a seat on the Scottish bench), has left a somewhat bizarre reputation. Pre-Dar-winian theories as to the simian origin of man, our ancestors having worn off their tails by sitting on them ; suppers after the manner of the ancients, satirised by Fielding in his novels ; rides from Edinburgh to London, coaches being despised as effeminate—these and other eccentricities are associated with his name. His latest biographer [1] does not seem to take his writings seriously. It will surprise many to hear that his book *Of the Origin and Progress of Language* contains acute analysis

[1] *Lord Monboddo and some of his Contemporaries*, by William Knight, LL.D. London (Murray), 1900.

and powerful reasoning. It is deficient in the method and lucid order of Kames's treatise. Its six volumes came out irregularly from 1773 to 1792, with no name or dedication, and by different publishers. The later volumes unblushingly repeat the former, traversing the same ground, often using identical language. A student of metre need hardly go beyond the first and second volumes, with perhaps the beginning of the third. Vol. I, treating of primitive man and the origin of speech, contains the speculations which so amused his contemporaries ; in Vol. II (published in 1774) he comes to the " Art of Language ". This second volume is divided into three " Books ", of which the first deals with the formal part of language (nouns, verbs, *etc.*), the second with the material part (" language considered as sound ", p. 226), the third with " the composition of language " (*i. e.* syntax). It is therefore to Vol. II, Book II, that our chief attention must be directed. Its first three Chapters treat mainly of articulation, of letters and alphabets ; with Chap. IV begins his examination of accent and quantity as elements of spoken sound.

Monboddo was a devoted Grecian, and with him accent means variation of pitch. He argues at great length that this was so in ancient Greek, but when he comes (p. 298) to consider English accent, maintains that our change of tone is on words or sentences only, not on syllables, which are simply pronounced louder or softer, the music of our language so far as syllables are concerned being " nothing better than the beating of a drum " (p. 300). Such alternations of force hardly exist in French, and probably did not in Greek or Latin, since " no antient grammarian speaks a word of [*i. e.* about] it " (*ibid.*). This doctrine excited very much comment. I do not think Monboddo was first to use the metaphor of a *drum*. Herries refers to it (*op. cit.*, p. 173), and there may be earlier instances.[1] But Monboddo made it his own, returns to it over and over again, and no idea is more often referred to by others in connection with him. It seems to me that all who make English *stress* purely and simply a matter of " force-accent " are bound to endorse Monboddo's description. He himself, however, was driven to modify it later, as will appear when we come to Steele [1775].

[1] I had imagined Sheridan its inventor, but cannot find that ne uses it in print before 1775.

In his next Chapter he takes up ' quantity ', conceived of as absolute duration of motion. His elaborate analysis of the five possible forms of rhythm—" it does not appear that the nature of the thing admits of any more " (p. 317)—with its clear distinction between frequency of percussions and continuance of one percussion, may be passed by, since he confines attention to this last-named, which he says is called *time* in music and *quantity* in speech, though it really forms only a part of the whole ' quantity ' of a language (*ibid., note*). Excellent are his remarks on the phenomenon so defined. Not for him the vulgar error that a Latin vowel became long when followed by two consonants, or the equally common fallacy that a doubled consonant in English means a double sound. The length of a syllable, he points out, even in Greek verse was relative and not absolute ; the proportion was taken as two to one, minor differences being neglected (pp. 318–19). Length depended either on the vowel, or on the consonants which follow the vowel, and which " retard the pronunciation so much, as to make the syllable long " (p. 319). " And so nice were the antients, that they distinguished by their pronunciation whether the vowel, in a syllable long by position, was of itself long or short " (p. 320). But he recognises that neither quantity of this kind, nor accent such as theirs, is necessary or essential. What, then, of English verse ? If we alter the quantity of particular syllables in a line, it does not change the metre (p. 326). Some syllables are long in themselves, but even these can be pronounced short without essential change ; and most are indifferent. Accented syllables are not longer than others, only louder, and " pronounced with more violence " (pp. 322–5). Foster was wrong in assigning absolute quantity to English syllables, just as in not keeping separate the rhythm of Greek verse from the tone-melody of its words (p. 322, *cf.* 329 *seq.*). Two things are essential to English verse : accent, and number of syllables. And by their combination we make the best verse of any nation in Europe (p. 325). French verse, owing to want of accent, needs the aid of rhyme ; their blank verse he thinks " miserably unsuccessful ". On the other hand, " there is a certain hardness or want of music in all the languages of Gothic or Celtic extraction " which disqualifies them from reproducing Classic metres (p. 327).

At the beginning of Chap. VI he shows how we substitute accentuation for quantity in reading Latin and Greek, making for example the first syllable of *Tityrus* louder and stronger, but not longer. Omitting this, and the earlier part of Book III, I come to Chap. VIII in the latter, " Of the composition of accents in English, and of English verse ". Applying his former analysis, he defines our verse as a " species of rhythm ", concerned with loud and soft syllables, these occurring at intervals which must be " equal or such as have some other ratio to one another " (pp. 384–5). This implies " a certain [*i. e.* fixed] number of syllables ". Here again he drags in his *drum.* Yet presently (p. 388, *note*) he distinguishes between " the accent, which is the elevation of the voice upon one *syllable* of the word, and the emphasis, which is the same elevation upon a *word* of a sentence ". So he does seem to recognise the function of *tone* in verse, as he recognises the existence of pauses " such as the sense requires " (p. 396). He praises Milton for securing variety by " breaking the measure ", and approves the cadence of

> Burnt after them *to the bottomless pit,*

which was so often censured (p. 388, *note*). The remainder of this Chapter enumerates various forms of English verse, characterizing them in the usual way as iambic, trochaic, anapaestic, though he seems to use these terms with some reluctance. At the end he recurs once more to his drum, and rebukes the heresies of " one John Mason " (p. 401, *note*). Succeeding Chapters wander off into other subjects, the " feet " of prose, the artistic development of language, Chinese, and Bishop Wilkins's " philosophical language " ; and the volume ends with three Dissertations on Greek. Throughout these pages, and in Vol. III (1776), which deals with *style*, there are many shrewd sayings, and Milton is quoted (often in unexpected places) as a model and master. A note on p. 409 in Vol. III refers to Steele, and distinguishes " syllabic tones, or accents, properly so called " from " tones of passion and sentiment ". Otherwise I have noted nothing of importance to add to the foregoing, though I cannot pretend to have read carefully the subsequent volumes, which seem mainly to repeat their predecessors. The gist of Monboddo's view I believe to be stated above.

That view, it will be seen, differs from the orthodox one mainly in substituting loudness for length ; and even this may have been suggested by Sheridan. Otherwise he does not seem to transcend the common notion of verse depending on a fixed number of syllables. His excellence is in phonetics rather than prosody. Yet he never objects to additional syllables ; and his glorification of Milton above Pope, blank verse above rhyme, together with his independent view of what constitutes ' quantity ', must have helped to encourage new conceptions. Had his six volumes been compressed into three, with more strict relation of ideas and merciless excision of digressions and repetitions, they might have ranked among the institutional works of our language. As it is, they remain a storehouse of vastly mingled materials, out of which may be picked some really sound and excellent stuff. I do not think they have ever been reprinted [1], but a selection of their best passages might have advantageously been made.

Perhaps *A New Dictionary of the English Language*, by William Kenrick, LL.D., (4to, London, 1773) should be added to our Bibliography for the sake of its " Rhetorical Grammar " (pp. 1–57). The Dictionary indicates pronunciation by elaborate symbols, anticipating a cherished design of Sheridan's. Prosody is considered briefly and generally in Chapter I, Section VI, of the " Grammar ", and somewhat more minutely in the last three Sections of Chapter II. But little definite doctrine can be extracted from these. As a critic of others, Kenrick is acute, and will not admit that our syllables form " what the ancients called a foot " (p. 48). Yet in lieu of this conception he offers nothing but vague talk about the " easy flow " of what he indifferently terms *feet* or *measures*, which are constituted by alternation of accented and unaccented syllables. Of any thing conditioning that alternation he seems unconscious, or of any need for a theory of metre. That this attitude was not peculiar to him my next paragraph will show.

In 1774 appeared the first volume of Thomas Warton's great *History of English Poetry*, in favour of which Gray had abandoned his own projected one. It was completed in four volumes, the last a posthumously published fragment. Long the standard work on its subject, it was reprinted several

---

[1] Vols. I and II went into a second edition almost immediately, but I fancy that was all.

times during last Century, and still holds the field in W. C. Hazlitt's edition of 1871. Students speak with respect of its survey of our elder literature, and at the time it was thought wonderful. But to us the most astonishing fact about it is that it contains absolutely no discussion of verse-structure. This erudite and accomplished historian of our poetry never asks himself what is the actual nature of the verse he is describing. Even when, in Vol. IV, he records the Elizabethan attempts at quantitative verse, he dismisses them with a remark on their " unnatural and impracticable mode of versification " (p. 289, Hazlitt's edition ; said of W. Webbe). Historically, his survey is admirable ; philosophically, it is naught. I do not think a more striking instance could be found of how entirely English scholarship had blinked the question of prosody, taking for granted a traditional view which applied Latin rules to English verse without ever inquiring whether as a matter of fact such application were possible and justifiable.

But the work left undone by Warton was taken up by others. The same year which saw his first volume issued saw also published, really anonymous, *An Essay upon the Harmony of Language, intended principally to illustrate that of the English Language.* Thirty years later it reappeared as *An Inquiry into the Principles of Harmony in Language, and of the Mechanism of Verse, modern and antient. By William Mitford, Esq. The second edition, with improvement and large addition.* In its original form, the *Essay* was chiefly a criticism of Foster. The enlarged *Inquiry* follows the same material arrangement, leaves out much detailed criticism, replacing this by more general statement. It is much fuller, and more authoritative. In many respects, however, the earlier *Essay* seems to me preferable, being simpler and clearer and more concise. Chronological fitness also makes it desirable to quote mainly from it, while reserving the right to refer to the later edition. Mitford being an acknowledged authority, his book deserves careful study. The *Essay* is divided into thirteen " *Sections* " or Chapters, the *Inquiry* into eighteen.

At the outset, Mitford complains of prevailing ignorance about the factors of speech, particularly of our own speech ; some make accent its efficient principle, some quantity ; " some affirm that there is no such thing as quantity in our language, and most hold that what quantity we have is always

determined by accent " (p. 7). A little later he denounces the
errors of " all who have written on English prosody, and their
utter inability to form any system for analysing English
verse " (p. 19). For himself, he distinguishes in language
melody, cadence, and *articulation* (p. 10). The third adds
beauty to speech, as does the tone [*timbre*] of a violin to sound ;
by attention to it the French and Italians have improved
their languages. But the first and second form his subject.
" Melody, in language, arises from the various tones of the
voice, which are called accents. Cadence is determined by the
quantity of time employed in the pronunciation of syllables "
(pp. 11–12). Hence arises a third incident to the harmony
of human speech called *meter* [*sic* throughout] or *measure.*
Following Foster into the question of ancient accentuation, he
notes that the Greek accent-marks " are daily growing more
out of fashion " (p. 19). For the most part he accepts Foster's
view, but complains that its author does not apply it to any
living language. He (Mitford) will therefore try to explain
" the particular nature of accent and quantity in the English
language " (p. 28).

What we commonly call accent, he says, is really *principal
accent.* " Every trisyllable " which has a strong accent on its
first syllable has " some " also on its last, and *vice versa* ;
e. g. *cónfidènt, èntertáin.* The principal accent he calls acute,
the other grave, and omits minor varieties. Accent being
" nothing more than the tone of the voice ", its " more minute
modifications are indeed almost infinite " (p. 30) ; for practical
purposes the above-named two suffice. Quantity is more
complex, depending either on vowels alone or on " the connexion of vowels with consonants " (p. 31). Most dogmatically
he lays down that there are *six* degrees of quantity, three of
which were reckoned short in ancient verse and three long ;
" we shall probably not err if we do the same " (pp. 39–41).
At great length he applies this to English speech, claiming
that a short vowel followed by two distinct consonantal
sounds make a long syllable with us as in Greek, this being
a rule " founded on nature and necessity ". Mute and liquid
are not distinct sounds, but coalesce ; we say *re-gret,* but
con-tend. And our doubled consonants represent usually one
sound. This last assertion he makes in capital letters, saying
it will startle the learned, and seemingly unaware that others

had anticipated him. As exceptions he notes *wholly* [pronounced *wholely*], *overrun*, and with careful speakers *irretrievable* but not *irritate* (pp. 41-4 ; *cf*. 55, 225 ; and *Inquiry*, p. 44). So *ng* is one consonant in *singer*, but two in *anger* ; and *dg* is a single sound in *sedgy*. As to vowels, he maintains that there is palpable difference of length, as in *fathom* and *father*, *pepper* and *paper*, *etc.* ; but that spelling is no guide, witness the last quoted pair of words, while others use the same letter for wholly different sounds (*ibid.*). Later he contends that vowel followed by vowel is short, except the diphthong *oi* ; *being* is as short as possible (p. 72), and " *die* of a rose " would be short but for the emphasis (p. 76). Thus he recognises emphasis as altering quantity, a fact which increases confusion.[1] We are scrupulous about our accented vowels, careless about our unaccented. This prolonged analysis occupies Sections III and V, Section IV being a protest against Foster's confounding accent with quantity. Then, in Section VI (p. 79), he proceeds to analyse English verse in accordance with the principles he has laid down.

" Meter ", he says, is irregular with us. " A certain rhythmical or measured disposition of the accents ", however, is necessary to the " very being " of English verse (p. 90). " Accent is the fundamental efficient [these two words in capitals] of English versification " (p. 91). The fact that " rhythmus ", with us, resides only in the " disposition " of accents makes our verse inferior to the " metrical versification of Greeks and Romans " (p. 93). Therefore trisyllabic feet are quite legitimate in heroic verse, and elision is condemned. He scans verse by feet, using symbols to show length and accentuation. In Sections VII and VIII Milton is exalted as the great model, his " inverted accents " giving all necessary variety ; yet he wrote " many harsh lines ", which " cannot be defended " (p. 102), while Shakespeare's verse was " calculated not to be read, but to be acted " (p. 118). Thus he condemns (p. 131) a line which he thus represents—

Gámbŏl'd | bĕfóre | thēm : th' unwíel-|dў ĕ́-|lĕphānt,

---

[1] In the *Inquiry* he makes emphasis moveable, accent immoveable (p. 64). He also admits that accent includes force as well as tone, while still contending that the latter is necessary, which he illustrates by óur pronunciation of the imaginary word *Alálal* (p. 57).

[the colon being meant to show *caesura*, while four accents are made to replace the usual five]. Similarly, in Section IX, where he deals with [oratorical] pauses and " cesura ", he declares that Milton's " bottomless pit " line " is to my ear not an English heroic verse " (p. 155). Section X is historical, and here the *Inquiry* (Section VII) is certainly fuller. In Section XI he comes to lyric measures, distinguishing between " common and triple cadence " (p. 181)—I will return to this immediately—recognising dropped syllables in the latter, and affirming that " the triple measures are wholly unfit for the sublime " (p. 190). Section XII deals mainly with Classic verse, asserting that " to an English ear a certain disposition of accents, without any regard to quantity, will raise the idea of a Latin hexameter " (p. 219), and that we read Latin verse " by an accentual rhythmus only " (p. 220). Finally, in his last Section, he deals more explicitly with the question of time, and makes what is perhaps his most important contribution to the subject under discussion.

This last Section deals with " Poetry and Music ". Both possess " rhythmus ", both exhibit common and triple time, and sometimes notes agree with syllables. But our iambic verse does not move to triple time, nor our dactylic to common (pp. 261–2). " The even and the triple foot can no more appear in the same verse than common and triple time in the same musical strain " [*query* as regards music ?], but a syllable can be added to an even foot or retrenched from a triple one, while the converse rarely happens (pp. 262–4). Triple-time verse is suitable for either riotous mirth or tranquil melancholy, as in music for either jig or " Sicilian movement ", but not for any thing intermediate (p. 266). Should the accented syllable begin the bar, as in music ? The other way is " more proper " and more convenient (p. 267). These remarks are interspersed with comments on " Anglo-Saxon " verse, on Greek metre, and on Greek music. Continuing to discuss this last, he thinks that it had no bars, or at any rate these were not distinguished by accent or emphasis as in modern music (p. 280). The Greeks measured cadence by length of time only, we by emphatical accent also. Therefore they could subdivide verse into many " meters ", while we have but two [common and triple] ; for their syllable divided the cadence definitely, ours does not (p. 281 *seq.*). Therefore, also, the relations of verse to music in modern times are quite different to what they were in ancient ; the two have grown apart. " What connexion subsisted between the accents of music and those of speech among the Greeks does not, that I know, appear from any of their writings ; " but their music " had no connexion with language but by means of versification " (p. 284). The power of their poetical measures we cannot understand, not knowing the just pronunciation ; they clearly admitted of more variety than ours. A few concluding sentences (pp. 287–8) express, though modestly, a belief that he has cleared away some difficulties regarding Classic verse, as well as thrown light on our own.

This belief was not wholly unfounded. Mitford does not, indeed, seriously modify the conceptions of his time. Much that I have quoted is common to him with others ; much more, not quoted, repeats traditional formulas. The same ideas, the same quotations and comments, appear in all writers of this epoch. But Mitford handles them with freshness, and does throw new light on them. He distinguishes accent from quantity as carefully as Monboddo ; both wholly reject the view of Bysshe and Johnson that accent makes quantity. In his recognition of " time " as conditioning verse Mitford has the advantage of Monboddo, and makes a distinct step forward. Most valuable of all, perhaps, was his explicit declaration that English verse-structure presents a problem to be solved ; that critics were wrong in thinking they knew all about it, or could explain it by Classic rules. This declaration alone counts for much. It is disappointing to find that between 1774 and 1804 Mitford made little progress. The *Inquiry* does not really carry us farther than the *Essay*, though it amplifies his argument and—especially in its earlier half—introduces some new ideas, *e. g.* " The poetical or metrical syllable is not precisely the same with the grammatical syllable " (p. 105). But he remains substantially at his earlier standpoint. To Steele he makes but one patronizing reference (p. 213), and his later " Sections " digress into cognate matters such as " euphony and cacophony ", grammar, *etc.* The last Section, with the Appendix which follows, can only be called a hodge-podge, but in the former he remarks that *jig* is a duplication of triple time, *minuet* a triplication of common time. Some remarks on foreign languages should be read with caution, as his knowledge hardly extended beyond the Romance tongues. On the whole, what is valuable in his views will be got most easily from the *Essay*, which has the directness and sharpness of a first sketch, and which—after all deductions—entitles Mitford to an honourable place among the pioneers of a rational system of scansion.

The year 1775 is memorable in the history of English prosody. Three books of note had birth in it. Of these Sheridan's *Lectures on the Art of Reading* must come first, for we have already neglected him too long. Thomas Sheridan, son and namesake of Swift's friend, father of Richard Brinsley Sheridan, Irish by birth and upbringing, retired actor and fashionable teacher of elocution, was a figure of some prominence in his day. Readers of Boswell should not be misled by Johnson's ridicule of "Sherry" the second, or by the repeated phrase "old Mr. Sheridan" used to distinguish him from his famous son. He was some twelve years junior to Johnson, from whom he was estranged by a foolish quarrel. Settling finally in London shortly before 1760, at the age of forty or thereabouts, he had lectured in the Universities and elsewhere on the need of better speaking, had published a *Dissertation* on the imperfections of our alphabet and *Lectures on Elocution* (both in 1762), was engaged in compiling his *Pronouncing Dictionary* (to be published in 1780 [1]), and taught a peculiar theory of accent to which attention must now be given.

From the first, while styling accent "that grand master-key to the pronunciation of our tongue, whose nature has hitherto been little understood, or grossly mistaken" (*Dissertation*, pp. 31–2 [2]), and contending that "it is by the accent chiefly that the quantity of our syllables is regulated" (*Lectures*, 1762, p. 41), he had rejected with scorn the idea that accentuation necessarily lengthens sound. On the contrary, when accent falls on a consonant it shortens the preceding vowel, as in *hat* and *habit*; only when it falls on a vowel, as in *hate*

[1] Sheridan's Dissertation contains his plan for a Pronouncing Dictionary, but Kenrick (as we have just seen) anticipated him in execution.

[2] This Dissertation is reprinted in the *Lectures* of 1762, being the last of several in that volume (pp. 223–62 ; the above quotation, p. 258). It was reproduced by Pitman in his *Phonetic Journal* for 1856, and issued as a twopenny tract. Its exposure of the shortcomings and inconsistencies of our alphabet makes good reading still.

and *hater*, does it lengthen that vowel. This is Sheridan's great idea, repeated in his *Dissertation*, in both sets of *Lectures*, and in the " Prosodial Grammar " prefixed to his *Dictionary*. He claims to have discovered it, and from it to have deduced this further " invariable rule " that when accent falls on and lengthens a vowel, all other vowels in that word are short, while if it falls on a consonant, no vowel in the word has its full long sound (*Dissertation*, as above). In the *Lectures* of 1762 he further develops this view, defining accent as " a peculiar manner of distinguishing one syllable of a word from the rest ", either by dwelling longer on it, or by " giving it a smarter percussion of the voice in utterance " (pp. 40–1). " There can not be any thing more false " than to say that accent always lengthens a syllable, though " all who have written on the subject " declare it does (p. 41). Only when accent rests on a vowel is this true ; when it rests on a consonant, the syllable is either short or doubtful—short, if the consonant itself be a short one, such as *k*, *p*, *t* ; doubtful, if the consonant be long, such as *l*, *m*, *n*, *r*, *v* (*ibid.*). Besides thus regulating quantity, accent is useful as dividing syllables into words, which the Greeks did by variety of tone, and " many modern nations " by pausing after each word, neither of which is necessary in English (pp. 44–6). Greek accent he understands to have been tone merely (" certain inflections of the voice like musical notes "), though the grammarians who say so do not tell us how to put it into practice (p. 39). At any rate, English accent is different. They distinguished three accents, we have one only[1], and its operation is as stated above. The difference between English and Scottish pronunciation is chiefly that the latter accentuates the vowel where the former accentuates the consonant (p. 42). " Nothing is of more moment in our tongue than to know when the accent is on the vowel, and when on the consonant " (*Dissertation*, as above).

These quotations are from the Third Lecture in the 1762 volume. The other Lectures deal mainly with elocution, the First and Second treating of letters, and the Fourth of emphasis, which " is to sentences as accent to words ". The Fifth and Sixth discuss " pauses or stops " as bringing out

---

[1] No distinction is made, as by Mitford, between principal and secondary accent.

the sense, and tones as ministering to expression ; the Seventh and last is on gestures. For us, therefore, Sheridan's contribution so far consists of his teaching about accent. I fear this cannot be deemed quite satisfactory. Do we really accentuate the *t* in *hat* any more than in *hate*, or is the difference not entirely in the vowel-sound (the final *e* is of course merely a typographical sign of a long vowel) ? We do certainly dwell longer on the vowel in *all* than in *add* (p. 44) ; but the difference is surely one of quantity alone. I do not gather that Sheridan's view satisfied critics at the time, or would pass muster with philologists now. His " invariable rule ", also, is by no means an absolute one. Does the second syllable of *twilight* lose any of its length, or the second syllable of *wayfarer* ? The first and third syllables of *privateer* are usually both sounded long.[1] Sheridan's rule usually holds good, simply because we love to emphasize one syllable and subordinate others ; but this usage is not invariable. These, however, are questions which scarcely affect prosody. What does make Sheridan's contribution metrically valuable is its clear perception that accent may shorten as well as lengthen a syllable. Whether his explanation of the fact be mistaken or no hardly matters. He saw clearly the difference between *ha-ter* and *hatt-er*, and invented a formula to account for it. Whatever we think of the latter, his recognition of the difference stands to his credit, and one looks with interest to see how it will affect his view of verse. This is not given in the earlier volumes. They are practical, concerned with the oratorical delivery of verse, not with its structure. Beyond a statement that " by the variety of the seat of accent, our words easily and naturally fall into all sorts of metrical feet " (Lecture III, p. 52), I do not think he refers at all to questions of prosody. When, however, we turn to the *Lectures* of 1775, the case is different.

The " First Part " of these later *Lectures*, indeed (Lectures I–IV), is taken up with how to read prose. Here the old ground is traversed, the former volume referred to, and accent again dealt with on the same lines. Foster's account of it leaves him "as much in the dark as before" (Lecture II, p. 73[2]). Ancient accent was " an elevation or depression of the voice ",

---

[1] Many other instances will suggest themselves, while in words like *edify, arrogate, emulate*, accent has deserted the long vowel.
[2] **My** quotations are from the third edition (1787).

ours is a " mere stress of the voice, without any change of note " ; ours is the drum, theirs the trumpet (pp. 74–5). Scottish speech has three accents like Greek, but irregular and without proportion ; English has but one, and " is utterly unacquainted with the circumflex " (pp. 76–8). In emphasis he now recognises a change of tone (p. 87). While unaltered in essentials, this later presentment of his view is more precise than the former ; he has profited by reading other definitions and discussions. But it is in " Part II " (again comprising four Lectures) that he comes to " the art of reading verse ", and begins with a characteristic flourish. " The principles and laws of our versification are either buried in obscurity or falsely seen through the mists of error " (p. 191). Our rules of prosody are taken from French or Classic verse. Because the French count syllables, we suppose that our heroic line must contain exactly ten syllables, which is absurd ; who says *ech'ing* for *echoing* (p. 192) ? A well-known line of Milton's contains thirteen syllables. And " a couplet of as fine sound perhaps as any in our language " [*viz.* Say's concocted one] disproves such numeration (p. 193). On the other hand, " not many years since, some essay writers showed [tried to show] that " English verse " was formed by feet, like that of the ancients ", and " boldly applied most of the rules of Latin prosody to our versification ; though scarce any of them answered exactly, and many of them would not square at all with the genius of our tongue " (pp. 193–4). Both views are wrong. " The Latin poetic feet are formed by quantity, the English by accent " (p. 194). He will explain the difference, and after doing so will conduct his hearers by " an unfrequented path " to " our part of Parnassus " (p. 212).

Such an exordium raises our hopes. Nor are they wholly disappointed. Sheridan still clings to *feet*, but these are conditioned by time.[1] " Numbers . . . consist in certain impressions made on the ear at stated and regular distances " (pp. 225, 230) ; " the other circumstances of long and short in the syllables, or diversity of notes in uttering them, are

[1] He also invents a distinction, afterwards adopted by Lindley Murray [1795], between quantitative and accentual feet, according as the accent falls on vowel or consonant. This gives us duplicates of the eight usual feet. " We have all that the ancients had, and something which they had not." *Cf.* pp. 230–1 *seq.*

not essentials " (p. 230). Quantity is always variable in our syllables, depending on emphasis (p. 208) ; and is not necessary to verse. Regular proportion is necessary, but our poets are justified in introducing " heterogeneous feet " for the sake of variety, as Milton does often. Two such feet following each other, however, are fatal to melody, wherefore Milton's double trochees are unhesitatingly condemned (p. 346). Heroic verse need not consist of iambs alone, but the feet should be proportionate ; trochee followed by iamb is just measure, so is spondee followed by pyrrhic (pp. 239–40). Yet this proportion may be sacrificed to expressiveness occasionally, that being " higher than mere melody " (p. 242). Melody, Variety, and Expression are all good, and he considers them at length. He distinctly recognises monosyllabic feet (p. 245), contends that Say's lines occupy exactly the time of pure iambic ones (p. 249), and asserts that a dactyl may always be substituted for a trochee, an anapaest for an iamb (p. 256). This variety, he had before said (p. 216), gives our heroic verse an " amazing advantage " over that of the ancients. Excellent are his criticisms of Dr. Forster [*sic*] (pp. 205 and 209), Pemberton (217), Kames (224). Of Pope he says that he " knew more of the art of versification than any of his contemporaries, though he seems not to have dived deep into the science of numbers " (p. 279) ; and evidently thinks him too monotonous. He insists on a " suspensive pause " at the end of every line, and claims that no one else has noticed this (p. 258 *seq*.). A recapitulation occupying pp. 298–304 concludes the Second Lecture, and summarizes his whole view. Two remaining Lectures treat of " expression ", and illustrate his attitude toward verse. Milton's description of Hell-gate is " exceedingly expressive, but cannot be called verses " ; his " Me, me only " would have read better as " Me, me alone " (pp. 350–1). He is naïvely surprised " in reading Milton, who was so perfect a master of numbers, to find so many lines that have not the least air of verse, and which could not have slipped from the pens of our middling poetasters " (p. 347) ; but this suggests no doubt of his own criteria. In these final Lectures he enumerates and characterizes various metres, on fairly familiar lines, the chief novelty being a contention that " amphibrachic " is a common type with us. On the whole, however, it is in the First Lecture of Part II that his most distinctive doctrine occurs. Its leading features are defence of variety as against monotony, and insistence on " Compensation " as the law by which one foot is shortened and its neighbour lengthened (p. 240) ; coupled with a sense of the importance of time as compared with mere syllabic numeration.

Had these views been proclaimed in 1762, Sheridan would have ranked high as a reformer. We do not know how far he may have taught them orally before 1775, any more than we know his attitude toward prosody in those earlier days when Johnson was a frequent guest at his house, and such questions must surely have been discussed. Published when they were, his Lectures only show that he shares a general movement, has assimilated its principles, but not advanced beyond them. To Johnson he refers once (p. 220), censuring him for calling " *most good, most fair* " iambs ; but he himself says (p. 299) that " all unaccented syllables are short ", so that the question between them is merely one of accentuation. In advocating variety, and approving trisyllabic feet, he duly follows where others had led, though he states the ground of his approval better and more convincingly than they. His indebtedness to Mason, Webb, Kames, Monboddo, is palpable ; I do not think he refers to Mitford. As a supporter of ' accentual feet ', Sheridan undoubtedly stands high ; later grammars copy him largely, and his authority carried weight. Most of his exposition would probably still commend itself to orthodox metrists, though in some points we have outgrown his standard. I had marked many more passages for quotation and favourable comment. But to me the surprise is that, having gone so far, he went no farther. Had he been more of an original thinker, less of a merely judicious critic and adapter, he might have seen for himself that English verse does not depend wholly on an ordered succession of syllables. That discovery he did not make. It was made—as will appear almost immediately— by a writer of much less note and authority, whose use of it, moreover, was by no means so successful as it might have been, and probably would have been, in Sheridan's hands.

In 1775 was also published *The Canterbury Tales of Chaucer : to which are added, An Essay upon his Language and Versification . . . etc.* The author was Thomas Tyrwhitt, a well-known antiquary, but as usual the title-page bore no name. The original edition comprised four volumes, the Essay and other introductory matter being in Vol. IV ; a fifth, containing glossary, *etc.*, came out in 1778. Often reprinted, it can be had in modern editions complete in one volume ; as the Essay is divided into short Sections, with numbered *notes*, references to these will suffice. Tyrwhitt was a writer of the same type as Warton, to whom he refers with high esteem, and his work is mainly historical. He holds our verse to be of Norman origin, copied from late Latin accentual metres, and owing nothing to " Saxon Poetry ", in which he can find practically no verse (§ 1, and *notes* there). He takes the usual view of the constitution of our metre, feet being composed of " syllables strongly and less strongly accented " (*ibid., note* 42 ; *cf.* first sentence of § 10). Yet he refuses to require an absolutely fixed number of syllables. While unable to conceive " that an heroic verse which wants a syllable of its complement can be musical, or even tolerable " (§ 8, *note* 60), he has no objection to " superfluous " syllables, quoting five lines from Milton in support of this, and laying down " one general principle, that an English verse, though chiefly composed of feet of two syllables, is capable of receiving feet of three syllables in every part of it, provided only one [*i. e.* one only] of the three syllables be accented " (§ 14, *note* 66). On this principle he scans Chaucer's lines, emphasizing the necessity of pronouncing " feminine *e* " and other dropped sounds. Previous writers had done this to some extent. In the extracts from Chaucer prefixed to Johnson's Dictionary accents were marked on " sweté breath," " allé night," *etc.* Tyrwhitt carried this immensely farther, while stipulating for an " obscure evanescent sound " (*note* 68) of final *e*, and restored proper accent to various words, thereby rendering Chaucer's rhythm intelligible to many who before had only " made shift " to read him. This, and his sanction of trisyllabic feet, are often referred to by his contemporaries. Yet his 73rd *note* shows him still trammelled by Johnsonian ideas ; at the best we can only say that, like a good many people, he practised better than he preached.

But the third book was far the most remarkable as touching prosody ; more remarkable, from that point of view, than any other book of the Century. In 1775 appeared *An Essay towards establishing the Melody and Measure of Speech, to be expressed and perpetuated by peculiar symbols.* Four years later followed a "second edition, amended and enlarged," under the title of *Prosodia Rationalis : an Essay . . . etc.* Its author was Joshua Steele, an Irishman, and Fellow of the Royal Society. The two editions are practically identical to the close of the first (p. 193) ; what follows in the second is headed "Additions" and dated September 1779. It looks as if the unsold sheets of the first edition had been used for the second, and new matter added. The leaf of *errata*, subjoined to the first edition and prefixed to the second, is in the latter revised and extended ; the index is enlarged to include the new matter, and the title-page is new. Otherwise I detect no change ; dedication [1], preface, and text (pp. 1–193) seem unaltered. As most of my references will be to the earlier pages, it is immaterial which edition is used. To meet with either is not easy, and the book has never been reprinted.

It began as a reply to Monboddo. The then President of the Royal Society, Sir John Pringle (to whom the book is inscribed), asked Steele to write remarks on Monboddo's view of verse (*cf.* p. 2). These—forming Parts I and II of the book, pp. 4–46 or possibly 55—were circulated in manuscript, and the author thought of printing them privately (p. 64). But Monboddo, to whom they had been sent, wrote frankly admitting some points and querying others ; Steele wrote Part III (pp. 65–84 or 89) in reply, and determined to publish (p. 92). The friendly correspondence continued, and in answer to further comments Steele wrote his long concluding Part IV (pp. 113–73). Meanwhile, proofs of the first three Parts had been sent to Monboddo, and his remarks on these rendered it necessary to add a Postscript (p. 174). Finally the book was published in stately quarto, the whole correspondence printed in full, Steele's reply to Monboddo's last observations concluding it (pp. 181–93). The additions to the second edition similarly contain criticisms by other correspondents, with Steele's replies, both sides being given fair play by his printing in full the remarks replied to.

The Essay, in either edition, is therefore less a consecutive treatise than a series of tracts, points being taken up as they are suggested by others. The correspondence between Steele

---

[1] Or rather *inscription*, to Sir John Pringle (see next paragraph). The British Museum copy contains also a formal dedication to the Royal Society, but this is absent from my copy.

and Monboddo is honourable to both.   It is amusing to see
that neither addresses the other by name ;   the letters are
always " to the author of ", *etc.*   Yet there is no concealment ;
Steele says " your l——p ", and Monboddo sends Steele a
copy of his book.   The anonymity was a mere etiquette.
Monboddo gets decidedly the worst of the argument, and
admits defeat on several points with engaging candour.   The
critics replied to in the " Additions " of 1779 are not named ;
one of them (p. 208) seems to have written *Remarks on
Mr. Steele's Treatise,* but I cannot find that these were ever
published.   The concluding pages of the second edition
(226–36) deal with Pemberton and Foster, the former of whom
he had not read before (pp. 208 and 226).   It is, however, in
the earlier pages of the Essay that we get Steele's own view
most distinctly stated, and a very remarkable one it is.   For
the first time (I believe) in the history of our literature a
writer proclaims that verse is essentially a matter of musical
rhythm, and applies musical methods frankly and fully to the
notation of metre.
    These ideas had been ' in the air ' throughout the Century.
Gildon had desiderated " prick'd notes " like those of music.
Say and the others of his group had referred much to music,
and had represented " feet " by notes.   Mason, as Mitford
later, recognised common and triple time in verse.   Foster
asserted that " every sentence uttered . . . is . . . capable of
musical notations " (*op. cit.,* p. 254).   Kames contended that
for accurate recording of pronunciation " notes must be
invented, resembling those employed in music " (*op. cit.,*
p. 272).   It was felt that, in modern England as in ancient
Greece, verse and music had been artificially separated, their
close kinship lost sight of ;   and it was desired to bring them
together.   But, while earlier writers merely played with this
notion, Steele put it into practice.   What they only desiderated
he tried to perform.   Discarding the whole doctrine of *syllabic
feet*—a doctrine, as we have seen, which was taken from
Classical prosody, and had never been shown really applicable
to ours—he substituted for this the conception of " *cadences* ",
similar in all respects to musical bars, and to be similarly
treated.   For their analysis he originally invented a " staff "
even more elaborate than that of music (p. 6), but came ultimately to regard the latter as practically sufficient (p. 30).

As regards time, he was content with four lengths of note, answering to semibreve, minim, crotchet, and quaver in music, any one of which could be made one-half longer by " dotting " ;[1] and, correspondent to the four lengths of note, he postulated four " rests or pauses " of like duration, with symbols to match.

This last idea was wholly new. The " pauses " spoken of by earlier writers were merely caesural divisions, affecting the delivery rather than the substance of a line ; Steele was first to treat them as factors of metre. That this should be so is truly surprising, and shows the artificialness of previous prosody. For, surely, it is a self-evident proposition that in any ordered succession of articulate or inarticulate sounds an interval of silence may on occasion be substituted for utterance, and may count toward the total result ; just as in dancing a measured interval of quiescence may form part of the ' steps ', or as in music ' rests ' are an integral part of the bar. Incredible as it may seem, this obvious fact had escaped notice, and was not admitted even after Steele called attention to it. Succeeding metrists, except a few avowed followers of Steele, ignored it in their teaching, as to this day it is ignored in the " Prosody " Section of our grammars. Coleridge never mentions it in his references to metre. Poe does not notice it in his protest against scholastic scansion, not even when it would seem impossible to avoid doing so. As lately as 1870, Prof. Sylvester appears to claim it as his own peculiar discovery. During recent years not a few writers have, as they were well entitled to do, recognised its obvious reality. Yet when in my *Study of Metre* I took it more or less for granted (as I have done since the first day I began to think about verse-structure), many of my reviewers pronounced this revolutionary. I should have deemed it a matter hardly needing demonstration that pauses as well as syllables go to make up a metrical unit.

The word *pause* is not free from ambiguity. In music, I understand, it denotes a prolongation at pleasure of either sound or silence, rhythmic movement being temporarily suspended. In ordinary English it is more loosely used. We speak of pausing on a syllable or pausing after a syllable, the

---

[1] This makes " eight different proportions of quantity " (*cf.* p. 144, *note*).

first being analogous to the ' dotted notes ' of music and the second to its ' rests '. That both of these exist in verse seems clear ; probably it is more or less optional which we employ in any given line. The first might be called ' dwelling on ' a syllable ; no convenient synonym suggests itself for the other. Personally, I use *pause* for both, following ordinary usage, and distinguishing when necessary by adding the musical equivalent. Even writers on music, I find, do not always restrict the term as above, but speak of " rests or pauses ", as Steele himself does (p. 8). The pause which follows a line of verse I regard as extra-metrical, when it exists at all ; the ' rests or pauses ' which occur during a line I regard as integral to structure, proved to be so by their taking places occupied in other lines by syllables or parts of syllables.

But Steele's notation was not restricted to expressing time. It was designed to show all the five " properties or accidents belonging to language ", viz. *accent, emphasis, quantity, pause,* and *force* (Preface, pp. viii and xvii). These, with their respective symbols, are explained in Part I. Accent is confined to tone, emphasis to pulsation and remission, in Greek phrase *thesis* and *arsis* [these words used in true Greek sense] ; the other terms explain themselves. With the ordinary division of verse into accented and unaccented syllables he has no patience (p. 20, *cf.* 86) ;[1] nor do " modern musicians " escape censure for a similar misuse of terminology (p. 11). The alternation in both cases is really between emphasis and remission, *thesis* and *arsis*, setting down the foot and raising it up. In verse, he proposes to express this by the terms *heavy* and *light* syllables, distinguishing this from accent on the one hand and on the other from force or loudness (p. 20). Remiss or light syllables may be highly accented and loudly uttered, but verse is not affected thereby. A general term is wanted to cover both *heavy* and *light*, as ' accent ' covers *high* and *low* and ' quantity ' *long* and *short* ; let that word be *poise* [spelt *poize*], and then " the poize of syllables is the most determined accident in our language " (pp. 77 and 144). The five sets of symbols are summarized and shown on p. 24. I cannot attempt to reproduce these here ; they must be studied in the book itself. " Heavy poize " is represented by ∆, " light " by ∴ , " very light " by ⋯ These, with the marks

[1] The popular use of these terms is " solecismatical " (p. 86).

of quantity, he finds sufficient for ordinary scansion ; it is only sometimes that he adds symbols of accentuation [in his sense] [1] and of *forte, piano, crescendo, diminuendo.* He notes, however, that "the meaning of a sentence may often be entirely altered by changing the accent from acute to grave, or *vice versa* " (p. 30) ; he does not say the same about loudness. It is interesting to know that he found in English intonation "at least as great " a range as the Greeks allowed to their accents, *viz.* a fifth (p. 17, *cf.* 149) ; also that, like them, he makes voice *slide* (as a general rule) from tone to tone in ordinary speech, but *jump* without intervening gradation from one to another in music.

This elaborate notation—which yet may be thought more complex than it really is—Steele applies to both prose and verse. Both move to either common or triple time (pp. 11, 25, *etc.*). The prose sentence on which he first illustrates his scansion gives his own view (p. 28), running thus—" Every sentence in our language, whether prose or verse, has a rhythmus peculiar to itself ; that is, in the language of modern musicians, it is either in common time or triple time ; videlicet, minuet time, or jigg [*sic*] time, or mixed." With this statement I cannot agree. All musical scansionists of prose seem to me apt to read into it a factitious regularity ; Steele's scansion of this passage is itself a case in point. No doubt in all speech there is a tendency to be rhythmical, and by exercising a little compulsion we can force prose words to keep time. But the true beauty of prose is lost when we do so. Fundamental irregularity is the law of prose, as fundamental regularity of verse. Certainly, good prose has its musical movements, which in ordinary parlance are vaguely called " rhythmical ", in obedience to which a sentence rises or falls, swells or dies away. Isolated phrases will form rhythmical passages, just as isolated words will form ' feet ' in our speech as in Greek ; but these are not therefore necessary or fundamental. Metre may exist in prose, without being more than an accident ; prose may be *metric* without being *emmetric.* Too great metrical regularity, we all know, is fatal to good prose ; I contend that too great rhythmical regularity is equally fatal.

---

[1] In one place, however (p. 150), Steele employs *accentuation,* " for want of a better word," in a wider sense, *viz.* as a general term to include *accent, quantity,* and *poise.*

Irregularity of rhythmic impulse is its distinctive note. In verse, syllables are set to equal time-measures, in prose to unequal. We can constrain them to act otherwise if we like ; but in doing so we destroy their proper effect. Add to this that no two readers will ' poise ' prose sentences in at all the same way, and it will appear how futile it is to force upon prose the temporal regularity which belongs only to verse. Those who seek to obliterate the dividing line between prose and verse must be somewhat insensible to the prime beauties of either.

With regard to verse, I accept Steele's principles of analysis, but not his application of these. He seems to recognise no law but his own ear. Our heroic line he makes consist sometimes of six cadences, sometimes of eight (*e. g.* p. 31). To an ordinary ' octosyllabic ' line he gives five cadences (*ibid.*), but only four to the same when ' trochaic ' (p. 32), and five to (p. 33)

> My time, O ye Muses, was happily spent.

His scansion of Hamlet's speech (pp. 40–6) ignores line-division, but Garrick's delivery of its first line (p. 47) is made to contain seven cadences. All this seems to me utterly wild, as wild as the division of Greek and Latin hexameter into eight cadences (pp. 80–3, and elsewhere). To place pauses wherever we choose to fancy them is to make verse a chaos. Steele was right in thinking that pause forms an integral part of every normal English line, wrong in thinking that this left him free to insert stops of any length at will. Temporal uniformity is the first law of verse. It might be possible to argue that every heroic line contains six periods ; it is clearly wrong to say that it contains sometimes six, sometimes eight. Steele's error comes partly from his libertine use of pause, partly from failing to see how the natural " heavy poize " of syllables was altered by metrical relation. Thus in his oft-repeated scansion of Pope's line—

> Oh, happiness ! our being's end and aim !

he assigns *thesis* or " heavy poize " to both the first and second syllables, which entirely destroys their metrical character. Throughout the book, one feels that his scansions are frequently forced and unnatural. His synthesis is not equal to his analysis. The admirable skill with which he dissected our complex speech fails him when he comes to reconstruction, and the monstrosities which he presents as specimens of scansion are enough to make careless readers reject his scheme entirely.

It was probably these extravagances which blinded contemporaries to his real merit. Enough has been said to show how profoundly original, how subtle and penetrating, was his analytic work. Nothing like it had been seen before. It might well have been 'epoch-making'; but it failed to become so. Monboddo accepted correction on some points; other writers praised " the ingenious Mr. Steele "[1] with dubious compliments. Most of them evidently thought his attempt impracticable and useless. He himself went off to the West Indies, and devoted himself to philanthropic work there. Prosody knew him no more, and forgot his teaching. A few followers, indeed, kept his name alive, and systematized his doctrine. Of these will presently be mentioned Odell [1806], Thelwall [1812], Chapman [1818], Roe [1823], of whom the first and last were the most valuable as regards theory. Through Thelwall, Coleridge may have profited by his teaching; but he never mentions him. Guest [1838] refers to him or his followers with contempt, not naming Steele. Poe seems never to have heard of him; Sidney Lanier surprises us by a slighting reference in his preface. On the other hand, Coventry Patmore gives him high praise, and students of phonetics have recognised his value. Rush [1833], an American writer on the voice, excepts him from his general strictures on prosodists; Alexander John Ellis, our highest authority on vocal physics, praised and adopted his analysis. Of late, Steele's star is certainly in the ascendant, but perhaps he is more often referred to than read. Even a meagre summary like the foregoing has not, to my knowledge, been attempted elsewhere.[2] His work was professedly tentative. The subject had occupied his thought for years (*cf. Dedication* and p. 1, also p. 204), and he aspired to lay a foundation for others to build on (pp. 3-4, *etc.*; *cf.* on pronunciation, pp. 166, 216). This at least he certainly did, faithfully and well. No " rational prosody " of the future, no prosody based on the actual facts of language,

---

[1] Mitford, *Inquiry*, p. 213; *cf.* Nares [*infra*, 1784]; *etc.*
[2] Compare, however, Prof. Saintsbury's hostile criticism in *History of Prosody*, Vol. II, pp. 547-8.

can neglect Steele's analysis. Those who substitute deduction for induction, theory for fact, may pass it by unnoticed ; those who judge only by results may turn from him in disgust. The real student will hail Steele as a master, however widely differing from his metrical conclusions, and will pronounce his the first really living work in the evolution of English prosody.

A few special *notanda* may be subjoined. The *thesis*, or heavy syllable, Steele of course makes begin the bar (p. 27, *etc.*) ; or rather, as he puts it more accurately later, the *thesis* rests on the " first sound or silence " of every cadence (p. 184). This idea would be new to most of his readers. He began his researches by attempting to devise a musical accompaniment for speech (p. 1), which he concluded must resemble the drone of a bagpipe, giving keynote and fifth (p. 46) ; our " speakers to the psaltery " may think this worth attention. He deprecated elisions in verse, taking the true ground of their non-necessity (p. 75). He recognised many forms of circumflex accent (p. 85), here anticipating later critics. He thought quintuple time impossible ; " a division into five equal parts nature will not admit " (p. 114). Recent music, as before said, disproves this assertion. The beginning of Part IV summarizes his analysis, but introduces an attempt to determine the absolute duration of measures (pp. 118–24) which seems to me both useless and hardly intelligible. Pp. 136–44 give representations of accent, *etc.* on isolated words, a very doubtful procedure. His view of *appoggiatura*, referred to by Guest, will be found on p. 145. In answer to Monboddo, he admitted that accent does not always slide by imperceptible gradations, but sometimes " rises or falls at once " (p. 192). There are some quaint scansions on p. 213, and on pp. 226 and 228. Steele's style throughout is clear, and his tone modest. He disclaims much knowledge of Greek (pp. 171, 200, 235, *etc.*), yet seems to read and translate it fluently. To Monboddo he is always polite, though sometimes firm (*e. g.* p. 168) ; and his " l——p " is the same, once apologising for the length of his remarks by saying he " had not time to make them shorter " (p. 93) [had this phrase been used before ? [1]]. To me it is

---

[1] Parallel phrases are common enough, *e. g.* Locke, introductory " Epistle " to his famous *Essay*, " I am now too lazy or too busy to make it shorter." But Monboddo's expression is neater.

particularly interesting that Monboddo was converted on the subject of pause forming part of rhythm (*cf.* pp. 110, 177). His gradual adoption of Steele's views on accent and " weight " does him very much credit. With such desultory remarks and imperfect appreciation we must leave the author of *Prosodia Rationalis*, certainly the most independent and acute inquirer into the phenomena of verse-structure whom we have yet encountered.

As a pendant to these three books I may name one of slighter content entitled *The Art of delivering Written Language ; or, an Essay on Reading, in which the subject is treated philosophically as well as with a view to practice* (Anonymous : 8vo, London, 1775). It is said to have been written by one William Cockin, a teacher in Lancaster, highly esteemed though not widely known,[1] and is dedicated to David Garrick. Quoting and following Sheridan, its author defines accent as " stress, energy, or force of utterance " (p. 22), but also recognises modulation of tone, consisting of " such restless inflexions of voice, through the smallest part of a note, as can by no means be suggested by the notes of a musical scale " (p. 121) [the contrast with Steele is curious]. Also, on p. 72 (*note*) he represents the actor's traditional delivery of a heroic couplet thus :

> Ti ti dum dum, ti ti dum ti dum de,
> Ti dum ti dum, ti dum ti dum te

[I quote *verbatim*, not professing to understand]. And in his last Chapter (pp. 135–6) he says that " Poetry " is to ordinary speech as dancing to walking, and is akin to music, though " modern refinement has in a great measure destroyed this union ". Beyond these rather suggestive remarks, the book makes little or no reference to verse.

I may also be allowed to mention that I possess a manuscript Essay[2] entitled *An Enquiry into the principles of English versification, with some analogical remarks upon the versification of the Ancients*, which begins by controverting Monboddo and contains references to Steele. Internal evidence shows it the work of Allan Ramsay, junior (son of the poet), a painter, author, and fine gentleman of those days ; Johnson's affection

---

[1] See obituary notice in *Gentleman's Magazine* for June, 1801 (Vol. 71, pp. 575–6).
[2] Now in the British Museum Library (1920).

for him will be remembered. He wrote miscellaneous articles, some of which were collected into a volume in 1762 [1]; but this is later, and has apparently never been published, or finished for publication. It is evidently a draft copy, with many excisions, additions, and alterations ; part is in a bound volume, part in loose sheets of the same size, these latter coming at the end. It is divided into sixteen Chapters or Sections [both words are used]. There is a title-page, but no preface, index, or table of contents. In its arrangement the book follows familiar lines, quoting largely from Classic verse [Greek words have no accent-marks], but the writer's fundamental conception is original. As against the Grammarians, he contends that division into feet is nugatory, unless we know the time which governs these. Metre is nothing without rhythm. " The natural sensation of rythm [*sic*, but elsewhere otherwise] gave the first rise to Poetry, and must always continue to be the directing soul of it." Practically, therefore, his main view is Steele's, but he explains matters differently. Besides objecting to Steele's " heavy " and " light " as merely metaphorical, he takes the more solid ground that the three qualities of *loud, acute*, and *long* really exhaust the possible chief properties of sound, and leave no room for Steele's fourth dimension. Monboddo had tried to make out that Steele's " heavy syllables " were *loud* ; he (Ramsay) contends that they are *long*, instancing " soil " and " toil ", which Steele (p. 166) had declared to be heavy by nature. Unluckily, however, he adds that all " important " syllables are long in virtue of their importance, which is merely the old confusion between accent and quantity. His analysis, therefore, cannot be called successful, and his examples are sometimes grotesquely incorrect, as when he makes the first syllable of " contribute " short and the second long. But when he comes to the rhythm of verse he is decidedly good. *Thesis* and *arsis* he explains correctly, and identifies them with beating of time. [It must be remembered that this view was not then the commonplace it is now ; Böckh and his successors were still in the future.] By these he really scans all verse, ancient and modern, explaining the former by the latter. Feet are in all respects like musical bars. Iambic and trochaic are one

---

[1] *The Investigator* (anonymous) ; contains four papers on widely differing subjects, not relating to verse.

measure, as also are anapaestic and dactylic. The Classic pentameter must either be two lines or contain six feet. Pause is thus recognised as constitutive of metre. Little is said of our heroic line, except that its fifth foot must be an iamb ; most of his English examples are taken from songs and comic rhymes. The best Chapter is on " the connection between Musick and Poetry ", where however he commits himself to the statement that " *accent* either means *quantity*, or it does not mean anything relative to the construction of verse ". Two final Chapters deal with " some doubts and difficulties ", mainly about Classic verse, and take up the cudgels against Bentley. On the whole, except for its view of rhythm, and its amusing examples (which I regret not having space to quote), this Essay hardly deserves to be rescued from its manuscript limbo. What is remarkable, and will seem surprising to many, is that at this time—different indeed from ours—prosody was a study that engaged the attention of men who were by no means pedantic ; that a court-painter to George III (for such Ramsay was), or a President of the Royal Society like Sir John Pringle, gave their hours of leisure to considering its meaning, and quoted Greek grammarians and English poets with equal gusto and with true apprehension.

We next reach books of greater celebrity but less value for our purpose. Dr. James Beattie, Professor in Aberdeen University, poet and philosophical critic, another friend of Johnson's ("we all love Beattie"), published in 1776 a volume of *Essays*[1] containing one on " Poetry and Music as they affect the mind ", written fourteen years earlier, but not previously printed. There is nothing novel in its subject-matter, but some interesting footnotes (*e. g.* on p. 90), a short account of rhythm in general (p. 158 *seq.*), and a final Chapter on the sound or harmony of verse. Even this last Chapter deals mainly with sounds which imitate sense, but metrical form is pronounced necessary to the perfection of poetry (p. 274), and in the last half-dozen pages Beattie compares the structures of English and Latin verse, treating both by accent, and

---

[1] There are two editions, both dated 1776. One, a fine quarto, includes his Essay on Truth, followed by the above and two other Essays, while the octavo edition contains only the last three. My references are to the third edition of the octavo (1779).

opining that a Latin dactylic hexameter line is rhythmically
represented by

> Multitudes rush'd all at once on the plain with a thundering
> uproar.

The concluding sentence refers to a " Treatise of Versification
and English Prosody, which I began some years ago, but have
not yet finished ". This was apparently never completed in
the form here proposed, but his later *Dissertations Moral and
Critical* (4to, London, 1783) include an Essay on " Language ",[1]
the fourth Chapter of which probably summarizes the treatise
in question. He there discusses English verse-structure,
making it depend wholly on " emphasis " [the term *accent* he
keeps for tone, see Chap. V, where he mentions having heard
of but not seen Steele's book], yet claiming the right to use
Latin names of feet and the symbols – and ◡ (pp. 72, 73). He
rejects numerical uniformity of syllables, but postulates regularity of stress, any departure from which makes verse not
" well tuned " (pp. 68–70). Much of his matter comes straight
from Sheridan, including quotations ; the examples of versification which conclude the Chapter are more fresh, but the
scansion frightfully wooden. Even " anapaestic " verse must
not drop a syllable except in the first foot (p. 83), though it
may sometimes add one (p. 84). Heroic verse, however, is
said to be capable of thirty variations (p. 76). The whole
Chapter is largely a compilation, and declines to " enter into
the niceties of English prosody " (p. 84). Its mechanical view
of verse prevents any regret being felt for this, or for the non-
completion of the larger treatise, which would probably have
contained nothing distinctively original, though its conclusions would doubtless have been expressed with characteristic
clearness and elegance.[2]

In 1776 appeared also the first volume of a *History of Music*

---

[1] Also published separately. I quote a " new edition " of the
separate Essay (1788).
[2] In case a reference by Beattie, or elsewhere, should suggest to any
one the idea of consulting a work by Beattie's co-Professor and Principal,
Campbell's *Philosophy of Rhetoric*, it may be well to mention that this
contains no allusion to verse. Published in the same year as Beattie's
earlier Essay, it is occupied wholly with the substance and rules of
rhetoric, and does not even, like the Greek rhetoricians, separate prose
sentences into ' feet '.

by Dr. Charles Burney, father of " Evelina " (a Doctor of Music, not of Divinity like his son who wrote on Greek metre). This volume was devoted to ancient music, especially Greek, of which he had the lowest opinion, citing passages to show that they beat time with bones and oyster-shells—" what a noisy and barbarous music ! " (p. 75)—and concluding that their tunes might have suited " Cherokees or Hottentots " (p. 103). The preliminary Dissertation (pp. 1–194) from which these remarks are quoted contains one or two references to verse, especially in § VI on " Rhythm ", often mentioned by contemporaries. " A poetical *foot* consists of a certain number of syllables, which constitutes a distinct part of a verse, as a *bar* does of an air in music " (p. 77). This is said of Greek verse, but he adds that we too have dactylic lines, and scans his example thus—

My | banks they were [are ?] | furnished with | bees.

Later, speaking of modern verse—" We no longer know Rhythm now under its ancient name," but as " time, measure, movement " (p. 82) ; and he seems to hold that common and triple time exist in verse (*ibid.*). His remarks, however, do not concern prosody in itself, but merely the setting of words to music. He is credited with saying that metre can exist without rhythm, but I have failed to identify this passage, or indeed to find much directly bearing on our subject. Apropos of a point already mentioned more than once, I note that he represents Tartini as saying—" Music has been composed of five equal notes in a bar, but no musician has yet been found that is able to execute it " (p. 82).[1] I find nothing else in the volume to quote.

The next book on our list is dated seven years later, but its true chronology is earlier. In 1783 Hugh Blair, D.D., an Edinburgh Professor, published the *Lectures on Rhetoric and Belles Lettres* which he had been delivering to students for the last twenty-four years. They ran through many editions ; I quote from that of 1830, in one volume. Blair is often called wordy and shallow. The same ideas, the same stock comments and quotations reappear in his pages as in so many others, and

[1] Burney refers to Benjamin Stillingfleet's *Principles and Power of Harmony* [Anon. : 4to, London, 1771], which expounds and comments on Tartini's musical theories. Verse is not mentioned in this book.

there is nothing original in his view. Yet it is sensible in its way. Of forty-seven Lectures the last ten are concerned with poetry, and nothing could promise better than the title of the first of these (Lect. 38)—" Nature of Poetry : its origin and progress : versification." Rightly finding the origin of verse in music, he (p. 462 *seq.*) accurately describes Classic quantity, though his view of *feet* is too mechanical (p. 463, *note*). He points out our quantitative vagueness, and says that " the only perceptible difference among our syllables arises from some of them being uttered with that stronger percussion of voice, which we call accent " (p. 464). " This accent does not always make the syllable longer, but gives it more force of sound only " (*ibid.*). Our heroic verse " is of what may be called an iambic structure " ; a succession, " nearly alternate," of accented and unaccented syllables. " The number of syllables is ten ; " where there seem to be more, " some of the liquid syllables are so slurred in pronouncing as to bring the verse, with respect to its effect upon the ear, within the usual bounds " (*ibid.*). Here he follows and quotes Monboddo, as on music he had followed and quoted Dr. Brown. It is all excellent of its kind, but does not go deep ; facts are stated, not their reasons. So with the usual exposition of " pauses " which follows, where he refuses to go farther than Pope allows. With Pope's versification he is entirely satisfied (p. 467). " Some liberty is admitted for the sake of variety," in accentuation, but " in general there are either five, or four, accented syllables in each [heroic] line " (p. 464). This is as far as Blair takes us ; I do not think anything more definite can be found elsewhere in the Lectures. The Thirteenth contains some remarks on prose feet (p. 141 *seq.*), the Thirty-third some hints on delivery of verse (pp. 400–1). If one had read no other book on the subject, these *dicta* would appear suggestive, if not quite satisfactory ; but one has met them often before. Blair's statements put the popular view pleasingly and moderately, but neither add to it anything novel nor discuss its meaning or authority.

Elements of Orthoepy, by R. Nares, A.M., " containing a distinct view of the whole analogy of the English Language, so far as it relates to Pronunciation, Accent, and Quantity," appeared in 1784. Rev. Robert Nares was an accomplished scholar, well up in his subject, not afraid to think for himself.

He refers to Mitford for the " laws of English versification "
(p. 142, *note*), to " the learned Dr. Forster " [*sic*] and Monboddo
for the nature of Greek accent (p. 144, *cf. note*, where he thinks
Steele's system " too obscure to be of general service "). But
on English accent he speaks confidently, in Part II of his book
(Part I deals with letters, *etc.*), and claims novelty for his view.
" It is to this hour disputed what accent is," yet no one
who sees an accent-mark placed on a syllable " feels any
doubt in regulating his voice according to that accent-mark "
(pp. 140–1). So begins Chapter I of Part II, and its second
paragraph may be quoted entire. " Accent, in English, is
only a species of emphasis. When one word in a sentence is
distinguished by a stress, as more important than the rest,
we say that it is *emphatical*, or that an emphasis is put upon
it : when one syllable in a word is distinguished by a stress,
and more audible than the rest, we say that it is *accented*, or
that an accent is put upon it. Accent, therefore, is to syllables
what emphasis is to sentences ; it distinguishes one from the
crowd, and brings it forward to observation " (p. 141). In
monosyllables, accordingly, accent and emphasis are obviously
identical. " So exactly is accent, in English, the same as
emphasis," that it changes with meaning, as Ben Jonson
pointed out (p. 143). Inflections, with us, affect sentences
rather than single words (p. 145). Particles have usually no
accent, therefore are " generally disposed in the unaccented
part of each foot ", *e. g.*

> Fár as the sólar wálk or mílky wáy (p. 142).

Ancient speech, on the other hand, as Monboddo shows, was
" more nearly allied to recitative than ours " (p. 146).

If this view is not so entirely novel as he supposes, it still
deserves attention. The long sentence quoted from p. 141
shows the word " stress " passing from its older meaning of
importance to its later meaning of *force*. With force accent
was being more and more identified, notably by Sheridan and
Monboddo, followed undoubtingly by Blair and others ;
Nares is somewhat more cautious. His solitary allusion to
verse in Part II [it is here that he refers to Mitford] shows him
concerned only with its accentual structure ; of other elements
he says nothing. The remainder of Part II (which contains ten
short Chapters) is taken up with practical rules of accentuation.

He recognises the "unstable" character of English accent (p. 147), therefore will point out the "general analogy" of our language, and frame rules for guidance. After going fully into these, he proceeds in Part III to deal with Quantity, which he well defines as "relative length of syllables" (p. 204). Here, unfortunately, he is misled by supposing that a short vowel implies a short syllable, so that *a, bad, barb, stands, strands*, are all to be classed as short syllables—though he admits "retardation of voice" by "concurrence of consonants" (pp. 205–6). On this, therefore, we need not dwell, except to note that he sees "how erroneous the common opinion is, that our accent always lengthens the syllable on which it falls" (p. 221) ; as just before he had remarked that, with us, even syllables apparently long by position are so "hurried on by the predominating force of our accentual emphasis" that they have neither the stability of long syllables nor the fluency of short ones (p. 220). Such criticisms lead one to expect a liberal prosody. But when, in the tenth Chapter of Part III, he deals with "syllables suppressed in poetic use", we find him an uncompromising supporter of elision. Of Milton's boldest experiments he can only say that the poet "melts two con-current vowels of different words into one syllable" (p. 252).[1] Numeration of syllables is evidently his creed ; *prayers* and *powers* "are now always monosyllables in poetry" (p. 253, *note*). So clear-sighted can a man be in subjects which he has studied for himself, so purblind when he merely accepts without challenge views dictated by others.

A book whose acquaintance I not long ago made contains nine "Critical Essays" by John Scott, of Amwell, post-humously published in the following year.[2] From the Intro-ductory Memoir by "Mr. Hoole" I gather that their author was of Quaker family, lived a retired and studious life, but occasionally visited London, there meeting Johnson and "the elegant Mrs. Montagu". He wrote poems of no great mark (*cf.* Boswell under date April 10, 1775), and Hoole notices "his predilection for laying an uncommon accent on words

[1] *Cf.* Part I, Chap. VII (p. 67), where in the line
　　　　Thou diest, and all thy goods are confiscate,
diest is said to be a monosyllable [like *died*].
[2] *Critical Essays on some of the Poems of several English Poets.* By John Scott, Esq. 8vo, London, 1785.

or syllables, which he thought gave strength to the line "
(p. lxv). The nine Essays deal with nine separate poems,
Lycidas being sandwiched between *Cooper's Hill* and *Windsor
Forest*, while two Essays deal with Dyer, the other authors
criticised being Gray, Collins, Goldsmith, and Thomson. The
criticism is mostly on matter, but in Essay V (pp. 120–1) he
makes some remarks on Milton's elisions such as " glory
obscured " or " the only ", which are " connected in pronunciation, so as to destroy the hiatus " ; while of a rugged
couplet by Dyer he remarks that " it has not the structure of
any English verse, consequently has no melody ", but admires
its onomatopoeic character. Also, in the previous Essay
(near the beginning), he finds fault with *Grongar Hill* for its
" irregular mixture of iambic and trochaic lines ; a circum-
stance rather displeasing to a nice ear ". I have not noticed
any other comments bearing on prosody, nor does it seem as
if much of importance from our point of view were likely to
come from this writer.

A striking and original paper " On Rythmical [*sic*]
Measures " was contributed to the Royal Society of Edinburgh's *Transactions* (Vol. II, Part II, p. 55) in December, 1786,
by Rev. Walter Young, of whom I know only that he was
a beneficed clergyman in what Southern writers like to call
the " Kirk " of Scotland. It is a real study of the relations
between verse and music. " Rythm, cadence, and measure "
are shared by both ; " tone " is peculiar to music. Our
power of dividing sound is very limited ; multiples of 2 and 3
are easy, of 5 extremely difficult, of 7 probably impossible.
Unaccented initial syllables in verse are like notes preceding
a bar [*anacrusis*], but in music these are always compensated.
A pause is assumed after each bar. Our heroic rhymed verse
contains three pairs of " times ", the sixth being silent. Blank
verse, omitting this silent space, comes nearer prose. This
makes it specially suitable for narrative ; it is enough if an
occasional line in strict measure reminds us of the rhythm.
Dactyl and spondee were the oldest feet, " march measure "
being the simplest form of rhythm ; here he quotes Burney's
account of a young prodigy named Crotch. Ancient hexameter (though the fifth and sixth feet may have been added to
an original shorter line) divided naturally into three pairs,
these again suggesting triple or " minuet " time, which in

verse produces a heavy effect by itself. On the other hand, when each unit is divided by three, we get tribrachs (or iambs and trochees), " gig measure " [jig ?], light and airy. In Greek trochaic verse a spondee is admitted in each even foot, that being unemphatic. In iambic the opposite is apparently true, but if we regard it as trochaic with extra syllable prefixed, both agree ; this is therefore probably the true view, but even so the combination is unintelligible to us, and he queries whether here the music did follow the verse. The object of " caesura ", in all verse, is to break a line into unequal segments. My notes on this paper are several years old, and may easily have missed valuable points. Even this short summary, however, should show how far this paper is from merely repeating traditional ideas, how practically it considers questions of structure. Would that there were more such Essays to cite, and that the author of this one had given more of his attention to our own verse. At least we may hail here, for once, a direct contribution to prosody.

Last of the great Eighteenth Century grammarians and lexicographers comes John Walker. Of humble birth and limited education, Walker's abilities and industry forced him to the front after a career rather like Sheridan's in a somewhat lower sphere. About as much junior to Sheridan as he to Johnson, Walker cherished toward Johnson an almost idolatrous veneration, while toward Sheridan his attitude was more critical. As early as 1774 Walker printed his proposal for a Pronouncing Dictionary, and in the next year published his useful *Rhyming Dictionary. Elements of Elocution* followed in 1781, and his *Rhetorical Grammar* in 1785 ; a tract called *The Melody of Speaking delineated* came out in 1787, the *Critical Pronouncing Dictionary* in 1791, the *Key to the Classical Pronunciation of Proper Names* in 1798. Even these do not represent all his productions, and most of them were largely altered in later editions. This makes it difficult to ' place ' Walker chronologically, but from 1785 to 1791 embraces his chief constructive work. The *Melody of Speaking* introduced one of his pet ideas ; the " Principles of English Pronunciation " prefixed to his *Dictionary* are mainly practical. His fullest discussion of accent and quantity is affixed to the *Key to Proper Names.*

On two " discoveries " Walker specially plumed himself ;

viz. (1) that tones of speech proceed by *glides*, not by abrupt leaps ; (2) that there are two forms of circumflex accent. In both he had been anticipated by Steele, to say nothing of others ; but only in his later books does he seem to know aught of Steele. The Preface to his *Melody of Speaking*—in which the two circumflexes are first mentioned—claims absolute novelty for a method which falls far short of Steele's. His doctrine of *glides* seems clearly laid down by Greek grammarians, whom he ignorantly despised ; but it is certainly strange that these grammarians knew but one form of circumflex, since there can obviously be several—Walker's two do not exhaust the number. As regards accent in general, he differs from most of his contemporaries by insisting that it includes tone as well as force. " If the word be pronounced alone, and without any reference to other words, the accented syllable is both higher and louder " than others (*Key to Proper Names*, " Preparatory Observations " to Accent and Quantity ; *cf. Elements of Elocution*, Part II, § 1, and *Rhetorical Grammar*, section " On accented force "). As a rule, however, he deals only with words in a sentence, distinguishes rhetorical emphasis from mere verbal inflection,[1] devotes to the former his whole attention, and prescribes absolute laws for its regulation— laws which seem to me apt to create what Sheridan called a " reading brogue ". His aim is elocutionary ; nine-tenths of his discussion deals with the delivery of sentences and the way to pronounce particular words. When he comes to deal with *quantity* (which I think he does only in the Essay affixed to *Proper Names*), he is as far from truth about English syllables as about Latin and Greek. Having " no conception of quantity arising from any thing but the nature of the vowels, as they are pronounced long and short " (§ 2), he naturally does not understand what quantity means in either ancient or modern speech. His remarks on matters of scholarship can always be safely neglected, while in regard of his own language his native good sense has in this instance been led astray by the same fallacy that imposed upon Nares.

All this, of course, matters to us only as it affected his view of English verse. But on this subject he is curiously silent. Apparently he accepted in the main Johnson's ideas. The

[1] In this way he admits degrees of stress, but without defining these as primary or secondary.

" Directions to foreigners " prefixed to his *Dictionary* assume
that accentuation is regular, " though a different position of
the accent is frequently to be met with in the beginning of a
verse." The " Rules for reading verse " which will be found
in both his earlier books (see their tables of " Contents ") are
intended for the actor or reciter. He recognises " regularity
of feet ", and " that measured harmonious flow of sound "
which distinguishes verse from prose ; and even proclaims
that " verse is a species of music " ; these phrases occur in
the sections just referred to. But he does not go beyond such
generalities. In the *Rhetorical Grammar* (" Of the accent and
emphasis of verse," Rule I) he asserts that " in verse, every
syllable must have the same accent, and every word the same
emphasis, as in prose " ; a most disputable proposition. In
Elements of Elocution (as above, Rules IV and V) he refers to
Sheridan's definition of " numbers " and to that writer's
" pause of suspension " at the end of a line ; but his remarks
apply only to delivery, and assume that two syllables may
be added to or subtracted from a line " without any indication
of false quantity to the ear " ! In both books he refers with
praise to Lord " Kaims " [1] on pauses, in both pronounces
against elision because " the syllable it forms is so short as to
admit of being sounded with the succeeding syllable, so as not
to increase the number of syllables to the ear, or at all to hurt
the melody ". On the other hand, every case of an ' inverted
foot ' implies that we " let the metre of the line shift for
itself " (*Rhet. Gram.*, *loc. cit.*, Rule II). These *obiter dicta*,
however, are never woven into a statement of principle. To
all speculations on the nature of verse, to all the discussions
which exercised his contemporaries, Walker turns a deaf ear.
None other of our leading grammarians has made so slender
a contribution to debated questions of prosody.

Nearly the same criticism, yet with a difference, may be
passed on Lindley Murray's *English Grammar* (1795). This—
which long held the field, passing through countless editions,[2]
and from which, or successors based on it, most of us probably
imbibed our first notions about English grammar in general

---

[1] Foster he always calls " Mr. Forster ".
[2] I quote the common (undated) 12mo " new edition ". The octavo
edition, in two volumes, which came out first in 1808, adds nothing
material as regards prosody.

and English verse in particular—is professedly a compilation, and in its " Prosody " Section acknowledges indebtedness to Sheridan, while Beattie is also drawn on for examples. This Section is divided into two Chapters, one on pronunciation, the other on versification ; neither contains anything that can be called novel. The former deals with " accent, quantity, emphasis, pause, and tone ", adopting unreservedly Sheridan's view of accent, but recognising a distinction between principal and secondary (p. 225). Quantity is made to depend on accent, and to be regulated by emphasis. " Though the quantity of our syllables is fixed, in words separately pronounced, yet it is mutable when these words are ranged in sentences ; " it is " not fixed, but governed by emphasis " (pp. 234, 235). Pauses and tones are treated merely from an elocutionary point of view. The second Chapter follows Sheridan implicitly as to feet, in respect both of number and of their formation by either accent or quantity ; and repeats the complacent remark " We have all that the Ancients had, and something which they had not " (p. 242). In scansion, however, both kinds of feet are marked by – and ˘, without any explanation, and with such appalling results as—

How lov'd, how valued once, avails thee not.

Be wise to-day, 'tis madness to defer.

From the low pleasures of this fallen nature.

On the warm cheek of youth, smiles and roses are blending.

Similar machine-like regularity is postulated throughout, relieved only by occasional intrusion of " secondary feet " (pp. 243, 248), which answer to Sheridan's " heterogeneous " ones. That writer's lead is followed in considering " poetical pauses " and " melody, harmony, and expression " (see under these headings), and the Chapter ends by referring " the ingenious student, for more extensive information on the subject ", to the *Art of Reading*. As Murray adopts (p. 245) Johnson's creed about the melodiousness of a line, " considered by itself," depending on regularity of syllabic accentuation, we may describe his teaching as Johnsonian orthodoxy expressed mostly in terms of Sheridan.

Such is the travesty of fact put forward by our principal

Grammar. Accent, quantity, and emphasis are jumbled up together and confused with metrical *ictus*, while verse is scanned not as it really is, but as the critic thinks it should be, written. The artificial nature of our traditional prosody receives striking illustration ; if facts do not square with rules, so much the worse for the facts. General principles are never mentioned ; even Sheridan's " stated and regular distances " are omitted by his pupil, and *time* is wholly ignored. Is it surprising that people turned in disgust from a theory so narrow, so frigid, so out of contact with reality— that prosody became a byword among readers of taste ? I anticipate by saying so, for the discrediting process was gradual ; sufficient for the day was the doctrine thereof. But an analysis of verse so crude, so rudimentary, so limited in its purview, was suited only to the mechanical age that produced it ; before the onset of new forms and new ideas it crumbled into hopeless ruin.

The chief Eighteenth Century critics having now been passed in review, it may be well to take stock of results. Discussions on prosody have had to do with details rather than with general conception. Our verse has been assumed to consist merely of clustered syllables, and the main question has been how the syllables in each cluster are related to one another. At first it was held that there was alternation between long and short syllables, as in Greek or Latin verse. Gradually this view lost favour, alternation of emphatic and unemphatic syllables taking its place ; some tried to amalgamate these views. The idea that an unemphatic was necessarily a short syllable, in particular, lingered long ; arguments about quantity were vitiated by confused theories of what created relative length, due mainly to the mistaken belief that a Latin vowel became long when followed by two consonants. The importance of accent to our verse was admitted by all who identified it with force or quantity ; those to whom it meant pitch found other terms to express the same conviction. Widely divergent views were held as to the function and operation of accent, but these were matters of phonetics rather than prosody, indeed mainly of nomenclature. Structural differences between English and Classic verse were mostly ignored ; from Webb onward, a succession of writers maintained that by arranging accented syllables in the order which was followed in a Greek or Latin line we should obtain, in English, all the effect of that line. Our poets were not quick to adopt this view ; when they did, as we shall see, the impulse came from abroad. Its adoption was but one incident in a revolution alike of theory and practice which set up accent as the sole factor to be regarded in English metre—a revolution whose progress we shall trace during the Century which follows. Eighteenth Century criticism paved the way for this revolution both positively and negatively ; positively, by its gradual substitution of accentual for quantitative groups ; and negatively, by failing to provide a theory which explained the variety and elasticity of our best verse. It was superseded by a criticism not less partial and one-sided, but which at least took the highest achievements of our verse as its subject-matter ; the stages of this supersession must be described as we come to them.

At present we need only notice that in the *Monthly Magazine* for June, 1769, appeared a " transversion " from Macpherson's *Ossian*, by William Taylor, of Norwich, the well-known " Address to the Sun " being rendered into accentual hexameters, avowedly on German models. This is memorable because it set Southey and Coleridge working on the same tack. I do not know whether Southey's " Sapphics " and " Dactylics ", published in his *Poems* of 1797 and satirised by the *Anti-Jacobin* next winter, were suggested by Taylor's performance ; his later hexameters certainly were. These, however, and the far more important poems published by Coleridge and Wordsworth, will be more suitably noticed in the beginning of the new Century. Before passing from the old one, there are still two or three names to mention, belonging in every way to it and its methods.

Peter Walkden Fogg, a teacher residing at Stockport, published there in 1796 *Elementa Anglicana ; or, The Principles of English Grammar displayed and exemplified, in a method quite original* (2 vols., 8vo). The second volume contains twenty-seven miscellaneous Essays which were also issued separately (the only difference being the page-numbers) in a thin volume entitled *Dissertations, Grammatical and Philological* [my references are to the separate edition]. Of these, No. XI (pp. 55–7) is on " Prosody," No. XII (pp. 57–72) on " Versification ". I do not find much novelty in Fogg's view

of verse ; indeed, in the Preface to Vol. II (p. xi) he makes
humorous complaint of the way in which his ideas have been
anticipated by other writers.   Sheridan and Steele, both
mentioned by him, were probably the chief offenders this way ;
for his explanation of syllabic length (pp. 55–6) follows
Sheridan's line of thought as to " dwelling on a final consonant ", and his division of syllables into " heavy, light,
and very light " (p. 56) is avowedly taken from Steele.   He
does not, however, distinguish weight from force, but identifies
both with *thesis* or stress, and says " By this force, thesis, or
weight, is the prosody of English conducted " (*ibid.*).   In
dealing with versification, he makes two feet the shortest
possible line (p. 57), whereas Herrick has lines of one foot ;
and his limits of length (*ibid.*) are too precise, as is his statement that " a single line is not acknowledged as verse " (p. 58).
Rightly, however, he makes feet and not syllables constitute
measure (*ibid.*), and regrets that " Our modern versifiers
have endeavoured, too successfully, to lay aside the trisyllabic
feet in heroic metre " (p. 59).   The " elegancies " of verse
are " melody, harmony, and expression " (p. 63), and harmony
includes variety (p. 66) ; but " a mixture of feet is prejudicial
to simple melody " (p. 65).   Beyond these general remarks,
I have noted nothing which demands reproduction.   Even
if " original ", they are far from constituting a new departure ;
and one must regret that study of Steele did not prompt to
bolder parting from old methods, and recognition of temporal
rather than syllabic structure as the basis of our verse.

In 1796 was also published a famous treatise *On the Prosodies
of the Greek and Latin Languages*, which we need only note
in passing as dealing with accent in English verse as well as
Classic.   Though published anonymously, it was known to
be by Samuel Horsley, Dean of Westminster and Bishop of
Rochester, and was dedicated to Lord Thurlow.   While
denying that accentuation necessarily lengthens sound (p. 18),
he still contends that in English " quantity and accent always
go together ", and that " we have no other rule of quantity,
but to lengthen the accented syllable " (p. 4).   He does not
deny that, when a word contains no long syllable, accent may
rest on a short one, as in *honey, clever, luckily* ; but if there
be a long one, accent chooses it, so that *gratifý* is more natural
than *grátify* (pp. 4–5).   We need not follow him into Greek

questions, nor into his criticism of Primatt (see his "Appendix"), whose book—published thirty-two years before—he had only just come across. His main assertion about English verse is that "we give the sharp stroke of the voice upon the syllable which, by its place in the verse, ought to be long " (p. 5). Beyond this *dictum*, which points toward unbroken regularity of accentuation, I find nothing which need detain us.

No one interested in the accent-quantity question should fail to read *Metronariston* ["best measure "]: *or a new pleasure recommended*, published anonymously in 1797, but ascribed to a Dr. John Warner (see Appendix B).   This most amusing writer urges that " there is nothing in common between Accent and Quantity " (p. 53), that " elevation without prolongation " is impossible to us (p. 6), that we read Latin and Greek as if they were English—an Italian priest said to him " You dactylize and trocheeize every thing " (p. 13)—, and that we should substitute for this reading by quantity.   Incidentally he pokes fun all round, at Jacob and Bryant (in his Preface), at " Mr. Sheridan . . . who, I thought, when I was his scholar, could not exemplify his own very good rules " (p. 22, *note*), at Scotchmen (p. 27, *note*), Bentley (p. 53, *note*), "unhappy Homer," who rarely made quantity and accent agree (p. 88), Handel (p. 108, *note*), and Bishop Horsley (see Postscript, pp. 113, 120).   His opponents he makes say *Nolumus stupiditates Angliae mutari* (p. 100).   English verse is often referred to, and paralleled with Latin in couplets like—

> *Ades, Pater supremè,*
> Thy head with glory beamy ;

or,

> *Beatus ille qui, procul negotiis,*
> Can to sweet lore apply, and live in letter'd bliss (p. 40).

As a pure dactylic hexameter he proposes—

Come we in pity now from the low palace of old Father Ocean (p. 23).[1]

---

[1] Before this is objected to, the reader should remember that this line is made up from two of Dryden's (in *Albion and Albanius*) which our common prosody would call dactylic, *viz.*—

> From the low palace of old Father Ocean
> Come we in pity, your cares to deplore.

Possibly the popular nomenclature may now be felt not wholly appropriate.

Every accented syllable he marks *long*, even in the line (quoted from Sheridan)—

The busy bodies flutter, tattle still,

while asserting that " our rhythmus " never lengthens short syllables, though it shortens long ones (p. 19). Quantity by position our language " utterly disclaims " (*ibid., note*) ; the first syllable of *constrains* is short. So again, " we have syllables which are short . . . where the vowel precedes no less than four consonants " ; and " some of the more northern languages ", he believes, extend the number to six (p. 112, *note*). The book is a medley of sense and nonsense, the latter largely predominating, since his fundamental position is that we cannot accentuate a short vowel without lengthening it ! But the wit and versatility of the writing make it unique among the dreary tomes of this controversy.

Lastly, in 1799 appeared *An Essay on the Nature of the English Verse, with directions for reading Poetry. By the Author of the Essay on Punctuation.* This connotes Rev. Joseph Robertson, writer of many small books, and of " near 3000 articles in the Critical Review " [see leaflet following Essay], that jejune periodical which laid down laws of taste to the readers of this time. The Essay may be shortly described as worthy of the *Review*. Rightly beginning with a statement that our verse does not depend on quantity— whence it follows that *iambic* and *trochaic* can only be applied to our verse in a figurative sense (pp. 3–4 and 15)—he spoils this by showing that to him quantity means merely length of vowels (pp. 1–2). And then he proceeds to dogmatize in the old irrational way. A "short final syllable is want of harmony " (p. 6). " For the sake of variety, the [heroic] line sometimes begins with an accented syllable " (p. 11) ; but if this is too often repeated, as by Pope, it becomes monotonous (p. 13). Whenever accent is misplaced, " the verse is lame and inharmonious," and he follows Kames in censuring

This nymph, *to the* destruction of mankind (p. 25).

As for Milton, while praising his " pleasing variety in pauses " (p. 10), he objects to " some archaisms and peculiarities in his versification ", censures his double inversions, and declares that many of his lines are " mere prose ", words being " protracted and extended in an arbitrary and capricious manner " (pp. 61–2). In an Appendix (pp. 124–6), while blaming Bentley's attempt to rewrite the concluding lines of *Paradise Lost*, he modestly suggests that it would be better if the last two pairs of lines were transposed ! The best thing in the book is its many quotations ; but nearly thirty pages (76–104) are occupied by a list of the Classical proper names that occur in English verse. Of anything beyond mechanical criticism there is no trace. Leaving this typical specimen of self-contented Eighteenth Century dogmatism, we now at the same time bid farewell to the Century itself.

CHAPTER IV

THE NEW VERSE

1800–1850

CHRONOLOGICAL divisions are seldom exact, and the revival of English poetry by no means waited for the dawn of a new Century. If in Gray and Thomson and Collins and Cowper novelty showed itself rather by substance than by form, yet Burns with his bold simplicity and Blake with his pure though singularly artless melody had definitely set aside Augustan canons of " correctness ". Delight in old ballads, ever since the publication of Percy's *Reliques*, told against artificial elegance ; and Macpherson's *Ossian*, here as well as on the Continent of Europe, produced an impression hardly credible by us. Besides, the very men who should inspire the new Century were already at work during the closing years of the old. Walter Scott was " making himself " in his Liddesdale excursions ; Wordsworth and Coleridge, Southey and Landor, were thinking and writing and publishing. Their impressionable years of youth and early manhood, with all these writers, belong to the Eighteenth Century. The first edition of *Lyrical Ballads* was published in 1798, the second—with Wordsworth's weighty Preface—in 1800. No work that Coleridge did in the new Century equals what he did in the old. For practical purposes, however, the new departure may be regarded as beginning with the new Century, which was well under way before the general public became aware of any change. Prosody always lags behind poetry, so not for many years shall we find the new methods recognised in books on metre.

However we may rank these writers otherwise, Coleridge was the most potent as regards form. *Christabel* was not published till 1816 ; but its First Part was written in 1797, its Second in 1800, and both were freely read and handed round in manuscript. From them Scott avowedly took the metre of the *Lay*, as from Scott's poems Byron unquestionably derived that of his Oriental Tales.[1] The seed of *Christabel* grew to flower and fruit in these and other writers. All the " Lake Poets " were experimenters in metre as in matter. Southey carried Coleridge with him into hexameters on Taylor's pattern, and several fragments, including a prelude to their projected poem on Mahomet, survive as a record of that attempt. But neither there, nor in Southey's own elaborate verse-schemes, nor in Wordsworth's ponderous rhythm, nor even in the *Ancient Mariner* (which, metrically, is but a prolonged ballad), can the new inspiration be found. This came, so far as metre is concerned, particularly from *Christabel*. When the preface to that poem was written does not appear. It may represent ideas as old as the Somersetshire days, ideas which—as I have already suggested—may have been partly shaped by Thelwall's account of Steele's views. In any case it affirms a " new principle " for prosody, which the poet had put into practice in those early days, whether or no he then formulated it explicitly. This principle was, in his own words, " that of counting in each line the accents, not the syllables." By the gradual adoption of this principle our verse, and later our theories of prosody, have been revolutionized.

Coleridge, of course, did not invent this principle. He may rather be said to have rediscovered it. Certainly it was " new " to the critics of his day. None of the Eighteenth Century metrists whom we have been studying—not even Steele or Mitford—had been aware of it. The whole discussion on ' trisyllabic feet ' ignored it. In essence, however, it was a return to older standards, observed by our poets, neglected

---

[1] Many people—including Moore, his biographer—credited Byron with knowledge of *Christabel* prior to 1815. But his own *note* to his *Siege of Corinth* [published early in 1816], § 19, negatives this, and is confirmed by Scott, who in a letter to Mrs. Hughes says " It was I who first introduced his Lordship to the fragment ". Byron and Scott never met before (or after) 1815, and it was probably at their first meeting that Scott repeated part of *Christabel* as well as *Hardyknute* (Lockhart, Vol. III, Chap. X). The earlier Tales therefore derive from Scott, not directly from Coleridge, though I feel some doubt whether Byron's above-mentioned *note* is accurate as regards the lines to which it is appended. As to this, *cf.* Introduction to *Siege of Corinth* in Murray's edition of Byron (Vol. III).

by our prosodists. It recaptured for the coming Century Elizabethan freedom and melody. Whether the description just quoted from Coleridge properly represents its nature and operation is, perhaps, open to argument. What, precisely, did he intend to convey by it ?

Everything turns on what Coleridge meant by " accents ". If he meant ' accented syllables ', in the ordinary sense of that phrase, his definition is at fault. That he did mean this has been commonly assumed, theories of " stress-rhythm " have been built on the assumption, and lines of *Christabel* which do not comply with these theories have been roundly censured. For, on this view, the poet's assertion that " in each line the accents will be found to be . . . four " is quite incorrect. So, unfortunately, is his other assertion that the syllables " vary from seven to twelve ". In the first five lines of the poem, one line has only four syllables, another six ; and similar ones occur again. There are also lines of an entirely different pattern from what he has described, *e.g.*

> Amid the jagged shadows
> Of mossy leafless boughs,
> Kneeling in the moonlight,
> To make her gentle vows.

We may conclude that these had escaped his remembrance, and that his description applied only to such representative lines as—

> From her kennel beneath the rock
> She maketh answer to the clock,
> Four for the quarters, and twelve for the hour.

Even here, it must be owned, the words " From " and " to " do not fulfil his conditions. They are not primarily accented syllables, and the lines containing them have but three such apiece. If we wish to look facts in the face, this must be frankly admitted.

Coleridge's description being in any case faulty, let us see for ourselves what his verse was. The novelty of *Christabel* lay in this, that it subordinated syllabic structure to temporal. Orthodox metrical criticism had forgotten this latter element of verse. A few timid references to the *time* of a line, a few assertions of identity between *feet* and *bars*, with a vague consciousness that verse and music had drifted too far apart, show dissatisfaction with prevailing theories rather than any attempt to mend them. Coleridge's practice, if not his definition, restored *time* to its true pre-eminence. He does not say that his accents occur at equal intervals, but our ears tell us that they do. The ' feet ' are uniform in length though diverse in the number of syllables they contain. That is what his somewhat loose description means ; that is what his magical verse builds on, with a charm all its own. In lesser hands the attempt might have failed, the result have been feeble, or harsh, or heavy. Coleridge, a master of verbal melody, carried it victoriously through, and in so doing vindicated for English verse its natural inalienable birthright.

It is possible to say, in another sense, that every normal line of *Christabel* (leaving aside for a moment those of a different pattern) carries four accents, because consisting of four equal bars or periods, each of which must theoretically have an accent appertaining to it. This is the musical view, and would be true of musical bars. But, firstly, there is no reason to think that Coleridge used " accents " in this sense ; and, secondly, the analogy is imperfect. If in music a note occupied the place which " From " or " to " occupies in Coleridge's lines just quoted, it could not fail to be accented. The fact that these words are *not* accented shows that verse has laws of its own. For, assuredly, the plain truth is that Coleridge meant these words to be devoid of accent. Even to style them ' metrically accented ' is fallacious ; they carry no accent whatever. Why should we force the laws of one art on the material of another, and imagine that spoken syllables must obey the same rules as musical symbols ? Let fact replace imagination. The actual fact is that our poets sometimes substitute a weak syllable for an expected strong one. Inferior writers doubtless abuse this liberty ; but our best poets use it, and it is not likely that they are all of them wrong. I do not think it is difficult to see why they do it. An occasional weak accent relieves the oppression of a too insistent beat, and makes welcome variety. However this be, the fact is indubitable. Musicians may talk of a " silent accent ", but the term hardly applies here. The theoretic rhythmical accent is not merely omitted, it is deliberately contradicted, in a way for which music seems to yield no parallel. Yet our perception of rhythmical uniformity persists ; persists, even though the syllables transgress instead of enforcing it. This reveals the fundamental law of English verse, opposition between syllabic and temporal structure. It is Coleridge's glory to have discerned this law, in practice if not altogether in theory. His verse obeys it, though his Preface does not clearly state it. His ear led him right, in this matter of omitted accents, where I maintain that he is nearer the truth than his critics. For, in our verse, time can be felt even when not signalized by accent, and every period need not necessarily contain a syllable of dominant stress. If we say otherwise, we condemn the work of (without exception) all our chief poets ; we must, like the Eighteenth Century critics, find fault with every line containing such cadences as

> This nymph, to the destruction of mankind.

But from theory I return to history. Coleridge's " new " metre, through the medium of its admirers, spread its influence far and wide. For long, indeed, it was considered a " light horseman " sort of affair, unsuited for the highest poetry ; just as triple-time verse was so regarded down almost to our own day. Only by degrees was it perceived that Coleridge's " principle " held good for all verse, that even our heroic line was subject to its sway. Still longer was it before these ideas found their way into manuals of prosody. It need not surprise us to find no mention of them in the books we have next to examine. Even at the present time they are imperfectly assimilated by our grammarians. Prosody is made a mere matter of accented and unaccented syllables ; the fundamental reality, the string which holds these together, passes unnoticed. Much less need we look for adequate views of verse in the prosodists of the earlier Nineteenth Century ; with a few remarkable exceptions, these writers continue laboriously to turn the old treadmill.

The exceptions were chiefly followers of Steele, who were already at work when the Century began. Thelwall has been named ; he printed tracts illustrating his scansions, but his one book on the subject will come before us under date 1812. Roe is credited with publishing a treatise on metre in 1801, but no copy is in our chief libraries and I have seen no account of it,[1] so must reserve him till 1823, when his one extant study was published. Odell, whose book appeared in 1806, tells us it

---

[1] As will be seen [*infra*, p. 138] a copy has now turned up.

was written four years earlier; and Chapman, whose two volumes came out in 1818 and 1821, had been teaching his views for many years before. All these writers, therefore, might be grouped at or about the outset of the Nineteenth Century ; and they form a group by themselves. But their work was little known, their influence small, so it hardly matters where we place them. Chronological order of publication has been my rule hitherto, and I propose still to follow it unless there is reason otherwise. The medley of widely differing authors thus presented is, after all, a fact of history not to be disregarded.

In 1804, as has been already noted, Mitford published his *Inquiry*. Next year it was caustically examined by the *Edinburgh Review* (Vol. VI, No. 12, Article X). This paper is reprinted, with an added Note about accent, and a Supplement of three pages written much later, in the *Works* of Dean William Herbert (Vol. II, pp. 31–78 and 212–15). If Classic instead of English prosody were our subject, this paper would need careful study. It propounds interesting views about the place of accent in Greek and Latin verse [anticipating those of Spedding, *infra*, 1861], while in the Supplement occur some good quantitative lines, for description of which see Appendix A. The young Oxonian—for such was Herbert when he wrote this review, though he adopts the standpoint of his periodical, calls the Scotch his countrymen, and speaks as though he lived in Edinburgh, " the metropolis of false quantities "—taxes Mitford with imperfect knowledge of his subject, and lays down the law about Classic, French, Celtic, Icelandic, and English verse with equal decisiveness. The last alone, fortunately, need engage our attention.

" The laws of English accent and versification . . . have perhaps never been rightly considered " (p. 377 : 65).[1] So begins his analysis, but it contains little that is really new. It is restricted to verse of Popian type, and blames even that when it transgresses his rules. Two accented syllables must never come together in a foot, and when they adjoin must always be separated by a pause (pp. 377–8 : 65-6). Three syllables may occur in any foot, so the above rule is observed ; the extra syllable " shall not be reckoned in scanning the verse ". Words like *heaven, prism, etc.* must be monosyllables

[1] I quote pages *first* of the *Edinburgh Review, second* of the *Works*, to facilitate reference.

in heroic verse, but must be dissyllables in " verse of the triple cadence ", in which no aberration of accent can be allowed (p. 379 : 68). Pope errs, therefore, in beginning a line with the words " Heaven's whole foundations " ; but " All heaven's foundations " would be " good metre, because the adjective remains grave before its substantive " (p. 380 : 69). In heroic verse " the tenth syllable shall be accented ; but the accent may be occasionally drawn back to the eighth " (p. 378 : 66). He scans specimen lines by both accent and quantity, but his accents come quite irregularly and his quantities are those of Latin verse. To these latter he attaches importance ; " quantity neither is nor ought to be entirely disregarded in our versification " (p. 380 : 70). In proof of this he compares the line—

O liquid streamlets to the main returning,

with this other—

The headlong torrent from its native caverns,

and asserts that the former would be objectionable in blank verse to a Classically trained ear (*ibid.*, *seq.*). I doubt if one such ear in a hundred would feel any difference, and certainly as English verse both lines are equally valid.[1] With more justice he says that in Greek and Latin verse the difficulty was to prevent too many short syllables coming together, while with us it is just the opposite ; with them variety had to be restricted, with us it is to be encouraged (p. 381 : 71, and *passim*). Yet his notion of variety is less wide than that of our chief poets, and his rules would restrict the freedom of even our most " correct " writers. If, finally, we ask whence these rules are drawn, the answer can only be, from the writer's imagination. No proof of them is offered, no justification of their authority ; the author's *ipse dixit* is their sole foundation.

While, however, no adequate view of the basis of English verse can be found in these pages, they well deserve reading on other accounts. The scholar will pause over the assertion that " the metrical rules observed in the South of Europe [*e.g.* in modern Italian verse, with which he parallels our own] were not modern inventions, but the old accentual laws of

---

[1] *Cf.* criticism by Guest (Skeat's edition, p. 109)

Latin verse, which survived those of quantity " (p. 376 : 63).
Classic accent Herbert believed to have been nowise different
from our own, and " the acute accent certainly does not
induce length of time " (p. 367 : 48). " The theory of Sheridan
[about accent] was so unintelligible, that it scarcely requires
notice " (p. 368 : 48). On every branch of his subject the
young writer is equally dogmatic. Klopstock's hexameter
is a " disgusting abortion ", which " has in a manner destroyed
all sense of good poetry in Germany " (p. 369 : 50). French
verse, through lack of accent, " affords little gratification to
other European nations " ; their Alexandrine is really two
lines, not one (p. 381 : 72). A final summary (pp. 384–5 :
77–8) resumes his chief conclusions. Students of Classic
verse should read also the " Note on Horatian metres " which
follows in Vol. II of the *Works* (pp. 79–90 ; dated 1841), and
the " Additional Note " (pp. 151–8). In the latter he repeats
his " position, that modern metres are accentual forms of
ancient temporal verse with little regard to quantity "
(p. 157), thus in mature age reaffirming conclusions at variance
with those of most critics, but which he maintains with no
little force and ingenuity.

    This same year, 1805, saw published Scott's *Lay of the Last
Minstrel*, which first popularized what we have called the
new verse ; and it also gave birth to *An Analytical Inquiry
into the Principles of Taste*, by Richard Payne Knight. Little
time need be spent over the latter, though it makes not
infrequent reference to verse-form. Shallow and sceptical
in philosophy, it applies Eighteenth Century canons to poetry
as to other arts, and finds Pope " the best versifier that ever
lived " (p. 112). Very little sensual gratification, however,
is afforded by even the most melodious versification (p. 51).
He ridicules pseudo-Classic structure in English (*ibid.*), and
echoes previous writers as to our violations of Latin quantity
(pp. 53, 127–31). Verse is well defined as being to prose as
dancing is to walking (p. 111) ; but his only notion of prosody
is that " English verse arises from a limited and regulated
distribution of accents and pauses, as well as of quantities "
(p. 112)—which really tells us nothing. Admitting the " great
and transcendent merits of Milton's poetry ", he yet blames
the " rugged anomalies " of his music, and devotes pages to
pointing them out (*cf.* pp. 112–20). Later, treating of the

sublime and pathetic, he pronounces our blank verse, " like Greek iambic, too near the tone of colloquial speech " (p. 395). Other remarks on metre are scattered through the volume, but I have noted nothing that requires mention. To all the higher side (as we now deem it) of verse this author seems insensible. His theory of art, and indeed of life, leaves little room for the nobler emotions ; and his view of verse is as mechanical as the rest of his thought.

After Knight, in 1806, comes the second published book of the Steele school. " J. Odell," author of *An Essay on the Elements, Accents, and Prosody of the English Language*, was an M.A. of Cambridge, beyond which fact my knowledge does not go. His moderate-sized Essay has a modest preface, but no index or table of contents ; it is not divided into Chapters, but takes each of its three subjects in turn. The *Elements* (pp. 1–54) are rightly defined as sounds, not letters merely, and his analysis of twenty-nine elementary sounds (p. 44) in English speech is original and suggestive. Six out of seven pure vowels, he says, may be either long or short. On *Accents* (pp. 55–123) he avowedly adopts Steele's view, regarding them as tone-inflections (of which there is an excellent description, with diagram, on p. 80), and constantly distinguishing them from emphasis. Monotony, in English speech, even for a single syllable, creates " intolerable dissonance " (p. 121). Steele's doctrine is summarized on pp. 93–102,[1] and Walker's discussed on pp. 104–23, as also in a " Postscript " (pp. 195–205). But it is the *Prosody* portion of this Essay (pp. 124–90) which specially appeals to us. Here he dissents markedly from Steele's teaching, both as to the difference between verse and prose, and as to the function of ' pause ' in verse-structure. Prose, he maintains, does not possess " rhythmical cadences in regular succession " (p. 152) ; non-metrical pauses affect the recitation of verse merely, not its actual structure (p. 156). Nor does he distinguish between force and ' poise ', like his master, though he bids us discriminate between " rhythmical and oratorial [*sic*] emphasis " (pp. 158–9). Moreover, he flatly rejects

---

[1] While adopting Steele's principles, he criticises his practice. " I confess that some of the examples of accentuation specified in his book seem to have been incorrectly noted " (p. 101). *Cf.* his remarks on a passage cited from Dionysius Thrax (pp. 89–92).

Steele's eight degrees of quantity, necessities of intonation limiting us to a proportion of four to one (pp. 154–5). In essentials, however, he adopts Steele's view, making "cadences" commensurate (p. 148), and actual time-beating the test (p. 151). Syllables possess quantity, but verse does not depend on these, but on "emphatic pulsations", regular as the beats of a pendulum ; "without such isochronism, there can be no regular rhythmical modulation" (p. 148). On syllabic quantity he is unsatisfactory, inclining to believe that "nothing but lengthening the vowel can possibly make the syllable long" (p. 137), though in the Postscript he ridicules the idea that a vowel changed its sound according to its position. Even Greek verse did not depend wholly on quantity, a trochee sometimes taking the place of dactyl or spondee (p. 149) ; while in "our iambic verse" tribrachs, spondees, dactyls, and double pyrrhics "are equalized with the leading iambic feet ; and sometimes a single syllable is made to fill a whole cadence" (p. 168). Common and triple time are, of course, distinguished ; "the first is the rhythmus of a march, and the second of a minuet" ; either may be quick or slow, and have "more or fewer steps" (pp. 130–1). Both occur in our heroic verse, but "without affecting the regular equality of the cadences" (p. 169). His excellent general principles, however, do not save him from supposing (pp. 173–4) that lines in *Paradise Lost* may consist, now of only three "cadences" or feet, now of four, now again of six, *e.g*—

> (Im-)|mutable, im-|mortal, | infinite.
> Fountain of | light, thy-| self in-|visible.
> Hail, | Son of | God, | saviour of | men, thy | name—

(the first and third feet of the last line being shown as eked out by a 'rest'). This, it need hardly be said, is simply flying in the face of fact. There can be no shadow of doubt that Milton intended every line of his poem, without exception, to be read as composed of five feet.

Toward the end of his Essay (p. 175 *seq.*), Odell maintains that Classic measures are quite possible in English, and have failed hitherto only because their writers violated natural accentuation, as in the 'sapphics' by Watts, or those others "I know not by whom" which were the work of Herries.

And he gives some specimens of his own [for which see Appendix A], which are certainly neater and smoother than those of his predecessors, though not quantitatively exact. He makes no allusion to German verses, nor to those of Coleridge, Southey, or Thelwall, and seems to have worked entirely on lines of his own. These, it is interesting to note, are—careful compliance with accent, coupled with avoidance of clumsily crowded consonants. Their basis is accentual, but quantity is not wilfully neglected, as was done by most of his successors. If Odell's lead had been followed, we should have been spared many jaw-breaking lines by authors of more note. The book ends with a lament over the cacophony introduced into our words by omission of the vowels in *-est*, *-ed*, etc., and some verses on " the old English language " (pp. 191–4) followed by the Postscript already mentioned.

Odell's Essay was originally written as an introduction to a Dictionary, and was primarily a criticism of Johnson's views. It replaces *a priori* dogmatism by study of facts. Our " numbers " consist of syllables in harmonious combination and of " rhythmical cadences in regular succession ", under " a system which has never yet been fully investigated " (pp. 125 and 152). Toward this investigation he makes a substantial and valuable contribution, though misled by false ideas as to the syllabic basis of verse. His criticism is always telling. The monotony of our heroic couplet he finds frequently " tiresome and disgusting " (p. 161) ; Milton's variety may sometimes be excessive, yet " less often than a cursory reader would imagine " (*ibid., seq.*). To Elizabethan writers he seldom if ever refers. His work has never been reprinted, though its freshness and vigour deserved longer life ; its teaching would now be old-fashioned. Yet no student of our prosody should omit glancing through it, so suggestive is it both in its truth and its error. To suppose it a mere repetition of Steele would be a great mistake.

[1] From the *Letters on Literature, etc.*, of Dr. George Gregory (2 vols., 1812) little of direct interest can be quoted. Posthumously published, they belong to the Eighteenth rather than the Nineteenth Century, surveying general questions of style and composition quite on the lines of Blair or Beattie, not without grace and liveliness. In Vol. I, Letter VIII,

[1] For Carey (1809) see under 1816.

pp. 93–4, he touches on prose form. "Something like a metrical arrangement may be traced in the style of our best prose writers." "The harmony of prose numbers depends on the judicious admixture of long and short syllables, and the musical or perhaps metrical conclusion of the periods or sentences." Macpherson's *Ossian* "is throughout metrical, and even monotonous". In the Bible, and Prayer-book Psalms, "you will find almost perfect hexameters." A grave uniform style abounds in iambs and trochees, as does English verse, while French verse "is all in dactyls". Again, in Vol. II, Letter XXIV, pp. 186–94, he points out the difficulty, not of distinguishing prose from verse, but of delimiting their boundaries, and defines the latter as "a metrical composition chiefly addressed to the passions", to which must be added that a poem is essentially a work of creation. For quantities of syllables, and rules for feet, he refers his reader to grammar, but warns him against supposing that English syllables are devoid of quantity, though in practice accent is more regarded. Our iambic verse he makes depend on number of syllables and management of pauses, "very little attention" being paid to quantity. All this, it will be seen, is merely what has been often said before, nor does Dr. Gregory put it forward as novel ; we need not, therefore, dwell on these volumes.

Next we reach "Citizen" John Thelwall, Radical and suspected revolutionary, friend of Coleridge and Wordsworth, editor of the *Champion* newspaper, where "Sapphics" by Coleridge and himself appeared,[1] lecturer on elocution, and disciple of Steele. His one book is usually cited by its half-title *Illustrations of English Rhythmus*, but the copy which I have seen—that in the British Museum—has a much longer title indicating that the book contains "Selections for the illustration of a course of instruction in the Rhythmus and Utterance of the English Language, with an Introductory Essay . . . etc.", the date being 1812. This copy, however, is

---

[1] Thelwall's "Song without a sibilant" used to be famous. I give the first stanza :—

> No, not the eye of tender blue,
>   Though, Mary, 'twere the tint of thine,
> Or breathing lip of glowing hue
>   Might bid the opening bud repine,
>   Had long enthrall'd my mind.

a patchwork affair, parts of another book, and sheets which had evidently been separate tracts, being bound up with it. The " Introductory Essay " is the only part with which we are concerned, and I take it that this belongs to the title-page, and appeared in 1812. The " Selections " are merely samples of prose and verse, in a few cases illustrated by Steele's symbols, but usually without these, though some are barred and characterized by hand as if at the teacher's dictation.

The Essay (pp. i–lxxii, but I shall use Arabic instead of Roman numerals for my quotations) adopts Steele's terminology throughout, and begins by saying that Steele, Odell, and Roe had alone had a " conception of the true nature and characteristics of a cadence, or English metrical foot " ; while even they had not " gone to the bottom of the subject ", through ascribing to mere taste what is really due to " indispensible [*sic*] necessities of organic action ". [The reference to Roe must be to his volume of 1801.] In all vocal efforts, the progress is from heavy to light, not *vice versa*, where there is alternation at all ; a duck utters heavy sounds only, but the single animal that reverses the above rule is a guinea-pig ! Therefore in English speech, and English verse, the rule is invariable. [Yet English sentences most often begin with a " light " syllable, *e. g.* " To be or not to be ".] " A cadence is a portion of tuneable sound, beginning heavy and ending light ; . . . a foot is a syllable or syllables occupying the space or duration of such a cadence, . . . and must be measured from the commencement of the syllable in thesis or heavy poise " (p. 6 ; *cf.* a fuller statement on p. 44). " Six proportional but varied cadences constitute (in its simplest form) an English heroic line " (pp. 3–4). General principles are thus laid down in pp. 1–20 ; then follow Sections on " praxis ", definitions, organs of speech. A beginning must be made with simple lines ; those of Shakespeare and Milton " can scarcely be treated thus in mechanical outline " (p. 22). " Appogiatura [*sic*] syllables " are mentioned (*ibid., cf.* p. 47) ; *caesurae* " sometimes do, and sometimes do not, increase the primitive number of the cadences " (p. 23). Pulsation and remission are explained (pp. 37–44), and are distinguished from long and short on the one hand, loud and soft on the other. But the most important Section of all is that on " Principles of Metrical Proportion, and of Rhythm " (pp. 44–58). Here he

restates his general theory with greater exactitude and more
detail. Common and triple time are distinguished, also quick
triple and slow triple (p. 45). These are recognised mainly by
the number of syllables in a foot, which, if not constant,
should be at least " so prevalent as to give its primary de-
nomination to the measure " (p. 46). Feet of one syllable are
freely admitted ; they must always contain " a single protracted syllable, beginning heavy and ending light ". Thus
he scans—

Arms and the | man I | sing, | who, ∧ | forced by | fate.

[the *caret* indicates a " rest ", which Thelwall represents by
the musical symbol defining its duration] (*ibid.*). Comparative
quantity is fixed, absolute quantity is " latitudinary " ;
" there is therefore no difficulty in giving to a trochee, or an
iambus, the same entire quantity with a spondee, or to a
spondee the same with a trochee, etc., though differing in the
proportions of their integral parts " (p. 49). Moreover " some
trochaics may be *inherently* as long as some spondees ", and
spondees may be pure or impure ; " syllables are not meted
out by a Winchester measure " (p. 51). Accepting Steele's
eight possible degrees of quantity, he yet finds *three* suffice in
practice, and notes that poise and quantity are often confounded (pp. 48, 51, 52). The Section ends with the following
" Definitions of the Rhythmus of Verse and Prose ", printed
mainly in italics. " (1) Rhythmus consists in an arrangement
of cadences, or metrical feet, in clauses more or less distinguishable by the ear, and of more or less obvious proportion,
in their periods and responses. (2) Verse is constituted of
a regular succession of like cadences, or of a limited variety
of cadences, divided by grammatical pauses, emphases, and
caesurae, into obviously proportioned clauses ; so as to
present sensible responses, at proportioned intervals, to the
ear. (3) Prose differs from verse, not in the proportion, or in
the individual character of its cadences ; but in the indis-
criminate variety of the feet that occupy those cadences, and
the irregularity of its clausular divisions. It is composed of
all sorts of cadences, arranged without attention to obvious
rule, and divided into clauses that have no obviously ascer-
tainable proportion, and present no responses to the ear at
any legitimate or determined intervals " (pp. 55–6).

The remainder of the Essay deals with other subjects.
From the foregoing it will appear how rigorous and logical is
Thelwall's analysis. I cannot, myself, endorse it throughout.
The claim with which he begins, that the divisions of cadences
can be written out exactly " in score " (p. 7), is practically
abandoned later in view of the difficulty attaching to syllabic
analysis (p. 50) ; and his treatment of single-syllable feet
seems to me arbitrary. Imperfect views of periodicity lead
him to hold that " pauses and emphases increase the number ",
though they do not alter the proportion, of cadences, so that
the following line contains *seven* cadences preceded by an
anacrusis (the third foot being constituted, and the fourth
supplemented, by a pause of the voice)—

(Ye) | airy | sprites | — | who ∧ | oft as | Fancy | calls (p. 55).

To contend that every heroic line contains six cadences is
reasonable, whether right or wrong ; to suppose that the
number of cadences is immaterial cuts away the foundation of
prosody. This heresy, we have seen, originated with Steele
himself ; his followers unfortunately adopted it. But, after
all deductions, and even questioning his fundamental postulate
of progress from heavy to light, how much there is to admire
in Thelwall's work ! How actual, how close to reality, it
seems after the *a priori* dogmatism of the Classical school.
His ideal, too, is lofty ; Shakespeare and Milton, not Denham
and Waller and Pope, are his models. " The divine Milton,"
especially, was the idol of his boyhood (pp. 4, 18, *etc*.), and
remains his master. In the opening lines of *Paradise Lost*,
it may be mentioned, he finds the prevailing cadence spondaic
(p. 49). Surely it is discreditable to English prosody that
work like Odell's and Thelwall's remained almost entirely
unnoticed ; unanswered, not because unanswerable, but because unread. So it was, however ; we shall find the high-
priests of criticism sublimely unconscious of their contribution
to metrical science, resolutely repeating old formulas which
had lost what little truth they ever possessed.

My Bibliography next mentions a book or books that have
wholly vanished. The titles are given in Watt's *Bibliotheca
Britannica*, the author's name being Richard Edwards, the
date 1813. No copy is known to exist ; advertisements have
failed to procure one. Guest mentions having tried to find

the third ; he does not refer to the others. What creates interest is that the author professes to give specimens of verse measured solely by quantity, as well as of verse measured solely by accent. Till a copy turns up, if one ever does, nothing further can be said.[1] The author's name is otherwise unknown to me.

Dr. John Carey, author of treatises on Latin prosody and the well-known *Gradus ad Parnassum*, published in 1816 a " new and improved edition " of his *Practical English Prosody and Versification* (the first edition, said to have come out in 1809, I have not seen) ; also a separate *Key* to same. As might be expected, both keep wholly to Classic lines. " Prosody teaches the proper quantity and accent of syllables and words, and the measures of verses ; " but " the quantity or length of syllables is little regarded in English poetry, which is entirely regulated by their number and accent " (p. 1). Accent he defines as " emphatic tone " (*ibid.*), and explains that the symbols – and ᴗ, in his book, denote accented and unaccented syllables respectively (p. 4, *note*). Of any real basis of verse, beyond mere numerical limit of syllables, he is unconscious. Rejecting Lindley Murray's absurd scansion [borrowed from Beattie] of

Frŏm thĕ lŏw | plēasŭres ŏf | thĭs făllĕn | nātŭre,

he proposes to substitute

Frŏm thĕ | lŏw plēas-|ŭres ŏf | thĭs făll-|ĕn nā-(ture) ;

but he does not tell us how rhythm is preserved when pyrrhics alternate with spondees (p. 13, *note*). Syncope, synaeresis, and the rest are freely invoked (p. 6, *cf.* Preface, p. xv) ; in " Full many a bard " the *y* is held to be elided. While opposed to trisyllabic feet in heroic verse, however, he admits that they sometimes occur ; nor does he object to Milton's intermingling of iambic and trochaic, for which he quotes precedent from Greek comedians (p. 27, *note*). He hints at a reason for the initial trochee (p. 42), and defends variety of caesura (p. 57 *seq.*). The amphibrach he rejects utterly, affirming that English versification requires an accent on either the first or last syllable of a foot (p. 52, *note*). On the whole, popular ideas are put not amiss in this short sketch of sixty-two pages,

---

[1] Compare, however, the note in Appendix B.

but it is amazing that any competent critic should believe its
main position tenable. How a line composed of heterogeneous
feet, restricted indeed in number but not in kind, could possibly
produce an impression of uniformity, one despairs to conceive ;
yet surely our verse does produce that impression. Critics
of Carey's school neglect half the problem ; they perceive
syllabic diversity, but fail to reconcile this with temporal
uniformity.

In 1817 Coleridge published both *Sibylline Leaves* (the first
collected edition of his shorter poems) and *Biographia Literaria*,
which contains much analysis and criticism of poetry. Here,
if anywhere, we might have looked to find a philosophy of
metre ; but we look in vain. In its Chap. XIV, metre seems
to be defined as " an exact correspondent recurrence of accent
and sound " ; which does not take us very far. Chap. XVIII
discusses the origin and function of metre, but not its nature.
And in " Satyrane's Letters " Wordsworth and Coleridge
discourse with Klopstock about the blank verse of Milton and
Glover [!], Wordsworth asserting that the merit of good blank
verse lies in " apt arrangement of pauses and cadences, and
the sweep of whole paragraphs," rather than in the even flow
of single lines. What constitutes that " even flow " we never
hear. In the " Table-talk " of Coleridge, it may be here
added, there are *obiter dicta* about prose being " words in their
best order ", poetry " the best words in the best order "—
complaints that the metre of some modern poems is to true
metre as dumb-bells are to music—much praise of Shakespeare's and Milton's rhythm, with strictures on Byron's and
on Tennyson's versification ; he sometimes " can scarcely
scan " the latter—and frequent mention of iambics, hendecasyllabics, and the like. But any real discussion of verse-
structure I have not found. He is familiar with technical
prosody, and discusses the nature of Greek accent ; but he
never philosophizes about rhythm in itself, or mentions
Steele's doctrines. It is equally difficult to believe that he did
not discuss these with Thelwall, or that they failed to interest
him. Some time might have been spared from ontological
discussion to these humbler themes. His pseudo-Classic verse,
printed in the *Leaves*, is no better than other people's ;
" Metrical feet : a lesson for a boy " is not particularly
happy. A false stress must be laid on the first syllable of

each line in the couplet translated from Schiller, and so often quoted—

In the hexameter rises the fountain's silvery column ;
In the pentameter aye falling in melody back.

And these things, at best, are mere toys. No man, surely, was better fitted than Coleridge to have given us a real analysis of metre, to have unravelled the harmonies that blend in such verse as his own. But he left the task unattempted, left it to writers such as the one who next meets us.

Rev. James Chapman, a teacher in Edinburgh, published there in 1818 *The Music, or Melody and Rhythmus, of Language,* and in 1821 *The Original Rhythmical Grammar of the English Language.* Both books may be considered together ; I have given the first words only of their somewhat voluminous titles. A follower of Steele and admirer of Thelwall, he draws largely on both. Not only is his " system " avowedly " taken from " Steele, but whole sentences and paragraphs are reproduced (without notice given), phrases like " I believe " and " I think " being transferred without alteration. The large print of the *Rhythmical Grammar,* indeed, is almost all Steele. The same is true, in less degree, as regards other writers ; sentences from Thelwall reappear, with the phrase " clausular divisions"; Webb and others are similarly honoured. I do not suggest that there was anything underhand in this wholesale plagiarism ; but it should surely have been acknowledged in his Prefaces. That to the *Rhythmical Grammar* gives a list of books which he has " consulted " (p. xiv) ; but it also boasts that he has " ventured to think for himself " (p. viii). As concerns theory, at any rate, the books unreservedly repeat Steele. His eight degrees of quantity, his six normal cadences of heroic verse, his readiness to let pauses increase the number of cadences, all are accepted unhesitatingly. No position taken by Steele, so far as I have seen, is challenged by Chapman. On the other hand, the pupil supplies orderly arrangement, copious examples, a lively style of controversy. He is amusingly contemptuous of all other systems of prosody, and amusingly confident in his own. It seems unnecessary to go through the volumes in detail, but of the *Music of Language* Chapters I to XII state his [*i. e.* Steele's] theory, the remaining nine are mostly occupied by illustrations, scansions, and pieces for recitation. (Chap. XIX deals with prose, Chap. XX

with Biblical passages.)   In the *Rhythmical Grammar*, which
is the fuller and larger of the two books, but abounds in misprints, the Chapters on Quantity, Emphasis, Cadence, Meter
[*sic*], and Rhythm are perhaps the most important ; and the
end of Chap. XIII, on " Errors of English Prosodians ",
should not be missed.   Both books, indeed, are eminently
readable throughout ; borrowed ideas are handled and explained with vigour if not with discretion.

How boldly Chapman adopts his teachers' doctrines is
shown by his actually asserting (*Music of Language*, p. 75 ;
cf. a similar instance on p. 20, and *Rhythmical Grammar*,
p. 203) that Milton's line—

> Rocks, caves, lakes, fens, bogs, dens, and shades of death—

is read precisely as if an *and* intervened after each of the first
five words !   This is Thelwall's view of single-syllable feet
pushed to an absurdity.   This line would thus contain eight
feet or " cadences ".   Similarly, for Milton's " I 'sdained
subjection " he bids us read " I dis-|dained sub-|jection "
(*Rhythm. Gramm.*, p. 215).   Nor does he ever stick at mere
number of cadences, but writes (*ibid.*, p. 124)—

> Great ∧ | source of | day ! ∧ | best ∧ | image | here be-|low,

and

> (The) | thunder | rolls ∧ | — | ∧ Be | hush'd the | prostrate | world

[my *carets* stand for " rests " of various length] ; or, in
Alexandrine metre (*ibid.*, p. 192)—

> Flies ∧ | o'er the un-|bending | corn, ∧ | ∧ and | skims a-|long the | main.

Individual lines, as will appear from these instances, are often
tortuously divided.   On the other hand, it must be understood
that these are the exceptions, not the rule.   Most of his
scansions are reasonable, if not certain.   But for his tendency
to make ' anacrusis ' a separate foot, line after line would pass
muster to-day.   His full recognition of the pause-element in
verse is admirable.   Most exposition in either book, his own
as well as that of others, is clear and cogent.   With his
strictures on our " Classical " prosodists I have naturally no
quarrel, though his condemnation of Carey's and Lindley
Murray's scansions lately quoted only leads to this no more
credible one (*ibid.*, p. 219)—

> ∧ | From the | low ∧ | pleasures | of this | fallen | nature,

which may give the prose value of the syllables, but surely not the prosodial. His remarks on Greek metre may be safely neglected. In one respect Chapman follows Thelwall rather than Steele, *viz.* in making the bulk of our ' iambic ' metre move to common instead of triple time. It is remarkable how persistent, in one form or other, is the idea that our commonest form of verse moves to " even measure ", though for three Centuries most of our grammarians have sought to identify it with triple rhythm.

In 1819 Thomas Campbell, the poet, published his *Specimens of English Poets*, in seven volumes [second edition in one volume, edited by Peter Cunningham, 1841], to which is prefixed an " Essay on English Poetry ". Like Warton, he deals entirely with the history of English verse, not at all with its structure. The same year gave a paper which interests as being the first from across the Atlantic. In the *North American Review* for September, 1819, appeared an article " On tri- syllabic feet in iambic measure ", which may now be read, altered and enlarged, in the Works of William Cullen Bryant [*Life and Works*, New York, 1883-4, Vol. V, pp. 57-67]. The writer contends that such feet should be allowed, but does not say *why*. He notes that they are frequent in Shakespeare and Milton, rare in Denham and Waller, " rigidly excluded " by Dryden and his successors [yet Pope has not a few]. " I find no traces of them in Thomson or Dyer." Akenside, after eschewing them in the first edition of his *Pleasures of Imagina- tion*, introduced them into the second ; Cowley used them " without scruple ". If the paper contain no theory, it at least protests against effete pedantry, and vindicates for the author of " Thanatopsis " [did any work of his later years equal in merit that youthful poem ?] his place as *doyen* of American prosody as well as poetry.

[1] In 1820 Southey wrote, in 1821 published, his *Vision of Judgment*, a poem in [accentual] " English hexameters ". This practically introduced that form of metre to the British public, and inaugurated a tremendous controversy. Hence- forward, the " Classic " problem assumes new shape, and becomes mainly a question touching the *raison d'être* of this

---

[1] A paper in *Blackwood's Magazine* for September, 1820, on " Sweet- ness of versification ", which does not call for comment here, is noted in Appendix B.

metre. I have discussed this question elsewhere,[1] and need
only summarize my view here. The metre has no claim
whatever to represent Classic hexameter. Apart from all
other differences—want of spondees, want of true caesura,
etc., etc.—it differs fundamentally in respect of time. It moves
to triple rhythm, Classic to quadruple. This has been overlooked, simply because so few people read Classic verse
according to quantity. They do not really give double duration to each long syllable, to the second syllable of a spondee
as well as the first. What they do is to place a strong accent
on the first syllable of each foot, and imagine that this represents quantity. The main difference between the metres thus
disappears, since most people read

> Arma virumque cano, Troiae qui primus ab oris . . .

to the very same time as

> This is the forest immense, where oaks and beeches assemble.

To realize what ought to be the difference, we need only try
to make the latter line move to quadruple rhythm, giving two
full beats wherever two are marked—

> This is the | fo-rest im-|mense, where | *etc.*

It is obvious that this is not the rhythm to which these words
are intended to be set ; but it is, beyond question, the rhythm
to which the Latin words were, and ought to be, set.
    While, however, Southey's metre has no claim to represent
Classic hexameter, it is perfectly admissible as an English
form of verse. It is simply a triple-time six-cadence line, with
falling accent, and without rhyme. It should be written like
any other English measure, with the usual latitude as to
syllables, and the usual reliance on time instead of finger-
counting. This the public, with its irresistible common sense,
has long since recognised. Whatever critics may say, this
metre is accepted and enjoyed by English readers ; from their
verdict there is no appeal. What future is in store for this
metre depends on poets, not on critics. By trial alone can
its possibilities be discovered, whether for good or evil, success
or failure. Hints in this direction can, in my opinion, be
derived from poems like Mr. Swinburne's " Hesperia " and

---

[1] In a pamphlet, now out of print, and in the Appendix to my *Study
of Metre*.

" Evening on the Broads ". No good will be done by relying
on rules of an alien prosody ; English verse must be ruled by
English speech-law. The above remarks will, at any rate,
relieve us from needing to follow with any minuteness the
often irrelevant arguments so copiously poured forth against
the " pestilent heresy " of Southeyan hexameters.[1]

Southey's poem was accompanied by an interesting Preface.
He claims priority as an experimenter, yet refers to two or
three (only) of his many predecessors.[2] In a foot-note he
asserts that the word *Egypt* is the only pure spondee in our
language ; twenty better ones could easily be produced. On
the other hand, he justly points out that words which seem
spondees when pronounced singly become accentual trochees
or iambs in verse. But the capital blunder in both Preface and
poem is that he makes syllabic feet the sole basis of verse, and
dispenses with " regular recurrence of emphasis ". Nay more,
he claims to use " any foot of two or three syllables " in any
of the " four first " feet, and most frequently in the first of
these—which is destructive of true rhythm. Constantly we
come on lines which can only with an effort be read to the
required tune. As a friendly critic [understood to be Words-
worth] told him, the first part of his lines is apt to be not
metrical enough in its effect, the last part too much so. This
is directly due to false theory. Striving to avoid the exotic
character of lines leading off always with a strong syllable, the
poet begins with a ' pyrrhic ' in place of a ' dactyl ', and so
ruins the structure of his line.

We have nothing to do with the theme of the poem, which
roused Byron to killing satire. But it may be noted that the
matter did little to help the metre. It is a fact—used as an
argument sometimes for, sometimes against, their adoption—
that accentual hexameters occur freely in ordinary prose.
Lines like

> Nay, it is better thus, the Monarch piously answered—

---

[1] Etymologically, ' hexameter ' means any line of six feet, but
practice has restricted it to one particular form of these. It is therefore
very undesirable to use the word in its general meaning ; and the same
applies to ' pentameter ', ' tetrameter,' and ' trimeter '. Why use
Greek terms at all ? *Six-foot* or *six-cadence* is just as good, and free
from ambiguity.

[2] *Cf.* the " Specimens " subjoined to the *Notes* which follow the poem.

show how natural is the swing of this measure, but also to
what danger it is liable. Except in strong hands, it quickly
degenerates into prose. Southey's subject should have prevented this happening, but his handling gave every chance
to it. The mixture of George III and heavenly mysteries
dispels poetry ; tumbling back into prose, we find the metre
insufficient to stay our fall, while some lines are positively and
unintentionally comic. Even in the admired opening passage
there is hardly a line which might not be bettered. There is
no victory in the march of its verses. At best we can read
them, admiring ideas rather than execution, and taking
pleasure in pictures of scenery—

> Derwent retaining yet from eve a glassy reflection
> Where his expanded breast, then still and smooth as a mirror,
> Under the woods reposed.

Such words—and they furnish a favourable sample—have no
magic in them, no " inevitableness ". This, indeed, is only to
say what we all know, that Southey was not a poet of first
rank. Enough, then, to realize that a poem of considerable
size, by the Laureate of that day, was bound to attract
attention ; and that its faults as well as its merits secured
special consideration of its metre.

The critics soon opened fire. First came the *Edinburgh
Review* (for July, 1821),[1] not averse to let Tory dogs taste
the lash. Metre is dealt with from a standpoint of pedantic
orthodoxy, ours being made a mere succession of accented and
unaccented syllables. " Versification consists in the recurrence of certain marked or conspicuous sounds, at regular and
fixed intervals " (p. 424) ; any " regular series of marked
syllables " would gratify the ear as much (p. 428). Yet time
belongs to Classic verse only, and ours depends on mere
number of syllables (p. 425). " No legitimate English measure
admits of any change in *the number* of syllables that make up
the line " (p. 426). When words like *heavenly, watery, etc.*,
occur in heroic verse they are " used as dissyllables, . . . the
middle syllable suffering a substantial elision " (p. 427).
A trochee can never replace a dactyl, for one unaccented
syllable can never be equal to two of the same description
(p. 432) ; nor can one or more unaccented syllables replace an
accented (p. 427). The reviewer's strictures on Southey's

---

[1] Vol. 35, No. 70, Art. IX, pp. 422–36.

poem, first as to its form and in the last few pages as to its matter, may be right in the main, despite their *animus* ; his own positions are no less vulnerable. To say that " wherever the structure of the verse requires an accented syllable, *nothing but an accented syllable* can be admitted " [the italics in these quotations are the *Review's*] (*ibid.*) is, as we have seen, simply to condemn the practice of all our best writers. On p. 430 it is truly remarked that spondees are frequent in our prose speech (in phrases like *vile slave, fair play, etc.*), and not unknown in our verse, *e.g.*

Thou First | great Cause, | least un-|derstood ;

while a *note* to p. 428 shows how the then current pronunciation of Latin mangled the cadence of its verse. But, as regards general principles, the dogmatic assertions of Southey's critic are mere echoes of Johnsonian narrowness, and will not bear testing by fact.[1]

Better in tone and scholarship are the *Remarks* of Rev. Samuel Tillbrook, B.D., Fellow of Peterhouse, Cambridge (1822), the first of many similar treatises devoted to the hexameter question. Without undue violence, and with far greater historical knowledge than Southey, he sketches the history of previous attempts, and sums up against the innovation. Italian Trissino is mentioned, our chief Elizabethan and later experiments described, and German models briefly referred to. He does not, however, explicitly distinguish between earlier quantitative and later accentual bases. Rather he assumes that the basis must be quantity in some shape, not necessarily as formulated by Classic rules, and asks Southey to state on what principles of quantity his verse is framed. The book being confined to this one question, its contents will appeal only to those who are interested in this particular branch of prosody ; but to them it may be commended as an informing piece of work, both in its history and its criticism, though the latter hardly takes quite wide enough views of its subject-matter.

In passing may be mentioned a translation of the first

---

[1] The objections to " double endings " and to the " singing and dancing cadence " of triple time (p. 433) were natural at this date, but have now become antiquated. Critics are seldom quick to appreciate novel music.

canto of an Italian poem called *Ricciardetto*, by Sylvester Douglas, Lord Glenbervie (1822 ; privately printed the year before), merely because the last of its explanatory Notes (No. 95) is said to be " an extract from an Essay I have in part composed on the different modes of versification in several of the modern languages " (p. 185). This Essay does not seem to have been published. Judging from the sample, it dealt with rules of versification, not with the nature of verse.

From these minor matters we turn to the latest and most systematic work of the Steele school. Comparatively little is known about Rev. Richard [Baillie] Roe, author of *Principles of Rhythm* (1823) ;[1] he seems to have been confused (*e.g.* in *Bibliotheca Britannica*) with another Richard Roe, a surveyor, who died in 1814. But, according to the *Dictionary of National Biography*, our Roe was a B.A. of Trinity College, Dublin, who later in life took orders, wrote on theology as well as a treatise on shorthand, was also a popular singer, and gave concerts in London, where he died in 1852. His first book on rhythm was a slender quarto ; that of 1823 is a goodly quarto volume, published in Dublin, and dedicated to the President and members of the Royal Irish Academy. The copy now in the British Museum was presented by the author. It contains preface, an elaborate table of contents, 189 pages of text, and some 30 of notes—controversial matter being mostly relegated to these last. Music is constantly referred to, and musical signs employed. Print and binding are both good, contrasting markedly with those of his three fellow-disciples. Seven out of eight Chapters deal with rhythm in speech, the eighth and last with music proper. Thelwall read the whole in proof (Note 19, p. 128).

Distinguishing tone from time, the Preface states that Steele and Odell sufficiently dealt with the former, theirs being " the only works extant in which it is clearly investigated " [*cf.* Note 2, which reproves Walker for disparaging Steele, while " actually purloining his explanation of the nature of accent "]. The present work, therefore, is confined to time or rhythm, in expounding which it is perhaps implied that these writers were less successful. Yet, by his own account

[1] For a short account of Roe's earlier and less important book, see Appendix B.

[Note 35], there are only two points where Roe differs from Steele, *viz.* in making an essential difference between prose and verse, and in not making grammatical pauses constituents of verse-structure. However this be, Steele's doctrines are at any rate recast in Roe's mind, and set forth in Roe's words ; and the practical results differ considerably when verse is scanned into feet.

Chap. I deals with " principles of rhythm in general ", points out that rhythm may be marked by " degrees of pulsation, of tone or of quantity " (p. 7), and praises Young's treatment of the subject [*ante*, 1786]. Chap. II, on " Elements of speech ", makes pulsation inseparable from quantity, and predicable of every portion of utterance (pp. 34–5, *cf.* 42). This double factor has two effects, elementary and rhythmical ; Sheridan noticed only the latter, but was right concerning it, since " a pulsated consonant is longer than the vowel which precedes it " (pp. 34, 39–40). So we come in Chap III to " English feet ", which are " simple or compound integers ", but in either case " all relatively equal " (p. 41). Dissyllabic intervals usually carry one pulsation, trissyllabic [1] two, the subordinate pulsation in the latter case not affecting rhythm (p. 42). Pulsations differ indefinitely in strength, but may generally be classed as *primary* or *secondary* ; the weakest " scarcely distinguish a pulsated from a remiss syllable " (*ibid.*). Of quantity there are three grades, long and short and *mean*, the last occupying either one-half or one-third of the ratio, while the others are respectively one-half longer and one-half shorter (pp. 43–4, *cf.* Note 24). " Entire intervals " are even or uneven, according as the syllables are or are not of a mean quantity (p. 44). These statements are illustrated by examples, not always very convincing, but clear and precise. Quantity is shown to be in one sense fixed, in another variable (pp. 49–51, *cf.* Notes 29, 30). " Length by position " is well explained on p. 48 (*cf.* Note 27), Mitford's view being fully endorsed.

There are said to be four modifications of feet as time-beaters (pp. 52–3). And feet are either perfect or imperfect ; in the latter, " rests, or measured portions of silence, supply

---

[1] In this and the next two paragraphs, Roe's spelling of *trissyllable* is adopted. The only objection to it is possible confusion of sound with *dissyllable*.

the place of absent syllables " (p. 53). Five sorts of feet are
enumerated, amphibrachs being added to iamb, trochee,
dactyl, and anapaest (*cf.* Note 31). " The misconceptions of
the Ancients on the subject of quantity have led most writers
to suppose dissyllabic feet to be in triple time, and trissyllabic
feet to be in duple time, whereas the very reverse is the truth "
(Note 31). All the foregoing applies to prose as well as verse.
In prose, imperfect feet " are *negatively* determined to the
most simple, that is, to the duple species " ; in verse, they are
positively determined to whatever species predominates, duple
or triple, for " no species of verse is wholly formed of feet
exceeding three syllables " (pp. 57–8). Prose feet are numberless, including all words of but one primary pulsation (on p. 42
he had claimed that no word naturally occupies more than
one foot). Imperfect dissyllabics are common to prose and
verse, imperfect trissyllabics are peculiar to trissyllabic verse
(p. 59). Finally, verse contains " irregular feet ", formed by
inadequate or super-adequate syllables ; this is due to
unavoidable defects of language (*ibid.*). A similar effect may
be observed in music (p. 65).

This elaborate analysis, open to doubt in parts—a foot of
nine syllables (p. 52) seems absurd ; and the doctrine of
" irregular feet " is surely a confession of inadequacy in
theorizing—leads to a discussion of " English lines " in
Chap. IV. This may be more briefly dealt with. It is here,
however, that he states his divergence from Steele, and makes
" incidental pauses " no part of rhythm (p. 74, *cf.* Note 35).
Lines are either pure or mixed, and are determined either by
sense or by modification of feet (p. 75 *seq.*). Trissyllabic lines
run on continuously (p. 83). Strangely, he makes lines of
three and five feet " possess a character of stability and
firmness " (p. 84). Caesuras with us are merely " greater or
less internal pauses ", not analogous to those of Classic verse
(pp. 86–7, *cf.* Note 36). The initial trochee is declared always
to form part of a trissyllabic foot (p. 89). Copious examples
are given, but in " mixed lines " he seems guided too much by
the airs to which verse has been set. Milton and Pope are
compared, the latter being " for blunt ears ", the former for
delicate (p. 103) ; yet some of the former's lines strike him as
hardly metrical in " just pronunciation ". Cowper too is
mentioned, and Southey's irregular verse, " imitated from

Percy's *Reliques.*" "The intermixture of different feet," in
our verse, "is more used in dissyllabics than in trissyllabics,
more in iambics than in trochaics, and most of all in heroics "
(p. 107). The first part alone of this Chapter contains much
that is of importance, the residue travelling mainly along
accepted lines.

What remains can be shortly summarized. Chap. V, " Of
English clauses," treats mainly of unrhymed stanzas, to
which he is evidently partial (Southey's *Thalaba* is mentioned).
Chap. VI deals with Classic verse, not helpfully, for he replaces
quantity by pulsation, and sees no difference between *turris*
and *turret*, *annual* and *annuus* ; pp. 142–3, however, show
that this view does not wholly satisfy him. Chap. VII compares prose with verse, their differences being summed up on
pp. 151–2 ; the same words are sometimes set to one time in
prose and another in verse (pp. 149–51). In Chap. VIII he
takes up the " second part of his subject ", Musical Rhythm,
but handles it concisely, principles having been already determined. Musical tones can be detached and combined with
a freedom which is impossible with spoken syllables, since the
poet finds these latter already formed into words (pp. 164–5).
Into purely musical questions we need not follow him. Of
the " Notes " which succeed the text those chiefly important
have been already cited ; in one (Note 50) he suggests a
" mixed Alexandrine " to imitate the *style* rather than the
form of ancient hexameter.[1] Many excellent remarks might
be quoted from these pages, and the whole book well deserves
reading ; but the most notable part of it from a prosodian's
point of view is certainly the Chapter on " feet ".

Of Steele's professed followers, Roe is the clearest and most
methodical ; his master's teaching loses nothing at his hands,
and wears a garb of scientific exactness. Some pitfalls into
which Steele fell are avoided by his pupil ; the difference
between prosaic and prosodial value of syllables is duly
recognised. If it were possible to attach a definite relative
length to every fraction of speech, Roe has shown how to
record it. The fault of his book, to my mind, is that it
attempts the impossible. Such precision as he seeks to find

---

[1] He mentions Taylor and Odell in this connection, and praises the
latter's verse (p. 147), but doubts the possibility of reproducing Classic
measures.

between long, short, and "mean" syllables is a fond imagination ; syllables do not in themselves express time thus precisely, though they may be so manipulated as to suggest more than they express. Even to fail in such an essay, however, is honourable, far more so than to linger amid vague generalities. Roe's strenuous attempt to analyse the actual facts of verse deserved a recognition which it never received. Hardly ever is his book quoted, even by "musical scansionists " ; yet their view of verse, now becoming so popular, was efficiently stated by him. Not till we come to Sidney Lanier [1880] shall we find it adopted so fully and unreservedly. If Steele first claimed a musical basis for verse, Roe first wove his ideas into a connected and only too elaborate system.

John Hookham Frere, friend of Canning and joint-author of the *Anti-Jacobin* [*ante*, 1797], professed himself a metrist and was a brilliant writer of verse, original and translated. His volume of *Poems*, published in 1824, contains one piece of so-called hexameters on " Malta ", a Note to which declares it to be " without false quantities " ; but it is difficult to know what rules of quantity sanction making *chivalry* a dactyl, or lengthening the first syllable of *honour*, the second of *precipitate*, and others. The second line begins with a redundant syllable (" Of chivalry, honour, and arms "), and in a Postscript to his version of the *Frogs* of Aristophanes (published 1830) he claims this as an allowable licence, and asserts that a Classic hexameter was somewhat longer, " or at least slower in enunciation," than an English heroic couplet, since it contained six bars of quadruple time, while each English line contains but two and a half. Beyond these statements (easily found in his *Works*, edited by Sir Bartle Frere) I have not found any utterance bearing on prosody in the writings of one who was scholar as well as poet, but whose just-quoted *dictum* about heroic verse seems to me doubtful in the extreme.

The *Treatise on English Versification* (1827), by William Crowe, D.D., Public Orator at Oxford, is the work of an old man (dedicated to a " friend of seventy years' standing ") who thinks that all experiments have been already made, and there is no room for further discovery (pp. 35–9). Not here need we look for fresh ideas ; the " new verse " of Scott and Southey he thinks unfit for epic strains (p. 3). A good historical Introduction (pp. 1–34) enumerates our chief prosodists,

Mitford being specially praised ; then in twenty-one Chapters he reviews orthodox verse on Eighteenth Century lines. Elision explains superfluous syllables, except in dramatic verse, where trisyllabic feet are admitted ; Classic rules of quantity are adopted without question, length by position being rightly explained (p. 53) ; Greek [printed without accent-marks, but with breathings] is read by accent instead of quantity. Letters, instead of sounds, are taken as units. The first four Chapters deal with elemental questions, after which rhyme is discussed through several more ; Chap. XI is on caesura, XIV on elision, XX on dramatic verse, XXI on Milton's versification. The style is pleasant, the criticism apt if not novel, but beyond dividing verse into feet there is no discussion of structure. Of feet he recognises the usual four, iamb and trochee, dactyl and anapaest ; amphibrachic verse is not acknowledged, because this foot never predominates (p. 62). Accent is identified with force,[1] but quantity is held to play its part in our verse ; instances, not very satisfying, are given of its effect (p. 57). He praises Milton's verse for its " variety ", but doubts whether this is not carried too far. If there is nothing novel in Crowe's exposition, there is much that is interesting and attractive ; old-fashioned ideas are handled with skill, and the diction is that of the Nineteenth Century. But the book shows how little even a capable critic can foresee what is coming, or rightly estimate new departures.

In *Blackwood's Magazine* for November, 1828, " Noctes Ambrosianae " No. 39, Prof. John Wilson, as Christopher North, prelects on the difference between prose and verse (pp. 642–52). He thinks that metrical phrases first occurred accidentally in speech, attracted notice, and were intentionally imitated (p. 642). Versification, he remarks, often proceeds historically from more complex to more simple structure. There is little else to our purpose in his disquisition, which toward the end becomes very ' flamboyant ' indeed.

---

[1] Accent he makes " closely akin to emphasis ", which may be defined as " a certain grandeur " given to syllables, it being so described by Holder (*Elements of Speech*, 1669). But Holder explains (*op. cit.*, p. 99) that this " grandeur " or largeness is given by " a more vigorous pronunciation, and a longer stay upon it ". The phrase is not metaphorical, and Holder distinguishes between accent and emphasis, reserving the former word for *tone.*

The Music of Nature, by one William Gardiner (1832), is
" an attempt to prove that what is passionate and pleasing in
the art of singing, speaking, and performing upon musical
instruments, is derived from the sounds of the Animated
World ". The bulk of its fifty-one Chapters deals with music,
but the last four belong to our subject, particularly Chap. 50
" on rhythm in language ". Here the handling is wholly
musical. Though the work of Steele and his followers is not
mentioned, the writer is in substantial accord with it. To
scan by feet alone is " mere visionary theory " ; " syllables are
as various in their duration as the notes in music," and a
classification into long and short is " much too rude for
a musician's ear " (pp. 500, 520). Instead, he scans by bars,
claiming that " the words which convey the sense invariably
fall upon the bar " (p. 510),[1] and that every verse must divide
into an *even* number of bars (p. 501). Our heroic verse he
makes always consist of four bars, *e.g.*—

> All are but | parts of | one stupendous | whole,

the second and third bars containing rests and ' dotted notes ' ;
while the apparent three units in

> I have found out a gift for my fair

become four through the addition of a silent bar. This seems
arbitrary, as does the setting of Pope's couplets now to triple
time, now to common (*cf.* pp. 501, 505, *etc.*) ; and one fails to
see why the demand for " equal times " precludes a strain of
five " measures " in verse or in music (p. 504). But the
importance of " rests " is duly felt (p. 502), and the distinction
between prose and verse referred to (p. 512) ; examples of
prose follow the latter reference, some being in common time,
some in triple. The final Chapter on " Quantity " gives
representative words with musical equivalents, as well as
sometimes with such phonetic transliterations as " pik-cher "
for *picture*. The whole treatment of speech, however, is far
too short and superficial to carry weight, and is interesting
mainly as recording a musician's hasty view. As such, it may
profitably be compared with those of more erudite and equally
dogmatic analysers.

America now began to send us important treatises on

---

[1] For explanation of this phrase see p. 503.

speech and grammar, notably those of James Rush and Goold Brown. The first edition of Rush's *Philosophy of the Human Voice* appeared, I believe, in 1827 ; the second came out in 1833, the third and fullest (which I quote) in 1845. It does not deal directly with prosody, but examines the material with which prosody is concerned, and as a study of intonation won the praise of no less a critic than the late A. J. Ellis [*infra*, 1873–4]. A practising physician, Rush first studied vocal physiology for himself, then read "all accessible treatises", finding none satisfactory, but those of Steele, Sheridan, and Walker valuable in parts (*Introduction*, especially p. xxvi *seq*.).[1] His own analysis distinguishes five features of sound, *viz*. Quality, Force, Time, Abruptness, and Pitch (text, p. 1). Into his elaborate discussion of these we need not enter. Perhaps Sections [*i. e.* Chapters] 4 on syllabification, 44 on accent, and 45 on quantity, contain most that is apposite. Accent he separates from emphasis, and makes depend on time as well as force ; while there are "six modes in which the force called Accent can be laid on the concrete" (p. 93). "Other audible means than force" can be employed to bring a syllable "under the special notice of the ear" (p. 318) ; the "accents of stress and quantity" readily give way to each other, but in English speech "the accented syllable is generally the longest" (p. 322). In an Appendix he states the difference between song and speech (p. 490 *seq*.), and incidentally makes some rather futile remarks about Greek accent (p. 488, *note*). Rush's phonetics are now naturally out of date, but were certainly remarkable at the time. Amid vague talk, or heedless dogmatism, he took nothing for granted, and tried to leave nothing undefined ; American prosodical study must have benefited by his investigations.

Goold Brown's *Grammar of English Grammars*, first published in 1836, was greatly enlarged in later editions ; the tenth (1875), which I quote, contains over eleven hundred closely printed pages. "Observations," in small type, following

---

[1] He thinks that Steele's "belief in certain fancied analogies between the system of music and the melody of speech . . . rendered his account of intonation meagre, indefinite, and erroneous" (p. xxvi). Sheridan neglected tone entirely, and Walker's view is less novel than he claims (pp. xxvii–viii). Accent on consonants is a ridiculous idea (pp. 323–4).

each paragraph, discuss other writers' opinions. An alphabetical list of Grammars (pp. xi–xx) is followed by a long Introduction (pp. 21–143), and this by the body of the work under the four usual heads of Orthography, Etymology, Syntax, Prosody. The last of these includes punctuation, utterance, figures, and versification, so that to Part IV, Chapter IV, our attention may be restricted.[1] The teaching of this Chapter, I imagine, has sustained little modification. It is highly dogmatic, and most questionable. Quantity is made to depend upon loudness. " A syllable fully accented cannot be reckoned short." " A syllable accented will always be found longer as well as louder than any unaccented one immediately before or after it." " The first syllables of *habit*, *borrow*, and *battle*, are twice as long as the last " (pp. 834, 835). This is the old fallacy of Eighteenth Century critics revived, and one is not surprised to find that he scans everything by syllabic feet (Section 3), and postulates absolute regularity in these (Section 4). Practically, the principles inculcated are those of Lindley Murray, so far as verse-structure goes, though with that writer Brown picked many bones of contention. However inadequate its theory, the fourth section of this Chapter is (in the said tenth edition) a perfect storehouse of examples, illustrating varieties of English metre. The " Exercises " with which it concludes, and the subsequent " Key " to these, belong to an elementary stage of study ; but in no book have I found so copious a collection of extracts. " Monosyllabic feet," it should be mentioned, are fully recognised (p. 841), some of the examples quoted having clearly accrued since the original edition was published.

Hallam's *Introduction to the Literature of Europe in the Fifteenth, Sixteenth, and Seventeenth Centuries* (1837–9) is too well known a book to need description. Questions of structure are scarcely mentioned. Yet, in Part I, Chap. I, the thirty-fourth paragraph summarizes the change from quantitative to accentual metre, and justly (as against writers like Goold Brown) remarks that " no want of emphasis or lowness of tone can render a syllable of many letters short ". In Part II, Chap. V, paragraphs *seventeen* and *seventy-five* note attempts

---

[1] Part IV, Chapter II, on " Utterance ", contains some brief remarks about accent and quantity ; but the sentences which I am about to quote will show that on this subject Brown is no safe guide.

to introduce Classic metres into Italy and England respectively, and leave us in no doubt as to his opinion concerning the wisdom of such attempts.[1] Beyond these incidental references I do not find anything which bears on the subject.

Among our older magazines the *Eclectic Review* held no undistinguished place. Its number for April, 1838 (Vol. III of a " new series ", Art. 3, pp. 395–414), contained a paper which I surmise to have been written by the late Prof. Blackie [*cf.* 1866]. Nominally a review of Foster's book on Accent [seventy-five years after publication !], it deals mainly with the question of Greek accent, but has some interesting allusions to English prosody. Three kinds of metre are recognised, dissyllabic, trisyllabic, and " mixed " ; the last, brought back by Coleridge and others, is " irregular style ", reserved for " wild passages " (p. 399). He notes " separation of accent from quantity " in the line

> Say, rush'd the bold eagle exultingly forth,

where *bold* must be lightly stressed (p. 400), as earlier he had pointed out that words like *balance, honors* [*sic*], *shadow* are accentual trochees but quantitative iambs. The same word may be now accented, now unaccented, in the same line, *e.g.*—

> Wild rushes the torrent, the boat rushes wild ;

especially in trisyllabic metre, which as compared with dissyllabic is " more removed from speaking and nearer to song ", and has more liberty of accommodating words to metre (p. 405). Accent rules our verse, yet quantity gives " expression, harmony, variety " (p. 401). Ordinary word-accents are often altered in verse, as when *wíld hórse* becomes either *wíld horse* or *wild hórse* (p. 404). A " trochee " usually comes after a pause, Milton's double trochees being therefore questionable, and it is even suggested that in one case the line would have read better as " *All* in their triple degrees " (p. 402). Southey's hexameters come in for censure toward the end of the article (pp. 412–13) as too careless of quantity, and for other reasons the metre is pronounced not likely to

---

[1] " A folly with which every nation has been inoculated in its turn " (par. 17) ; " an injudicious endeavour . . . met with no more success than it deserved." Our language, " abounding in harsh terminations, cannot long observe the law of position " (par. 75).

succeed. From papers like this one can often gather hints of more value than can be got from professed treatises on metre, and such studies become more plentiful as the Century advances. On the other hand, books and papers with attractive titles sometimes turn out useless for the purpose of our quest.

Hexametrical Experiments, published anonymously in 1838, and understood to be by James Blundell, M.D., an eminent physician, translate four of Virgil's Eclogues into lines professing to regard both accent and quantity. The Introduction boldly tries to make quantitative rules for English verse, recognising that these must differ from the familiar rules of Classic prosody, and must not run counter to accent. Syllables it divides (p. 11) into long, short, double-short, and " common " or doubtful, claiming the right to use an extra short or double-short syllable in any foot (as in the phrase " | glory of the | earth "), as well as to prefix redundant syllables to the initial eat. Both these licences, I need hardly say, accord thoroughly with the practice of our chief poets in ordinary verse. Accented syllables are to be accounted long, and are so marked, others being left unmarked, while redundant syllables have a dot under them, *e.g. radiant* (a further distinction of " redundant feet " by two dots seems uncalled for and unnecessary). The last line of the First Eclogue will sufficiently illustrate his ethod—

> Ạnd, lēngthening apāce, from the tōwery Ālps sēe shādows
>   descēnding.

Sticklers for quantity must rebel at such a dactyl as " shadows de-", and certainly accentuation there entirely replaces length. Yet, to my mind, Blundell's lines read more happily than most, because less at variance with real English prosody ; despite many eccentricities of diction, such as *godden* for *gods*, which are duly preannounced in the introductory remarks. At all events, the experiment interests as coming at a time when the current set in favour of loose and shapeless ' accentual ' structure.

A landmark of great importance is reached with Guest's *History of English Rhythms* (2 vols., 1838 ; revised edition, with Notes *etc.* by Prof. Skeat, in one volume, 1882 ; my references are to this latter edition). Till lately, this book, by a Cambridge scholar and philologist of high rank, was our chief—indeed, our only—masterful and exhaustive treatise on English metre. If we exclude the work of foreign scholars, which in the present survey is deliberately left out of account, it remained our standard textbook till finally superseded by Prof. Saintsbury's standard *History of English Prosody*, which on the narrative side at least re-traverses the same ground with ampler because later knowledge. Guest's views have profoundly influenced all students of his subject. It is unfortunate, therefore, that they were based on a theory which must be pronounced defective and misleading.

In one sense Guest was the last of an old school, in another the pioneer of a new. His rooted objection to trisyllabic feet in dissyllabic verse linked him with Eighteenth Century critics. He began, as Prof. Skeat points out, by totally denying the existence of such feet. He maintained that Shakespeare pronounced a word like *delicate* in two syllables, and asked Wordsworth and Coleridge whether they did the same, implying that otherwise they should not use it in place of a dissyllable (p. 176, *cf. note*). From this view he was gradually driven, and it is significant that his book was not republished during his lifetime,[1] though offers to do so were not wanting. With him one had thought this view died, but it has been resuscitated in our day. To me it seems clear that any word may be used which can be readily pronounced in the normal time of dissyllabic feet, even quadrisyllables like *ministering* or *spiritual*, and that there is not the slightest reason to suppose that such words were ever pronounced by readers of our verse *m'nist'ring* or *sp'ritval*. A contrary opinion verges on paradox.

In another direction, however, Guest was revolutionary. For the traditional scansion by feet he substituted division into versicles or " sections ". Enthusiastic in the study of " Old English " verse, he found there a loose syllabic structure punctuated by alliteration and strongly marked by a midway pause ; this structure he sought to find in all English lines. So far as this conception encouraged syllabic elasticity, it did good ; but as a theory it will not hold water. A great change admittedly came on our verse between (say) 1100 and 1400 A.D. What is called Old English verse is not what we now know as English verse, though related as sire to son. Modern long

[1] He lived till 1880.

lines tend, like all long lines, to have optional breaks ; but these are not essential, and often a poet's whole art is given to avoiding them.[1] Our verse is made up, not merely of sections, but of smaller units recurring with regularity, whether these units be primarily syllabic or temporal. The causes of this change historians must declare, but the fact is evident. Even if the influence of Anglo-Saxon verse (to use a name which at any rate emphasizes racial and linguistic change) survive in the tendency to weaken the medial accent, to write lines like

> The glass of fashion and the mould of form—

even so that is not the whole story. The five feet are there, though one be not signalized by accent ; are there, though some critics recognise only four, others claim to find six. Our verse is not merely rhythmical prose ; it differs from such by its metrical structure. The verse of *Piers Plowman* may represent an ancestor of the verse of *Paradise Lost* ; but it is absurd to suppose ancestor and descendant one and the same person.

Guest's exposition should therefore be studied, not taken for gospel. And it makes delightful reading. The four " Books " into which it is divided are arranged on a scale of descending importance from our point of view. Book I deals with general questions and the factors of rhythm. In Book II his doctrine of " sections " is formulated and expounded, while treating of " origins ". Book III discusses different metres, beginning with the shortest ; its seventh Chapter is concerned with heroic verse (" metres of five accents "), its tenth and last with " metrical experiments ". Book IV explains old forms of verse, rondels and virelays and the rest. In all there is interesting matter, and lavish quotations add to enjoyment. The first half of the work (the first volume of the old edition) contains most that is of interest to us. Even there, it will be found that fully half the space is occupied with discussion of verse that preceded English verse proper. For Guest was primarily a philologer and only secondarily a prosodist ; and his book is a " history of rhythms ", not a study of rhythm.

[1] *Cf.*, *e. g.*, the metre of Tennyson's poems " To Virgil " and " God and the universe ", or Mr. Swinburne's " March, an Ode ", and parts of " The Armada ", " The Garden of Cymodoce," *etc.*

Yet he begins with a definition. " Rhythm in its widest sense may be defined as the law of succession." Applied to motion, it gives us the dance ; to matter, sculpture and architecture ; to sound, music ; to articulate sound, prose and verse. In verse, the rhythm is so definite that its suc‑ cession can be anticipated ; in prose, so wide that this rarely happens. " Rhythm may be marked either by the time or the accent ; " Sanscrit, Greek, and Latin used the former, all other languages the latter. Its parts are " proportional ", not necessarily equal (pp. 1–2). Introductory remarks of this kind occupy Chap. I in the First Book, while Chap. II deals with letters, Chap. III with syllables. The last takes up " elision ", which to him is absolute contraction, as when Burns shortens *Edinburgh* to *Embro'*. Similarly, the *i* in *Niobe, lion, riot,* even *having,* and the *e* in *heaven* and *given,* are left out by poets, the first being made a dissyllable and the rest monosyllables (pp. 40–51). Chap. IV discusses accent, Chap. V quantity. Accent, in our " prevailing dialect ", he considers to be essentially loudness, though sharpness of tone usually accompanies it, and though the muscular action it involves tends to make us dwell on sounds so marked, whence the " vulgar notion " that accent always lengthens a syllable (pp. 74–75).[1] " Our earliest writers, almost to a man, confound accent with quantity " (p. 75, *cf.* 284). He, on the contrary, distinguishes these, tries to differentiate accent from emphasis (p. 79), and also (like Greek and Roman writers) distinguishes actual from metrical quantity, denying the latter to our verse while admitting the former. " We have most certainly both long and short vowels " (p. 103). Our treatment of consonants differs from that of the Ancients ; Mitford is right about the doubled consonant. The first syllable of *hilly* cannot be long. But rules depend on usage, and ours has laid down none (p. 107). Accent is therefore " the sole principle that regulates English verse " (p. 108), though a skilful use of quantity " embellishes " it (p. 111). Apropos of this, he quotes the attempt made " in one of our leading Reviews " [*cf. ante,* 1805] to prove quantity vital to English verse, and totally rejects its illustration by the line " O liquid streamlets, *etc.*" (pp. 109– 10). Of the two remaining Chapters in Book I, Chap. VI deals

[1] Note his remark (p. 22)—" I am far from sure that our English accent pervades the syllable."

with rhyme and alliteration, Chap. VII with pauses. The last he considers merely as caesural, and finds fault with latitudinarian views. "When we see how nearly the freedom of our elder poets approached to licence, we may appreciate . . . the obligations we are under to the school of Dryden and Pope " (p. 157).

Having thus laid his foundation, he proceeds in Book II to show how English verse uses rhythm. It does so by dividing lines into definite " sections ", indicated by accent. From this follows, one would think, that exact number of syllables is immaterial, and that three syllables may easily be ' equivalent ' to two. But Guest draws no such deduction. He lays down precise rules as to both number and relation of syllables. " Two accented syllables may come together, if they have a pause between them. . . . Adjacent accents must be separated by . . . not more than two syllables which are unaccented " (p. 159 ; *cf.* pp. 78, 86, 284). Apparent exceptions in Spenser and Shakespeare, Milton, Burns, and Moore are sought to be explained away. The whole of this exposition, like his system of scansion in general, I consider unsatisfactory,[1] so will not redact, merely noting salient points. His use of the bar-mark in scanning is peculiar but intelligible ; compare Prof. Skeat's remarks in Preface, pp. x–xi. He rejects Mitford's view of common and triple measure as unhistorical (p. 161, *cf.* 550), yet himself often uses both terms. Substitution of trochee for iamb is considered on p. 165. Elision is again taken up (p. 172 *seq.*), such contractions as *om'nous* (for *ominous*), *pill'r* (for *pillar*), *sp'rit, etc.* being insisted on, and a sneering reference made to " Thelwall's fashionable *appogiatura* [*sic*] syllable ".[2] Book II, Chaps. IV and V, treat of " verse of

---

[1] He ridicules (p. 75) the idea that Milton's words " both turned, both stood " carry equal accents. So far as certainty is attainable in such matters, I deem it certain that Milton intended them to do so.

[2] With this compare two later passages, where he evidently refers (without naming names) to the Steele school. " With them rhythm is rhythmus, and an elided syllable an apogiatura [*sic*] . . . Much which they advance, I do not understand, and much that I do understand I cannot approve of " (p. 299, end of Book II). " Some of these theories I have vainly tried to comprehend, and others I have found wholly inapplicable " (p. 532, in Book III, chap. VII). This shows how entirely unfamiliar, even to a critic like Guest, was the whole notion of temporal periods.

five accents ", according as the section containing two accents
precedes or follows that containing three ; while Book III,
Chap. VII, discusses,'" the metres of five accents "—an arrangement which involves much repetition. Both deal with heroic
verse, which is elsewhere said (pp. 160, 561) to contain 1296
possible variations or varieties. Milton is frequently praised,
and defended against Dr. Johnson's strictures. But, as the
book advances, he is more and more excepted against. For,
indeed, Milton's verse collides with Guest's doctrine, being
often devoid of regular sections and medial pauses, and is
condemned accordingly.[1] In Book II (p. 230) it is admitted
that " our heroic metre was from the first a mixed one, . . .
though . . . it has approached nearer and nearer to the common
measure ". But in Book III, Chap. VII, Milton is said to
have carried this mixture beyond all bounds in his " passion
for variety " (p. 531). And toward the end of the same Book
his " fatal example " is made a warning, his violation of
metrical orthodoxy asserted. " He split the sections, and over-
laid the pauses, and the law of his metre was broken, the *science*
of his versification gone. The giant put on the habiliments of
the dwarf—what could he do but rend them ? " (p. 560).
    A view of metre which ends by condemning the work of
one of our greatest and most ' musical ' poets cannot deserve
respect. Where it fails, I must maintain, is in ignoring *time*.
This he leaves entirely out of reckoning. Even when he says
(p. 109) that " the time is occasionally of great importance
to the beauty of a verse, but never an index of its rhythm ",
he refers merely to syllabic quantity. Similarly, when (p. 169)
he denies that any " temporal rhythms " are to be found in
our literature, he is thinking merely of quantitative feet, and
probably feels that pseudo-Classic attempts lie outside of our
real " literature ". But of time in the musician's sense, time
as the real basis of verse, he has no conception ; Mitford's
partial acceptance of it, we have seen, he denounces. For
want of this, he can see no difference between a line devoid of
his sections and a prose sentence ;

> Such verse we make when we are writing prose (p. 560).

That the book is full of information goes without saying.

---

[1] *E.g.* (p. 445) he reprobates the absence of caesural pause in those
otherwise " exquisite " poems, *L'Allegro* and *Il Penseroso*.

I would fain quote many passages, as on "tumbling verse" (Book III, Chap. VIII), "triple [*i. e.* trisyllabic] verse" (*ibid.*), "riding rhyme" (p. 526), *etc.* His strictures on pseudo-Classic verse (Book III, Chap. X) are much to the point [1]; an experiment by himself will be found on p. 553. (A page earlier he says, " I have seen few German hexameters which, to my ear, were satisfactory.") On all historical matters his verdict carries weight, except when biassed by his theory. But on the main question of prosody; the question of the absolute basic foundation of verse, his view seems to me altogether at fault ; and this has been a great misfortune for English metrical science.

It would be difficult to fix limits to the extent of this misfortune. For two generations Guest has been the chief ruler of our prosody. Students of verse, as distinct from mere general readers, have gone to him for authoritative doctrine. The great merits of his book, its philological and historical excellence, its bold theorizing, its catholicity of quotation, secured for it general acceptance, the more so because its seed fell on prepared ground. The tendency of the time was to exalt accent to exclusive supremacy. Those who make ' beats ' the sole reality in metre—those who talk of " stress-rhythms ", usually meaning thereby a verse which has stresses but no rhythm—shelter behind Guest's shield. His rigid views about syllables have been discarded, but his theories of accentual basis pass for absolute truth. We shall see, as we go on, how widespread has been their domination. Yet theories which leave out the one fundamental factor of English verse, and which can find in Milton's harmonies only a violation of prosodic law, should not have been received without challenge, nor have coloured our whole notions of prosody as they have done. To Guest every student of our poetry owes much ; his learning and labour must be gratefully acknowledged ; but his whole view of metrical structure rests on unwarranted assumptions, and presents neither a true nor a complete account of the phenomena of English verse.

---

[1] Of modern " hexameters " he says (*ibid.*, near beginning) that they move to triple rather than common time, but this is so because syllables lack length ; because, as he puts it, accent is in them taken as equivalent to quantity, whereas it is really equivalent only to *ictus* or sharp tone. [For his own experiment see Appendix A.]

With the Forties of last Century we seem brought nearer our own time. Latham's *English Language* [1] is still an accepted class-book, yet its first edition appeared in 1841. Succeeding editions greatly modified and enlarged it, without however altering its method of prosody. Adopting the crude popular dichotomy of syllables into accented and unaccented, Latham calls the former *a*, the latter *x*, then resolves verse into such feet as *a x, x a, x x a, etc.* And, certainly, such a line as

> The weight of all the hopes of half the world

may fairly enough be described as " 5 *x a* ", that is, a line containing five pairs of syllables thus related. But English verse does not long preserve such ideal regularity—very insipid it would be if it did. Already in a line like

> Now trebly thunder'd on the gale

we find the third foot escaping his category ; and the vital fact in English verse seems to be less its compliance with these categories than its habitual and persistent departure from them. Nor does Latham explain in virtue of what principle *a x* and *x a* alternate in the same line, much less how *a x a* is possible along with *a x x* or *x x a*. This " innocent " theory, with its unquestionably convenient if otherwise permissible nomenclature, seems to confound verbal accent with metrical stress ; a confusion which existed before Latham, and has had only too many exponents since.

In Latham's first edition the Section on Prosody (" Part V ") is extremely meagre. By 1855, when the fourth edition appeared, this Section had become " Part VI ", and had received many additions, including a Chapter on imitations of Classic metre, said to be reproduced from the *Transactions* of the Philological Society (1843) [but the reference is incorrect as regards date]. The analysis of " caesura " there contained, with his deductions as to its place in English verse, may be left for scholars to study. As to English metre generally, his conception is wholly limited to syllables, and postulates an artificial regularity among these. " No English measure [*i.e.* foot] can have either more or less than one accented

---

[1] This should be distinguished from his *Handbook to the English Language* (first published in 1851), a separate book, which also went through numerous editions. Prosodical teaching is the same in both.

syllable " (p. 701 [1]). " On every even syllable," in heroic verse, " there shall be an accent " ; and " the end of lines should coincide " with " the breaks in the sense " (pp. 706–7). He recognises no quantity in English except that of vowels (Prosody, Chap. II), and rejects the whole idea of division into feet. " The classical names are never used with impunity " (p. 669). In his Seventh Chapter there is much talk of " convertible metres " and " metrical combinations ", by which are apparently meant lines that violate his imaginary rules. Deservedly esteemed as the book is otherwise, its view of prosody seems to me wholly insufficient ; I cannot even see that it furnishes a criterion to distinguish verse from prose.

This closing decade of the Half-Century brought a considerable epidemic of ' hexameters '. Longfellow in America did much to popularize them, and many writers in our country worked at them. I do not propose to follow in detail either these attempts or the criticisms of them which appeared in magazines ; the chief ones are enumerated in my Appendices. Among writers, Shadwell and perhaps Lockhart [2] deserve note as trying to maintain some regard for quantity, when most writers rejoiced to

> Flounder at will over consonant, vowel, and liquid,

relying on accent to cover all deficiencies. The verses of Whewell, Herschel, and others who worked under German inspiration (conveniently sampled in the volume published by Murray in 1847) show all the faults of their Teutonic prototypes, and rarely give us a smooth or memorable line. Dr. Hawtrey's short specimen from the *Iliad*, often held up as a pattern, seems to me only a degree better than the others. In contrast with this " mob of gentlemen ", Clough stands forth as a true though not great poet and an independent investigator and experimenter ; but his experiments were too often forced, being out of accord with natural English prosody.[3]

---

[1] My references are to the fifth edition (1862).
[2] Clough may have taken a hint from such lines of Lockhart's as
> This was her answer from Priam, the old man
> godlike in presence.

Lockhart's basis is accentual. For Shadwell's, see Appendix A [1844].
[3] Much criticism has been passed on one line of Clough's—
> With a mathematical score hangs out at Inveraray.

The only remarkable feature in this line is that the normal strong

The charm of his *Bothie* is perennial ; his later quantitative verses will be referred to in next Chapter. Charles Kingsley (to overstep for a moment the Half-Century) in his *Andromeda* achieved perhaps as great a success as is possible to any one starting with Classic verse as his ideal ; sundry Letters, given in his *Life*, show real and remarkable thinking. But, on the whole, verse of the *Evangeline* type represents what most writers at this time aimed at, and what most critics either decried or exalted. Its facile, sugary, somewhat nerveless and monotonous lines were well adapted to become popular, having that singing cadence which Longfellow seldom lacks. And they certainly did more than any other verse to commend so-called hexameters to the million.

The magazine articles of this decade are often most interesting. Around verse of Longfellow's type the battle of prosody raged keenly. Whewell with his breezy dogmatism scouted the notion of relying on aught but accent ; others pointed back to Classic perfection, and scoffed at the modern bard with his

> . . . Mamma has forgotten her tea-spoons,

or

> Softly, Louisa, be careful, and mind you don't trip in the bushes !

The contention of Whewell's school was that English hexameters should " read themselves " ; his opponents urged that this did not differentiate verse from prose. Glimpses of prosodic theory emerge in these disputes, but no complete survey of facts. Meantime Lowell impartially satirized both sides, and Longfellow himself confessed, in the Notes to his " Children of the Lord's Supper ", that in verse like his " the motions of the English Muse are not unlike those of a prisoner dancing to the music of his chains ". Not from such fetter-dances can natural verse or sound criticism arise ; for these we must look elsewhere.

---

initial syllable is replaced by two weak ones. Substitute such a word as *His* for *With a*, and the line becomes ordinary ; the second half is frankly trochaic. A more natural prosody would have simply prefixed the word *With* to the first beat, as is so commonly done by our poets in ' trochaic ' and ' dactylic ' verse. But I doubt if a single instance of such prefixing can be found amid all the wild metrical libertinage of the *Bothie*, though occasionally such a syllable is appended to the preceding line.

Few general treatises on metre appeared during these years. In his " Introduction " to *Poems of Chaucer, modernized* (1841) [*cf.* especially pp. xxxvii–xci ; I shall substitute Arabic numerals] " Orion " Horne discourses lengthily on trisyllabic feet, speaking of syncope (p. 23), " appoggiatura " (pp. 45, 83) and " musical time " (p. 68), and obviously recognising temporal periods, yet without definitely saying so. One pregnant sentence may be quoted. " It would be far nearer the truth were we to call our scanning gear by such terms as systole and diastole,—metre being understood as muscle, and pulsation as rhythm,—varying with every emotion " (p. 84, *note*). That suggests much, but it is not followed up, and Horne's ideal of structure is loose ; he praises the " new metre " of Leigh Hunt's *Legend of Florence*, and desires a theory of prosody from its author, as from " the hand most competent to instruct us " (pp. 86, 89). I know of no response to this request, though in an Essay of seventy pages on " What is poetry ? " published in his *Imagination and Fancy* (1844) Hunt refers slightly to metre, remarks that " the whole real secret of versification is a musical secret " (p. 49), and credits Coleridge with " dividing by time instead of syllables " (p. 55). These sayings are not explained, but writers of this group—among whom may be included Elizabeth Barrett [1]—evidently held advanced views about the *technique* of verse.

O'Brien's *Ancient Rhythmical Art Recovered* (Dublin, 1843), though concerned with Classic verse, of which he sought to demonstrate the rhythmic as opposed to the metric structure, refers several times to English. Isochronism of bars is generally held essential (*cf.* Editor's Preface, pp. xiv, xix) ; a completed cadence must always contain two parts, just as a soldier halting first advances one foot, then brings the other up to it (text, pp. 13, 16). On p. 19 *seq.* the writer discusses our heroic verse, refuses to call its structure iambic, and claims that its beats are separated by equal intervals. These, however, are but *obiter dicta*, and his scansions are not very conclusive. In the recently started Philological Society's *Transactions* for May, 1847 (Vol. III, p. 95), is a paper by Prof. Malden on " Greek and English versification ", of little interest

---

[1] Both the theory and practice of this lady (afterwards Mrs. Browning) show a tendency to experiment in prosody, witness her defence of imperfect rhymes as forming a species of " assonance ".

save to Classical scholars ; time is made synonymous with syllabic quantity. A small book called *Essentials of Phonetics* (1848), by A. J. Ellis, on the other hand, would repay examination, but I reserve it for mention under date 1873-4, when its author's matured views on prosody received their fullest expression.

America contributed independently to discussion at this time, notably by one remarkable paper (see next paragraph), also by other writings of less consequence. *English Prosody*, by Asa Humphrey (1847), I have failed to see, but *A System of English Versification*, with rules and examples, by Erastus Everett (New York, 1848), does not seem to go much beyond Lindley Murray. The Preface complains of our having no system of quantity, yet on the first page of text comes the fatal assertion that " the quantity of each word depends on its accent ", and his very first example runs—

Whĕre slāves ŏnce mōre . . . ., *etc.*

Far more interesting is a short article in the *American Review* for May, 1848 (pp. 484-92), signed with the initials of the editor, James D. Whelpley, and entitled " The art of measuring verse ". Nominally a review of Everett, it really gives its author's own ideas about English verse-structure, which he asserts to be wholly based on quantity, that word, however, comprising both time and accent, " the two elements of musical metre " (pp. 488-9). Words he divides by their sounds, which in verse are continuous, so that in the above quotation the first syllable is unquestionably long. These sounds create musical impressions, apart altogether from their meaning ; and it is by no means right or necessary that feet should coincide with complete words, in English any more than in Latin. There is much that is suggestive in this short paper, though its ideas seem hardly worked out. It concludes with the remark " We propose to revert again to the subject ", but so far as I can ascertain this promise was never fulfilled.

But incomparably the most noteworthy contribution to prosodic study at this time was the " remarkable paper " referred to in last paragraph, by Edgar Allan Poe. Handy English editions of his " Poems and Essays ", unluckily, rarely or never include this paper on " The rationale of English verse ", even when they profess to contain his " Complete Poetical

Works and Essays on Poetry ", contenting themselves with including three other papers of less consequence, these being indeed only notes for popular lectures.   The " Rationale " must therefore be sought in one of the really complete editions of Poe's *Works*, such as Ingram's in four volumes (1875), or some later and still more exhaustive collection ; or it may be procured from America in the single-volume edition of Poe's *Best Poems and Essays* by Sherwin Cody (Chicago, 1903), which contains critical remarks by the editor on this as on other articles.   The date of its first publication I have ascertained to be 1848 [*cf.* Appendix B] ; with its examination we may close our record for the first half of the Nineteenth Century.

This rather discursively written paper, occupying some fifty pages (331–82) in Mr. Cody's edition, to which my references are made, attempts to dissect the actual structure of our verse.   The work of a brilliant analytic genius, famous in other fields as in poetry, it abounds in striking passages, but has equally striking defects.   To begin with, its author attends only to syllables, neglecting the pauses which form equally essential parts of a line.   Thus (p. 361 *seq.*), while rightly scanning as a continuous measure Byron's lines—

> Know ye the land where the cypress and myrtle
>   Are emblems of deeds that are done in their clime ?
> . . . .
> Where the virgins are soft as the roses they twine,
>   And all save the spirit of man is divine—

he objects to the foot " twine, And " as too short, whereas it is obviously filled out by silence to equal time with its neighbours.   This preoccupation with bare syllables vitiates his whole analysis, prompting him, for example (p. 361), to find inequality of time in this couplet—

> The water-lily sleeps in pride
> Down in the depths of the azure lake—

where I venture to say every untutored reader is conscious of perfect equality.   Still more serious is his failure to distinguish between quantity and accentuation.   Here his self-reliance and contempt for traditional teaching lead him far astray.   Like many others, he cannot conceive any verse-scheme save our own.   He evidently read Latin verse wholly by accent ; for proof, he thus misquotes (p. 376) a familiar line—

Parturiunt montes, et nascitur ridiculus mus.

We must not follow him through this argument, but when he assures us (p. 375) that Horace wrote " Sunt quos curr- " as a dactyl, and would have made " great eyes " if told otherwise, it is clear that the essayist fails to perceive the initial difference between English and Classic verse-rhythm.[1] So failing, while rightly contemning the wooden scansion of the schools, he substitutes for it one which ignores the whole structure of Classic speech. And this, in turn, reacts fatally on his conception of English verse.

It is with this conception that we are concerned. As will be seen, it borrows nothing from music or from Classic prosody, and deals wholly with syllabic value. It makes such value depend almost entirely on accent. He does, indeed, recognise (p. 341) that a syllable clogged by many consonants must take longer to pronounce than one composed of fewer ; to the other element of natural quantity, which makes *far* a perceptibly longer syllable than *fat*, he remains wilfully deaf.[2] But the main element of length, to him, is accentuation. " Accented syllables are of course always long " (p. 343), *naturally* if their structure so permit, *unnaturally* if it do not. Such a long syllable is accounted exactly equal to two short, being made so by any just reciter ; and verse depends for its effect wholly upon this contrast between long and short syllables (*ibid.*, and *passim*).

So far there is nothing novel in this view. He proclaims the nullity of all previous investigations into our verse (p. 332), yet himself repeats their fallacies, nor do we know how far his reading went—Steele and his school are never mentioned. It is in working out his view that originality appears. Passing by criticism of others, we find him (p. 339) make verse originate in enjoyment of *equality*, under which term he includes " similarity, proportion, identity, repetition, and adaptation

---

[1] " To melody and to harmony the Greeks hearkened with ears precisely similar to those which we employ for similar purposes at present " (p. 339). But this does not prove that their mode of utterance was identical with ours.

[2] He grasps, however, the fact that in ' length by position ' it is the syllable, not the vowel, which is long (p. 342).

or fitness ". This enjoyment it shares (p. 340) with the simpler
forms of music—" scientific music has no claim to intrinsic
excellence "—and verse " cannot be better designated than
as an inferior or less capable music ". [This solitary reference
to music is, unfortunately, not followed up.] The rudiment
of verse, it is suggested (p. 341), may have been the spondee,
and the next step the collation of " two syllables differently
accented (that is to say, short and long) ". Thus came iambs
and trochees, from which the transition was easy to anapaests
and dactyls ; and these five feet—with one previously mentioned (p. 337), the " caesura " or foot of a single syllable—
exhaust the real feet, others being combinations of them.
These feet had next to be divided into lines, which (p. 344), in
defiance of history, Poe assumes to have been done by *rhyme*.
He protests, indeed (*ibid.* ; *cf.* pp. 349–50), that dates are
immaterial, and that even if rhyme be modern his " positions
remain untouched " ; but he does not explain how. Lines
thus secured, progress was easy to couplets, quatrains, stanzas ;
and the rest of this imaginative history of verse is occupied
mainly with explanations of what are called " bastard feet ",
where three or even four syllables replace two, and *vice versa*.
Such replacement, I need hardly say, is possible only in virtue
of a higher law, that of temporal equality ; but, conscious
though Poe the poet must surely have been of this as a guiding
principle, it is never explicitly stated by Poe the prosodian.

Summarized thus baldly, Poe's view appears crude and
narrow ; but it is expounded with spirit and ingenuity, as
well as flashes of true insight. Absurdities, indeed, are not
wanting. His notion that dactyl and anapaest may meet in
a line is as monstrous as his illustration of it (p. 337) by the
example—

Sīng tŏ mĕ | Ĭsābēlle,

which I do not believe would be so rendered by any reader.
His contention (p. 360) that length in a syllable is perceived
absolutely, shortness only by contrast with length, would
have been ridiculed had he found it in another writer. That
the " sum of the syllabic times " in *whether* is equal to that
in *thou choose* (p. 354) cannot be admitted ; while the sugges-
tion (*ibid.*) of his being the first to use two initial inversions
shows extraordinary ignorance of Milton, to go no farther.
On the other hand, his recognition of single-syllable feet is

throughout excellent, though his term "caesura" is misleading, and though he ascribes varying length to the syllable
(p. 337), instead of to the foot containing it. His vindication
of trisyllabic feet (p. 350 *seq.*), where the syllable is not elided
but adjusted to time by rapid pronunciation, shows clear
perception of temporal law in this case, as does a later statement (p. 358) that feet must be "*made* to occupy the same
time".[1] Wherever Poe trusts his ear he goes right, as in his
scansion (*ibid.*) of the line—

> Many are the | thoughts that | come to | me.

But his theory makes scansion depend on fictitious syllabic
values (*e. g.* "the sixth of long", p. 359) instead of on overruling rhythm. He quotes (p. 358) the immortal

> Pease porridge hot—pease porridge cold,

actually without making a silent interval follow any word.
How little Poe's notion of scanning really differs from the
traditional may be seen by comparing the samples of each on
p. 369. His merely refines on the orthodox view by denoting
sub-varieties of accentuation. In all other respects the two
methods are absolutely identical.

Some extravagances of criticism need but bare mention.
"The nicety of Byron's ear" (p. 364) contrasts with the
"roughness" of *Christabel* (p. 356), and Coleridge's system
of scanning by accents is roundly pronounced "nonsensical"
(*ibid.*). Horne's *Orion* is "the most happily versified long
poem in existence" (p. 353). The French "have no verse
worth the name" (p. 378). Such utterances, like the reference
to "German Greek prosodies" (p. 338), must be taken with
a large grain of salt ; nor do I see why Leigh Hunt is censured
(p. 341) for speaking of "the *principle* of variety in uniformity".
More to the point are his strictures on the "Longfellownian
hexameter" (p. 381), but his own attempt in that metre
(p. 382) is singularly weak. Well may he say that "some of
the dactyls are not so good as I could wish", for *hope to make*
and *men of sense* are as little like dactyls (in any sense of the

---

[1] *Cf.* the phrase (used once only, p. 366) "equality between two or
more pulsations ". That Poe had a true sense of metrical rhythm I do
not doubt, yet his theorizing all but ignores it, as witness his definition
(p. 339) that rhythm concerns merely the "character of feet, that is,
the arrangement of syllables ".

term) as can well be imagined. A critic like Poe should have realized that the measure of his lines is derived, not from their syllables, but from a preconcerted rhythm with which these syllables are somewhat violently forced to keep time.

My citations have done scant justice to the *verve* and brilliance of Poe's Essay. But these cannot hide the fundamental weakness of his position. It is weak, *first*, through omitting all notice of silent spaces—as though one should read a page of music by its ' notes ' alone, neglecting ' rests '. It is weak, *secondly*, in its analysis of syllabic quantity. In English verse, accentuation usually reinforces metrical *ictus* ; Poe assumes that this implies temporal protraction of the accented syllable. In other words, he mistakes conspicuousness for length. The first weakness could be easily remedied ; not so the second. It constantly affects his judgement, and sets him to the impossible task of " expressing to the eye the exact relative value of every syllable employed in verse " (p. 367)—impossible, because such value fluctuates with each reader, and with the same reader at different times. Indeed, Poe's whole view of verse is made artificial by it. He begins by saying (p. 331) that nine-tenths of prosody " appertain to the mathematics ", and follows this up by a demand that long and short syllables shall be mathematically proportioned (p. 342), and by the assertion that in perfect verse there would never be any disagreement between " the rhythmical " and " the reading flow " (p. 360). Is this, perhaps, why he seems to prefer the melody of " Mr. Cranch " and " Miss Mary A. S. Aldrich " to that of Coleridge ? In Poe's own verse, is there not sometimes too obvious an effort to provide luscious syllables, too apparent joiner-work in the carpentry of his lines ? So does theory influence practice ; so important are just views of prosody. The greatest singers may not need them, but they certainly help others. How wedded Poe is to his theory, how fearless in following it, is shown by his complaint (p. 355) that " many even of our best poets do not scruple to begin an iambic rhythm with a trochee ", a dactylic with an anapaest, and so forth. The common practice of our best poets is more likely to be right than the criticism of even a Poe ; sounder views of metrical structure easily justify such apparent licences as are found (for example) in the opening lines of Mr. Swinburne's " Hesperia ".

I have thought it needless to give a *précis* of this paper, or recount its many amusing divagations and incidental felicities. These no student will fail to enjoy, as he will profit by what is said about " quick trochees ", " bastard dactyls ", and the like. By his main issue Poe must be judged. He aimed at nothing less than a complete analysis, making " the scansion and the reading flow go hand in hand " (p. 371). No English writer for at least twenty years had made such an attempt ; those who earlier had done so he does not seem to know. All credit, therefore, must be given him for originality, and his paper marks a stage in our inquiry. It shows men ready to inquire, aware that there is a problem to solve, casting aside conventional explanations. If the problem is not solved by Poe, at least he shows how to attack it. And no contemporary of Poe's known to me made so bold and thoroughgoing an attempt to lay bare the heart of English verse.

So ends the Half-Century, its " new verse " having as yet found no trustworthy analyst. The most familiar phenomena of English metre are still ignored by the prosodist, even by one so able and iconoclastic as Poe. It remains to see what may reward our search in the fourth and last Half-Century included in this survey.

CHAPTER V

THE NEW PROSODY

1850–1900

DURING the second half of the Nineteenth Century a more adequate conception of metre gradually emerged. It appeared neither suddenly nor from the first full-grown. Following, as hitherto, an order mainly chronological, we shall still find ancient ineptitudes furbished up anew. But, with and among them, more rational and real methods of scansion slowly assert themselves ; critics are less apt to assume beforehand how English verse ought to be written, more ready to discover for themselves how it actually has been written by our chief poets.

A Treatise on Versification, by Rev. R. W. Evans (1852), illustrates these assertions. Verse is to him still merely an affair of syllables, the " regulated recurrence of a syllable " constitutes metre (p. 3), and " the stress on a single vowel necessarily prolongs its time " (p. 20). " Our literature has long ago reached its maturity " (p. 169), and its rules are fixed. He sees how we habitually neglect quantity (Chap. II) and exalt stress (Chap. III, *cf.* Chap. XIV), the latter alone guiding our prosody. There are some singular remarks on " the modern hexameter " (Chaps. XV, XVI), accentual succession being taken as the sole regulative principle. It is needless to recapitulate familiar views, or quote just criticism on particular points. Shortcomings of theory are best seen in the concluding Chapter, " Of lyric poetry ". Ignoring temporal structure, he finds no room for such verse in English. " Our truly lyric poetry must ever be almost a blank " (p. 169). " An evil genius " presided over its birth (p. 165). The choruses of *Samson Agonistes* are not verse at all (p. 166). To such conclusions can false theory force a man brought up on Shakespeare and Milton, and in whose ears Tennyson's youthful melodies had for a decade been sounding. The only possible reply to them is—there are none so deaf as those who will not hear.

Poetics, by E. S. Dallas (1852), on the other hand, leaves old lines entirely, but not always advantageously. Book III, Part II, Chap. II, on *Verse*, contains some striking remarks, such as that metre, in its simplest form, is "*time heard*" (p. 164)—a definition to be pondered by those who ignore temporal relations in their analysis of verse—and much excellent discussion as to why poets use metre at all ; but such speculation leads him away from the practical question, What exactly is this same metre ? When he does touch on actual structure, his views are apt to be wild, as when he contends (p. 185) that blank verse should be written in lines of irregular length, and should never contain a pause ; that dramatic verse alone has *feet*, while epic has *bars*, and lyric has *stanzas* (p. 176) ; that Shakespeare's dramatic verse, even when most melodious, is merely "metrical prose " (p. 179). We get from Dallas little help regarding actual verse,[1] but many suggestive hints about principles of poetry—which, after all, form his subject. With his book should be read Prof. Masson's enlightening criticism in *Essays Biographical and Critical* (1856) ; the last three or four pages deal with metre. And the student should go on to the next paper in this volume, on " prose and verse ", which well vindicates the naturalness and appropriateness of metre in moments of emotion. The Essay on " Milton's versification and his place in the history of English verse ", in Prof. Masson's edition of that poet, though published much later, may be mentioned here. It is mainly practical and tabulative, but contains some remarks on Milton's " metrical management " (p. 212) and on the difference between accent and ictus (p. 219), and may profitably be read even after the yet more elaborate treatise of Mr. Robert Bridges on the same theme.[2]

[1] He combats Guest's view that rhythm is equally real in whispers, and with regard to accent lengthening syllables says " an acute sound is naturally louder than a grave one ; a grave one is longer lived " (p. 164). With less justification he blames "the absurd practice of letting one line run over into the next " (p. 175), and asserts that Milton's " bars " are not of equal length (p. 179). These " bars ", however, are not what most people mean by that term, but represent " the dance or motion of verse between pause and pause " (p. 175).

[2] I see no need to particularize other books on Milton, such as Thomas

Criticism of the variances in Shakespeare's versification at different periods of his life practically began in this decade, the works of William Sidney Walker and Charles Bathurst leading the way.[1] Though such criticism, since become so continuous and confident, bears directly on prosody, it rarely discusses structure, or at least principles as distinct from details of structure. " Weak endings " and " double endings " as characteristic, " end-stopt " lines giving place to " run-on lines ", are matters interesting historically, but of small consequence from a theoretical point of view—hardly of more than the question whether a particular word is to be pronounced as monosyllable or dissyllable. Before we determine the value of such things for prosody, we must know what prosody is. I mention these inquiries here, that the reader may bear them in mind, but he need not expect to find in such investigation what Poe called the " rationale " of our conception of metre.

In 1855 Walt Whitman published the first instalment of *Leaves of Grass*. Our survey cannot omit writings which raise in such acute form the question whether metre is essential to poetry. Whitman himself is credited with saying that the *Leaves* contain both prose and verse ; his warmest admirer, therefore, need not contend that everything in them is poetical. And surely, it is beyond question that poetic feeling and rhythmic utterance, as a rule, go hand in hand throughout them. Neglecting some purely metric passages— such as " O Captain ! my Captain ! " and " Joy, shipmate,

Keightley's *Account of the Life, Opinions, and Writings of John Milton* (1855), though this is specially mentioned by Prof. Mayor in his *Chapters of English Metre* (1886), and contains a few remarks on prosody (*e. g.* pp. 440–50). It is impossible to notice every critical edition of every English poet ; nor is it necessary to do so, unless they throw fresh light on familiar questions. All students of Milton's metre should possess Canon Beeching's one-volume edition of the *Poems* (Clarendon Press, 1900), which reproduces typography supervised by the poet himself, often throwing light on matters of scansion.

[1] It is needless to quote titles of books which do not concern us. Craik's *English of Shakespeare* (1857), similarly, deals only with questions of articulation, *etc.*, as regards form. What has just been said of Milton applies far more to Shakespeare, works on whom form a separate literature. Unless incidentally, I do not intend referring to these, or to the discussions of his metre which they frequently contain. As a rule, these discussions are concerned with practice alone.

joy ! ''—the rhythmic pulse certainly beats strong in lines
like—

> When lilacs last in the dooryard bloom'd,
> And the great star early droop'd in the western sky in the night,
> I mourn'd, and yet shall mourn with ever-returning Spring ;

or

> Come, lovely and soothing Death,
> Undulate round the world, serenely arriving, arriving.

To ignore the temporal structure of such lines is as absurd
as to talk of shaking off the trammels of metre, form being
a help not a hindrance to true singers.   Whether irregular
rhythms such as those favoured by Whitman will ultimately
oust the more regular—whether, to go farther, recondite
harmonies of prose, often nobly illustrated by Whitman, will
finally supersede the more definite rhythms of verse—these
are questions which no critic can answer.   So long, however,
as high emotion craves appropriate utterance, so long as in
moments of excitement it is more natural to dance than to
walk, rhythmic expression of some sort will assuredly
continue.   And as yet there is no sign of the old forms being
effete.   At the very moment when Whitman was trying to
cast them from him, the author of *Atalanta in Calydon* was
preluding a music soon to fill them with new life.   Did verse
answer to no instinct of our nature, it might well be abandoned
as a thing outworn.   Prophecy is the most futile of literary
amusements, but we may at least be sure that fundamental
instincts of our nature will demand satisfaction.   The precise
form which that satisfaction may or may not take cannot be
foreseen ; we can feel sure only that, in some shape or other,
it will exist to gratify an ineradicable longing.

Imitations of Classic verse were less common in this
decade.   Kingsley's *Andromeda* has been already mentioned ;
two or three magazine articles, specified in Appendix B, are
readable but not important.[1]   Scholars will like to consider
two tracts by Lord Redesdale,[2] a nephew of the Mitford

---

[1] Clough's '' Letters of Parepidemus '', published during his short
American sojourn, can be read in his *Poems and Prose Remains*.   The
second Letter discusses quantitative verse, of which he afterwards
attempted some examples (*cf. infra*, 1861 ; Appendix A, 1853).

[2] Bibliographical details, omitted here and elsewhere for brevity's
sake, will be found in Appendix B.

whose Essay on the harmony of language we discussed at length ; they make measure depend on quantity, melody on accent, and refuse to word-accent the function of marking rhythm. Two poems by " Owen Meredith " may profitably be compared with each other in respect of structure. The paper by Barham, and still more the introduction and notes to his much earlier edition of Hephaestion, approach the subject of English verse from the Classic side, and are hardly suited to the general reader ; but they handle both ancient and modern verse in a way quite other than the usual, insisting that both must be rhythmized to " isokhrony " [so spelt], even in such a couplet as—

> Come unto these yellow sands,
> And there join hands.

He apparently assumes that rules of Classic quantity apply unaltered to English speech, but the breadth of his general conceptions differentiates him entirely from the tribe of traditional prosodists.

By far the most remarkable contribution of this decade, however, was Coventry Patmore's *North British Review* Essay, later reprinted (with slight alteration) [1] as an appendix to his collected poems (Vol. II, pp. 215–67),[2] with a Note in which, misdating the original publication as 1856 instead of 1857, he characteristically expresses pleasure at finding that, between then and 1886, " its main principles have been quietly adopted by most writers on the subject in periodicals and elsewhere." If this be true, the adoption is usually without acknowledgement, for the Essay is strangely seldom quoted by subsequent writers. I suspect, however, that the " adop-

---

[1] Originally the paper reviewed Dallas's *Poetics* ; some introductory matter referring to this has been omitted. Two whole paragraphs at the end have been left out, making the Essay now close rather abruptly, also some sentences from the present last paragraph, while the parenthesis in it referring to Shakespeare is new. The entire paragraph on p. 244 beginning " The iambic ode " is new. On p. 246 a paragraph has been omitted which, among other things, remarked that " much modern writing, professing to be verse, is, in fact, no such thing ". All these changes, I think, were made when the Essay was first reprinted as a preface to his poem *Amelia* (1878), where the introductory note is different. The Appendix in its present form dates from 1886, and has remained without further alteration since then.

[2] I quote the edition of 1900 (2 vols.). Later editions of the *Poems* usually omit the Essay, but *cf.* a subsequent foot-note.

tion " was often merely coincidence of thought ; Patmore voiced ideas that were in the air, and was sometimes less original than he fancied. However this be, his Essay is one of highest importance, and requires careful study. Its author was a poet, who some think has not yet reached his full measure of fame. He was also a learned critic, had read carefully the chief authorities, and does justice to Steele (p. 219) and O'Brien (p. 239). And he was a consecutive thinker, expressing his views clearly, if sometimes too dogmatically. Add that he observed and thought for himself, and we have a combination of qualities not easy to parallel. Accordingly, his Essay is a thing by itself. I regard it as inaugurating what I have called the " new prosody ". Note, for example, his assertion that " the metrical expression of emotion is an instinct, not an artifice " (p. 223), and can be understood only after profound study, first of sounds in themselves, then of " the philosophical grounds and primary laws of such expression " (p. 220). Here we are poles removed from the old idea of verse as a mere ingenious exercise, to be constructed as one puts together the pieces of a Chinese puzzle. A view of metre so serious as Patmore's postulates a thoughtful and thorough examination of all its constitutive elements. Such an examination is attempted in this Essay, and will be found carried out with increasing precision by writers who hold like views.

After brief tribute to precursors, Patmore develops his own view. This is, that " the co-ordination of life and law . . . determines the different degrees and kinds of metre " (p. 221). Primarily, metre is " a simple series of isochronous intervals, marked by accents " (p. 224). As such, it exists in all speech, when adequately rendered ; time is as essential as tone, the two being inseparable. This brings him (p. 229 *seq.*) to consider accent, which he defines as that which marks, " *by whatever means,* certain isochronous intervals." [1] " Metre implies something measured " ; " the thing measured is the time occupied in the delivery of a series of words ; " and that which measures it, being itself unmeasured, is an " ' ictus ' or ' beat ', actual or mental," which divides speech into " equal

[1] " Those qualities which, singly, or in various combination, have hitherto been declared to *be* accent, are indeed only *the conditions of accent* " (p. 231).

or proportionate spaces " (p. 230). But this is not all. Bare rhythm, mere succession of intervals, is not pleasing till distinguished by difference of tone. This, therefore, is an essential factor in metre. " The music of verse " is a truer phrase than " the rhythm of verse ". " Rhythmical melody," not rhythm solely and by itself, is what makes verse agreeable (pp. 231–2).

Illuminative as this statement is, I must pause to express partial dissent. Patmore seems to me to attach undue importance to mere delivery, and not sufficiently to discriminate between word-accent and metrical beat or ictus. His " accent " is simply ictus. He himself identifies it with musical accent (p. 231), and this confusion leads him to say later (p. 238) that " the marking of the measure by the recurrent ictus may be occasionally remitted, the position of the ictus altered, or its place supplied by a pause "— remarks which are perfectly true of spoken word-accent, but surely not of that " mental beat " which, as he truly says (p. 231), most often " has no material and external existence at all ". This confusion between mental and vocal punctuation leads him to think that metre is a matter wholly of elocution. Quoting two sample passages (p. 226) he opines that the sentence " Her ways are ways of pleasantness, and all her paths are peace " receives " entire metrical effect " from our ordinary reading ; and that in a remarkable extract from " St. Jude " all accented syllables must, in proper reading, be separated by equal measures of time. Neither proposition seems to me certain or necessary. His identification of this " metrical accent or ictus " with change of tone also seems questionable, and still more his assertion that it always coincides with " long quantity " (p. 227). With much in these pages I entirely concur. The statements that in Greek verse " ictus, accent, quantity, and verbal caesura advanced . . . in parallel order " (*ibid.*) ; that our words have no fixed tones, these varying with sense (p. 229) ; that the time-beater of rhythm is mental ; these and other points are admirably put. But the claim that prose and verse, when properly delivered, have the same temporal foundation (pp. 224–5) seems to me untrue to fact, and the scansion on p. 236 of

For one restraint, Lords of the world beside,

assumes that word-accent and metrical beat must coincide. On the other hand, Patmore sees clearly that the rhythm of our so-called dactyls and trochees is totally different from that produced by the Greek or Latin feet bearing these names, and rightly explains that difference as one of " time " ; while he properly insists that the " very distinct character ", in verse as in music, of iambic as against trochaic rhythm (and similarly in triple metre) requires us to find distinctive terms for each (pp. 236–7).

In considering how far the actual articulation of a syllable represents its metrical value (p. 237) Patmore makes the mistake of ignoring short ' rests ', and is driven (p. 238) to hold that the equality of metrical intervals is " no more than general and approximate ". Here, again, he seems to judge too much by spoken effect. And, though he professes to broach novel doctrines on the subject of pause, his considera-tion extends only to caesural and final pauses. He distin-guishes, indeed, between metrical and grammatical pauses (p. 240), but by the former he means immensely protracted stops, often embracing a whole foot. That such do exist, as in ' poulters' measure ' (p. 241), I fully believe. But his claim that every line containing an odd number of feet is followed by such a pause seems to me quite untenable. In advancing it (p. 242) he formulates with much complacency the thesis that English verse has for its unit a " dipode " or double foot, and must contain two, three, or four of these. It follows that every line of three, five, or seven feet comprises also a silent foot at the end, completing the " dipode ". This I cannot for a moment accept. There is, doubtless, what Sheridan called a " suspensive pause " felt or expressed after every line of verse ; but the expression may be, and in dramatic verse often is, infinitesimal in duration, and there is no reason whatever to hold that we feel it equivalent to an entire foot. Patmore's pompously announced " law " seems to me nonsense. It misreads a principle truly stated by O'Brien [*ante*, 1843], that a verse-unit must contain in itself two actions. But a single foot may be such a unit. It is absurd either to hold that our heroic line consists of two and a half units, or that it is supplemented always by a " silent foot ". The only rational view regards each foot as complete in itself, containing action and reaction, systole and diastole ;

proof of this, if proof be wanted, is supplied by the fact that English poets have written pieces in which every line consists of one foot only, while the assertion that each of these is followed by an equal measure of silence must by the nature of things remain a mere assertion, incapable of demonstration.

With the rejection of this thesis some of Patmore's argument falls to the ground. His example of " six-syllable iambic " on p. 243 (taken from a poem of his own, Vol. II, p. 183) is hardly fair; since the seventh line is prolonged ; if he means that pure six-syllable lines are necessarily mournful, facts are against him.[1] He was too fond of such rash generalizations. In the original essay, " jaunty choriambics " are pronounced totally unsuited for a dirge ; this remark disappeared from the reprint, Mr. Swinburne having meantime utilised them for this very purpose. In a paragraph added to the reprint, on the other hand, it is actually maintained that a " catalectic pause " may cover the time of twelve syllables (p. 244) ; a contention which is surely theorizing run mad. The statement that " unmixed ' trochaics ' or ' dactylics ' have seldom been written by poets of fine musical feeling " (p. 245) I regard as equally disputable ; practical difficulties have probably more to do with the matter than fineness of ear. And the immediately sequent scansion of lines by " sections "—as he there proposes to call his *dipodes*, possibly borrowing the term from Guest—attaches far too much importance to a poet's natural desire of avoiding monotonous agreement between word-accent and verse-beat. It would be a very ' wooden ' verse where these always coincided, but a hardly less wooden which was bound by Patmore's sections. All such attempts to minimise liberty fail, and deserve to fail ; our business is to discover the principle which justifies liberty, not to fetter it with bonds of our own devising.

The second and shorter half of the Essay (from p. 246 onward) deals with rhyme and alliteration, for the most part excellently.   A. C. Swinburne may well have profited by

[1] In Cowper, for instance, this metre is not restricted to mournful subjects. Patmore's friend Tennyson ridiculed the idea of such limitation, and sent him some six-syllable lines of a very opposite character. See Tennyson's *Life*, single-volume edition, 1905, p. 395. The prosodist might have remembered a victory-song by Mrs. Hemans, beginning
Io, they come, they come !
Garlands for every shrine !

Patmore's vindication of the true place of alliteration in our verse, while the account given of Anglo-Saxon structure, and the criticism of Rask's view of " anacrusis " (p. 252), seem unimpeachable. Dealing with Anglo-Saxon rhythm (p. 254), Patmore sides with Mitford against Guest, but speaks in a singular way of " ' common ' or ' iambic ' time " (p. 255), whereas true iambic time is necessarily triple. I take this merely to mean, however, that (like other critics before noted) he recognised " even measure " in our standard type of verse. For his remarks on four lines from Scott (*ibid.*), and his italicised statement that " an entire line may be in common or triple cadence, according to the cadence of the context " (p. 256), go to the root of the matter. On rhyme he is less entirely trustworthy, attempting to show that it constitutes as well as signalizes metre, and that octosyllabic couplets are non-metrical without rhyme, because they have no " catalectic pause " (p. 258, *cf.* 265) ; while he also commits himself to the view that " the verbal accent . . . gives length wherever it chances to fall " (p. 259). So, too, he contends that the true " Alexandrine " is a line of four sections, " having a middle and a final pause each equal to a foot " (p. 262). The scansion of triplets in common-time verse as " real anapaests " (p. 263) may confuse a reader who quite sees that the tri-syllabic feet in triple-time verse are not either accentually or quantitatively anapaests (*ibid.*), because it seems to make syllables actually constitute rhythm ; but the explanation that " two syllables are read into about the time of one " (p. 264) puts matters on their true basis. While these paragraphs, therefore, like their predecessors, must be read with caution, they yet contain much that is true, and much that is suggestive. The reference to Shakespeare in the Essay's final sentence, it should be noted, considerably qualifies previous confident assertions about " major and minor accent ". The paper ends, as I have already said, somewhat abruptly, without anything like peroration or final summary of views.

However one may differ from particular conclusions of Patmore's, it is impossible not to admire the spirit and plan of his Essay. We have in it a real study of metre from an independent and intelligent critic. Its chief defect, in my judgement, is non-recognition of minute intervals of pause.

The extraordinary assertion (p. 237) that " in music played *staccato* on the pianoforte, the actual duration of sound in a crotchet or quaver note may be the same ", shows this clearly. Not the duration of sound, but the interval between the beginning of one sound and the beginning of the next, is identical ; and that interval is partly occupied by silence. So it is and must be in verse. Hearers are slow to admit the reality of such pauses. They will often deny the existence of any silent interval, even when phonetic considerations prove that such interval *must* occur. Recognition of these silent spaces is essential to just prosody, and often revolutionizes our ideas of a line's actual structure. It is therefore a mistake to concentrate attention on syllables so exclusively as Patmore did ; and his peculiar view of accent tended farther to mislead him in this respect. But, after all deductions, his Essay remains a most important contribution to English prosody. Its importance was not at once recognised. So far as my reading shows, it was but seldom referred to, and only of late years has its value been properly appreciated. Those who now appreciate it are, perhaps, too much inclined to take all it says for gospel ; I have therefore emphasized my dissent where its teaching seems to me erroneous. But I heartily agree in giving it a very high place among English studies of prosody, ranking it among the few papers of abiding value which the subject has elicited. By far the ablest contribution during the decade to which with it we bid adieu, it well deserves the permanent position given it in the best editions of Patmore's poems.[1]

The Sixties of last Century saw culminate the rage for pseudo-Classical forms of verse, and criticism of prosody was then mainly concerned with these. Here, again, I must decline to consider in detail the mass of ' hexameter ' verse written by Cochrane, Dart, E. W. Simcox, and others, or the discussion of these in contemporary magazines. But it is necessary to point out that some of our chief poets at this time made experiments in this direction, while some very eminent critics entered into controversy on the subject. That controversy began with an assertion by a great Classical scholar,

---

[1] *Cf.* a previous foot-note. I am glad to learn, however, that the Essay is still obtainable in the " collective edition " of Patmore's complete *Works*.

Munro of Cambridge, that modern speech had lost all sense of syllabic quantity. This theorem was assailed by James Spedding, in an article reprinted (with additions) in his collected *Reviews and Discussions*. Postscripts on either side continued the argument, which was taken up by Matthew Arnold in his *Lectures on Translating Homer* (see especially the " Last words "), and by Prof. F. W. Newman in his vigorous reply to Arnold's criticisms. Of these, Spedding's paper has most relevancy for us. Munro's total denial of quantity in English syllables save as produced by accentuation (see his " Appendix ") can only be called extraordinary. Arnold does little to elucidate this part of his subject, and his own model lines are singularly weak ; he actually makes " To a " stand for the first foot of one line. Prof. Newman's reply deals mainly with ancient verse.[1] Spedding's modestly written plea for an interrelation of quantitative and accentual structure, however, interests both on its own account—however little one may accept his conclusions—and because of its influence on others, shown so recently as in the work of W. J. Stone (*supra*, p. 5) and his pupils. It was this paper, and similar efforts made by Clough,[2] which led Tennyson to write his well-known lines about lame hexameters :

Hexameters no worse than daring Germany gave us.[3]

Tennyson's own " Experiments in Quantity " took a different line. Instead of contrasting accent and quantity, he sought to unite them on one syllable—a task in which he

---

[1] One should also mention " Lectures on Poetry " [1869 ?], now reprinted in this author's *Miscellanies*, Vol. I. The second Lecture is on " forms of poetry ", and contains some remarks on metre (pp. 82–4), distinguishing *duplicate* from *triplicate* forms. He contends that too uniform succession of accents is displeasing in verse, and that " equable times ... are to us an offence " [the latter statement is surely fallacious]. On the other hand he recognises that our English so-called dactylic and anapaestic measures move to " minuet or dancing time ", therefore do not reproduce the Greek rhythms bearing these names.

[2] Two of these being dated " Freshwater, 1861 ". See Clough's *Poems*, " Essays in Classical metres." Both Clough and Spedding were dear friends of Tennyson's.

[3] I owe students of my previous writings an apology, on the following score. People who read in the ordinary editions of Tennyson's poems his lines beginning " These lame hexameters " must infallibly suppose that

was later followed by Prof. Robinson Ellis in his complete translation of Catullus (1871). Certainly Tennyson's "Alcaics" have a majestic, his " Hendecasyllabics " a dainty swing, but one may doubt how far that is due to supposed structure, in which also flaws are perceptible ; [1] poems like " The Daisy " and " To F. D. Maurice " appear more happily to unite Classic inspiration with native metre. " Boadicea ", as the writer himself said,[2] is hardly intelligible without a key of some sort, teaching us for instance to say *célebratéd* not *célebrátéd*.[3] With these should be compared Mr. Meredith's " Phaethon ", and some other poems in annotations to which that author plays the prosodist so far as to indicate accented syllables but not pauses. Mr. Swinburne's " Sapphics " and " Hendecasylla-bics ", with his later " Choriambics ", show a fine natural ear for quantity, not trammelled by supposititious rules. Matthew Arnold made no further attempt in this line that I know of, and Browning essayed such verse only in his much later " Ixion " and possibly " Pheidippides ". No subsequent work of great importance has followed these patterns, though accentual ' hexameters ' and ' elegiacs ' are always with us ; though Mr. Watson reproduced Swinburnian cadences with fine effect in his " Hymn to the sea ", and Mr. Meredith sub-joined some fragments to his *A Reading of Life*.[4] Still more

he is referring to his own lines—and lame enough they are ! I so took it ; and spent much time in wondering what particular German " quanti-tative hexameters " he had in view, turning over the pages of Platen and others in the vain search to find such. But, happening to look up the original place of publication (*Cornhill Magazine* for December 1863, pp. 707–8), I was surprised to find appended a note from which it is clear that the " lame hexameters " referred to were those of Herschel and others then so common ; and I find that the Eversley edition confirms this. The matter is now clear. Led away for the moment by the example of his friends Clough and Spedding, he made this attempt at " quantitative hexameters ", and ridiculed the " accentual hexa-meters " then in fashion, with their prototypes in Goethe, Schiller, and Co. *Cf.* the Note in Appendix B (1864).

  [1] It should be noted that Tennyson professed to follow the structure of *Greek* alcaic verse, not the more restricted Horatian model (see *Life*, as before, p. 425). [2] *Life*, pp. 367, 386.

  [3] Students of Latin verse should compare *Catullus : the Attis* by the late Grant Allen, on Galliambic Metre. (See Appendix A, 1892.)

  [4] *Edith*, by Thos. Ashe (1873), and *Dorothy*, by Arthur J. Munby (1880), are two of the longest poems written in these metres during the last generation. For others, see my Bibliography in Appendix B, which is far from exhaustive, or even representative.

recent work by Mr. Robert Bridges, on the other hand, harks back to the tradition of Clough and Spedding, and shows what life may lurk in embers that had seemed altogether dead.

That tradition had been worked for most that it was worth by a writer now seemingly forgotten. Charles Bagot Cayley's "Remarks and Experiments" in the Philological Society's *Transactions* for 1861–2,[1] his Preface to a translation of the *Prometheus Bound* (1867), with his later *Iliad Homometrically Translated* (1877), seem to me pretty well to determine the issue. It is amazing that they should not have been cited by Messrs. Stone and Bridges. Cayley's rules (given in the first two publications) differ somewhat from theirs ; following Classic tradition, he shortens long vowels before a following vowel, and neglects *h* as a consonant. But in all essentials his verse is one with theirs. Accent is combatively opposed to quantity, and he is sound on the " doubled consonant " question. The experiment suggested by Spedding, and revived by Stone, was systematically tried by Cayley for nearly twenty years. There seems little likelihood of fresh fruit from a plant that has been already so assiduously cultivated.

I have declined to enumerate magazine reviews of hexameters during this decade—the veteran Whewell was still writing in its earlier years—nor need I quote the opinions of men like Dean Alford, Philip Worsley, Lord Derby, the first Lord Lytton, and others, in prefaces prefixed to their works. A tract by Lord Lindsay " On the theory of the English hexameter, and its applicability to the translation of Homer ", suggested by Arnold's Lectures, is interesting on personal rather than critical grounds, since it quotes unpublished opinions of several critics ; its own theory and practice are alike defective. As an " ideally good " hexameter it quotes one which I can neither understand nor scan—

> Oh, by Abs ! Oh, by Adnan ! I am the lover of Illa !

[1] Though this paper is for scholars only, it contains some very acute remarks on English speech and verse. In the latter he recognises " positive pauses (like the rests in a bar of music) " (p. 67), but these are only caesural or final. To say " that accent in the modern languages is the same thing as quantity in the ancient . . . seems to me something like saying that noise on the pianoforte is equivalent to time on the kithara " (p. 83). His main positions are too technical to be discussed here. Another paper by him on " The pedigree of English Heroic Verse " (Philolog. Soc. *Trans.* 1867, pp. 43–54) is good but now out of date.

The last Dissertation in Vol. I of Prof. Blackie's *Homer* (1866) treats the hexameter question pretty fully, and kindred papers (reprinted from these or earlier years) will be found in his *Horae Hellenicae* (1874) ; but this vivacious writer was sometimes run away with by theories. Calverley's paper " On Metrical Translation ", published in 1868 and now reprinted in his *Works*, is to my mind the ablest discussion of this question from the purely Classical side, and disposed of any pretence that our accentual hexameters reproduced the structure of Greek or Latin verse. That question is but a side-issue for us, and Calverley's paper contains little that will profit the student of real English verse ; but it is well to know where the arguments affecting this particular limited question can be found most convincingly stated.

I have tried to gather here all that remained to be said about this side-issue. Far be it from me to preach finality of criticism. Poets have every right to try experiments, and success is the only criterion. But this particular question does seem to me thrashed out. Neither quantitative verse, nor accentual lines as our German school understood them, can be expected to take root in English. The first, because it transgresses our fixed speech-habit ; the second, because their constitution comes short of true prosody. The latter fault can be easily remedied, as readers from the first discovered, and the lines can be treated as native English lines, their supposed structure being a myth ; the former fault is irremediable. Such is my belief, and I hope not again to return to this question, during what remains of this volume. Readers should now, at any rate, be able to distinguish between two such different things as accentual and quantitative hexameters, though eminent critics of our own day have sometimes failed to make this distinction.

A few treatises of wider outlook were published during this decade. *Lectures on the English Language*, by George P. Marsh, had gone through more than one edition in America before it came to us in 1862. Mostly occupied with grammar and vocabulary, it touches on verse in Chapters 23, 24, 25, dealing mainly with rhythm and alliteration. There are, however, a few remarks on structure, and some apposite quotations. Had not my attention been specially directed to this book by a correspondent, I should hardly have thought it worth mention here.[1]

In 1862 also appeared a book by Thomas Arnold, brother to Matthew, entitled *A Manual of English Literature, Historical and Critical. With an Appendix on English Metres.* A seventh edition of this came out so lately as 1897. The Appendix is short and slight, in the latest " revised " edition as in the earliest. Guest is referred to as the sole authority, his " natural system of prosody " being adopted as regards *sections*, while yet the " classical system " is " retained provisionally ". " Metre is the arrangement into verse of definite measures of sound, definitely accented " (opening words). Six kinds of feet are described, to the ordinary four being added spondee and amphibrach—which last he proposes to call *amphiambus* —but the examples given of the last are not convincing. Some remarks about hexameter verse, ancient and modern, have accrued since the first edition. As the whole Appendix occupies only some dozen pages, these references will easily be found. Nothing of consequence is to be learned from it.

Not forgetting the impetus given to metrical study at this time by Mr. Swinburne's early poems, as well as by those of some elder contemporaries, we pass on to 1869.[2] *The Rules of Rhyme*, by the younger Hood, published in this year [2nd edition, 1877], covers wider ground than its title implies, but hardly does more than illustrate traditional rules of verse by old and new examples. " Feet and caesura, metre and rhythm, rhyme and figures " are dealt with in the nine Chapters which form the first portion of the book, some lines of Pope's being quoted and commented on by way of general introduction. " Guides and handbooks " are enumerated to the extent of four [!], beginning with Bysshe. Twelve kinds of feet are specified, but it is admitted that neither these,

---

[1] From about this time onward, most grammars and literary manuals divide verse by accents alone ; this may henceforth be considered orthodox prosody. It is needless to multiply examples. Fairly typical is a *Handbook of the English Tongue,* by Joseph Angus (1862), the " Prosody " Section of which (pp. 343–65) is based on Latham. Classical terms are pronounced misleading, but are still used. I shall mention only books which depart more or less from this tradition, as does the one specified in my next paragraph.

[2] For *A Manual of English Prosody* by R. F. Brewer, published in 1869, see under 1893 (foot-note).

nor the Classic rules of caesura, quite apply in English verse ; in Chap. II the writer inadequately conceives the difference between Latin and English metre, and his illustrations are faulty.[1] These nine Chapters (pp. 1–63) are followed by a Rhyming Dictionary, and an Appendix (pp. 153–206) based on *The Young Poet's Guide* [this I have failed to identify ; it is apparently not by T. Hood, senior], dealing mainly with the expressional value of sounds. While this book cannot be considered trustworthy, even for beginners, it is modestly and pleasantly written, and shows acquaintance with contemporary poems—a feature not too common in books of prosody. But its view of verse is narrow and defective.

Much more ambitious and noteworthy is a book published in the same year—*English Versification : a Complete Practical Guide to the Whole Subject*, by E. Wadham (Longmans, 1869). Here indeed is apparently a " new prosody ", with nomenclature of its own ; instead of iamb, trochee, anapaest, and dactyl we have *march, trip, quick,* and *revert, forward* and *backward* accent instead of rising and falling, while names like *midabout, outabout, odd-over, partlet,* occur freely—a weak accent is styled *the hover.* But when we dip below the surface this apparent novelty vanishes, and we find old ideas under new names. The writer has no conception of *time* except as *tempo* or pace (*e.g.* p. 65) ; ' rests ' are deliberately rejected (p. 127). The melody of verse, according to him, is wholly due to vowel-sound and rhyming (p. 113) ; metre is a matter entirely of syllables. His " pauses " are the usual caesural divisions merely (pp. 8–9). There are no real units in our verse except lines ; " divisions into lines appears to be the prime principle of metre " (p. 142). This too narrow view misleads his analysis throughout, often blinding him to temporal equality (*e.g.* in Shelley's " Away, away ! " on p. 103), and making him believe that " the measure is broken " whenever two accented syllables come together (p. 121). Like Poe, he postulates rigid syllabic proportion, and censures any breach of it (p. 60). Yet there is much excellent stuff in this volume. The writer has thought as well as made

---

[1] Thus " Hapless lasses " is given as an equivalent for " Miserarum est " (p. 12). My references are to the earlier edition. To the later, which seems otherwise substantially the same, was added a copy of Bysshe's " rules for making English verse ".

names for himself. His first Chapter might lead us to expect success. " Rhythm, run, or singsong " is there made " the most characteristic quality of verse ", it being noted that " all exaltation is rhythmic " (p. 2). The difference between Greek and English prosody is well explained (p. 4, *cf.* p. 56 and Chap. XXIII), and the tendency of English verse to accent the last syllable of a foot insisted on in opposition to the " backward run " of music (pp. 7–8, *cf.* Chap. VI). The historical origin of English verse is shortly sketched in Chapter II, and blank verse (epic and dramatic) carefully examined in Chapter III, while these and all succeeding Chapters are enriched by a profusion of apposite quotations—in some cases, if I mistake not, from the writer's own pen. Forms of versification are gone into at great length, the " hexameter " being included under " false metre and dubious " (Chap. VII). The " assertive bounce " of rhyme is a good phrase (p. 115), and though the true structure of a line like

> The sun *sets*, the shadow flies,

is not recognised, its cadence is defended (p. 125). But, throughout my reading, I find myself continually registering dissent, which culminates on reaching the author's treatment of what he calls " cesural ", " free ", and " main " verse (Chaps. XIX, XX, XXII). Here the distinction between prose and verse seems to me entirely lost, through neglect of temporal equality. The " stress-rhythm " theories of a later day are most curiously anticipated and illustrated in these Chapters. Holding the opinions I do, it is impossible for me to consider the author's view of verse adequate or even sensible, and to these final Chapters I confidently appeal for proof of its insufficiency.

Equally peculiar in terminology, though of a different kind, was a tract entitled *The Laws of Verse, or Principles of Versification Exemplified in Metrical Translations*, by J. J. Sylvester, of Cambridge, then resident in Baltimore, U.S.A., afterwards Savilian Professor of Geometry in Oxford. Prof. Sylvester's Preface and Notes to the first part of this tract (which is followed by a paper on a vastly different subject) deal, not with verse as a whole, but with one feature of it called Phonetic Syzygy, which merely means easy junction of syllables. " Rhythmic," or the technical side of poetry, it is explained in the Preface (pp. 9–19), divides into " Metric, Chromatic, and Synectic ", the first (concerned with accent, quantity, and suspensions) treating the discontinuous aspect of the Art, and the last the continuous ; while this last is subdivided into Anastomosis, Syzygy, and Symptosis, the first of which deals with passing from one word to another, and the third with rhyme, assonance, *etc.* His translations (from Horace, Goethe, Schiller, and others) seek to illustrate these, especially Syzygy, and the Notes explain his method. They are therefore only of comparative interest to us. As regards " Metric ", he endorses Poe's view, " rendered more complete by my introduction into it of the theory of the silent syllable or rest " (p. 10)—almost as if this theory was his own discovery. In effect, his teaching goes little beyond Poe's. When he says (pp. 64–5) that " the substratum of measure is time ", he refers mainly if not solely to syllabic quantity as determined by accent ; and so when he says that " feet in modern metre are of equal length " (p. 66, *cf. note*). Yet I think he would have been ready to take a wider view, unless the mathematical preconceptions which he shared with Poe prevented ; for he distinctly refers to musical time in some of his notes, and speaks of " acopation " and " tempo rubato " (p. 67). It is to be regretted that he did not develop his view of *metric* as well as *synectic*. The tract is dedicated to Matthew Arnold.[1]

It was during the eighth decade of last Century that a really new prosody, after some false starts, fairly began its course. The researches of Helmholtz—made accessible to English readers by A. J. Ellis's translation in 1875—had laid bare the nature and working of those " tones " which create verse among other forms of vocal music ; Alexander Melville Bell, by his *Visible Speech* alphabet, had for the first time given

---

[1] I have seen another *brochure* by the same author (privately printed, N.D., British Museum Catalogue says 1880), *Spring's Début : A Town Idyll, in Two Centuries of Continuous Rhyme* [*i. e.* two hundred (and odd) lines all rhyming more or less perfectly to the termination *-een*]. A Note at the end of this speaks of " two distinct schemes or strands of time and accent, in general coincident, but occasionally showing themselves independent " (p. 27). Unless *time* be here restricted to syllabic quantity, this anticipates a doctrine which I have myself tried to preach. He does, however, usually so restrict it (*cf.* p. 69, *note*, in the earlier book), and I suspect does so in this case also.

a notation capable of expressing any articulate sound. Building on such foundations, English as well as Continental scholars attacked *de novo* questions of metrical rhythm. Ellis himself, by this time President of the Philological Society, led the way ; in the *Transactions* of that Society will be found papers by him, as also by Professors Skeat, Mayor, Sweet, and others.[1] Deferring for a moment further reference to Ellis, and reserving the work of these others for examination when their separate books appear, I pause to notice briefly in chronological order one or two volumes which shared the influence of this school.

The Philology of the English Tongue, by Prof. Earle of Oxford (first edition, 1871 ; I quote the third, 1880), contains a Chapter on " Prosody, or the musical element in speech ". This title suggests the new outlook. Verse seeks to construct musical cadences, to emphasize the modulative element in speech—an " accordant, concentive, illustrative element ", which exercises " a formative, almost a creative power " (p. 587). This it does by using *time* and *tune*, quantity and accent. Of these the latter is identified with tone, as also is emphasis, the two differing only in the objects to which they are applied ; " an accented word is emphasized by the intensification of its chief accent " (pp. 595-6). Quantity is the note-mark of primitive speech (p. 589), prominent in Greek and Latin (pp. 603-4), but " a period comes . . . when the sonorousness of words gives place to the sentiment of modulation, whereby a musical unity is given to the sentence like the unity of thought " (p. 621). So in Anglo-Saxon verse " word-sound " was a chief feature, while its prose developed sentential rhythm ; when verse adopted this, the " restraint of metre " became necessary, for " metre is to rhythm what logic is to rhetoric " (p. 623). Rhythm is a national thing, metre can be transplanted ; French influence " gave us a new music ". Metre is " ultimately resoluble into a speciality of modulation or rhythm " (p. 624). Earle's discussion is entirely general, as is his summing up (pp. 634-40), and there is much that is highly questionable in these statements. But the point of view is widened, the *conception* of verse is broad ; analysis of parts is not substituted for analysis of the

[1] The Minutes of " Proceedings " are also often of interest, giving discussion by experts, *e. g. Transactions* for 1873-4, pp. 644-5.

whole. In this we may trace the effect of new ideas and discoveries.[1]

More of practical guidance is given by two City of London School men, Dr. Abbott and Prof. Seeley, in their *English Lessons for English People* (1871). Intended primarily for boys, this book contains much that will benefit older readers, Part III being on metre. General rules applicable to English verse are formulated, but are stated much too absolutely. Thus we have the assertion that two consecutive syllables in a word cannot be metrically accented, and that when a polysyllable has two accents, these must rest on alternate syllables (*sólitáry*, not *sólitarý*, paragraph 100) ; while with all the emphasis of italics they state that " *three unaccented syllables cannot be found together in any English metre*, if they are all fully pronounced " (par. 107). None of these rules is invariable. To their further rule that " a pause is necessary before a trochee " they themselves quote " remarkable exceptions " (par. 138) ; but they admit none to the dogma " in most strict dissyllabic metre [*disyllabic* is their spelling], a trisyllabic foot at the end of the verse would injure the effect " (par. 144). Their general tendency is toward a too mechanical view of syllabic structure ; their proposition that " any extra syllables may be admitted that are felt not to interfere with the regular recurrence of the accent " (par. 202) might have been extended to other than dramatic verse. Particular scansions are often dubious ; Tennyson repudiated their analysis of his line (par. 204)—

> Down the long turret stair, palpitating.[2]

In the main, however, sound principles are stated, and there is a refreshing absence of pedantry ; ' anacrusis ' is styled *the catch*. A too rigid view of syllabic structure, often leading to wrong analysis and division, is the chief fault I find in this book.[3]

---

[1] In a good phrase he says, " The Gothic ear enjoys a precipitous consonantism " (p. 612).

[2] See the discussion referred to in recent foot-note. The line is altered in later editions.

[3] The " Prosody " Section of Dr. Abbott's *Shakespearian Grammar* (1869 ; third edition, 1870, revised and much enlarged) goes on the same lines, and seems marred in places by the same fault. Mono-

Here also may be mentioned a study possessing very different characteristics. The *Fortnightly Review* for December, 1874, contained a paper by J. A. Symonds on " The Blank Verse of Milton ", reprinted more than once, and finally in a separate volume called *Blank Verse* (my references are to the latest and best edition, 1895). This volume contains three Essays, the first a " Prefatory Note ", the second historical, while the third represents the original paper. All three may be considered together, for the writer's position did not alter. It amounted, practically, to a negation of prosody. Recognising that " the notes and bars of the musical composer " give a " truer basis of measurement " than syllabic feet (p. 88), he fails to follow this out into detail, preferring to bid us trust our ears, " attend strictly to the sense and the pauses " (p. 90), and observe the " balance and proportion " of syllables, the " right proportions and masses of sound " (p. 87). Excellent advice in itself, but—as he gives it—tantamount to denying that a sonata can be resolved into its constituent notes. " Analysis by feet " is odious to Symonds ; he deals with the " rhetoric of verse rather than prosody " (p. 1). His Prefatory Note shows small technical knowledge. Originally, he had laid it down that " quantity forms no part of our prosody " (p. 84) ; now, he admits that " both Quantity and Accent have a common element of Time " (p. 10), but thinks that " in many words quantity is hardly distinguishable from accent " (p. 7), selecting curiously as his example the Latin word *Tityre*. This attempt at technicality, made with " diffidence ", carries no weight. On the other hand, the historical account of our blank verse, from Marlowe to Tennyson (" the most original and greatest living writer of blank verse ", p. 67), is full of interest, and there is much excellent criticism both there and in the third Essay. The volume deserves reading as an exposition of the general effects of verse, of the mutual relations between sense and sound ; but it deliberately abandons any attempt to analyse these. (For his own statement see p. 85 *seq.*) The

syllables are frequently made dissyllables, even in so strong a case as—
    Twelve *year* since, Miranda, twelve year since,
which should surely be accounted a nine-syllable line. As a collection of instances, and monument of careful study, this book (especially in the later edition) deserves all praise.

original Essay is well summarized and criticised by Prof. Mayor in his *Chapters of English Metre* [*infra*, 1886], Chap. IV, being there ranked as a production of the " aesthetic or intuitivist " school. From that school students of practical prosody get little or no help.

Returning now to A. J. Ellis, I would first single out his paper on " The physical constituents of accent and emphasis " (Philological Society's *Transactions* for 1873–4, pp. 113–64) as representing his mature views of these. Length, pitch, and force, with other ingredients, are here (pp. 115–26) clearly defined by our foremost phonetic scholar, and he considers these three mutually independent (p. 148, *note*). " Specific varieties, due to pitch and force, are the main sources of accent ; emphasis requires, in addition, the use of expressional varieties of *form* [*i.e.* quality or *timbre* of the voice], and also the adoption of differences of length " (p. 118). Specific differences of pronunciation may be either " fixed " or " free " (p. 125). English Accent can be shortly defined as " fixed force with free pitch " (p. 128) ; in French speech, pitch, force, and length seem all " practically free ", so that it has " no accent, only emphasis " (p. 138) ; ancient Greek speech is considered in p. 142 *seq.* Classical students will learn from these last what speech meant when (as a general rule) each syllable had its relative length and pitch determined beforehand, independent of expression, while varieties of force were left to the speaker's choice. Only thus can they fully realize the nature of ancient ' quantity ', only thus measure the gulf which yawns between Greek verse and ours, even when the rhythmic as well as metric relations of the former are duly taken into account.

But it is with Ellis's view of English verse that we are directly concerned, and for this we must go to a later paper. Brief reference is indeed made to our metrical structure in the one just referred to (pp. 130–2), but it is treated more fully and systematically in pp. 435–49 of the *Transactions* for 1875–6 (*cf.* also pp. 456–69), the main substance of which is reproduced in Prof. Mayor's *Chapters on English Metre*, Chap. V. It must be owned that his treatment is heroic. In his *Elements of Phonetics* (1848) he had distinguished three degrees of both accent and quantity—the latter there termed " long, brief, and stopt "—but now he would have us distinguish no less than nine degrees of each, with correspondingly numerous gradations of " pitch, weight[1], and silence ", making altogether forty-five differing possibilities to be taken into account.[2] Rather than be tortured with such minute analysis, Prof. Mayor would " rush into the arms of the intuitivists ". But of course this analytic detail is not put forward as necessary to enjoyment of verse. For all practical purposes, Ellis himself says, three gradations instead of nine will serve, thus reducing the variations to a more manageable number. And, after all, the question is one of fact. Can it be denied that Ellis's complicated tabulation corresponds to possible varieties of syllabic sound ? It is well that all critics, especially those who regard syllables as constituting the entirety of verse, should be made to realise how exceedingly complex the relations of those syllables can be. Something more simple and definite than these relations must inspire the quick appreciation of verse shown by children and savages. How does Ellis handle this simpler element ?

In his earlier paper (*loc. cit.*) Ellis had made our verse-rhythm depend " mainly on periodical succession of clear force-accent or emphasis. . . . Length [of syllables] has no part in the fixed laws of English verse-rhythm, but has much influence on the oral effect." He now says that " English rhythm is primarily governed by alternations and groups of strong and weak syllables ", but " materially influenced by alternations and groups of long and short, high and low, heavy and light syllables, and great and small pauses " ; the tabulation of these in the case of simple alternations has just been dealt with. In a previous paragraph he had stated that " our English verse, though based on alternations of force, is materially governed by length and pause, . . . and is more than all perhaps governed by *weight* ". On this last element

---

[1] This word he borrows from Steele (to whom he does justice), but employs it in a sense of his own ; see my next paragraph.

[2] Prof. Mayor speaks of " forty-five varieties of *stress* ", making this word cover all Ellis's five qualities. It *force* alone be dealt with, it is obvious that the possible combinations of ascending force in a dissyllabic foot would be thirty-six, with the same number of descending ; while if the other four qualities may be combined with these in any order, the total of possible combinations would be counted by millions ! I do not, however, imagine that Ellis conceived all five qualities to be necessarily present in every such pair of syllables.

he insists much, defining it with precision in the remainder of his sentence. To me it seems that the " very complex phenomenon " so defined is really a combination, partly of metrical *ictus*, partly of elocutional expression which, as Prof. Mayor says, forms no necessary part of verse-rhythm. Adornment is insufficiently distinguished from essentials, delivery from structure. And this brings us to what I think most open to criticism in Ellis's view, *viz.* its indefinite treatment of rhythm. That he was conscious of temporal relations is clear ; his recognition of " rests ", his use of the word " periodicity ", sufficiently prove that. But they find no prominent place in his analysis. Rhythm is to him wholly a matter of syllables, created and conditioned by their relations, whether or no they adjoin each other or are separated by intervals of silence. Apart from them it would cease to exist. This point of view is natural to the metrist, still more to the philologer whose whole life has been spent in studying syllables ; but I cannot think it a true one. Analysis of individual bricks does not give us the secret of the arch which is made of these. Even if we take into account mortar as well as bricks [that is, in this case, silences as well as sounds], and reckon the strains and thrusts to which they are subjected, we are still far from having realized the meaning of an arch. To form an adequate idea of verse, we must survey it as a completed whole as well as in its component parts.

In all that affects individual syllables, however, Ellis is a master. I leave readers to study his exposition in detail ; the sentences cited will be easily found in Prof. Mayor's book. In the discussion already twice referred to, Ellis gave it as his opinion that the unit of heroic measure was " indiscriminately either dissyllabic or trissyllabic " [his spelling] ; [1] and his views throughout are similarly liberal. Indeed, they became increasingly liberal as he went on. In an Appendix subjoined to this later paper he owns himself convinced, on further consideration, that " my rules do not form, as I thought, the sole conditions of rhythmical verse ". He clung to the idea

---

[1] He subsequently explained, in a passage not cited by Prof. Mayor, this statement as meaning that *any one* foot could be one or other, not that all five feet could be trisyllabic at once (*Transactions*, 1875–6, p. 435). Neither critic was prepared to admit the possibility of the latter alternative.

that the last foot of a line should be typical, but admits that even this rule has exceptions. In his scansion he adhered to the orthodox *foot* (which he preferred to call a *measure*), instead of reckoning altogether by accents ; but he thought the Classical names both " misleading " and " utterly insufficient for English purposes ". He " found it of great practical advantage to be able to speak of a *strong* syllable, quite independent of the origin of its strength " ; with most writers that practical advantage would be apt to accompany evasion of true analysis.

It may be said, therefore, that Ellis did invaluable work as regards details—work which should have finally exploded some antique fallacies—though he left much still to be done toward perfecting a general conception of verse. How far this latter work has since been done my succeeding pages will seek to show. Meantime, all that he wrote about verse deserves study. *Essentials of Phonetics* has been already mentioned. In his great book on *Early English Pronunciation* (1869 *seq.*), which threw a flood of light on much that had been dark before, occur some passages which are superseded by the later and fuller expositions we have passed under review. His *Basis of Music* (1862) is perhaps sufficiently popularized in two undated books, *Speech in Song* and *Pronunciation for Singers*, both containing much that is *ad rem* for us ; his Preface to the second reviews his own work of thirty years. The article on " Speech-sounds " in the *Encyclopaedia Britannica* (1887) is by him. His tracts entitled *Hints on the Quantitative Pronunciation of Latin* (1874) and *The English, Dionysian, and Hellenic Pronunciations of Greek* (1876) still remain unequalled to my knowledge for general handling, though some minor points may need revision. If his early devotion to mathematics left traces on both his matter and his style, they are not unwelcome in regions where clear thinking is somewhat a stranger. As a prosodian we consider him, and as such his place is a high one. He did much, and suggested more. For the most part, subsequent English prosody has progressed along lines marked out by him. Where it has been fruitful, it draws fertility from his ideas, from his way of regarding the subject ; where these are neglected, it remains sterile and unprofitable.

Singularly different is the line taken in *A Treatise on*

Versification, by Gilbert Conway (1878), the single-sentence Preface to which announces its author's desire to show " what are the laws which rule, *or ought to rule*, the mechanism of English verse " [I italicise four words of dangerous import]. The 113 pages of this book are not divided into chapters, nor furnished with index or table of contents ; but they contain elaborate foot-notes referring to the opinions of very many writers. Conway's own view makes our verse wholly the creation of force-accent. He goes so far as to declare that English speech is uttered in " strict monotone " (p. 5), and that no word has ever more than one accent (p. 7) ; also that " there can be no rhythm where there is no forcible sound " (p. 16, *note*), though most of us have seen a bar of music containing only ' rests '. Accordingly, the idea that our heroic line contains " five feet necessarily " seems to him as absurd as Steele and Chapman's ideas with regard to Latin hexameter (*ibid., note*). The type and model of English verse is Italian, from which he derives rules which he thinks ought to be obeyed, and for transgressing which he is quite ready to blame our chief poets. A large part of the book (pp. 60–88) discusses hiatus and elision, the latter being distinguished from contraction. " Elision " is merely *blending* unaccented vowels by rapid articulation, as we all do constantly in speaking (p. 61, *note*) ; but actual contraction is claimed in the case of " hypermetrical syllables " (p. 88 *seq.*). Thus, in Say's often-quoted couplet, he allows *many a* to stand as a case of blending, but *amorous* must be written " am'rous ".[1] Milton comes in here for criticism (p. 96 *seq.*), as earlier he had been accused of inconsistency.[2] " English hexameter " is briefly referred to on pp. 107–8, and onomatopoeia on pp. 109 *seq.* While the learning shown in Conway's foot-notes commands respect, his main contention seems to me altogether faulty, and singularly at variance both with the work last reviewed and with other work almost immediately to be considered.

The year 1880 is memorable in our prosodic history. Not

---

[1] His rule is, " elide the elidable syllables, and cut out the mute " (p. 92, *note*). As if the mid-syllable in *amorous, delicate, beautiful, manifest*, etc., etc. were in any sense " mute " !

[2] " Consistency of practice . . . it is vain to seek in the versification of Milton " (p. 67).

because Ruskin then published his *Elements of English Prosody*. This tract, indeed, is the work of a man of genius, brought for the first time in his life face to face with metrical questions, and attacking them with characteristic self-reliance. How little his attempt satisfied himself, how little also he had studied such matters as the effect of accent, his Preface tells. The acute intellect of Ruskin fastened at once on essentials. He saw that metre and music were akin ; that the former, too, contains " measured rests, filling up the time required, as in bars of music " (p. 2) ; that " the primal essence of a poet is in his being a singer " (p. 32), actually and not metaphorically. He recognised that usually [he says "always"] it must " depend on the reader's choice to fill up the time with his voice, or to give an interval of silence " (p. 3). But when he comes to apply these excellent principles he is soon in difficulties, which his wayward genius disposes of anyhow. He starts by assuming that the most beautiful verse violates its own law, and this notion remains with him throughout. Employing somewhat peculiar terminology—*feet* he calls " metres ", a *trochee* he prefers to name " choreus ",[1] keeping the former term [which he writes " troche ", though a *spondee* is with him always " spondeus "] for what most writers call *pyrrhic* or *dibrach*—and representing " metres " by musical symbols, as others had done before him, he reduces all quoted verse to his Procrustes-measures, letting the accent fall where it will. Readers should never accept his statements without scrutiny. They need not believe that the first example on p. 7 is rightly divided ; or that " bonnie lassie " and " Aberfeldie " are reversed in accentuation (pp. 8–9) ; or that a word like *crustacean* could not begin a " really melodious " heroic line (p. 10) ; or that there is entire difference of cadence between

> The Assyrian came down like the wolf on the fold

and

> Should the soldiers of Saul look away from the foe (p. 18) ;

or that the structure of Scott's " Coronach " ought to be called " a trimetre with two syllables in rest " (p. 24) ; or that Byron wrote " purely constructed and errorless verse "

---

[1] This term properly applies to any foot used in a chorus, and some writers make it include three-syllable feet.

(p. 54). His whole scheme of defining the time of " metres " positively as well as relatively (p. 5) seems to me fallacious, as much so as making *deliberateness* characteristic of ancient Greece (*ibid.*). Technically, indeed, I should say that Ruskin more often goes wrong than right ; what redeems his tract is its emotional receptivity. He *felt* the cadence of particular lines, felt it deeply and truly, and tried (arbitrarily and capriciously) to translate his feelings into prosodic theory. Not thus is true theory reached ; yet the record of feeling has its value, coming from such a man. And, with all its faults, Ruskin's wild speculation at least aims in the right direction ; students " in St. George's schools " will get from him a truer idea of what verse really is than if they had read a hundred treatises based on the old lifeless orthodoxy. But they must not think him infallible.[1]

Nor was this year rendered so memorable by the work of Edmund Gurney, though his book on *The Power of Sound* (4ᵗᵒ, Macmillan, 1880) is full of interest. Chapter VII discusses rhythm in general, making it consist in " stimulation of fixed degrees of time ", its essential quality being " continuous satisfaction of expectation " (pp. 127, 128). Chapter XIX is on " the sound-element in verse ". Not the mere presence of accented syllables, but their regularity of occurrence, constitutes verse ; they come " in the vast majority of metres at equidistant places " (p. 425). Going on to compare music and verse, he thinks it immaterial whether we place the accented syllable first or last in a foot, and proposes an extraordinary scansion—

By the wá-|ters of Báb-|ylon we sat dówn | and wept—

remarking that such a case of four unaccented syllables occurring together is rare (p. 427 [2]). He asserts that stress

---

[1] *Rock Honeycomb* (1877), referred to on the title-page of the *Elements*, and forming Vol. II of *Bibliotheca Pastorum*, will not reward search metrically, though it comments on " some broken pieces of Sir Philip Sidney's Psalter ". The " Essays on Scott and Byron " mentioned at the end of the *Elements* appeared in the *Nineteenth Century* under the title " Fiction, fair and foul " ; but only the third of these (Vol. VIII, p. 394) contains even casual reference to prosody.

[2] Compare, by the same author, *Tertium Quid* (2 vols. [of essays], 1887), Vol. II, p. 213. This comes in an Essay on " The appreciation of Poetry ", where he breaks a lance with Theodore Watts[-Dunton] over Poe's " Ulalume " (p. 201, *note*), and discusses Shelley's " Thy

is " never reversed " in the last foot of English blank verse,
an assertion which from his lips shows considerable ignorance ;
and makes some rather questionable statements about our
" trochaic " verse (pp. 430, 431). He declines to admit
" rests " as integral to structure (p. 432, *note*). On the whole,
I cannot think Gurney adds much to our actual knowledge of
English verse, though his remarks on Classic metre are noteworthy, and his treatise may rank high as a contribution to
the study of sound in general.

What makes the year memorable from our point of view
is that it saw published *The Science of English Verse* (New
York, 1880 [1]), by the American poet Sidney Lanier. This
book seems still insufficiently known here ; in its own country
it has long been a textbook, and has founded a school of
critics, prosody being much more earnestly studied there than
with us. The distinctive note of the book is that it makes
rhythm not a mere accident or ornament, but the essential
basis, of verse. That idea, trite as it may seem, had not been
systematically and scientifically worked out by any previous
English writer known to me. Many had dallied with it, but
none had followed it up to its legitimate conclusions. If I
cannot, with some of his American admirers, think that
Lanier has spoken the last word about English verse, I gladly
join them in proclaiming the importance of his book, which
to many people came as a revelation.

Lanier was at this time a teacher in the newly founded
Johns Hopkins University at Baltimore, which has had a long
and honourable connection with prosody. He was a practical
musician, playing the flute in professional orchestras. As a

---

brother Death came and cried " (pp. 211–12), and " Fresh spring, and
summer, and winter hoar " (p. 214, *note*). But the paper deals with
matter more than form. Earlier in the same volume, an Essay on
" Poets, critics, and class-lists " refers to " regularity of recurrence "
as common to verse and music (p. 158, *cf. note*), and opines that the
musical element in verse constitutes but a small part of its effect. I
have enjoyed making acquaintance with these volumes, though by no
means concurring in their conclusions as regards metre.

[1] Succeeding editions are apparently page-for-page reprints of the
first. My copy, dated 1898, has nothing to show that it is not a new
book, except the words " copyright, 1880 ". It contains an error in
pagination, the first leaf of text being pp. 21, 22, while the last leaf of
contents bears the same figures in Roman numerals. There is a full
table of contents, but no index.

poet his posthumous fame has steadily increased. In every way, therefore, he was well qualified for the task he undertook.[1] A singer who knew that he sang, he studied the mechanism of his singing, studied English verse as it was made by himself and others. He sought to analyse its musical structure, approaching it almost entirely from that side ; there lay, perhaps, his weakness as well as his strength. It was work that greatly needed doing ; let us see how he did it.

His Preface defines his aim, which is to give " an account of the true relations between music and verse ", and deals shortly with a few predecessors, Steele's attempt being strangely disparaged. Then the first Chapter treats introductorily of sound, and the next eight Chapters (grouped as " Part I ") of our English verse-sounds and rhythms. " Part II ", in one Chapter, describes the "tunes " of verse, and " Part III ", in five Chapters, its " tone-colors "—a phrase more familiar in music. These last Chapters—dealing with rhyme, alliteration, and syzygy—show especial marks of haste, as if time or strength failed their writer. For the same year that saw this book published saw also its author's death. He died, leaving his task unfinished, his best songs perhaps unsung. But enough is left to judge him by, in prosody as in poetry ; the main lines of his theory of verse-fabric are clearly marked out.

The assertion with which Chapter I opens, *viz.* that verse impresses wholly by its sound apart from its meaning, is perhaps too absolutely made, but takes us at once into prosody's true domain. " The study of verse must begin with the study of sounds ; " and they should be studied with reference to duration, intensity, pitch, and *timbre* or " tone-color" (p. 24). These are accurately distinguished and defined,

---

[1] Details of Lanier's life will be found in the memoirs by William Malone Baskerville (1876) and Edwin Mims (1905). A Southerner by birth, he fought in the Civil War, and suffered permanently in health from hardships and imprisonment. In youth he " could play on any instrument ". See also his *Letters*, edited by his widow (1899). The lectures from which his book is formed are said to have been written in six weeks. Another set of lectures on *Shakspere and his Forerunners* (2 vols. 4to, London, 1902—the other books mentioned above are published in America) show full and careful reading. They repeat briefly his main views on prosody, but add nothing to his exposition. Personally, Lanier was much beloved. I shall refer later [*infra*, 1888] to a memorial volume written by friends and admirers.

the first being expressly stated to include " the correlative
duration of the *silences* between sounds, which . . . are quite
as necessary to many forms of verse as are the sounds thereof "
(pp. 32–3) ; and verse is affirmed to consist of " such sounds
and silences as can be co-ordinated by the ear " (p. 33). Now
force, or intensity, cannot be so co-ordinated with exactness
(pp. 38–9), and therefore plays a subordinate though important part in verse, whose primary factors are duration, pitch,
and tone-colour. Rhythm depends primarily on duration,
and only secondarily on other elements (pp. 39–40) ; and
verse-rhythm contains all the factors of musical rhythm,
spoken words being sounds uttered by instruments of one
particular class, to wit, our vocal organs (pp. 48–50). The
characteristics which distinguish these sounds from other
varieties of musical sound relate to *timbre* and *tune* (pp. 50–2).
Speech, and therefore verse, has an elaborate notation of
tone-colours (the alphabet), and uses every interval of tone,
not only a chosen number. These characteristics distinguish
verse from music ; as for prose, " scientifically considered, it
is a wild variety of verse " (p. 57). To observe and classify
the phenomena of rhythm, tune, and tone-colour, so far as
they can be indicated through the medium of spoken words,
is therefore the aim of prosodic science (p. 58).

These important conclusions, developed in the three
" Parts " which follow, are in substantial accord with the
work of A. J. Ellis (to whom he refers in this connection,
p. 27, *note*), Lanier's " color " being what Ellis calls " form ".
The composite structure of this last is duly noted. Parts II
and III, however, dealing with the " tunes " and " colors "
of verse, occupy collectively only about a fourth part of
Lanier's exposition, three-fourths being devoted to Part I on
rhythm. On this last our attention must be concentrated.
What Lanier says about tune and tone-colour is for the most
part admirable, though I must ask readers to receive with
incredulity the assertion that " no rhyme but a perfect rhyme
is ever worth a poet's while " (p. 299). But it is in Part I
that his really constructive work is done, and done with
thoroughness, though he modestly asks that it be considered
as only an outline to be filled up by further research (p. 251).
It is from Part I that we learn, both generally and in detail,
what was Lanier's conception of English verse.

Though a musician, Lanier does not wholly adopt musical methods and rules. He does not, like musical textbooks, make time depend on accent. Only in " secondary rhythm " does accent, like other factors, play its part ; " primary rhythm " consists entirely of co-ordinated durations. When a clock beating uniformly says " tick-tick " (p. 63), we instinctively make it say either " tick-*tick* " or " *tick*-tick " ; but this apparent difference is imaginary, and merely shows our tendency to superimpose secondary on primary rhythm. " Accent can effect nothing, except in arranging materials already rhythmical through some temporal recurrence " (p. 65 ; *cf.* the syllogistic " demonstration " in the long *note* which begins on that page). English speech habitually utters syllables in definite and simple relations of equality or proportion (p. 60), and it is by this definiteness of relative duration that rhythm in prose or verse is created. These syllables therefore possess " quantity " (p. 68 *seq.*), not fixed but shifting, yet determinable by the ear, in virtue of which they can be grouped into divisions of equal or different length. Verse groups them in equal divisions or *bars*,[1] each of which is " exactly equal to any other bar " (p. 82). In doing so, it employs " secondary rhythm " (pp. 69–78), and also " tertiary rhythm " or phrasing (pp. 79–87) ; but its essential base is equality of duration. It further groups these bars into lines, stanzas, and whole poems, so that six methods of grouping have to be considered (p. 95), *viz.* by quantity, rhythm, phrase, line [which he designates " metre ", pp. 88, 91], stanza, and poem. To these the next six Chapters are devoted, what has been summarized in this paragraph occupying Chapter II, while Chapter IX [the last of " Part I "] briefly discourses of " rhythm throughout . . . Nature ".

Chapter III continues the discussion of primary rhythm, and illustrates how English words in themselves constitute a system of rhythmical notation, their accents being arranged so as to enforce the rhythmical accent. Here he protests against the common notion that our verse is created by accent, even as expressed more guardedly by Ellis (p. 98), and insists that (in verse as in music) rhythms " exist in virtue of the simple time-relations between the units of sound " (p. 99). Then he expounds at length the temporal structure of verse-

[1] *Cf.*, later, p. 150, *note.*

units, taking as his first example Tennyson's " Break, break, break ". His exposition assumes that syllables correspond to and can be represented by musical notes, the time-values of which he therefore explains, noticing particularly the " triole " or group of three sounds uttered in time of two. This occupies the rest of the Chapter (summed up on p. 117), toward the close of which (p. 114) he anticipates future discussion by asserting that English blank verse moves to triple time, and that its feet are accented on the second syllable.

These two assertions square with orthodox tradition, but the first departs from the opinion of some of our best critics, who have recognised " even measure " in our commonest type of verse, while the second departs from the almost invariable custom of musical scansionists. All Lanier's previous exposition and examples have prepared us to find the accented syllable made to begin the bar, his early illustrations of rhythm having been restricted to ' dactylic ' cadences, *e.g.*—

Rhythmical | roundelays | wavering | downward.

Now, dealing with ' iambic ' verse, he surprises us by writing—

To whom | should I | complain,

instead of, as might have been anticipated—

To | whom should | I com-|plain.

No reason is assigned for the new departure ; we are simply told (pp. 114–15 ; *cf.* also pp. 230–1) that the facts are so. It strikingly illustrates, some will say Lanier's inability to free himself from old tradition, others will say his clear perception that English verse-units are most commonly signalized by a rise of accent. Which view is correct need not be at present debated, but readers should note and bear in mind Lanier's practice.

His identification of our commonest verse-movement with " triple time " is made with similar confidence throughout Chapters IV and V. There is little matter for surprise in this, since any one listening merely to the syllables of a line would in most cases come, as our orthodox prosody came, to this conclusion. Yet it is disappointing that Lanier, who has so clearly taught us that a line does not consist merely of its syllables, should not have at least recognised the possibility of another view. If " even measure " underlie our iambic

syllables, half the difficulties of our prosody are at once
resolved, and the radical difference between metres like

The stag at eve had drunk his fill

and

At the silence of twilight's contemplative hour

is satisfactorily explained. Lanier, however, did not take
this view, and we must continue studying his.

Chapter IV divides secondary rhythm into " 3-rhythm and
4-rhythm ", 2-rhythm being identified with " pyrrhic " feet
and pronounced intolerable (p. 130), while 5-rhythm and
7-rhythm are too difficult for use in verse (pp. 132–5). A clear
distinction is made between rhythmical and logical accent,
the latter term covering both syllable-stress and verbal
emphasis (pp. 120–3) ; and as clearly it is explained that the
actual number of sounds [*i. e.* syllables] in a bar need not
correspond with its typical number of time-units (p. 136).
The general drift of this short Chapter is summed up at its
close (pp. 138–40), and the consideration of 3-rhythm is
continued in Chapter V—much the longest in the book—
which traces its prevalence from " our father Cædmon " down
to Morris and Swinburne, and finds identity of movement
where most people feel diversity. Criticism which asserts
sameness of structure in the metres of " The Battle of Maldon "
(p. 147) and the " Ormulum " (p. 159), the " Cuckoo song "
(p. 161) and the " Canterbury Tales ", the " Song of ever and
never " (p. 171) and Hamlet's soliloquy, seems to me to miss
its mark. Even were fundamental rhythm the same in all
these, their differences would outweigh that sameness. The
gulf that separates Langland's verse from that of Chaucer
(p. 165) is not bridged by saying that both wrote in 3-rhythm,
or even that one is " ancient heroic measure " and the other
" modern " (p. 183). Of course Lanier knew this well, indeed
he states it himself on the page last cited ; but this does not
suggest to him any doubt. It does not prevent his declaring
(p. 184) that the overwhelming bulk of English poetry since
the 14th Century is written in 3-rhythm. He goes on to deal
with Shakespeare's verse by methods that would make metre
of almost any words. That famous line in *Measure for Measure*

Than the soft myrtle ; but man, proud man . . .

is pronounced undoubtedly correct, because " rests " occur

freely in verse (pp. 189–97)—as if they were usually " rests "
of this kind ! What remains of this Chapter is taken up with
analysis and glorification of Shakespeare's verse, in which
I find little to quote except his remark that " in every line,
five rhythmic accents are always present or accounted for "
(p. 215), and his recognition of inverted accent (p. 217). At
the end he asserts that variation from type must have been as
common in Greek and Latin verse as in English, and quotes
Elizabethan authorities as to the prevalence of dissyllabic
feet, especially that " cunning" testimonial given by James VI
(of Scotland) when he assumed that no other foot need be
taken into account.

Three short Chapters conclude Part I, and need but brief
mention. Chapter VI treats of 4-rhythm verse, distinguishing
(p. 225) the true classic dactyl from the spurious triple-time
' dactyl ' of English prosody, but strangely finding the former
in " Hame came my | gudeman, and | . . ." (*ibid.*), and mis-
dividing Jean Ingelow's " It 's we two, it 's we two " (p. 228,
e.g. 3rd line). He recognises the " ponderous pulse of march-
time " in Classic hexameter (p. 227) ; our quadruple rhythm
he considers to have usually a comic effect (p. 229). Judgements like this last are apt to be falsified by events, and the
great development of 4-rhythm since Lanier's day (as in the
hands of Mr. Rudyard Kipling) makes it open to question.
Chapters VII and VIII deal very slightly with " tertiary
rhythm ", noting the time-beating functions of rhyme and
alliteration, and desiderating omission of line-division in such
" rhythmic but unmetric verse " as Shakespeare's (p. 235).
Chapter IX refers (as had been done before, p. 186) to the
" patting " of rhythmical periods by negroes, and notes the
universality of periodic rhythm in the processes of Nature.
The comparatively brief remainder of the book, as said before,
is concerned with matters bearing only indirectly on rhythm.

It will be seen that it is for principles rather than conclusions
that I hold Lanier's book valuable. Particular scansions often
seem to me quite erroneous, as when he makes consist of
trisyllabic feet the poem beginning " Agincourt, Agincourt "
(p. 179) ; and his habit of letting accents come irregularly in
successive feet [1] seems to me destructive of true analysis.

[1] He represents the first line of *Piers Plowman* as divided thus—
In a sóm-|er séson | whan sóft was | the sónne (p. 163) ;

And, though he fully recognised *rests*, he does not in my opinion make nearly enough use of them, actually (for example) showing " ocean " a spondee in his notation on p. 232. His musical preconceptions, I think, led him too much to make syllables embody rhythm—as in this word " ocean "; and I doubt if he sufficiently realised that suspensions of sound may occur when in no way dictated by meaning or sentential rhythm. Other and larger regions where I question his analysis have been already indicated. But criticism must yield to praise so far as fundamentals are concerned. It is Lanier's glory to have brought these finally to light. Temporal relations are shown by him essential to verse; whether or no we accept his reading of these matters comparatively little. The " new prosody " takes in his book a step which can never be retraced. I have said that to many the book came as a revelation; its reading first showed myself how far prosodic science had advanced during the eighth decade of last Century. The name of Sidney Lanier is imperishably associated with that advance; he led its triumphant attack upon the fortresses of prejudice and superstition. If he made mistakes, they may well be forgotten in view of his great achievement. He showed, once for all, where the foundations of true prosody lie, for which reason 1880 must always be memorable in the annals of our subject.

During the final twenty years of last Century speculation about verse was constant. The elaborate metres used by our chief recent singers—by Tennyson, Browning, D. G. and Christina Rossetti, Swinburne, and others—had compelled inquiry and made tradition of little account. My notes will become briefer as we reach well-known books by living writers; here, my wish is to concentrate scrutiny on what helps insight into true principles. Sometimes I have failed to get sight of articles mentioned by correspondents, particularly those printed in the United States; more fortunate students may profit by my bare enumeration of these. Let me add that

a line of Shakespeare's thus—
    Would bé | as heávy | to mé | as ódi-|ous, bút (p. 215);
and so on. His *feet* are of course represented by musical notes; Classical names are not so much rejected as quietly put aside. The gain in accuracy and precision is immense, but must be considerably neutralized for musical readers by eccentric occurrence of accent.

I shall always be delighted to hear of any important additions to my printed lists, but it is hopeless to attempt making these lists cover all ephemeral journalistic work or guide-books to English literature. Most of the latter only repeat old ideas about prosody, as do even the latest grammars ; where there is anything novel, I shall be glad to have my attention drawn to it.

Outcast Essays and Verse Translations, by Shadworth Hodgson, appeared in 1881, and the volume has been several times reprinted. I quote the first edition, in which pp. 207–360 are occupied with a discussion of " English Verse ". Distinguishing three kinds of " stress " which correspond in an ascending scale to language, metre, and poetry (pp. 215–16), the writer also (like Ellis and Lanier) distinguishes four elements in language, *viz.* time, pitch, force, and colour (p. 223). Of these last, time is quantitative, the others qualitative (p. 224). Unlike his predecessors, however, he does not make time the basis of verse, but assigns that function to colour (p. 231). " English metres do not aim at dividing time into equal or proportionate lengths ; they aim at a response of phrase to phrase, and sound to sound " (p. 236). Patmore's isochronous bars are rejected ; did they exist, they and not stress would be the chief source of metre (*ibid.*). The whole conception of *feet* is therefore set aside, and replaced by counting " stresses ". I cannot deem this analysis right, and think it errs through regarding " time " as synonymous with syllabic quantity. It is quite true that our verse does not depend on quantity of syllables, and I agree with most of the remarks to this effect on pp. 293–8, where it is shown that such quantity is not a factor essential to English metre, though still " a condition which must be reckoned with ". But it does not follow that our verse bears no relation to time. The writer's exclusive devotion to stress sometimes affects his scansion. I doubt his division of the " Bush aboon Traquhair " (p. 281) and " Come into the garden, Maud " (p. 283), also whether each pair of lines in Browning's " After " corresponds precisely to one line of " Saul " (p. 287), and whether Lamb's

> I have had playmates, I have had companions,

repeats the structure of Latin hendecasyllabic metre (p. 336). It does not seem to me helpful to say that both

> She bounds before the gale

and

> This is a spray the bird clung to

are "lines of three stresses" (pp. 285, 286). I certainly challenge the statement that "stress laid on a short acute syllable makes it long, e.g. *cano*" (p. 258). Though the main prosodial teaching of the Essay must be held defective, there is much excellent criticism of verse otherwise, and of such matters as our English "impatience of form" (p. 229), and our tendency to "rush at the meaning" in speech (p. 232). Particularly good is the distinction made between *colour* and *tone* (p. 301), and the proof that mere pitch without emotional "tone" does not create emphasis (p. 302). Hexametrical and other experiments are discussed on pp. 329–42. The Essay is followed by some translations from Homer and Horace which, like most 'accentual' lines, often postulate imaginary stresses to the reader's bewilderment, *e.g.*—

> A'nd as whén in heaven, around the moon in her brightness.

Perhaps the 'elegiacs' on p. 386 are the most satisfactory of these attempts.

The *Saturday Review* during February and March, 1883, contained some papers by Prof. Fleeming Jenkin of Edinburgh. reprinted in the *Memoir* of him by Robert Louis Stevenson (1887), Vol. I, pp. 149–70. Beginning as a review of Guest's book, the second edition of which had just been published, these papers go on to expound a new and original theory of English verse-structure, which is held to contain both feet and sections. The latter are word-groups, just as in prose, but shorter, five syllables being the outside limit (p. 159); feet are formed by accent and occupy "dissimilar and irregular periods" (p. 150). Thus we get "two coexisting rhythms, one due to the grouping of sections, and one to the grouping of feet"; while caesura is due to the fact that "the number of sections never coincides with that of the feet" (p. 159). These sections are not joined at random, but show continuity of beat throughout a line. "In beating time from beginning to end of each line one stroke will fall on each accented syllable," except where it falls on a pause; "but neither in verse nor prose does a beat ever fall on a weak unaccented syllable" (*ibid.*). "Time, number, and rhythm" are thus the three elements of verse (p. 161). "The beat upon the accents marks the time, the feeling of number is given by the constant number of feet and . . . of sections. The group of syllables within the section, and the group which these syllables form within the line, give the primary sense of rhythm ; and underlying this varying rhythm we have the secondary rhythm due to feet which by their approximately uniform arrangement assist in giving " a " sense of unity " (*ibid.*). In a normal line, he had already said, " the number of sections is constant " (*ibid.*). Applying this theory to our heroic metre, he finds that " the normal English heroic line is an iambic of five feet, broken into four sections by one major and two minor pauses " (p. 162). Representing the minor pause by one dot, the major by a colon, he thus divides a line from Pope (p. 160)—

> Gó·, wóndrous creáture, : moúnt· where scíence guídes :

Here there are six beats ; some lines have only three, others have seven or even eight. The proof of his theory, he thinks, is that unless lines are read by their sections they cease to impress us as being metrical ; read Milton's blank verse otherwise than by its proper sections, and it becomes prose (p. 169).

It is a striking theory, and strikingly put. The crude view which finds five accented syllables in every heroic line Jenkin rejected ; " those who classify by accents are fain to call many syllables accented whose sole claim to that honour is given by their length " (p. 156). He saw that two elements combine to form our verse. Had he reversed their functions, making rhythm invariable, syllabic structure changeful, I think he would have come very near the truth. Why he refused to let the rhythmical beat fall on a weak syllable I cannot understand. It surely does so in a line he quotes from Milton—

> Of Oreb or of Sinai . . . ,

and in many other instances. His recognition of pause is sometimes too arbitrary, as when he insists on expanding into an ' Alexandrine ' the line—

> Crouch for employment : ʌ but pardon, gentles all—

declaring that, otherwise, " scansion seems . . . impossible " (p. 165). An enthusiastic actor, he evidently gave chief attention to verse as delivered on the stage. He rightly strove to " search for the main laws of rhythm by listening to the actual sound " of verse (p. 156) ; but the child crooning its sing-song must be listened to along with the " well-graced actor " if we would grasp the full meaning of these laws. Jenkin believed that " scansion was originally based upon a measurement of time " (p. 167), but not that it remains based on it to this day. That the number of beats in heroic metre may vary from three to eight is simply incredible. The test of every line in this metre is that it can be adjusted to five beats ; what we cannot so adjust ceases, for us, to be heroic metre. Failure to give due importance to time leads Jenkin to identify quantity with accent, to write *fămine* and so forth, to " count any syllable long which receives a secondary accent " (p. 165)—in fact, to invent imaginary criteria of " length ". As against Dr. Johnson, he explicitly maintains that " the beauty of a line cannot be determined by noting how closely it approaches to the central type " (p. 162) ; but any line which transgresses his canon he condemns, be Pope or Milton the culprit. So that this gallant attempt to throw off traditional fetters was not wholly successful ; the essayer remained a slave to accentuation, and in his devotion to it neglected the true basis of verse. To make grammatical pauses constitute rhythm is to confound elocution with structure, and this seems to me the fundamental error in these ingenious and captivating papers.

To the same year may be assigned a paper on " The Physiology of Versification " by Oliver Wendell Holmes, since it came out in his collection of Essays styled *Pages from an Old Volume of Life* (Boston, 1883) ; the real date is doubtless earlier. This short Essay of six pages treats of " the relations of verse to the respiratory organs ", claiming that length of lines is determined by rate of breathing, and suggesting that accentuation may have to do with arterial pulsations. The normal proportion of respirations to pulse-beats being one to four, and twenty octosyllabic lines occupying a minute in average reading, accents and pulsations during that time will both be eighty. Personal equation plays its part ; Spenser must have habitually breathed more slowly than Prior, Anacreon more quickly than Homer. Such speculation may seem fanciful, but it is precisely the application of phonetics and physiology to verse that has made prosody practical ; whether Holmes's conclusions are scientifically valid I cannot pretend to determine.

The title of a small book by C[harles] Witcomb *On the Structure of English Verse* (1884) raises hopes which are hardly fulfilled. Structure is made to depend wholly on accent ; accentual feet are postulated in the usual way. Good examples are given, but criticism otherwise is unnecessary. The last Section is on " imitations of Classical metres ".

Not much about prosody will be found in the Philological Society's *Transactions* for 1885–7, but I would draw attention to one paper read on December 19, 1884, by Mr. James Lecky, of which only an abstract appears in the " Proceedings ", pp. ii–vi. Beginning by desiring a phonetic notation for prosody, and contending that the stress-mark should be placed before rather than on a syllable, he proceeds to define rhythm and metre in unusual terms, making *metre* signify pulses of equal length, and *rhythm* denote stress-groups of proportional length (pp. iv–v). The latter is divided into *binary* and *ternary*, but " a stress-group may have a ternary effect when only containing two syllables, and a binary effect when containing three " (p. v). Five grades of stress are recognised, degrees of length and pause being also shown by symbols. *Basic* and *anacrusic* verse are illustrated by

> Hence in a | season of | calm | weather,
> Though | inland | far we | be.

" Archaistic influence " affects our verse, lyric poetry alone being now spontaneous and natural (*ibid.*) ; it is queried whether Classic prosody was not determined by accent, since " the grouping of syllables into metres [*cf.* above] is only possible by means of stress " (p. vi). Much is debateable in these statements, and there seems some confusion between quantity of syllables and length of groups in the opening remarks, but the condensed report may be to blame. I regret that this striking paper has not (to my knowledge) been published in any fuller form.[1]

R. L. Stevenson published in the *Contemporary Review* for April, 1885, a paper " On some technical elements of style in Literature ", now reprinted as the first of his *Essays in the Art of Writing* (1905), to which edition I refer. With his accustomed grace of diction, he dwells on points too often forgotten

---

[1] A short report of it appeared in the *Academy* for January 10, 1885 (pp. 31–2).

by professional prosodists. He founds, indeed, on Prof. Jenkin's theory, and pushes it beyond truth when he says that heroic lines cannot contain less than three or more than five word-groups, that five is the " forbidden number " (pp. 21–2), and that a line of heroic metre could not begin with feet like " Mother | Athens " (p. 24).[1] But his general view of verse is fresh and helpful, being shown in such sentences as the following. " Music and literature, the two temporal arts, contrive their pattern of sounds in time " (p. 9). " The rule of scansion in verse is to suggest no measure but the one in hand ; in prose, to suggest no measure at all " (p. 26). " The eccentric scansion of the groups is an adornment ; but as soon as the original beat has been forgotten, it ceases to be an adornment " (p. 25). " The laws of prosody . . . have one common purpose ; to keep alive the opposition of two schemes simultaneously followed " (*ibid.*). [This last sentence recalls Prof. Sylvester's theory, *cf. ante,* 1870, foot-note.] With these compare such phrases as " the double pattern of the texture and the verse " (p. 17), the illustration of a juggler keeping up several oranges at once, and the final reference to a versifier's " five preoccupations " (p. 32). I venture to think that a more adequate view of prosody than any yet met with is hinted at in these extracts. The last pages of this Essay deal with recurrent sounds in prose and verse, *e. g.* Milton's " FugitiVe and cloistered Virtue ". Such matters are beyond our present purpose, but must assuredly be reckoned with in any complete analysis of verse.

---

[1] A line of heroic metre may consist of only *one* word, as in Carey's burlesque—

> Aldiborontephoscophornio,
> Where left you Chrononhotonthologos ?—

or of *two* words, as in Wycherley's line [this reference I owe to a newspaper quotation]—

> Inhospitable hospitality.

I see no reason why it should not consist of *ten* words, each bearing an equal prose-accent. As to " Mother Athens ", heroic lines beginning with similar cadences can be found, as already noted, in our best writers. " Five word-groups " are of course quite legitimate, *e.g.* Milton's—

> And swims, or sinks, or wades, or creeps, or flies—

though it may be noted that Milton himself printed this line without a comma after " swims ".

The nineteenth volume of the *Encyclopaedia Britannica*, published in 1885, contained Mr. Watts-Dunton's famous article on " Poetry ". Its merits have been universally recognised, but small part indeed of its space is given to metre. The question whether metrical structure can be dispensed with by poetry is examined in the first pages, without our being told what that structure is. We hear later of " caesuric effects ", of " recognised and expected metrical bars " (p. 262, 2) ; also of " those lighter movements which we still call, for want of more convenient words, anapaestic and dactylic ", the use of alliteration being commended as helpful to these latter (p. 258, 1). " Questions of versification," it is said in this connection, " touch . . . the very root of the subject " (*ibid.*). The " rhythmic life " as well as the " inspiration " of poetry are insisted on throughout, Dionysius and Hegel furnishing apposite texts. The common origin of verse and music, and their gradual growing apart, are handled on p. 260. It is noted that in a line of George Eliot's—

> Of the unspoken ; even your loved words . . .

" the main accent falls upon a positive hiatus " (p. 257, 2). Nothing like a reasoned analysis of verse-structure, however, is attempted in this article, nor is any theory of scansion put forward ; its pages are occupied with discussion of higher subjects. The *Encyclopaedia*, it may be added, contains no article on Prosody.

A paper dated 1885 on " Quantity in English Verse ", by Thomas D. Goodell, appears in the *Transactions* of the American Philological Association (Vol. XVI, pp. 78–103). Prof. Goodell being an accomplished Grecian,[1] his paper naturally starts from and refers to Greek metre, but by no means in a narrow spirit. Indeed, he blames older prosodians for approaching our verse with Classical prepossessions instead of " simply listening " to its own cadences. Equally, however, he blames those who ignore all resemblance between ancient and modern metre ; Greek verse had its accentual beat, ours has temporal structure. Lanier first [?] showed this, taking the true starting-point, though his method was

---

[1] I can here only mention his *Chapters on Greek Metric* (New York and London, 1901), a book full of suggestive hints about verse-rhythm generally. A review by him in the American *Nation* for 12th October 1911 led to an interesting discussion in subsequent numbers.

faulty (p. 80). In English verse as in Greek, " rhythm is a definite arrangement of times," each time-group containing at least one syllable of increased " force or stress ", so that our verse is really " based on word-accent " (pp. 81–2). An English versifier must so arrange words that their chief accents " shall coincide with and distinctly locate enough of the rhythmic ictuses to enable the voice unconsciously, or at least with slight effort, to locate the other rhythmic ictuses " (p. 83). Substituting " mind " for " voice ", this last sentence seems to me unexceptionable. Following Lanier, he finds only $\frac{2}{4}$ and $\frac{3}{4}$ time in our verse, the latter immensely preponderating (p. 85) ; for notation he uses four (Greek) signs of syllable-length, with four of pause-length. This coincides with Steele, whose work seems unknown to him, for he believes himself first to suggest that the ' initial trochee ' is part of a trisyllabic foot (p. 89). Initial feet, and anacrusis, often " insist on more than their due share of time " (pp. 90–1). I shall not debate particular scansions, but cannot think that the last line of Emerson's " Rhodora " varies in time from its predecessors. Rules of quantity are laid down on pp. 100–2, seven for triple-time verse, six for quadruple rhythm. In this latter " the rhythmizing instinct favours equality, . . . as in triple time inequality " (p. 102). Among questions omitted (see last paragraph of paper) are the relation of ictus to word-accent, that of verse to prose, and the employment of " rest or pause " within the line. These are serious omissions, but even so the paper is most instructive, whether or no one can accept all the writer's conclusions. Its terminology appeals to scholars rather than to the general public, but its clearly stated argument can be followed by even the casual reader.

Prosodic discussion was now being warmly taken up in America, from which in the same year 1885 came two first books by writers who continued its study, Prof. Gummere's *Handbook of Poetics* and Prof. Raymond's *Poetry as a Representative Art*. In the former, " Part III " is on metre, the other two Parts dealing with subject-matter and style ; of the three Chapters into which Part III is divided one discusses general principles of metre, the next classifies English metres, the third deals shortly with one or two special types of versification. The first of these Chapters forms an admirable introduction to the study of our verse. Concisely and without undue dogmatism—indeed, pointing out dubieties as he goes—the writer analyses the actual structure of our metre, starting from the postulate that " measured intervals of time are the basis of all verse ", and laying down that " Time is thus the chief element in Poetry, as it is in Music and Dancing" (p. 135). With excellent caution he states that " when the ear detects at regular intervals a recurrence of accented syllables, it perceives Rhythm " (p. 134), not making rhythm a creation of accent (*cf.* p. 141). Word-accent and verse-accent are distinguished (p. 139), without prejudice to the avowal " Accent is the chief factor of modern verse " (*ibid.*). Rightful deduction is perhaps exceeded when the indubitableness of Greek feet being signalized by stress is unhesitatingly assumed (p. 138) ; and, though pauses are well recognised (pp. 145–7), such recognition does not necessarily imply approval of the disputed line—

> Than the soft myrtle ; but man, proud man. . . .

When, in the next Chapter, metres are classified, the reckoning is by " stresses " ; these, however, are not the actual prose-stresses of particular words, but those found in " the simple plan of the rhythm, uninfluenced by the actual words " (p. 200). From this " metrical scheme " a poet continually departs, urged both by need of variety, and by the intractability of language (p. 199) ; but it remains always in his mind. Two such departures are to be found in " hovering accent " and " wrenched accent " (*cf.* p. 142). The difference between iambic and trochaic metre is said to be " very slight " (p. 169). On the whole, without professing concurrence in every position taken up, I do not know where to find a safer and better textbook of prosody than this. Published by Ginn and Co. of Boston, I imagine that it can be easily procured from their London Agency.[1]

---

[1] Interesting papers by Prof. Gummere will be found in *The American Journal of Philology* for 1886, No. 25, pp. 46–78 on " The translation of Beowulf ", and *Modern Language Notes* (Baltimore) for 1887, No. 6, pp. 159–62 reviewing Prof. Mayor's book. Both refer much to verse-structure. Compare also in the latter for 1886, pp. 35–6, his " try " at defining the basis of English prosody. A later volume by the same author will be noticed in the Postscript to this Chapter. His Essay on " The Ballad and Communal Poetry", in the *Child Memorial Volume* (Boston, 1897), I have been unable to see, but there is a very full summary of it in "Gayley and Scott" [*infra*, 1899], pp. 266–70. [I regret to learn of Prof. Gummere's recent death.]

George Lansing Raymond is the author of a whole series of books on comparative aesthetics, whose dates of publication do not indicate their place in the series. The volume I have named is logically preceded by two more general books, one of which appeared only in 1900, and followed by four others, of which *Rhythm and Harmony in Poetry and Music* (1895) alone concerns us. His books are published in both London and New York. Covering so wide a field, they naturally paint with a broad brush ; and, their author being a teacher of oratory, approach verse mainly on its elocutional side. *Poetry as a Representative Art* deals chiefly with the expressional function of verse, and dwells almost entirely upon its accentuation. Time is not wholly ignored—" a poet has only to arrange his words so that the accents will recur *at like intervals* " (p. 28 ; *cf.* 25, 45), but it is usually made merely a matter of pace, and force as well as duration is considered " essential to the effects of rhythm " (p. 35). It is fair to quote the author's own saying : " some may doubt that accent is the basis of rhythm and tune, but it is really about all that the majority of men know of either " (p. 27). Every speaker has " a rhythm and a tune of his own " (p. 20), and verse-forms are " traceable to the pause and accent of ordinary conversation " (p. 32). Differing profoundly from this view, as from the statement that accented syllables necessarily are longer than unaccented (p. 33), I find myself differing often from Prof. Raymond's analysis. He does not seem to realise the difference between ancient and modern verse (*e. g.* pp. 29–31, 46–7), or between the prosaic and the prosodial value of syllables (p. 31). Trisyllabic feet are supposed always to represent rapidity (Chap. IV), whereas triple time has its slow as well as its quick movement. The " endeavour to interpret the meanings of metres " (p. 64), dividing them by initial, medial, and terminal accents (p. 60), is surely pushed too far. (Musical scansion, it will be observed, is rejected ; iambic is distinguished from trochaic metre : p. 67.) Condemnation is prompt when a poet's practice violates the critic's theory, as in the case of run-on lines (p. 40) [1]. When the writer goes on to discuss pitch and tune, figures, indirect and alloyed

[1] In the first line so quoted, a misprint has survived successive editions. I have noticed some others, not surprising in a work of such proportions.

representation, *etc.*, there is less to except against ; quotations
are profuse and delightful.   But his view of fundamental
structure does not change, nor do I find it materially altered
in the later volume, though that is well brought up to date,
and makes more use of *rests* (*e.g.* in a passage from " Marco
Bozzaris " on pp. 41–2).   It is strange that one who has
studied Lanier should remain insensible to his demonstration
of " time " in its true sense.   The aesthetic effect of verse
not seldom depends on its temporal fabric.

My record for 1886 contains only one separate book, which
has been already mentioned, *Chapters on English Metre*, by
Joseph B. Mayor [second edition, " revised and enlarged,"
1901 ; my references are to the first edition].   Its breadth
and catholicity, within self-assigned limits, deserve all praise.
But the limits are strait.   To Prof. Mayor, as to others whom
we have reviewed, syllables constitute verse, and their accents
its regulative principle.   " Where the accent recurs in obedience to a definite law, there we have verse.   And the kinds
of verse are classified according to the intervals which separate
the accents, whether an interval of one syllable or of two
syllables " (p. 4).   Scansion means dividing lines into syllabic
feet, which he notates by three figures indicating degrees of
stress, and also calls by the familiar Classic names, metaphorically used.   *Time*, in his exposition, is only pace or
duration ; as rhythm, it is explicitly rejected (p. 53).[1]   That
this view is insufficient I need hardly again argue ; its want
of finality is shown in these " Chapters ".   Feet which Prof.
Mayor thinks *iambs* other writers make *spondees* or even
trochees ; verse which most critics call iambic he pronounces
anapaestic (p. 32, referring to a line in *Samson Agonistes*).
He is himself occasionally in doubt whether a metre be
anapaestic or iambic (pp. 109, 115, about Tennyson's " The
Flower ").   For, in truth, accentuation is an uncertain guide.
Our word-accent, and still more our sentence-accent, are too
fugitive and capricious to be made the sole basis of verse.
If metre depends wholly on them, it becomes a chaos, and
prosody is impossible.   Prof. Mayor acutely recognises syllabic
diversity, but ignores the temporal uniformity which gives
that its whole value.   This is clearly shown in, for example,
his dissection of Tennyson's " Cauteretz " (pp. 104–5), and

[1] *Cf.* (p. 55) " Nor do I recognize any given time for two syllables."

amusingly by his confession of the difficulty he long felt in scanning Byron's poem beginning "Bright be the place of thy soul!" (p. 112). Because in this latter piece sometimes one, sometimes two, and sometimes no syllables precede the first beat, doubt was felt about the metre. When *time* is given its due place, such doubts are not felt. The lines are seen to be all in one and the same metre, whether particular places be filled by sound or by silence. Whether the poet writes "E'er burst" or "Ever burst" at the beginning of the third line is a matter purely of euphony; metrical structure remains absolutely the same. The "routine scansion" which Prof. Mayor rightly defends (p. 6) is primarily based on time.

Otherwise prosody in this volume is sane and liberal. Trisyllabic feet are admitted to every station, even the last, in heroic verse. Monosyllabic feet are recognised, though a sentence on p. 53 referring to them disappears from the second edition. Only "amphibrachs" are barred (pp. 45, 94–6),[1] being avoided by such desperate dividing as "the ra-|pid of life |" (p. 109) and "With such | *dexte-|rity* | to inces-|tuous sheets" (p. 179), or by supposing an "extra-metrical syllable", *e. g.* (p. 153)—

But how | of Caw-|*dor ?* | The thane | of Caw-|dor lives.

Having no test of metre except feet, the writer would fain limit the number of exceptional feet in a line (p. 73), but honestly quotes lines which disprove his canon (*ibid.*, footnote); change of feet is to him change of metre. This may avail in ordinary verse, but in less usual metre soon breaks down. Thus, in the hymn "There is a happy land" (p. 127), the sixth line of each stanza is pronounced irregular. A time-scansionist sees that they are in the same metre with the lines which precede and follow. Supply obvious 'rests', and the three lines in the first stanza run thus—

Oh ! ʌ | how they | sweetly | sing ʌ,
Worthy | is our | Saviour | King ʌ !
Loud ʌ | let his | praises | ring ʌ !

---

[1] I suspect a misprint in one exceptional case (p. 78)—

Epic|ure|an and | *the Stoic* | severe.

Prof. Mayor's usual scansion would be "the Sto-|ic severe".

There is no irregularity in these lines, any more than in Browning's couplet—

> Morning, evening, noon and night,
> " *Praise* God ! " sang Theocrite.

Attention to time removes all difficulty. On the other hand, the words of " O come, all ye faithful " (p. 133) have no claim to rank as English verse. Apart from the tune, its second stanza produces no metrical effect whatever, but is simply prose.

A prominent feature of this book is its discussion of other prosodists, and admission of their replies. The short introductory Chapter is followed by criticism of Guest, Abbott, Symonds, Ellis and others ; then we have Prof. Mayor's own views upon " metrical metamorphosis ", naming and classification of metres (the illustrations to this Chapter are from hymns), and the blank verse of Surrey and Marlowe, Shakespeare (two Chapters), Tennyson and Browning. No pretence is made to completeness (Preface, p. vii). The book is based on lectures, some read before and criticised by the Philological Society ; Ellis's remarks on Shakespeare's blank verse will be found on pp. 165–71. The second edition adds three new Chapters, on the views of Messrs. Skeat and Bridges, Shelley's metre, and the English hexameter ; the last adds little to previous discussions. " Revision " is of the slightest, but a list of feet has been added. No fairer-minded or pleasanter guide than Prof. Mayor could be desired, and his book abounds in copious quotation ; the student is given every opportunity of forming an opinion for himself. But the doctrine of verse set forth in its pages appears to me radically defective.[1]

Though no other separate book appears on my list for 1886, I should like to mention an article entitled " Studies of Rhythm ", by G. Stanley Hall and Joseph Jastrow, which appeared in *Mind* during this year (Vol. XI, pp. 55–62). This short paper is the first of a series of experimental inquiries into rhythm by American scholars, to which I shall refer again later [*cf.* Bolton, 1894, and references there], and which show how much more seriously (as already said) prosody is taken by our Transatlantic cousins than by us. At present

---

[1] Prof. Mayor's *Handbook of Modern English Metre* (1903) will be mentioned in the Postscript to this Chapter.

it may suffice to say that this paper claims to find a good deal of subjective " illusion " in what we have been wont to regard as objective rhythmical facts.[1]

Under date 1887 I formerly placed references to various books by Prof. Saintsbury. Others would now have to be added, with particular mention of his " Introduction " to a new *Rhymers' Lexicon* (1905). But all are superseded by his elaborate *History of Prosody*, noticed in the Postscript to this Chapter. The earlier passages merely hinted at a view of " equivalence " to be some day developed and expounded. They cannot, therefore, have influenced contemporary theorizing, except by showing that a critic and scholar of high rank was dissatisfied with current methods and results ; so we need not at present stay to examine them.

The first appearance of *Milton's, Prosody*, by Mr. Robert Bridges, was as an appendix to the Clarendon Press edition of Milton (1887). Through successive editions as a separate issue it retained marks of its birth, and of continual additions, even one so late as 1901,—which I shall quote,—speaking of " to fill up the spare pages of this sheet " (p. 82). Originally a " tabulation of Milton's practice ", it has grown by multiplied Appendices, each separate and independent, into a discussion of verse-structure generally. The original tabulation was a masterly piece of work. If " laws " are sometimes made too absolute, the guiding principles of Milton's practice are analysed with loving care, and amply illustrated.[2] But it is with the Appendices that we are mainly concerned, particularly with those on " metrical equivalence " and " rules of the common lighter stress-rhythms ". In these, as elsewhere, Mr. Bridges champions a view in which time is ignored. It is, I think, only twice referred to, and that hypothetically (*cf.* pp. 33, 103) ; and it certainly plays no part in his theoretical exposition, which makes verse depend either on feet or " stresses ". The fact that stresses do not occur when expected only moves him to condemn the practice of our best poets (p. 73 *seq.*, *cf.* p. 96, *etc.*), and to proclaim the desirability

---

[1] A paper in the same volume (pp. 393–404), " On the time-sense," by Lewis T. Stevens, contains nothing that bears directly on verse-rhythm.

[2] Two points of detail are " corrected " by Mr. Bridges in the *Athenaeum* of January 30, 1894 [*cf.* Postscript to this Chapter].

of a reformed verse, in which stresses are to be constant. How such verse is to differ from prose I do not find stated ; it can differ only by virtue of temporal relation between the stresses, and then comes the question whether the stresses are really indispensable. Besides, who is to guarantee perception of the stresses ? All previous attempts in this direction have failed, because the stresses were not self-evidencing. Even the choruses in *Samson Agonistes*, to my mind, do not make their structure clear. Divorced from time, stress in English has never proved a sufficient basis of metre ; lines do not " read themselves ". And, divorced from time, no mere succession of prose accents will create an impression of verse. Ingenious as the rules given in " Appendix J " are, and sound as is the incidental criticism of other systems, these rules by themselves only explain how to make verse smooth ; they do not touch its guiding principle.

The high place held by Mr. Bridges both as critic and poet makes his teaching carry weight. Yet experience seems to me against him. As with his later quantitative essays (before referred to), so here, the experiment has been well tried already. Leigh Hunt worked on similar lines in dramatic verse. Frere, in his renderings of Aristophanes, wrote blank verse of similar looseness. Nay, did not the successors of Shakespeare, Ford and Massinger and Webster, trust too much to stresses in their verse, and did not Milton restore temporal structure ? Are we to run the same cycle ? Not Mr. Bridges himself, but some of his followers, write verse which is indistinguishable from prose ; some of them deny that the two differ. Even in the master's beautiful poem " London Snow " I for one miss temporal fabric. Critics are slow to appreciate new departures ; my judgement may be biassed. But poets, also, sometimes depart in wrong directions. I cannot believe that, even in the hands of a singer like Mr. Bridges, verse which lacks the foundation common to all verse can be more than tuneful prose.

Apart from theory, *Milton's Prosody* is a book to spend hours over. Consummate metrical skill is in evidence throughout ; criticism often seems divination. Students should remember that with Mr. Bridges " elision " does not mean cutting out but some form of slurring ; it is used as " a term of no definite meaning " (p. 52). " Stress " is also a general term (p. 78). They must be prepared to learn that Milton " came to scan his verses one way, and read them another " (p. 18) ; also that in *Paradise Lost* he attempted " to keep blank verse decasyllabic by means of fictions " (p. 19). With the fuller statements given in this book they may like to compare its author's Note at the end of his *Feast of Bacchus* and of *Nero, Second Part,* and to study the " six-stress " lines of the former along with the " five-stress " lines of the latter. Among the *Shorter Poems* some are of great interest metrically, and have much influenced younger writers. The verse as well as the prose of Mr. Bridges must be taken into account in dealing with English prosody, and critical differences need not blind any one to the great merits of both.[1]

The *Andover Review* (Boston, U. S. A.) for March, 1887, contained a paper on " The Laws of English Tone-color ", by Albert H. Tolman. Prof. Tolman has, I believe, written much on prosody in the *Atlantic Monthly* and elsewhere, but this is the only magazine article of his I have seen. Into short compass it packs much illustration of the phenomena in question, observation of which he seems to consider modern, and due to German guidance. The scientific explanation of such facts we owe to Germany, but the facts themselves— alliteration, " vowel-echoing," *etc.*—were noted by Eighteenth Century metrists. Rhythm is not a subject of study in this paper.

Next year, however, in a memorial volume already referred to, *The 46th Birthday of Sidney Lanier* (Baltimore, 1888), this writer ably criticises Lanier's conception of verse.[2] A pupil of Lanier's, he duly honours his master's work, pointing out that he " sought to explain English verse as a present fact " (p. 39), and declaring that " so long as man's heart-beats are separated by equal intervals, he will never distribute accents without reference to time " (p. 40). But he also points out that Lanier, essentially a lyrist, laid too much stress on the singing elements of verse. " He treats the rhythmical accent of verse almost as if it were a thing independent of every-day accent." " In rendering music, we add accent to musical

---

[1] For quantitative verse by Mr. Bridges see Appendix A, 1903.

[2] This paper now appears in a volume entitled *The Views about Hamlet, and other essays* (see Appendix B), in which is also a paper on " The symbolic value of English sounds ".

sounds ; in reading poetry, we find it in spoken sounds."
" In free blank-verse . . . not so much of the expression is
committed to the rhythm ; the words have a substantive, an
independent meaning, which the separate tones of a piece of
music do not have " (p. 41). Hence come " frequent omissions of the rhythmical accent even in bars that are filled
with sound ", and " a bewildering variety of equivalent forms
of the bar " ; but " the fundamental rhythm . . . is clearly
heard through all interruptions ". Such original and telling
criticism makes one wish to know more of Prof. Tolman's work.
On the fundamental fact of ' isochrony ' he is evidently sound.

In 1888 appeared a remarkable book entitled *Accent and
Rhythm explained by the Law of Monopressures* (Blackwood,
Edinburgh ; published anonymously, but understood to be
by a Scottish clergyman ; " Part I " only). The teaching of
this book has been adopted by Prof. Skeat, first in the
" Introduction " to Vol. VI of his *Chaucer*, then in a paper
on " The scansion of English poetry ", read before the Philological Society in January, 1898. As prosody owes in other
ways much to this veteran philologist, and his work should
precede that of younger men, I take the above together, there
being no substantial difference in their views. Both writers
reduce the " monopressures " or accentual units of our speech
to four types and no more, exemplified in the first book by
the words *mind, remind, minded, reminding*, which may be
represented by the simple signs I, ⌐, L, ⌐ (Prof. Skeat prefers
figures *one* to *four* [1]). They claim that all verse is resoluble
into these forms, which give a true scansion as opposed to
the conventional false one. A familiar line would then be
thus divided [it will suffice to link the words]—

The-curfew tolls the-knell-of parting day,

sense and " monopressure " coinciding. Two objections to
this analysis surely present themselves. Does not a word
like *unity* present a different type ? Is the pressure on its
final syllable more obvious than that on the final syllable of
a word like *abundant* or *remorseful* ? [2] May not a word of even

---

[1] He also uses *T, A, C,* and *E*, being initial letters of the illustrative
words *tone, ascent, cadence, extension*, while a Roman t denotes secondary
stress.

[2] The anonymous author's way of dealing with such words will

four syllables contain but one " monopressure " ? Apart from this, does resolution into these groups throw light on verse-structure ? They are not distinctively units of verse. They are merely the raw material which verse and prose alike use. *How* the maker of verse constructs from these a fabric essentially different from that of prose speech is the very question which prosody asks, and it is not answered by saying that prose and verse use the same raw material. I cannot, therefore, see that this method is helpful, though phonetic details are ably handled in the anonymous author's book, and though Prof. Skeat's later paper deservedly ridicules our ordinary scansion. If their view be pushed so far as to deny the possibility of three consecutive unaccented syllables, our recent verse is conclusive against it. Whenever a fourth syllable is squeezed into triple-time measure, three out of the four syllables must be without metrical accent ; and such instances are far from uncommon.

In 1888 was also published Prof. Sweet's *History of English Sounds*, rewritten and greatly altered from its first form of 1874. In this new edition paragraphs are numbered throughout, at an average rate of nearly four to a page, making reference easy ; and there is a fuller table of contents. Noticeable among additions are the recurring paragraphs on " metre and stress ". While Prof. Sweet does not, like his elder colleague just dealt with, advance any complete theory of verse-structure, he gives in these paragraphs hints from which a true phonetic basis of verse might, I think, be well constructed. Take such sentences as the following. " Quantity and stress are as essential elements of metre as time and barring are of music." . . . " In practice it is impossible fully to harmonize the natural quantity and stress of a language with the artificial quantity and stress of metre ; one or other must go to the wall." . . . " The stress-groups of ordinary speech amount to nothing more than prose ; " to make them into feet, we " lengthen or shorten syllables without scruple " (356). Yet " unconscious respect for natural quantities influences our best poets " (357). " Syllables that are quite stressless in ordinary speech can in verse take the full stress that is required by the metre " [this is said of

be found on p. 46 of his book. I am not sure whether Prof. Skeat endorsed it.

" Middle English four-stress metre "] (609). Compare the references to Chaucer and the *Ormulum* (614 *seq*.), to " Modern English " (755–64), and to " Living English " (935–44). Prof. Sweet recognises three degrees of both quantity and force (16, 19), and seems to identify accent entirely with the latter. He enters into niceties about long and short consonants as well as vowels which have perhaps little value for us, metre depending on broad and simple principles. No detail, indeed, is too small to be noticed by metrists, and even these probably should not escape attention. It is, however, to the general view of metre typified in the above extracts that I would particularly direct remark, and that seems to me as sound as the rest of the book is above any criticism of mine.

Amusing is the contrast between these books and one on *The Poetry of the Future*, by James Wood Davidson (New York, 1888). Its writer wishes to abolish " the trammels of metre and stanza " (p. 109), and with these are to depart also rhyme, alliteration, refrain, and most other embellishments of verse (pp. 96–7). We have really, he thinks, only " four feet, each accented on the last syllable " (p. 40) ; for it is a " universal law " that " the pause produced by the stress of accent marks and makes the end of the foot " (pp. 58–9). Trochaic and dactylic metre he scans as commencing with a monosyllabic foot, and recognises only two possible forms of rhythm. Whatever clashes with this he condemns, and would fain amend, even in Milton's verse. " Had the poet not been in too great a hurry," he could have written the line as Mr. Davidson thinks better (p. 87) ; when he does not, in another case, we are told—" It is unrhythmical. It is prose " (p. 158). Such criticism needs no comment ; yet much in this book shows acute observation. But to its author verse is merely a " succession of syllables " (p. 29), and " accent is the foundation-idea of the whole system of English prosody " (p. 176). He has, in fact, still to learn what really constitutes the " metre " which he seeks to abolish.

For the next year or two my notes are confined to American writers. A *Theory of the Origin and Development of the Heroic Hexameter*, by Fitzgerald Tisdall (New York, 1889), I have not seen ; nor yet a book on *The Versification of Pope in its*

relation to the Seventeenth Century, by William Edward Mead
(Leipzig, 1889). *Modern Language Notes* (Baltimore) for 1890
contained a paper on " Certain considerations touching the
structure of English Verse ", by William Hand Browne, the
late Emeritus Professor of English Literature in Johns Hopkins
University (Vol. IV, pp. 97–101, double columns numbered
193–202 ; I use the latter for reference). Vigorous and confident, this paper lays down rules of much precision. Though
Lanier is praised at the outset as the first person who studied
English verse as it is, not what other people said about it,
his method is not followed in detail. *Feet* are said not to
exist in our verse ; the amphibrach in particular is pronounced
wholly impossible (col. 193). English verse is " decorated
prose ", decoration involving symmetry and proportion (194).
Its decorative patterns are framed by contrast of strong with
weak syllables, in the proportions of one to one, one to two,
or one to three, the last being a recent invention (195–6).
Variations are got by dropping either one or two accents,
reversing either one or two, or by combinations of these (197).
" Any variation is allowable that does not obscure or equivo-
cate the genus " (198), as Milton does with his " bottomless
pit ". [The present love of multiplying trisyllabic feet in
heroic verse would have got short shrift from Prof. Browne.]
' Time ' has not yet been mentioned, but comes in when
twenty lines from " To be or not to be " are examined. *To
die* " is the exact analogue of the short appoggiatura in music,
the time of which is taken [subtracted] from the following
note " (*ibid.*). In *natural shocks*, " three syllables are uttered
in the time of two ; . . . this is the triplet, the exact analogue
of the triplet of music " (199). Pause may replace a whole
foot (*ibid., cf.* 201). So he comes to deal with *caesurae* (199–
201), making an incidental remark on French caesura which
is no longer correct ; and here at length he finds his unit of
structure. The " stave " formed by caesura is " the unit
of verse-formation " (201). This conclusion recalls that of
Fleeming Jenkin [*ante*, 1883]. I cannot agree with it, or with
division by syllables instead of beats ; nor do I think rhythm
adequately treated. But the paper throughout is full of point
and suggestiveness.

Briefer mention may serve for some other writings. A
paper in the same volume of *Modern Language Notes* on

" The inventor of the English hexameter ", by F[elix] E.
Schelling,[1] contains nothing *ad rem* for us ; nor is there much
to our purpose in a paper on " Beginnings of the Classical
Heroic Couplet in England ", by Henry Wood, printed in
the *American Journal of Philology* for 1890 (Vol. XI), though
it discusses Waller's reputed improvement of that metre, and
his debt to French poets. *English Versification for the use of
Students*, by Rev. James C. Parsons (Boston, New York, and
Chicago, " copyright 1891 " ; second edition, 1894), needs
mention only as an unpretentious summary of accustomed
rules. *A Primer of English Verse, chiefly in its Aesthetic and
Organic Character*, by Hiram Corson, LL.D. (Boston, 1892),
adopts Latham's notation by *a x* and *x a*, and deals mainly
with assonances and other " colors " of verse, not without
interesting criticism of these. And Edmund Clarence Stedman's book on *The Nature and Elements of Poetry* (Boston
and New York, also London, 1892 ; a reprint, with additions,
of lectures which had appeared in the *Century* magazine during
that year) deals with higher matters than the technique of
verse. In the second Lecture, indeed, it is pointed out that
rhythm means vibration, and vibrations both cause and
express emotion, wherefore in passionate utterance speech
grows rhythmic (pp. 51–2). But the lecturer soon after
declines to " enter the workshop of the poet ", though,
speaking to a Baltimore audience, he praises the teacher who
there demonstrated laws of rhythm (pp. 61–2). For the most
part, however, like Mr. Watts-Dunton—whose article he calls
" the best modern essay upon the subject " (p. 25)—he deals
with the matter and not the form of poetry.

A book called *Orthometry*, by R. F. Brewer [2] (London, 1893),
is a substantial compilation on old lines, adding little or
nothing novel. Regularity of accentuation is pronounced the
differentia of verse (p. 1), but quantity is recognised (p. 22),
and a pause is allowed " rarely " to take the place of a syllable
(p. 143). Trisyllabic feet in which vowels come together are
said to be made dissyllables by a " nice ear " (p. 121) ; whence

---

[1] Other papers by this writer (not seen by me) are mentioned in
Appendix B.
[2] This is a reissue, greatly enlarged, of *A Manual of English Prosody*,
by Robert Frederick Brewer, B.A. (12mo, Longmans, 1869), in which
its view of verse was already defined.

the following line is practically taken to consist of nine
syllables thus divided (p. 145)—

I | whŏse vāst | pĭtў ăl-|mŏst mākes | mĕ dīe.

The book contains a rhyming dictionary, and—what deserves
special mention here—the fullest bibliography yet published
in any English treatise on metre (pp. 280–96). Some entries
in it need explanation. " Okell " is probably a misprint for
Odell. " Haslewood " must be the editor of Puttenham's and
other *Ancient Critical Essays*, who did not himself write on
metre. " Trussler " and " Longmuir " merely edited rhyming
dictionaries. If " Bain " means Prof. Bain of Aberdeen, I
know nothing of consequence on metre by him ; in one book
he has a chapter on " The definition of poetry ", but declines
to go into questions about metre. Why should " Canon
Daniel's Grammar " [1881] be mentioned more than a score
of others which have the usual Section on Prosody ? Any
attempt at a list of prosodists, however, is welcome in the
almost total dearth of such ; this list is later and fuller than
that of Crowe [*ante*, 1827], and there is hardly another
between.

It would be hopeless to keep count of articles and reviews
in the daily or weekly press, but I may mention that during
some ten years from 1893 onward the *Literary World* (London),
then a weekly journal, contained a succession of papers
dealing with the rhythmical structure of verse, explaining
double and treble beats and freedom of " syllabism " within
these beats, and laying much stress on " relative accentuation "
as a key to syllabic cadence. References to these will be found
in that Journal's issues for June 5 and 26, 1903. Their
writer seems to have been unaware that any prosodist except
Ruskin had anticipated any part of his view—which shows
that a survey like the present one may have its uses. A book
or pamphlet based on these papers would be a desirable
addition to prosodic literature, for there is fresh work in them,
though I cannot accept all their conclusions in matters of
detail. The writer, however, would do well to acquaint himself with what has been accomplished by predecessors along
the same lines.

A singularly interesting paper on " Rhythm ", by Thaddeus
L. Bolton, appeared in *The American Journal of Psychology*

for January, 1894 (pp. 145–238).[1] Some thirty pages at first sketch the physiological basis and historical development of rhythm. Statements not in themselves novel combine here to fresh result. With Lanier's view of primary and secondary rhythm (p. 157) is linked a Guestian theory of syllabic groups (p. 158), while feet are also recognised, and assumed to be separated by pauses (p. 173). It is stated that " the two-rhythm was apparently the prevailing rhythm in the history of our language " (p. 160) ; but by ' two-rhythm ' is apparently meant, here, merely a grouping into couples. " Poetry has never lost the time-element entirely " (p. 169) ; " the simplest unit of English poetry is the time between two accents, . . . and this must be constant " (p. 172). The emotional effect of rhythmic utterance, its origin in and production of a " trance " condition, are ably explained (pp. 163, 165, 171). The attempts by Lanier, Corson, and Poe to " construct philosophies of English verse " are shortly noticed (pp. 174–6), disagreement being intimated with Corson's view that " feeling unifies, intellect analyses ". The bulk of this paper, however, is taken up neither with theory nor criticism, but with a record of experiments ; and this gives it great value. Observation was applied to determine " what the mind did with a series of simple auditory impressions in which there was absolutely no change of intensity, pitch, quality, or time-interval ", and then how it treated " regular variations with respect to the intensity or time-interval of the sounds in this series " (p. 178).[2] The results are exceedingly interesting. Absolutely uniform sounds were mentally arranged in groups. The net result of a long series of experiments with varied intensity (pp. 186–228) was to show that increased force suggested a fictitious idea of prolongation ; while conversely, as appears from the shorter record of experiments with varied time-interval (pp. 228–34), prolongation suggested fictitious increase of force. An accented sound tended to come first in a group, a longer sound last ; " if the recurrent difference is one of duration, the longest impression comes last " (p. 232). Curiously enough,

---

[1] *Cf.* also pp. 310 and 488 for some additional memoranda.
[2] Details cannot be given here. The sounds were *clicks*, produced by a machine, and as far as possible the auditors were kept in ignorance as to what results were observed or expected.

" a change from a 3-group to a 4-group gave rise to a feeling of slower pace " (p. 236) ; while a succession of changes from 2–groups to 3–groups, or *vice versa*, produced " a very disagreeable feeling " (p. 237). These facts have obvious bearings on metre. The writer holds they prove that " the most common foot in modern poetry is accented on the last syllable " (p. 234). Might it not be safer to say that when we attend mainly to stresses we incline to make these begin feet, but to terminate them when we attend mainly to time ; that both methods are legitimate, but the latter preferable (unless otherwise shown invalid) because in our verse temporal relations are more important than stress-values, though both are essential ? Some further applications of the " general principle " to verse are suggested on pp. 237–8, tending perhaps to inculcate a too rigid theory of verse-structure, rather akin to Poe's. But the whole discussion is fruitful in a great many ways, and the paper must be considered a ' document ' by all interested in verse-rhythm.[1]

The *Contemporary Review* for November, 1894, contained an article by William Larminie on " The development of English metres " (Vol. 66, pp. 717–36). This seems written with two purposes—to inculcate regard for quantity, and to advocate a form of *vers libre*. The first part, with its " fourfold " division of quantity (p. 720), pushes criticism too far. It is quite true that Browning was apt to let stress override quantity (*ibid.*, *cf.* p. 736, *note*) ; but when it comes to rewriting cadences of Poe, Swinburne, and Tennyson (pp. 722–5), one should remember that smoothness is not the sole virtue for a poet. Quantity is perhaps made too much a fetish ; but recognition of it is so rare in our prosodies that one welcomes even an exaggerated respect for it. Why should Mangan's lines be praised above others, when they contain quantities like those marked in the following ?—

> Shall I hear the thrŭsh sing from his lair . . .
> No more sēe the bēe bearing honey.

As for the proposal to substitute Biblical or Ossianic prose for verse, on the ground that " the burden of technique . . . has become too heavy to be borne " (p. 727), poets must be left

---

[1] Those so interested should refer to Hall and Jastrow [*ante*, 1886], to Hurst and MᶜKay [1899], and to a group of writers named together in the Postscript to this Chapter.

to consider it.   Certainly, if it is adopted, alliteration and
assonance will have to play a larger part even than they now
do in our verse.   National partiality, one suspects (as *in re*
Mangan), has something to do with the praise of assonance
(pp. 731–5) and the question (p. 736) " Can the august poetry
of England condescend to take a hint from the Cinderella
of the West ? "   It should not be above doing so, and it would
have to learn no unfamiliar lesson ;   meantime, need we
despair of old forms ?   Some of Mr. Larminie's statements
seem rather questionable, *e.g.* " Italian has no quantity, but
it has stress ;   French has neither " (p. 726).   Nor will all
agree with him about " the unnecessary burden of rhyme "
(*ibid.*).   But as a whole the paper is fresh and interesting,
provoking thought even when it does not convince.

In *English Poetry from Blake to Browning,* by William
Macneile Dixon, Trin. Coll. Dublin (1894), the first Chapter
discourses on " Poetry and its relation to life ", making
rhythm the essential quality of verse, and stating—almost
in the very words of Mr. Stedman [*ante,* 1892]—that " rhythm
represents emotion, and it gives rise to emotion " (p. 9).   I
do not, however, find any attempt made to determine the
precise nature of this rhythm.

A paper in *Mind* for 1895 (New Series, Vol. IV, pp. 28–35)
on " The difference of time and rhythm in music ", by
Dr. R[ichard] Wallaschek, might seem beyond our province,
but will be found to contain apposite matter.   It insists that
our sense of ' time ' is wholly subjective, speaks of " the merely
mental character of time-division in music ", even says that
" in spite of an accentuation which is likely to suggest triple
time, the observer may still follow duple time in his thought "
(p. 29).   There is, according to this writer, only one musical
time, *viz.* " evenness " ($\frac{5}{4}$ and $\frac{7}{8}$ time being designedly irregular :
p. 30).   " There is no ' time ' in the heart-beats themselves,"
though from Aristotle onward men have said that there is
(p. 32) ;   bird's songs have *tempo* but not *Takt,* the latter
denoting our perception of the motion (p. 34).   It will be
seen how this affects the question of relation between spoken
words and rhythmical periods.[1]

---

[1] Readers who wish to pursue this subject farther are referred by
Dr. Wallaschek to his book on *Primitive Music* (Longmans, 1893),
which contains " an inquiry into the origin and development of the

In 1895 was published the first volume of Dr. Courthope's great *History of English Poetry*. Chroniclers of our literary annals seem rarely to find time for prosodic study ; as with Warton's and other histories, scant room is given to metre. The denial of any link of connection between Anglo-Saxon verse and Chaucer (p. 4) will stagger many. The latter half of Chap. II (pp. 70–8) sketches the change from quantitative to accentual verse, and suggests that our heroic metre derives from iambic trimeter as modified by French poets. Vol. II (1897) mentions briefly Surrey's reforms in verse (p. 92), and in Chap. X deals cursorily with the Elizabethan quantitative attempt, Fraunce being singled out for praise. It is not, I think, till Vol. III (published in 1903), in the first half of Chap. XIV, treating of Milton's verse, that questions of scansion are referred to ; and then—besides a reference to Mr. Bridges—we merely have a contrast drawn between the views of Guest and Prof. Mayor, preference being given to the latter. It seems clear that, with so many large matters to consider, the historian has not found time to study the philosophy of verse, or to read our principal prosodists.[1]

During 1896 I find for mention only an anonymous tract of twenty-four pages, reprinted from the *Manchester Quarterly Review*, and understood to be by Mr. H. D. Bateson.[2] It consists of two parts, the first an " Introduction to the study of English rhythms ", the second a discussion of the metre of *Christabel*. Both are very slight, and raise more questions than they solve ; the general tendency is to rely on accent, coupled with caesural pause (pp. 7–8). " Isochronous divisions of accents " are said to be " familiar to the English ear " (p. 12). A distinction between common and triple rhythm is suggested (p. 2), and elasticity of structure highly praised, while yet the writer tries to state " limits within which the variation of the metre is confined " (p. 21).

The closing years of the Century saw pamphlets, magazine

music, songs, instruments, dances, and pantomimes of savage tribes . . . with musical examples ".

[1] *Life in Poetry : Law in Taste* (Macmillan, 1901), by the same author, refers in the second Lecture of Part II to " Poetical expression ", discussing the necessity of metrical form. An earlier volume, *The Liberal Movement of English Literature* (1885), hardly touches prosody.

[2] This has since been separately published (1904), without alteration except by a preface prefixed and a short list of prosodians added.

articles, and newspaper correspondence about metre in considerable profusion, among them some efforts of my own. As a whole, these served chiefly to show how uncertain were most people's ideas about English prosody. Not staying to enumerate these, I pass to more outstanding contributions. It will be borne in mind that, also, some first or second editions of books already mentioned came out during these years. Prosody was to a certain extent ' in the air ' at this time, and in the air it rather tended to remain, seldom touching solid earth. Yet, as will be seen, some publications had importance.

New Essays towards a Critical Method, by John Mackinnon Robertson (London and New York, 1897), contains an Appendix on " accent, quantity, and feet " which shows thought and wide reading. It evidently began as a defence and eulogium of Poe's " Rationale ", and too much adopts his view. For want of any clear distinction between stress and quantity, the first three Sections—dealing with Classic verse, the Foster-Gally controversy, and accent generally—leave us pretty much where they found us. And when the writer passes to modern verse, he seems at first to adopt Poe's fatal premiss " there is no time-unit " (p. 361), and legitimately to conclude that " prosodical method . . . is essentially incapable of reduction to scientific bases " (p. 355). But foot-notes added later show that reading Lanier's book has modified this view. He indeed defends Poe against Lanier, and successfully criticises the latter on particular points (pp. 355, 364, *notes* beginning on) ; but the conception of rhythm as a series of sounds and silences, which he mistakenly believes Lanier the first to state clearly (p. 362, *note*), has evidently impressed him. I feel sure that a critic so able as Mr. Robertson will come increasingly to lay weight on this side of the balance. Unless we realise that verse is a stringing of words to time, and that this may be accomplished by divers methods, varying with varying speech-habits, prosody cannot be sound. Mr. Robertson had originally gone far in this direction ; he was aware of the " fluctuant relativity " of metre (p. 361), he knew that " time-space between syllables " was a factor of verse (p. 362) ; it needs but to give this due importance. There is much that is interesting in his fourth Section, dealing with our own verse, and still more in the fifth and last, which discusses French verse with ripe knowledge, disposing of some ancient crudities. I cannot, however, believe that Racine's line—

> Je ne le croirai point ?   Vain espoir qui me flatte !

" comes pretty near *Arma virumque cano* in total rhythm " (p. 374, *note*). Neither French nor Latin metre falls within the purview of my present work, but a remark like this seems to manifest settled confusion between two different things ; which confusion mars the effect of much that is otherwise admirable. One may hope in future editions to find it replaced by that clearer view to which the author's judgement already inclines.

A small book of much learning is that on *The Foreign Sources of English Versification, with special reference to the so-called iambic lines of eight or ten syllables,* by Charlton M[inor] Lewis (Halle, 1898).[1] Building on German authorities, the author in five of his six Chapters traces the progress of metre from primitive forms, through Classical verse, to our own day. Only in the sixth and last does he reach English verse ; indeed, only in the last Section of it (p. 99 *seq.*) does he discuss its structure, treating of " the syllabic principle in modern English verse ". It might suffice to quote his pronouncement : " Our verse is of a very complex constitution, and any description based upon feet or accents alone, or on both together, is not adequate to cover all the phenomena " (p. 103). With this I heartily agree, but wonder if our meaning is the same. For, speaking (p. 102) of a line in Shelley's *Cenci*—

> The house-dog moans, and the beams crack ; no more—

he says that the first words would be pronounced in precisely the same way if they occurred in a line of 4-foot *Christabel* metre, *e.g.*—

> The house-dog moans, and the beams are cracked.

Here I must differ. The essential difference between the two metres lies in this, that the words are adjusted to a slightly different rhythm in each case ; and it is precisely this process of *adjustment* which has to be reckoned with in addition to

---

[1] For the same author's *Principles of English Verse* see the Postscript to this Chapter under date 1906.

prose feet and accents. This may seem a small matter, but
it is one of vital importance ; for it is this element, apt to
be ignored by the scholar in his study, which constitutes the
life of our verse.[1] Coming to details, it is hardly correct to
say that no 9-syllable heroic line has been written since
Elizabethan days ; Keats has a famous one (with redundant
final syllable), and one or two others exist. I doubt if Milton
wrote " Belus or Serāpis " ; in any case, better instances
of ' treble initial inversion ' can be found than either that or
" How the lit lake shines, a . . ." (pp. 99–100). Shelley, for
instance, has the line—

> Harmonizing silence without a sound ;

and Mr. Watts-Dunton has—

> Water, water ! Blessed be God, he says.

When points like these, however, are the only ones to mention,
criticism might almost as well be silent ; and this last Chapter
seems on the whole as judicious as its predecessors are erudite
and informing.

Laborious study is also shown in a treatise on *Word-stress
in English*, dealing with " the accentuation of words in
Middle-English as compared with the stress in Old and Modern
English ", by George J. Tamson (Halle, 1898). Following
German models, Dr. Tamson collates examples from our
verse with admirable industry, but leaves general conclusions
to be drawn by others.

In 1898 was also published a pamphlet *On the Use of Classical
Metres in English*, by William Johnson Stone. I shall not
be suspected of favouring its attempt to revive quantitative
metre when I say that no more remarkable Essay had appeared
for years. The whole notion that Latin laws of quantity can
be transplanted into English seems to me absurd. The young
writer's historical knowledge was incomplete ; some of his
chief predecessors were unknown to him. His view of accent
was crude, and soon underwent modification, as appears in
the second edition,[2] printed (posthumously) along with the
1901 edition of *Milton's Prosody* [*ante*, 1887]. What made the

---

[1] I am glad to notice that, both as regards this point and as regards
that next mentioned above, the author has modified his statement in
The Principles of English Verse.

[2] Where the title becomes *Classical Metres in English Verse*.

Essay remarkable was its clear grasp of ' quantity'. At a time when few English writers recognised its existence, most prosodians subordinating it to or mixing it up with stress, Stone fastened intuitively on it as a fact. To this day critics stumble over his complete recognition of it ; they will not believe that he meant his verses to be read " with the natural accent unimpaired ". I regret that these verses do not appear in the revised edition. No doubt they had faults, but the paper seems incomplete without them. Reviewers were terribly puzzled by them ; even the best came to grief in scansion. Not one, that I saw, noticed the few occasional slips, of which one occurs in the line—

As the arrow-scattering goddess Artemis hunts on a hill-side.

To me, this shows the unreality of the whole attempt, but another explanation is obviously possible. Stone's rules I shall not discuss, but they showed true phonetic feeling ; the " doubled consonant fallacy", in particular, surely received its quietus from him. It is this sense of phonetic quantity, quite apart from the use he made of it, that I find altogether admirable. " Will. Stone " was a born prosodist, and his death at twenty-six was a loss to science as well as to his friends. His paper is sparklingly written, and entertains where it does not convince. In correspondence—I did not know him personally—he was fair and open-minded, ready to receive as well as give. The alterations introduced into his revised text show widening reach and deepening insight. Fundamental disagreement with his methods and aims should not blind any one to the ability with which they are planned and carried out.[1]

A view of verse as unique as Stone's, though in a different way, came from a teacher of long and high repute, Prof. James Wilson Bright of Baltimore. Readers in this country first noticed a condensed review in the *Athenaeum* (July 8, 1899) of a paper submitted by him to our Philological Society. This paper has apparently not been published, but its conclusions were doubtless those stated in the same writer's articles on " Proper names in Old English verse " (*Publications of the Modern Language Association of America* for 1899, Vol. XIV,

[1] Appendix A [1899] notes some quantitative lines by Mr. Stone's father.

No. 2, pp. 347–68), and " Concerning grammatical ictus in English verse" (see *An English Miscellany presented to Dr. Furnivall in honour of his 75th birthday*, Clarendon Press, 1901, pp. 23–33). Utilizing ideas furnished by Sievers and other grammarians of the German neo-philological school, Prof. Bright denies that ' inverted accents ' are either real inversions or parts of a trisyllabic foot, claiming that in such cases the usual force-accent is supplemented by a pitch-accent on the apparently unstressed syllable. He also rejects trisyllabic feet in strict heroic verse except after a pause, reducing them to dissyllables by synaeresis, syncope, *etc.* ; this is not mentioned in these articles, but in works by his pupils [see next paragraph]. " Unbroken continuity " of practice is said to exist " from Swinburne back to the *Beowulf* " (first paper, p. 357) ; by studying it we shall find " the true basis for the scansion of English verse " (second paper, p. 25). Such a thesis, maintained by so learned a critic, must indeed give us pause ; we seem back in the Eighteenth Century. I do not know what " essential laws of rhythm " (p. 362) require absolute uniformity of syllabic recurrence. As to " pitch-accent ", Prof. Bright would probably not make too absolute the distinction between that and " force-accent ", but would be content to say that pitch predominates in one case, force in the other. Even so, how shall his proposition be established ? Familiar instances like *rose-gardén* and *well-watér* prove nothing ; they admit of other explanations. Is it credible that in every case such as Milton's

> And tow'rd the gate *rolling* her bestial train

we have a specialized pronunciation—that metrical stress somehow falls on the second syllable of *rolling* ? Besides, Prof. Bright surely gives away this part of his case when he admits that ' inversion ' may occur in one foot, the first (p. 362). If in one foot, why not in others ? Why, particularly, not in the second foot, when it is obvious that Milton's ' double trochees ' imitated Italian models ? What grounds are there for making ' inversion ' possible only after a pause? The grammatical facts put forward by Prof. Bright are, I think, of great value in helping us to understand the phenomenon of ' hovering accent ', but do not justify the conclusions drawn from them. After reading carefully the Professor's two papers and some by his pupils I remain unable to see that his view of syllabic structure has been proved or even made probable.

Some pamphlets by pupils of Prof. Bright are mentioned in Appendix B. One of them, by a writer no longer living (George Dobbin Brown), tries to prove dissyllabic Milton's pronunciation of *Aegean* in the well-known phrase—

Of Lemnos, th' Aegean isle.

The fact that Milton himself spelt the word with a diphthong in the second as well as the first syllable seems fatal to this hypothesis. A vast amount of research is evidenced in these pamphlets, but their central position is always assumed, never established by argument.

In a class of its own stands a paper by Prof. W. P. Ker on " Analogies between English and Spanish verse (Arte Mayor) ", dated December, 1898, but printed in the Philological Society's *Transactions* for 1899–1901, Part I, pp. 113–28. Favourers of ' amphibrachic ' verse will like to know that Prof. Ker gives the structure of the lines he is considering, double feet being separated by caesura, thus [I correct an obvious misprint]—

∪ <u>∕</u> ∪ ∪ <u>∕</u> ∪ | ∪ <u>∕</u> ∪ ∪ <u>∕</u> ∪ (p. 114).

Much useful information about the origin of pure triple-time English verse is given in this paper, with appropriate quotations. A significant sentence may be noted. " The triple time of common dance tunes, with periods of eight bars, was found congenial to verse, and was allowed to shape the prosody of verse " (p. 124).

Experimental research into rhythmical facts found expression in an article on " Time-relations of poetical metres ", by A. S. Hurst and John M⁰Kay, which appeared in *University of Toronto Studies* for 1889 [*cf.* Appendix B]. Observations conducted by tapping in connection with inaudible scansion (to avoid vocal distracting elements) produced some curious results. Dactyl and trochee were found of shorter duration than anapaest and iamb (p. 66) ; the rhythms of dactylic and anapaestic metre revealed themselves as different (pp. 70–1). In amphibrachic metre, there was " a tendency . . . to speak the accented syllables a little shorter than the others " (p. 65). The writers' general conclusion is that accent is not the sole regulator of our metre (p. 68). As their methods and results have not escaped challenge, further consideration of them may be reserved for the Postscript to this Chapter, but their paper well repays perusal.[1]

A book of prodigious importance for students was and is Professors Gayley and Scott's *Introduction to the Methods and Materials of Literary Criticism* (Boston, U.S.A., 1899). Into small compass is packed an amazing mass of information, critical and bibliographical, on verse as well as on wider matters of literary interest. While Chapter VII, on " The principles of versification ", naturally contains most that is relevant for us, other Chapters should not be neglected, and will not be by any one who even glances at them. This is a book which the student should " sell his bed " to buy ; it is simply invaluable to every literary worker.[2] Messrs. C. M. Gayley and F. N. Scott, who have here laid us under so deep a debt, are also known by independent publications. Among other things may be mentioned Prof. Gayley's *Classic Myths in English Literature* (Boston, 1893), which contains some ' hexameter' translations by the author ; and his *Representative English Comedies* (Macmillan, 1903), in which there is an appendix on Greene's prosody. For two striking papers by Prof. Scott, see the Postscript to this Chapter.

One or two minor publications, later than the foregoing, remain for mention. *A Note on the Scansion of the Pentameter and its Use in English Poetry* (1900), by F. K. Harford, is sufficiently characterized in my Bibliography, but should be read by any one to whom its contention is novel. The second of two papers in the *Cambridge Review* (March 1, 1900) " On English Hexameter Verse ", by Edward Carpenter, has some thoughtful remarks on the possibilities of this metre, with specimen lines. Among Essays not treating directly of structure is one in *Longman's Magazine* for December, 1900, on " Rhyme ", by Frank Ritchie, which pleasantly puts together a good deal of information. This might fitly close the Century, so far as date is concerned, but two books of larger scope have still to be noticed.

---

[1] Two papers by Dr. Scripture, occupying Vol. VII (1899) of *Studies from the Yale Psychological Laboratory* (of which he is director), deal only with elocutional matters. Important work by him, however, will be mentioned in the Postscript to this Chapter. For further details see Appendix B.

[2] In a work of such magnitude, a few mis-references are inevitable. I have noted one or two only, but would suggest that any found should be reported to the authors, as a small acknowledgement of great obligation.

My last entry for 1900 is one which doubtfully comes within a survey limited to native writers discussing their own prosody ; but since Messrs. van Dam and Stoffel's *William Shakespeare : Prosody and Text* is written in English and published in England it can hardly be omitted, and with it may be named a later work by the same authors, *Chapters on English Printing, Prosody, and Pronunciation* (1550–1700), published at Heidelberg (1902). In these books a gage of defiance is thrown down before our chief critics, the former one asserting that " no editor has up to now thought it worth his while to make a full and close study of Elizabethan prosody " (p. 428) ; while the latter wages unflinching war against any " extra syllable " in heroic verse as quoted by scansionists hitherto, without actually denying the possibility of such a syllable (p. 112). It is a pretty quarrel, which we can leave to those concerned ; Prof. Churton Collins, as will be noted in the following Postscript, was not slow to reply. Us it does not directly concern, since we deal with modern English ; trisyllabic feet are undoubtedly used by modern poets, whatever Chaucer or Shakespeare did. The " burden of proof ", however (p. 113), it seems to me, rests with those who assert a difference between Elizabethan and Victorian verse in this respect. And personally I should query this initial statement in the former book : " The rhythmical arrangement of syllables is the sole essential principle that determines the outward character of poetry as compared with prose " (p. 3). Unless " arrangement " here covers much more than the syllables themselves, this statement is seriously defective ; its prosody is unreal, a concoction of the laboratory. The authors' main thesis is defended with determination, and cannot be lightly set aside. Taken along with Prof. Bright's view, it shows how little certitude, how little finality, has been reached by prosodic study. Here is a cardinal point on which contradictory opinions still prevail. At the end of the Nineteenth Century, people were still asking whether a bar of verse may—or, at least, for several Centuries did—contain now two and now three syllables. We may think that the question answers itself ; but such is not the belief of all experts. The very foundations of English prosody are still in doubt. Its " essential principle " cannot be said to have been placed beyond question.

POSTSCRIPT

WITH the Century I originally meant to stop. But the considerable number of important publications which had come out since suggested carrying the record down to date, and seemed to argue increased attention being given to prosody. Some of these have been already mentioned, but others await remark, while still more recent volumes may swell this Postscript to the size of a Chapter. A briefly summarizing conclusion also was thought desirable.

Prof. Gummere must lead the way. *The Beginnings of Poetry* (Macmillan, 1901) is a weighty work, gathering together the results of long research into " the rise of poetry as a social institution " (Preface). Its first two Chapters discuss various theories about the origin of verse, from the " sexual cry " to the tribal dance ; the second Chapter, particularly, traces with infinite learning all accounts and explanations of primitive metre, the " latest word of science " being sought in Meumann (p. 81). The writer's own view is fully given. Verse is " rhythmic speech, with mainly emotional origin " . . . " By *rhythmic* must be understood a regular recurrence which clearly sets off such speech from the speech of prose " (p. 30). " All writers on poetry take rhythm for granted until some one asks why it is necessary ; " then, after discussion, " a respectable minority (but still a minority) " holds it nonessential (p. 31). Prof. Gummere is not one of that minority. As a contribution to the philosophy of verse this book ranks high ; but it is a book for scholars rather than the general public. The ordinary student will be content to let specialists discuss the matters of which it treats, and will still use the author's *Handbook* [*ante*, 1885] for immediate necessities. And our survey, confined to practical issues, must dismiss this work with short notice but sincere praise. It were easy to quote pages of interesting matter, but they would not advance our search. The book is beyond all else a storehouse of information and thought on its particular subject.

In 1901 was also published *The Musical Basis of Verse*, by Julia P. Dabney. As the title indicates, this deals wholly with the rhythmical aspect of verse-structure, looks to Lanier as sole precursor, and credits him with being first to use time-scansion (Preface, p. viii). It does not, however, follow him slavishly, but rejects his view of 3-beat rhythm, and his accentuation of feet on other than the first syllable (*ibid.*). Musical methods are adopted wholesale, accent always beginning the "bar", and metre on its technical side being made matter of *vibration* (p. 17); differences are recognised between music and verse (pp. 24, 26–7), but they are differences only of degree. In the main, I need hardly say, this commends itself as a right view, if less altogether novel than the writer supposes; but it is urged with too unquestioning faith. Nothing which seems to conflict with it can be good. Measuring from accent to accent, and drawing no distinction between rhythm-accent and word-accent,[1] the author postulates uniform structure, and condemns all departure from this. "It is bad writing to put upon the accented beat of the measure any weak monosyllable" (p. 32); yet our best poets do it. "Wrenched accent" is "inadmissible" (*ibid., note*); they think otherwise. "If we adopt direct attack [*i.e.* verse without 'anacrusis'], direct attack must be uniformly preserved" (p. 48); Milton's *L'Allegro* and *Il Penseroso* contradict this. Historical knowledge is not this author's strong point, nor has she studied comparative metre. She is not even aware that ancient hexameter moved to common time, but identifies it with our triple-time metre (pp. 63, 181, *etc.*). J. A. Symonds and Prof. Mahaffy are her authorities for ancient times, Mr. Gosse and others for modern. But within its own limits the book is excellent. Insistence on *movement* as a line's chief feature shows true insight. The distinction between 2-beat and 3-beat rhythm [4-beat being apparently not recognised] (p. 30) is practical, and avoids the frequent fallacy by which a trisyllabic foot is supposed to imply triple time. Indeed, some scansions will surprise in an opposite direction, as when Coleridge's—

'Tis the middle of night by the castle clock,

is pronounced to be in 2-beat rhythm (p. 42), and also Shakespeare's—

Come away, come away, Death (p. 45);

---

[1] This distinction she positively rejects (p. 58), declaring that "syncopation in verse is not conceivable" (p. 31, *note*).

while the assertion (p. 50) that Pippa's song—

Overhead the tree-tops meet,

is " really in 3-beat rhythm " seems hazardous. Differences over such matters, however, must be expected ; principle is the great thing, and that is embodied in the words, " The 2-beat and the 3-beat rhythm are as antipodal and as distinct from each other as oil and water " (p. 53). I see little use in crowding pages with rows of crotchets and quavers ; the question arises—Do these represent syllables, or only beats ? My belief is that they represent the latter, and that identification with syllables is misleading. Still, musical notation teaches the rudiments of rhythm, and so far this book is helpful. Its second and third Chapters are the most distinctive ; their weak side appears in such statements as that Scott took his four-foot verse from Wordsworth (p. 70) and that Byron was " a master of technique " (p. 85), their strength in descriptions like that of the " bounding swiftness " of most 3-beat rhythm (p. 76). The Chapters which follow are interesting in themselves, but add little to previous knowledge. Unequal as the book is, and even dangerous sometimes as a guide, it is refreshing through its whole-hearted devotion to rhythm. *Pause* is of course recognised as integral, but is used with comparative rareness. There is very much apposite quotation from elder and recent writers.

The *Modern Language Quarterly* (London) for December, 1901, and April, 1902, contained two papers by R. B. McKerrow on " The Use of so-called Classical Metres in Elizabethan Verse ". Mr. McKerrow, to whom I am indebted for several pieces of information (*cf.* Appendix A), is a distinguished student of the period referred to, and these papers give an independent scholarly account of that curious eddy in the river of our poetry. I do not always agree with their phonetic judgements, and think injustice is done to Stone in this connection ; but these are points not worth dwelling on here. I trust these papers will be published separately some day, or rather will form the basis of a more detailed and exhaustive account of the Elizabethan quantitative experiment. Such an account is still a desideratum.

Experimental scrutiny of our verse-measures produced some striking results during 1901 and 1902. To the former year belong papers by Messrs. Wallin, Triplett and Sanford, and Squire, particulars of which will be found in Appendix B ; to the latter belongs *Elements of Experimental Phonetics*, by Edward Wheeler Scripture (New York and London, 1902). This latter work sums up results obtained by investigators, including the above-named, to whom its author was guide and friend. Dogmatic theorists about rhythm—particularly those who approach it from the musical side—would do well to study these results. They will find that things which they have been accustomed to regard as objective facts are relegated to the domain of subjective impressions. Dr. Scripture distinguishes between physical and mental constituents of accent, and between auditory and motor factors of the same, the most characteristic property of auditory accent being " impressiveness " (p. 506). This bears out the view of accent suggested provisionally in the earlier pages of our study. He does not find it sufficient to identify accent with force. Where Bolton heard only greater intensity in the ' tick-*tick* ' of a clock, he claims to find pitch and quality slightly altered too ; we seem to hear it say ' tick-*tock* ' (p. 522). And he recognises but three " necessary properties " of a tone—pitch, duration, and intensity ; quality, *timbre*, or tone-colour is one of the extra properties which " may be added " (p. 89). It is very interesting to find the latest belief of science coming back to agreement with earlier ones ; this tripartite division is as old as the Latin grammarians, perhaps as Aristotle. Dr. Scripture's large book is full of suggestive ideas ; space allows me to cite only these few. His governing notion is division into " centroids ", that is, groups not unlike the " monopressures " of an earlier critic [*ante*, 1888], but considered as resulting from other elements in addition to *force*. This conception naturally reappears in the work of his pupils or co-workers, and will be much canvassed. I doubt myself if it is a complete representation of the facts. But the observations and conclusions of this writer are of the highest importance.

The researches on which his book is based were conducted mainly by *tapping*. There is an evident danger in this method, that the act of tapping may influence mental or audible recitation, creating fictitious regularity. Of this the observers were aware ; one couple remark, with much acuteness if some *naïveté*, that their method would be " fatal to poetry ". Of

course no great verse is a matter merely of temporal rhythm ;
other elements differentiate " Propria quae maribus " from
a line of the *Aeneid*. Nursery rhymes, with their bold rhythmical effects, are well suited to this method, and this pair of
writers apply it mainly to them, recording their " auditory
forms ". Mr. Wallin got some amusing results from setting
people to read a crabbed passage from Browning which was
new to them ; the difference was very marked when they read
it as prose and after discovery that it was verse. Mr. Squire's
is the longest and most philosophical of the three papers. He
experimented first with German then with American children,
and found that the former showed more tendency to " qualitative accent " and greater intervals of pitch. Little is said in
any of the papers about the relation of verse to musical time.[1]
Messrs. Triplett and Sanford scan by stresses ; to them, " peas
[*sic*] porridge hot " is identical with " the short meter stanza
of the hymn-book " (p. 365). They find, however, that " there
is a rough equality in the figures for the intervals, except
where they are lengthened by pauses ", or made irregular to
bring out the meaning (pp. 375–6, *cf.* 379). Mr. Wallin holds
that prose is measured as well as verse, and that " centroid
intervals " are not uniform (p. 113 *seq.*) ; yet " no recurrence
of centroids can be rhythmized unless the length and regularity of the intervals fulfil the requirements of the rhythmical
time-sense ", which " may differ slightly for individuals "
(p. 128). To Mr. Squire, on the other hand, " temporalness,
in its connotation of regular succession, is the basal principle
of rhythm," and " temporal changes can alone (intensity and
pitch remaining constant) produce a pleasing rhythm "[2]
(p. 541). All the writers agree that there is much self-decep-
tion ; Mr. Squire thinks that " the objectively long may
appear shorter and unaccented " (*ibid.*), and noted that
" some individuals were inclined to hear the high as the more
intense, others the low " (p. 549). In opposition to Messrs.
Hurst and McKay [*ante*, 1899], Messrs. Triplett and Sanford
found iambs quicker than trochees (p. 380), and Mr. Squire

---

[1] They agree in making the 2-group naturally precede the 3-group ;
Mr. Squire alone identifies these with Lanier's 3-rhythm and 4-rhythm
respectively. He speculates on the probable origin and development of
these groups (pp. 535, 540).

[2] So can also " intensive co-ordination " by itself (*ibid.*).

found it impossible to get his children to group by amphibrachs at all. The differences of opinion among these papers enhance one's feelings of their good faith and vivid reality ; they read like what they are, transcripts from life. I regret that we have as yet nothing of a similar character to show in this country.

Bold departure from tradition characterizes *An Introduction to the Scientific Study of English Poetry*, by Mark H. Liddell (New York, 1902), in which it is maintained that " accent is not the determining element of English verse-forms " (p. 22). " Thought-groups," not temporal periods, are made the units of verse in our language, and " rhythm-waves " are considered without reference to their duration. I do not think the writer was cognisant of the researches last mentioned ; he makes no reference to them, and seems to work on lines of his own. Realising the essential difference between Greek verse and ours (Book I, Chap. V, and *passim*), Prof. Liddell pushes this to a denial of quantitative relations in our metre. In simpler words, he ignores the fact that our syllables, too, are set to time after a fashion of their own. Through ignoring this, his able analysis fails to carry conviction as a complete account of the matter. The first half of his volume (Book I) deals with general questions, the second half (Book II) with English verse-structure more particularly. In the second Chapter of the former he makes his leading assumption (see especially p. 45 *seq.*), and I think the example on p. 47 may test its truth. He finds only " rhythmic prose " in the following [I alter one phrase to avoid bisecting a word]—

> Duncan is in his grave. After the fitful
> Fever of life he sleeps in peace. For fate
> Has done its very worst—nor steel, nor poison,
> Malice domestic, foreign levy, nothing
> Can touch him further.

I submit that this would pass anywhere for verse ; not good verse, but still verse ; and that this is so, not because we count the syllables, or because the printer has arranged them in lines, but because we relate them to equal time-periods. Shakespeare's music, his " rhythm-phrases ", and the rest, are superadded to this ; they beautify the verse, make all the difference between doggrel and poetry, but they do not create the structure. That depends on our perception of *time.*

Without that, even the best words are prose ; with it, even the weakest may be verse. Shakespeare himself cannot evade this law ; it is because he uses it so subtilely, so masterfully, that his verse is so wondrous. Here, if anywhere, is the " one factor " so often " overlooked in studies of Verse Form " (p. 85).

There is much that is valuable in this book, with much that invites criticism. Its introductory Chapter seems rather captious. Who, nowadays, makes poetry " supernatural ", or upholds Lindley Murray's scansion ? In Chapter II, ' inversion ' is supposed to occur only " after a pause ", " where the thought took a new turn " (p. 48) ; is this true of Shakespeare's—

> And yet dark night *strangles* the travelling lamp,

or of Shelley's line—

> And wild *roses*, and ivy serpentine,

or of many similar instances ? The analysis of speech-significance in this and succeeding Chapters may seem protracted, but is necessary for the writer's purpose, to demonstrate his " five rising waves of attention-stress " (p. 59)—a conception which, taken by itself, is surely no whit less mechanical than counting feet or syllables or accents. In the one place where, speaking of English verse, allusion is made to the element of time (pp. 171–3), this is identified with capacity for being set to music ; but the two things are quite different. On the other hand, the analysis of stress in Chapter XI is perspicacious, especially the distinction between a force and its result (p. 208) and the proof that accent can shorten sound (pp. 212–14). But what gives chief value to the book is its dissection of speech into " thought-moments ", " emotional pulses ", " waves of attention energy ", illustrated by painstaking analysis. I do not, indeed, accept the identification of these with " rhythm-waves " (p. 217), or believe that in itself a " grouping of thought-moments would be a rhythmic Verse Form " (p. 87). Still, we have here a fact of speech, for which room must be found in our theory. Comparing this book with that on *The Musical Basis of Verse* recently mentioned, we see how complicated is the problem. Miss Dabney and Prof. Liddell represent opposite wings of the prosodic army ;

the main line of advance, I think, is between their extremes, each of which has truth, but not the whole truth.

The Relation of the Rhythm of Poetry to that of the Spoken Language, by C. W. E. Miller (Baltimore, 1902), I have been unable to see. It will be noticed that in American literature ' poetry ' is, more frequently than with us, used for ' verse ', and ' verse ' for ' line ' ; both usages are hostile to clearness. Turning home, what have we to show in these years ? New editions of chief books [*cf.* Mayor and Bridges] provoked much newspaper reviewing ; but little solid teaching resulted. In an edition of *Milton's Lycidas*, by H. B. Cotterill (1902), Appendix I " On Rhythm in English Verse " gives a bright but sketchy view of verse regarded musically, and speaks of " counter movements of stress and length, like the cross-play of wavelets on an ocean roll " (p. 105). The " Ptolemaic " theories of Mr. Bridges are rejected, triple time is assumed for our ' iambic ' measure, and anapaestic retardation is invoked to explain every case of ' pyrrhic *plus* spondee '.[1] Mrs. Woods, on the other hand, in her Preface to *The Princess of Hanover* (1902), adopts Mr. Bridges' view of verse, and adds little of her own. Defending " nine-syllabled lines ", she does not tell us why these are not found in *Paradise Lost* ; defending Cockney rhymes, does not advert to Tennyson's repudiation of these. Rightly ridiculing " rhymes to the eye ", she with equal justice vindicates imperfect rhymes from wholesale condemnation, but might have added that many of them are conventional survivals of what once were perfect rhymes. It will be noted that this Preface is only the second piece of work by a woman-writer chronicled in this volume. Great advantage may be expected from women turning their attention to prosody ; they bring fresh minds, not dulled by traditional fallacies. They have already begun to discuss Latin metre ; surely English is worth their examination. Since Mrs. Browning can hardly be said to have entered the field, we may hail in Mrs. Woods our first native English woman-prosodist, and trust that her example will be largely followed.

Imaginations in the Dust, by L. H. Victory (1903), contained an " Essay on Elementary Metres ", based mainly on Ruskin, but short and practical. My own *Study of Metre*, in the same

---

[1] This author's translation of the *Odyssey* (1911) should not be overlooked.

year, attempted to popularize more ' actual ' views of verse-form. Prof. Mayor followed up his larger book with a *Handbook of Modern English Metre* (Cambridge, 1903), intended for educational use, which covers wider ground than his *Chapters*, going on to consider the aesthetic effect of particular metres and of individual words. Rhythm is still wholly a matter of syllables, scansions seem sometimes most questionable [*e.g.* the lines said to be " in the same metre " on p. 91], and there are one or two slips, such as thinking that Wordsworth never closed a sonnet with rhyming couplet (p. 147). The examples are good and up to date, but the method of analysis far from adequate. " Some remarks on the study of English verse," by Henry van Dyke, in the *Atlantic Monthly* for October of this same year, begin by asserting that " the science of English verse is still in its formative stage ", and rightly urge that it must be based on the practice of poets, yet do not get beyond counting by syllables and their stresses, these last being " structural factors ". But four papers by Ernest Newman, in the *Weekly Critical Review* (Paris) for the four weeks of September, 1903, discuss " The rationale of English verse-rhythm " in a manner far removed from ordinary journalism, and constitute a real study of the subject. Mr. Newman is evidently a musician, and pushes the musical view as far as it will go. In the last analysis, he is " left with the trochaic line alone as the skeleton upon which English verse is hung " ; in other words, nearly all our lines are in ⅜ rhythm, and what seems departure from it is usually but variation of it. This rhythm may be determined either by accent or quantity, or by " the two in coincidence " ; and all bars are equal to one another. I do not think this view gives the whole truth, or that it could withstand such experimental investigation as we have lately considered ; but he puts one side of the truth forcibly. The other side relates to that quantity, that syllabic residuum, which Mr. Newman would fain subordinate entirely to rhythm ; and to the possibility of maintaining a double time in our consciousness. The essayist's style is clear, his comments on other prosodists pertinent and pointed ; Lanier receives due credit. These papers should certainly be extricated from their obscure place of lodgement, and re-issued after consideration of the other works mentioned in this Postscript.

In 1904 appeared *English Verse* by Raymond Macdonald

Alden, a Professor in California, followed in 1909 by *An Introduction to Poetry* (both Holt & Co., New York), and minor publications. These two books are very valuable. The earlier one contains well-chosen examples, illustrating in Part I the nature, and in Part II the historical development, of our verse ; and a still more noteworthy Part III on " The time-element in English verse ", the excellence of which may be judged from two extracts. " The sounds of verse have constantly to effect a compromise between the typical rhythm to which they are set and the irregular stress- and time-variations of human speech " (p. 394). " The fundamental principle of verse is that it sets up a new order of progress which constantly conflicts with, yet without destroying, the order of progress of common prose speech " (p. 408). The *Introduction to Poetry* deals in its earlier portions with larger and more general questions, in its later with types of versification and the significance of rhyme ; but in its Chapter IV deals competently with the rhythm-foundation. Better teaching than these two volumes contain cannot easily be found, and in the later one the author departs a good deal from mere classification by stresses.[1]

In 1903 Mr. Bridges published his first quantitative poem, *Now in wintry delights* [Daniel Press, Oxford ; for others see Appendix A], which I name here only to mention the beautiful sample of phonetic script which it contains. In January, 1894, he contributed to the *Athenaeum* newspaper three articles headed " Miltonic elision ", maintaining that in real tri-syllabic feet " the extra (elided) syllable is always to be slightly pronounced " (p. 114, first column) ; his cogent and well illustrated argument in support of this should surely be conclusive. Prof. Churton Collins, in his *Studies in Shakespeare* (1904), condemns Messrs. van Dam and Stoffel's " amazing theories about Shakespeare's metrical system, and their still more amazing re-arrangements of his verse as prose " (p. 331), but himself opens the door to chaos by denying that laws of rhythm can be definitely formulated (p. 327). I do not understand what is conveyed by such scansions [or rather *pictures*] as

Ĭf ăftĕr ēvĕrў̆ tĕmpēst cōme sŭch cālms ;

---

[1] For a later article by this author, see the year 1914, *infra*.

and cannot admit that in

From Dis's waggon ; daffodils . . .

" the ear tells us that rhythmically there is no deficiency "
(pp. 329, 330). On such principles anything may be verse ;
meantime, the uncertainty of Shakespeare's text makes all
such discussion rather nugatory.

A book entitled *How to Write Verse*, by George J. H. Northcroft (1904), does me the honour to borrow my account of the
basis of English metre, especially in its fifth Chapter, without
further acknowledgement than a complimentary reference at
the end of that Chapter. It covers the whole field of verse-
making, and forms a useful introduction to that art. *Forms
of English Poetry*, by Charles F. Johnson, N.D. [1904], gives
a good summary of metrical types for young readers. *Feet*
are discussed on pp. 12–14, " equal time-beats " being held
fundamental ; " scanning is simply pronouncing the accents
at isochronous intervals." In his short Preface the author
remarks that " an ingenious physicist may at any time prove
that the acoustic basis of verse is something different from
what it has been supposed to be ", but that will not affect our
enjoyment of metre. A booklet *On Anglo-Saxon Versification
from the Standpoint of Modern-English Versification*, by Edwin
B. Setzler (Baltimore, 1904), hardly comes within our scope,
as it deals wholly with Old English verse, of whose syllabic
structure it makes a careful study. The author is not a disciple
of Prof. J. W. Bright [*ante*, 1899].

Late in 1904 was published a substantial pamphlet on *The
Basis of English Rhythm*, by Mr. William Thomson, of Glasgow.
I discussed it in a slighter pamphlet [1] which hardly did justice
to the author's wonderfully clear and elaborate system of
notation. Using either musical or numerical symbols in this
and later publications (for which see Appendix B), he depicts
chosen utterances with a subtle skill which I had not deemed

---

[1] *Metrical Rhythm* (1905). Some slips require correction. On p. 8,
line 20, " seven quavers " should be *six*. On p. 16 I assumed that
Milton's word " melancholy " was scanned like one of Mr. Gilbert's
four-syllable feet ; but they are four syllables in time of four, it is
four in time of three—this distinction I should not have overlooked.
On p. 23 Mr. Thomson says I overstate agreement between us as to
temporal equality ; this is due to his not recognising the distinction
between subjective and objective rhythm.

possible and have never seen equalled. If such a method had existed in Tennyson's time, he need not have complained that no one would know how to read " Boädicea ", and a faithful record of the poet's utterance might have been preserved for posterity. Whether such a record of even typical utterances can avail instead of ordinary prosody is another matter. Mr. Thomson claims " Rhythm " as his particular province and is somewhat intolerant of intruders on it. His tract entitled *Laws of Speech-Rhythm* contains twenty-four weighty pronouncements, whose exposition I understand occupies a volume now awaiting publication ; its early issue is certainly desirable. In that mental rhythm to which I and others conceive every line of English verse to be instinctively set he has no belief.

In June, 1904, and again in December, 1905, Prof. F. N. Scott of Michigan University [*cf. ante*, 1899] contributed two remarkable papers to *Modern Language Notes* (Baltimore). The earlier is on " The most fundamental differentia between poetry [not merely verse] and prose ", which he traces to a radical difference of impulse, that which produces prose being the desire of communication, that which produces poetry the desire to express feeling, separately or in communion with others. The later paper, on " The scansion of prose rhythm ", claims to find crescendoes and diminuendoes in prose speech which obey fixed laws, and which collectively he designates the " motative arc " (*nutation* and *motation* are his names for the rhythms of verse and prose respectively). He makes prose rhythm depend mainly on pitch, verse rhythm on " stress " [force] ; but surely goes too far when he says (p. 717) that " stress or energy " is " the principal element " of our metre. The " simple experiment " by which he seeks to demonstrate this introduces time as well as stress under the name " pauses ", and this other " element " is essential to its success. Both papers, however, deserve attentive reading.

The limits of my survey have not allowed me to mention any work by foreign writers, even the monumental *Englische Metrik* of Prof. Schipper [*cf. infra*, 1910], or the brilliant critiques of some younger French writers such as M. Paul Verrier. But they do not forbid my including a *brochure* by a compatriot, though written in French and (privately) printed abroad. This *Étude comparée de la versification française et de la versification anglaise, par* Thos. B. Rudmose-Brown (Grenoble, 1905), was reviewed in the *Athenaeum* of September 16, 1905, and contains a careful study of some writers previously unknown to me, particularly Fredrik Wulff. Mr. Rudmose-Brown has since become Professor of English Literature at Trinity College, Dublin, and has contributed criticisms of prosody to the pages of the *Modern Language Review* and elsewhere.

What is one to do when foreign writers present us with contributions in impeccable English ? This applies to M. Verrier and to M. Thomas of Lyons. The latter's study of Milton's prosody in *M.L.R.*, Vols. II and III, supports what I believe an impossible view, and mistakes the meaning of Milton's phrase " fit quantity of ˙syllables ", but is written in the purest English. M. Verrier's gigantic *Essai sur les principes de la métrique anglaise* (three large volumes, Paris, 1909-10) lies outside our province, but from his English papers (see Appendix B) it is easy to gather his views. Firmly convinced of isochronism, he makes rhythm the essential foundation of metre. Rightly stigmatizing the chaotic scansion of too many English prosodists, he himself sees no difference between heroic lines which begin with accented syllables and the nine-syllable lines in Tennyson's " Vision of Sin " ; and he insists on such scansions as " | suitor of | old | times ". Prof. Saintsbury's rather gratuitous cavil at his examples being the work of French readers is disposed of by the fact that several readers were English, including Madame Duclaux (*née* A. Mary F. Robinson). The *Métrique* is a storehouse of information, but M. Verrier cannot be allowed to rule out perfectly legitimate English lines as not complying with his theories.

In 1906 Mr. John Davidson appended to his *Holiday and Other Poems* a Note " On poetry ", in which he declares rhyme a " decadent " thing, though capable of being used for " crescive " work, and praises the " nude " beauty of blank verse—as if *Paradise Lost* were less richly clad than the *Essay on Man* ! A paper in *Macmillan's Magazine* for June on " Rhythm and rhyme ", by George Bourne, vindicates the place of temporal beat in verse, without touching disputed questions. But the metrical event of the year was the commencement of Prof. Saintsbury's great *History of English Prosody* (1906–10). This long-projected and long-expected work seems to have been planned as a history rather of our verse itself than of what critics have said about it ; the first volume carries the tale from the " Origins " down to Spenser. It would be idle to attempt to summarize the contents of these three substantial volumes. Their author's profound knowledge of his subject—his racy style, often dropping into delightful slang—his contemptuous dismissal of syllable-counters and (mere) accent-counters—his firm adherence to the great truth that " in English, by the grace of God and the Muses, the poetry makes the rules, not the rules the poetry " —these have universally met with the praise they deserve. No praise can be too high for the jewels to be found in this Golden Treasury, which (as I anticipated) has finally displaced Guest (*ante*, p. 148 *seq.*). And he has followed this up by an equally valuable *History of English Prose Rhythm* (1912) in one volume, and a *Manual of English Prosody* (1910) which gives the results of the larger work in succinct form. (For other books of his see Appendix B.) Yet I think most readers of his volumes will share my surprise at the resolute way in which their author declines to discuss the phenomena which he chronicles. All the questions which have interested us during this survey, and which we have seen battled over during two Centuries of inquiry, he puts aside as " previous questions ". A true Englishman, he confines himself to fact, and eschews philosophy (*cf.* Vol. I, p. 7, *note* ; the Introductory Chapter generally ; and *passim*). When he came to consider prosodical criticism, to traverse the ground we have traversed, it was surely incumbent on him to express opinions of some sort, to say on what foundation he conceives his doctrine of " equivalence " to rest. No such foundation is described. He talks of " long " and " short " syllables, without saying what they mean, and says he might as well have called them " abracadabra and abraxas ". His scansions are a glorious higgledy-piggledy of iambs and trochees, or dactyls and ana-paests, without any clue given as to how these can be inter-changeable. He not only does not know how " feet " are constituted, but he resolutely refuses to inquire. His really reckless use of the terms " long " and " short " with deliberate avoidance of their meaning leads him into terrible pitfalls

when he comes to deal with quantitative verse, as appears
from a significant misquotation (Vol. III, p. 417) of a line
already misquoted by Calverley. It is only too apparent that
" quantities " have no meaning to this prosodist. Matchless
as an historian of our verse, as an analyst he is not only naught
but wishes to be so. No adequate account of our verse-
structure is therefore to be found in these otherwise admirable
volumes.

It were ungracious to dwell on this deficiency. Rather let
attention be given to the many merits of the historical account
—to the excellent sketch of the beginnings of our verse—to
the description of how foreign influence brought in more
rigorous syllabification, yet never (despite grammarians)
conquered the native freedom of our poets, or ousted the
" blessed trisyllabic swing and swell "—to the painstaking
survey of our older poets which occupies Vol. II, and the
equally exhaustive and competent discussion of the verse of
our younger poets in Vol. III (but omitting his Chapter on
the " English Hexameter ")—and to numberless hints like
that one in which he shows how a slight change in a familiar
metre of Praed and others gave us the new music of " Dolores ".
If, on the other hand, it is desired to see how *not* to scan verse,
let the reader look at the treatment of " Phyllida flouts me "
(Vol. II, p. 336), of three passages from Dryden (*ibid.*, p. 373),
and of " Philip, the slighted suitor of old times " (Vol. III,
p. 418). With this wholly inadequate mention I must leave
Prof. Saintsbury's great work.

In 1906 appeared also *The Principles of English Verse*, by
Charlton M. Lewis [*cf. ante*, 1898]. This is a small but able
book, for " general readers " as well as scholars (*Preface*).
It has six chapters. Rhythm is " a recurrence of similar
phenomena at regular intervals of time " ; " regularity of
time-intervals is a *sine qua non* of rhythm " (p. 2 ; *cf.* p. 16
on the " ideal rhythmical scheme "). " Time," however, is
still identified with *tempo* (*e.g.* p. 15), and in the first Chapter
the rhythms of prose and verse are accounted equally regular,
neither perfectly so (p. 14 sums up this view). Much is said
about " conflict " (first mentioned on p. 16), held to be between
thought and expression. Metrical beat is assumed to create
" stress " of some sort (p. 25) ; the effect of a weak stress is
" as if a runner should put one foot in a hole and so fail to

touch ground. We can perhaps imagine him going on without breaking step " [I cannot ! He would certainly fall] (p. 21). " Inversions " in ' heroic ' lines cause irregularity " in the metre, not in the rhythm " (p. 27), and in these the poet " does not change the total number of syllables " (p. 30). [The term ' heroic ' is restricted to couplets, the other being styled " blank verse ", and both " pentameter ".] Yet the objection to nine-syllable lines is " purely a matter of convention " (p. 31). " Hovering accent " is discussed on pp. 35–8 ; Classic names of feet are admitted (pp. 39–44), with cheerful defiance of " system " (p. 44). This ends Chap. II. The remainder of the book is mainly practical, and should be useful. " Trochaic rhythm " is asserted to be less natural and agreeable than iambic (p. 104) ; the " rhythmical scheme " [identified with " average tempo "] of triple-time verse is pronounced to be slower than that of " iambics ", though the syllables of the former are more rapidly uttered than those of the latter (p. 111). [The former's " gallop " (p. 109 ; *cf.* 117), therefore, must be slower than an " iambic " march !] There is some candid criticism of Browning and Swinburne in Chap. V, where also the " little book " of R. Bridges is pronounced " utterly wrong in some of its fundamental principles " (p. 121). Like Gurney, the writer finds but four stresses in the line—

By the wáters of Bábylon we sat dówn and wépt (p. 119),

which, in my judgement, reduces it to prose. The last Chapter contains a wholesome protest against doctrinaire views about tone-colour.

In 1907 was begun the publication of *The Cambridge History of Literature*, the prosodical Chapters in which are the work of Prof. Saintsbury, and need not be further characterized. The same year produced my *English Metrists* (18*th and* 19*th Centuries*), of which this book is a redaction. A certain amount of discussion followed the appearance of both volumes, but I do not find anything in my notes requiring separate chronicle.

1908 was more fruitful. Prof. Saintsbury's second volume roused the usual reviews in the *Times*, the *Athenaeum*, and elsewhere. That autumn, too, a perfect epidemic of letters about metre broke out in the *Academy*, and was continued

into the next year, a New Zealand critic named Johannes
C. Andersen taking a prominent part ; who also wrote several
pamphlets, which I had hoped to see combined into a larger
work.[1]　Among separate publications was one on *Time in
English Verse Rhythm*, by an American experimenter, Dr.
Warner Brown (particulars in Appendix B).　His weighty
treatise is concerned only with spoken sounds, but recognises
clearly that the sensation of equal periodicity forms part of
the phenomena to be investigated, and in opposition to some
recent teachers lays down that " if the initial *and final* [my
italics] points of a sound are well defined, further details can
be dispensed with so far as the rhythm is concerned " (p. 18).
He is apt, however, to call stress a quantitative factor, and
even to talk of longer and shorter beats—as if beats could
have duration.　Into his actual experiments we need not
enter, but the general conclusion is that verse produces on
us the effect of a series of equal time-intervals (p. 76).　From
a later and slighter tract on *Temporal and Accentual Rhythm*
(1911), by the same author, giving his views more succinctly,
I quote the final sentence : " the time aspects are fundamental,
and the accentual features while necessary are not at the root
of the phenomena."

The various publications by Mr. Bridges on quantitative
verse inspired attempts by several writers, among whom may
be mentioned Mr. R. C. Trevelyan, who in his *Sisyphus* (1908)
and other poems introduced cunningly concealed " quantities " without notice to the unsuspecting reader.　The ordinary
Englishman is callous to such attempts, but may be reminded
why these efforts to imitate Classic verse are abortive.　It is
because speech-accents in Latin verse (of those in Greek verse
we know nothing) were unquestionably much lighter than ours,
while the succession of " quantities " had an importance
totally denied to our speech and verse.　Seeking to reproduce
in our verse the effect of theirs is therefore impossible and
harmful.　I may be allowed to refer to an unsigned article of
mine on " Accent and Quantity " in the *Academy* for 20th February, 1909, in which I tried to make this clear.

1909 was unproductive at home except in newspaper controversy, but 1910 had several things of interest besides

[1] My criticism of M. Thomas came out in the *Modern Language
Review* for October 1908 (Vol. IV).

discussions of Prof. Saintsbury's final volume. A painstaking scholar, too soon removed by death, Mr. E. P. Morton of Chicago, produced an inquiry into *The Technic of English non-dramatic Blank Verse*, which deals with much more than 'end-stopt' and 'comma-stopt' lines. Its first ninety pages discuss general questions, the remaining forty or so examine selected poets from Surrey to Swinburne. Dramatic requirements are said to "subordinate, or modify, or sometimes even destroy the verse pattern", and may cause Blank Verse to lose most of the things which make it unmistakeably verse (p. 64). The writer claims to be first in pointing out that trisyllabic feet in heroic metre differ from anapaests in " triple time measures " (p. 70),[1] and he recognises cases where logical and metrical accents do not coincide (p. 73). On the great question of fundamental time he is thoroughly sound. Continual slight divergence between syllables and time is repeatedly insisted on, and his most definite conclusion is that " in modern Blank Verse the contrast between stressed and un-stressed syllables has grown less sharp " (p. 88). Amusingly he avers that he has " never yet seen a page of verse scanned exactly as I should scan it ", which " common experience " shows the complexity of our metres (p. 73, foot-note). His chief other papers traced the history of the Spenserian stanza in our literature.

It may seem strange to cite here *Rhythm in English Prose*, by P. F. van Draat (see Appendix B), but the introductory pages have much about verse also, which repays reading, before one comes to the bountiful wealth of prose quotations, especially from recent writers. In excellent English he tells us that " our striving after rhythm is quite as natural . . . as breathing itself ", and that " almost all rhythmical movement is more or less emotional " (pp. 3 and 4). He shows well how rhythmical flow determines accentuation, though he goes too far when he says that we *never* get more than two unstressed syllables between stresses, and that in both prose and verse we must avoid a succession of three unstressed syllables. He naturally points out the predominance of two-syllable feet in our verse. Later on, it may be added, he defends the " split infinitive ", from the view-points of both theory and practice.

[1] I had myself made the same remark in my *Study of Metre* (1903), p. 115.

A difficulty again arises with regard to English translations of foreign writers, conspicuous instances of which are the *History of English Versification*, by Prof. Schipper (translated apparently by himself from his smaller *Grundriss*), and the *Short History* of the same by Prof. Kaluza of Königsberg, which appeared respectively in 1910 and 1911. I do not feel it necessary to dwell on these. They show Teutonic thoroughness, and perhaps little more need be said. Prof. Schipper's scansions are of the most wooden order, as when he thus accentuates Coleridge's line :

It ís an áncient márinér,

saying nothing of any difference between these stresses. Fully two-thirds of his book is occupied with the early stages of our literature. This last remark applies equally to Prof. Kaluza, only the last section of his book dealing with modern prosody, though this section is comparatively interesting and suggestive, quoting recent writers, and recognising different degrees of stress. His is distinctly the more up to date of the two books.

In 1911 was published *English Poesy*, by Dr. Winslow Hall, with a short preface by myself. This book essays the immensely difficult task of disentangling all the various threads that go to make up the fabric of our verse, while clinging closely to the fundamental principle of periodic rhythm. It is not for me to say how far the author has succeeded in his attempt. Readers will be prepared to find much subtle analysis, and they will not be disappointed. The book has no index and but a short table of contents, but a " glossarial index of technical terms " is appended.

The same year produced valuable articles on prosody in the *Edinburgh Review* for January and the *Quarterly Review* for July, the latter claiming that " so long as the mind hears the implied accents in their places " actual accents do not matter. Mr. Gosse's article on " Verse " came out in the *Encyclopaedia Britannica*, and gives a readable popular account of European verse-history. Prof. Kaluza's book mentioned previously rightly belongs to 1911. To redress this displacement, I here quote a sentence from a literary journal at the very end of 1910 : " The verse *is* the poem, as the paint is a picture ".

In 1911 was also published *A Study of Versification*, by Prof. Brander Matthews of Columbia University. The title correctly describes the book, which deals with forms of verse rather than structure, though there are some good remarks on rhythm generally on page 9. It is an interesting popular book on its subject, though it calls syllables " *long*, even though they may owe their value to other elements than mere duration of time " (p. 14), which is surely throwing dust in his readers' eyes. And, though on p. 4 he disclaims telling "how verse ought to be written", in his Chapter IV he demands that only perfect rhymes should be used, disagreeing here with all our recent great poets. Otherwise the book is readable and pleasant, and may well serve as the " simple textbook for beginners " which his Preface claims for it.

1912, besides reviews in the *Modern Language Review* and elsewhere of books lately published, and discussions in that magazine which were prolonged into subsequent years, protagonists being M. Verrier and Prof. Rudmose-Brown, saw appear in the *English Review* for January, March, June, and August four articles entitled " A new study of English poetry ", by Sir Henry Newbolt, since published in book form. Their subject being " poetry " and not verse, it is perhaps unreasonable to expect much about structure, yet I cannot help wondering why so distinguished a poet does not tell us why he writes verse, or why he thinks other people do so. The nearest approach to this is in the second article, but there he is led away by theories of " stress-rhythm ". He thought the then age was one of " rebuilding " (p. 299) ; how far has the presage been justified ? More illuminating, to my mind, was a paper in the June number of the same periodical in the previous year on " Form in poetry ", by Mr. John M. Robertson, but his statements must not be always taken for gospel. When he asserts absolute metrical novelty for the opening lines of *Maud* (p. 380), and when he postdates *Enoch Arden* to *The Princess* and *In Memoriam* (p. 385), he slips. His other books have been mentioned before [1897], and he is always a forceful and interesting writer, with much that rewards perusal about matters other than metrical.

This year also saw produced the first of a series of thick pamphlets or paper-covered volumes [see Appendix B] by Thomas Fitzhugh, Professor of Latin in the University of Virginia. These, though bearing on verse, are for fully equipped scholars only, as they broach a new and startling theory of the foundation of Latin metre. To set critics on their track I need only quote one sentence (slightly abbreviated) from the latest of these : " In the rank soil of this artificial and unhealthy tradition with its brachysyllabic, instead of pyrrhic, single instead of continuous accent, philology has come to be filled at the hands of Hellenizing and Indogermanizing grammarians with accentual and rhythmical fictions, boldly masquerading as ' Laws ' and assumed as axiomatic ".

Perhaps a word should be said here about the cadences of prose, apropos of Prof. Saintsbury's already mentioned book on prose rhythm. It has been often pointed out that recurrences in prose are irregular as compared with verse, and that lapsing into metre injures the effect of a prose passage, as when Dickens in pathetic mood " drops into poetry " like his own Silas Wegg ; Prof. Saintsbury shows how a skilful prose writer interjects a syllable on purpose to break too close resemblance to verse. But several writers have lately sought to find special recurrent cadences in prose, among whom may be specially mentioned Mr. John Shelly and Prof. A. C. Clark, particulars of whose publications will be found in Appendix B. Their discussions tend rather tö turn on comparisons with the cadences of Latin prose. Apart from this, it must be conceded that even good prose sometimes simulates metrical effects, as may be illustrated by a passage from Landor arranged into lines—I begin in the middle of the passage, though some preceding sentences are equally to the point.

> And when we shall go forth on our long journey,
>   will not some guardian Deity lead the way ?
> Yes, Hermes will lead us to the unseen land,
> Hermes the interpreter of gods and men ;
> Many a message has he brought from Olympus,
> And this last saddest will he also bring.
> Athens is dear with its fruitful olive,
> Dear are the hills and the Arcadian plains,
> But in Hades there are meadows where heroes meet,
> And the amaranth flowers for the livelong year.
> I shall go down to the shades in peace,
> And I ask no more.

Admirers of *vers libre* will probably claim that this is actually verse ; it may interest readers to consider for themselves why the claim is fallacious.

Several publications appeared in 1913. First came *Thomas Campion and the Art of English Poetry*, by Thomas MacDonagh, in which some selected poems of Campion's are embedded in a long disquisition on metre. Mr. MacDonagh was an enthusiastic young Irishman, who fought in the rebellion of 1916, and paid the penalty. The chief point in his long essay is a distinction between " speech-rhythm " and " song-rhythm " poems, less novel than he apparently imagined, and surely given away when he had to postulate an intermediate form which he called " chant-verse " (pp. 45, 59, etc.). More interesting are some remarks on recitations by W. B. Yeats and " Æ " (p 52 *seq.*), and on the way we English have of over-stressing our accents. The rest of the book is rather an *olla podrida* of points that have occurred to the author in the course of his reading or thinking.

In the Classical Association of Scotland's *Proceedings* for 1913 was printed a paper (also published separately) by the late Prof. Ross Hardie on " What is Metre ? " Prof. Hardie was a most accomplished scholar (for his other books see Appendix B), reciting Greek and Latin verse as freely as other people recite English ; and, while firmly convinced that Greek verse supplied the norm for all metre, was by no means inclined to accept all that Greek grammarians said on the subject. But when he came to deal with English verse, he trod with less sure foot. He began, indeed, with such excellent principles as that " To read verse as if it were prose means to misplace the emphasis at every turn. Prose has its way of arranging words, and verse has its way of arranging words, and the two ways are very different " (pp. 2–3) ; and on the essential difference between English metre and that of Greek or Latin (p. 10). [Compare also, in *Res Metrica* (1920), his remark about " empty forms or time-spaces ", " rendered visible or audible by some kind of movement or sound " (p. 268).] He is good, too, in *What is Metre* (p. 8), on the first line of *Paradise Lost*, where recent critics too hastily assume the presence of a monosyllabic foot. But, as he goes on, he slips into the common error of regarding syllables rather than time-spaces, and suffers accordingly. He mocks at isochronism being claimed as a novelty ; I know no instructed writer who makes that claim. His aim was to demonstrate a foundation **for all** European metre, but when he comes to French verse he frankly owns himself puzzled. And indeed it is not easy to find any dependence there on iambs and trochees, or any formula to cover both

> La Mer, partout la Mer ! Des flots, des flots encor !

and

> Oui, je viens dans son temple adorer l'Eternel.

On Greek metre, at any rate, Prof. Hardie was an acknowledged master.

(An article on " English Prose Numbers ", by Prof. Oliver Elton, in Vol. IV of the English Association's *Essays and Studies*, is mentioned here because of the reply which it called forth next year, as mentioned immediately.)

Equally remarkable, but in other ways, is the paper on " Rhythm in English Verse, Prose, and Speech ", by Mr. D. S. MacColl, in Vol. V (1914) of the English Association's *Essays and Studies*. It is too much a mere review of Prof. Saintsbury, but branches into wider questions. Without Prof. Alden's ripe knowledge of the subject and its history, Mr. MacColl rides gaily through the *mêlée*, hitting hard all round, and making many good strokes. I wonder where he found Lanier's " singling out " (p. 29) of " The Battle of the Baltic " ; my impression is that Lanier never refers to this poem. And of course he assumes a monosyllabic foot (p. 41) in the first line of *Paradise Lost*. Vigour of style and love of combat are the chief features of this paper, and criticism is more in evidence than constructive ability.

In 1914 came also *The Theory of Poetry in England*, by R. P. Cowl, a useful compilation of passages dealing with its doctrines from the Sixteenth to the Nineteenth Century. These limits prevent the citations coming down to date, so that we stop at Leigh Hunt for principles of versification, Matthew Arnold for ideals of translation, F. Myers for " the functions of metre ", and Pater for criticism. " Metre and Versification " occupy pages 224–62.

The *Modern Language Review* for July contained a paper of great interest on " The Mental Side of Metrical Form " by Prof. Alden, who has been mentioned before [1904]. The thesis of this paper is that we cannot " be easily certain that the expressed rhythm, when it finds vocal utterance, is identical with that which has been mentally perceived in silent reading or with that which is mentally conceived at the moment of oral expression. We may even be fairly sure that to some extent it is *not* the same " (first page). This thesis is expounded with great skill, the writer stating that " all respectable treatises " now accept ' rests ' in verse-lines, and going even farther than I dare do when he admits the validity of omitting an accented syllable in heroic metre (second page). That such omissions occur elsewhere any reader may satisfy himself by comparing two lines from Macaulay's " Ivry " :

> Hurrah, the foes are moving. Hark to the mingled din
> Of fife and steed and trump and drum, and roaring culverin.

Not to recognise the ' rest ' after " moving ", answering to a syllable in the second line, would be indeed fatuous. This paper is so valuable throughout that I content myself with advising all readers to study it carefully. It seems to me the best thing recently done on the subject, and I do not say this merely because it contains references to myself.

A small book entitled *Ventures in Thought,* by Francis Coutts, which came out in 1915, is made up of short swallow-flights of criticism, some of which touch not unhappily on the relations between verse and music, between speech-accent and metrical accent. But " the long and short of it " (pp. 122–7) entirely mistakes the function of quantity in Classical Latin verse.

The Technic of Versification, by William Odling (1916), is the work of an elder amateur, fond of poetry, but knowing nothing of the science of his subject, and not having advanced beyond counting accented syllables. He gives such " innocent " analysis as

> Neárer, | my Gód | to Thée,
> Neárer | to Thée !

not explaining how trochee and iamb can alternate in one line. The best part of the book is the numerous examples which fill the second half of it, and the arrangement of these under different headings, but his scansions should be totally ignored.

For 1917 my records are mostly of newspaper discussion, but 1918 made amends by giving us by far the most valuable book that has lately appeared on our special subject, *The Foundations and Nature of Verse,* by Cary F. Jacob (New York and Milford, London). Beginning at the very beginning

with inarticulate utterances, it traces the development of
these into verse, prose, and music, the exposition being richly
documented by references of all kinds, particularly to recent
American magazine articles, with many of which I am unacquainted. Readers should supplement my deficiencies by
consulting the foot-notes to this book ; a bibliography by its
author would be indeed welcome. Perhaps there is a little
parade of reference to books of limited relevance, such as
accounts of travel, but this is a fault on the right side. The
author's own views are stated with admirable clearness,
though it is long before we reach them. Rhythm he defines
as " constituted by the consecutive occurrence of phenomena
which are perceived as forming a succession of distinct, related
patterns in time " (p. 101), accent being merely " one of several
phenomena which may mark the recurrence of the time-
intervals " (p. 100). Thus, though evidently a deep student
of music, he differs from those of its professors who make
accent the creator of rhythm. The Chapter on *time* is particularly good, and of course Dr. Jacob takes account of
silences as well as sounds. With it should be read the one on
" Duration ", and I should have said sooner that the data on
which he relies are from experimental researches into sound—
facts, not theories. It would be a pleasure to quote whole
paragraphs, but I must content myself with a few leading
sentences. " Music and speech did not arise the one from the
other, but both from (or together with) an identical primitive
stage in one of their common elements " (p. 27, quoted with
approval from Wallaschek's *Primitive Music*). " In poetry
the vowels are [should be ?] pronounced with the greatest care.
They are deliberately prolonged beyond the time-lengths
usually assigned them in conversational speech, in order to
make their tone-color prominent " (p. 53). Investigation
" must seek to determine what are the phenomena marking
the end of single time-intervals and how these phenomena
affect our perception of time " (p. 86). " Any theory of
English poetry which assumes for the syllables either equality
of time-length or the existence among them of any degree of
simple proportion is without foundation in fact ", therefore
Prof. Saintsbury and the followers of Lanier respectively
" must seek elsewhere for justification of the faith that is in
them " (p. 117). " Usually the marking off of the measures is

by mere increase of loudness ; but this means of accentuation is not at all obligatory " (p. 124). Neither " for prose nor verse nor music is there any accuracy of time-lengths between the accents " (p. 134). " Relative periodicity of accent is not the sole and controlling factor in verse any more than it is the sole factor in music " (p. 187). I could wish that Dr. Jacob recognised more fully the " sing-song " effect as the chief feature in our mental rhythmizing, and in the following sentence I should like to substitute " felt " for " heard ": " The only problem for the scanner ought to be, What is the best way of writing down the rhythm as it is heard ? " (p. 198). For this reason several of his scansions seem to me arbitrary. " Sing-song " is undoubtedly the natural beginning of verse, and I believe we carry it in our heads through much syllabic diversity. As he himself says, " the ear occasionally demands the supplying of an accent at some point where neither the word accent nor the logical accent would naturally fall " (p. 141). Nor can I agree that division of verse into lines is a mere accident, and that " to one reciting from memory the lines are nonexistent " (p. 167). But I have no fault to find with the statements that in verse there must be " the perception of a succession of distinct, related patterns in time " (p. 192), and that while " admitting that there is no absolute equality of time-length to be found anywhere in either verse or music ", he " can still make equality of time-length one of my major premises " (p. 212). So I end by counselling the student of verse to regard this book as one of the indispensable weapons in his armoury. It has a sufficient Index.

In this year also appeared *A Study in English Metrics*, by Adelaide Crapsey (New York), a young lady whom delicate health and an early death prevented from carrying out elaborate proposed researches into verse-structure. (She also published a small volume of poems.) Her " Study " is mainly taken up with estimating the part played by monosyllables and polysyllables in our verse, and the comparative tables show the indomitable patience with which she worked. Likewise, at Ann Arbor, Michigan, edited by Prof. F. N. Scott, a study of the rhythmical function of " pause " in verse, by Ada L. F. Snell. It is based on experiments made with a recording apparatus, so judges mainly from delivery. I do not quite understand her criticism (p. 65 *seq.*) of my own views about " compensating pause ". Certainly I never meant to teach that every metrical unit is uttered in the same duration of time, any more than a pianist plays every bar at the same *tempo*. If she means to deny that in " Kentish Sir Byng " a pause after " Byng " equals its period with " Crop-headed " in the next line, I fear we must part company.

1918 brought also the *Poems* of Gerard Hopkins, with introduction and notes by the Poet Laureate. Readers who enjoy fantastic new would-be developments of metre will study these poems and their author's teaching about " Sprung Rhythm " and other mysteries, and will find ample material in the one poem entitled " The Wreck of the *Deutschland* " ; others, neither intolerant of nor unhopeful for new experiments, will turn from them with repugnance. The Editor's introduction and notes are, as always, clear and helpful, expounding his friend's metrical theories, and not infrequently registering dissent from his eccentricities, especially in rhyming. The double rhymes in " The Loss of the *Eurydice* " are simply atrocious, and curiously enough the Editor has singled out for special censure one of the least offensive of these. I cannot believe that these poems deserve or will receive attention from even the most determined seeker after novelties.

A book published in 1919 raised questionings about metre. This is *The Song of Roland*, translated by Capt. C. K. Scott Moncrieff in the original metre, with assonance instead of rhyme tying lines into longer or shorter paragraphs. An introductory " Note on Technique " by Prof. Saintsbury says all that need be said about prosodical details. The metre is simple decasyllabic. The translator's prefatory " Note " compares it to the Scotch second version of the 124th Psalm, beginning

> Now Israel may say, and that trulie ;

but the tune to which that is sung so transforms the words that I doubt if many worshippers realise that they are singing decasyllabic verse, or would not be puzzled in trying to sing to it any such line as

> High were the peaks, and shadowy and grand.

Experiments should be tried, and this one has been tried faithfully and well ; but I cannot think that the experiment is likely to be often followed, or deserves to be, as a type of English poetry.

Considerable sensation was caused during 1919 and 1920 by two books of Mr. Bayfield's. *The Measures of the Poets* (1919) contains much that is interesting and a fine wealth of quotations, but the author's ideas of structure are rudimentary. Both he and Prof. Saintsbury seem to think (though neither says so) that when we " read scanningly " we necessarily pause after each foot, and therefore to them iambic and trochaic are essentially different metres. If they realised that, in verse as in music, the bar-mark is not a sign of division— that " the | nóble " | and " | the nó | ble " are the same thing —discussion might be much clarified. Also, Mr. Bayfield seems unaware how frequently our poets put into a foot two equipollent syllables, and when these begin a line he at once claims to find a monosyllabic foot, as in " And his | great ∧ | love ∧ | " *etc.* The insistence on trochaic scansion seems rather puerile, since almost every line of blank verse can be read either iambically or trochaically, but it should be noted that this author distinguishes accurately between the real trochees and iambs of Greek and Latin metre and the supposititious trochees and iambs of our accentual verse. Real trochees and iambs of course abound in our lines, and the only reason for preferring one method of scansion to the other is if it can be shown that the foot or " measure " is thus more accurately divided.[1] I cannot believe that the author really regards as " inferior " (p. 26) such a line as

> The weight of all the hopes of half the world,

or even as

> The busy little bodies bustle still.

His larger book on *Shakespeare's Versification* (1920) I cannot claim to have read through. I note that he still favours such scansions as " Then | you, and | I and | all of us | fell | down ' (p. 49). As to the resolution of Shakespeare's contractions, we know that such contractions were common in his day, that *'gin* for *begin* and *'sdained* for *disdained* occur in non-dramatic verse, and who is to say what contractions were tolerated on

---

[1] In dealing with " acephalous " lines, why does the author ignore the fact that no " unresolved " initial measure beginning with an accented syllable is to be found in *Paradise Lost* or *The Idylls of the King* ?

the stage ? The discussion which followed the publication of these volumes in the *Times Literary Supplement* and elsewhere did not seem particularly well informed.[1]

Much more satisfactory and helpful is *The Writing and Reading of Verse* (1920), by C. E. Andrews, Professor in the Ohio State University, and apparently also Lieutenant in the American Army. Its *raison d'être* is exposition of the artistic elements in good verse-making, and its second half, devoted to " technique of special verse forms ", with apposite examples of each, should be especially valuable to young poets. The last Chapter is on " free verse or vers libre ". The first half, however, dealing with " principles of verse ", has much good matter about the actual structure of verse, in which connection the first part of Chapter V (" Prose and Verse ") should be carefully read [2]; the remainder of that Chapter is to me less convincing. Very sensibly the writer states at the outset (p. 4) that no one reading of a line of verse is necessarily correct ; different readers read differently, and his readings are merely those which he himself prefers. He defines the basis of verse by saying " a line is metrical when divided into sensibly equal time parts " (p. 9). Omitting much detail, I come to these excellent sentences : " Verse, then, has an ideal pattern, very largely subjective, of metre [3] and rhythm, to which the poet must fit his thought. If the words fit into the pattern too perfectly, the verse is monotonous ; good verse has a constant struggle between the sense of the words as brought out in the prose reading, and the ideal metrical and rhythmical pattern that must be felt in the verse reading " (p. 51). This " constant struggle " is what so many critics fail to recognise, and a good reader of verse is one who gives sufficient value to *both* elements.[4] Chapters VI on " Move-

---

[1] If Mr. Bayfield would attend less to speech-accents, and would work out the view excellently put in his *Measures* (p. 38) that " the movement of verse is essentially orderly ", while the time-values " are not slavishly and inartistically observed when the words are spoken aloud ", I think his scansions would have more reality.

[2] A whole line has been accidentally omitted from the second quotation on p. 53.

[3] I apologise for occasionally substituting English spellings, for my readers' comfort.

[4] " The finest Shakespearian verse when spoken on the stage to-day usually becomes merely fine rhythmical prose, because most actors

ment " and VIII on " Tone-colour " will be found interesting through their wealth of illustration. I do not pretend that the author's " readings " are always mine, but his individual scansions are usually unimpeachable—a good specimen is that of Kipling's lines on p. 46—and this latest production of the American school certainly deserves the favourable reviews which I have no doubt it will receive.

A discussion on *vers libre* in the *Athenaeum* during July, 1920, might fitly close this survey. It began with a review of a book called *Other-world Cadences*, by Mr. F. S. Flint (Poetry Bookshop, 1920), followed by letters from Mr. Ford Madox Hueffer and others. What strikes one in such discussion is lack of psychology. The revolutionary writers never seem to ask why a poet writes verse at all. If they would pursue that inquiry, they would find that he does it in obedience to fundamental instincts which men have felt in all ages and will probably continue to feel, which do not prompt slavish adherence to accepted forms, but whose ' urge ' favours measured cadences rather than the amorphous lines dear to some poets to-day.

I am able, however, to add reference to yet another discussion of " *vers libre* ". Replying to some obviously ill-informed adherents of this, Mr. Llewellyn Jones, literary editor of the *Chicago Evening Post*, in his *Free Verse and its Propaganda* (1920), not only annihilates their random definitions of our regular metres, but puts forward good ones of his own. Blank Verse, for example, he defines as " a free movement emphasized and made more measurable to the ear by being written against a metric scheme which . . . is not always apparent but exists as a convention in the mind of the poet and of the auditor " (p. 14) ; and he remarks that " if blank verse were actually in three-eight time—as Lanier asserts— *Paradise Lost* would be slightly more suggestive of a waltz than it is " (p. 8). Each page of this short pamphlet has point, and the summation of argument on its last page must surely carry conviction.

What, then, is the upshot of the whole matter ? This, for certain ; that we have as yet no established system of prosody. Much analytic inquiry has yielded no synthesis authoritative

seem unable to give it properly expressive interpretation without obscuring the pattern " (p. 68).

and generally accepted. It is a strange fact, so late in the history of our literature ; Greek metrists would have viewed it with surprise. That the synthesis will come is surely past question. When it does come, I suspect it will be found less and not more complex than its many predecessors. It will not come on lines of Greek prosody. Our syllables do not directly express time, are not regarded by us as primarily measures of time ; any attempt to prove that they do so in our ordinary verse must fail, and any attempt to make them do so in verse of novel pattern seems to me ill-judged. Yet—keeping to our ordinary native fashion of verse—syllables must be some-how marshalled and arranged, if they are to produce patterns differing from those of prose speech. They must be brought into relation with some overruling law, through whose dominance they become materials of prosodic structure.

That this law is a temporal one I cannot doubt. Verse without time-measure is about as conceivable as weaving without thread. All talk of stresses and thought-groups and emotional climax and centroid recurrence is so far beside the mark ; it omits the most necessary factor. Verse depends first and always on time-rhythm ; it " contrives its pattern of sounds in time ". Different ages, different speech-habits, modify its manner of doing this ; but it must always do it somehow. Failure to apprehend this truth has made lifeless much of our metrical criticism. Verse considered apart from time is a dead thing, a corpse for the dissecting theatre of grammarians ; the life is fled, how then can their analysis find it ? The same mistake was made by Greek and Latin prosodists of the later Empire ; they dealt with part of the question as if it were the whole.

Whether we have yet rightly apprehended the relation of our verse to time is another matter. We may have formed too narrow conceptions of rhythm. Hitherto we have bor-rowed these mainly from music ; do all its methods necessarily hold good in dealing with speech ? That there is close kinship between verse and music is evident, and as yet we have no language save that of music in which to express temporal occurrences. But this language does not always seem appro-priate. In any case, English syllables do not by themselves create or constitute rhythmical periods. They are, at most, set or adjusted to such periods, often with perceptible coercion.

This enforced adjustment, in my belief, gives our verse its charm and character. Theories which consider only one or other side of this double structure cannot be adequate. The correlation, the interaction of both elements is the very thing we have to analyse. Most prosodic investigation takes too limited a view of the problem ; some of it has got so out of contact with truth that it sees no difference between the effects of verse and prose.

The reality of this double structure seems easily demonstrable. Does not some of Swinburne's most brilliant verse suffer from the perpetual hammer-beat of syllabic accent, leaving the ear no liberty, but mechanically enforcing rhythm ? Such verse is felt to have the hardness as well as the clearness of resonant metal. On the other hand, in the work of our most accomplished singers—even in such exquisite work as that of Christina Rossetti—is there not sometimes a tendency to let syllabic and temporal beats wander too far apart, so that occasionally the ear is puzzled to bring them together ? In all verse, are we not conscious of slight divergence between the uniform temporal beat and the varying syllabic accent ? To say that these habitually coincide is surely doing despite to our judgement.

There is, therefore, still room for much independent inquiry. We have first to determine, theoretically and experimentally, what is the real basis of our verse. Laboratory work can be of use here, if free from preconceptions, and if its methods do not create phenomena instead of recording them. The basis once made clear, endless labour can be expended on contributory factors. All details of syllabic structure, vowel and consonant character, stress-value, ' tone-colour ', expressional significance, and the rest, will find place in a complete theory. Much has been already done in this regard, and much remains to do. But these things can be rightly seen only in perspective of the whole. Our first need is to view verse intelligently as a composite total—now at length, looking back on the experience of Centuries, to discover what English verse really is. That the discovery has still to be made, may well seem surprising ; but the fundamental disagreements revealed throughout our survey show plainly that such is the fact.

We may reasonably look with expectation to what the next few years will bring. Prosody has certainly made advance

since the first edition of this book was published. No longer
the despised Cinderella of the arts, it takes its place now
among sister sciences. If the whole truth has not yet been
reached, it is now recognised as attainable ; our best analysis
is saner, wider, more catholicly minded than ever before.
Study of temporal sequence, in particular, has made more than
a beginning. It is in that direction that advance may be
most confidently expected, as it is in that direction that advance is most desirable. Many experts, fortunately, are aware
of this, and are seeking to extend our knowledge on this side.
From their efforts much gain should result. To them more
especially, but also to all who are interested in prosody,
I trust this book may be of some use, and I proffer cordial
salutation.

APPENDICES

BIBLIOGRAPHICAL APPENDICES

It will be seen that these lists are confined to English writers.

Books may be presumed octavo and published in London, unless otherwise stated.

Entries marked by an asterisk are of books not mentioned, or not discussed, in the text. A short notice is appended to these.

The arrangement is by date of publication, each author being represented by his first or chief work on the subject, and reference made in that place to his other works. For alphabetical list of authors see Index.

Notice of *important* errors or omissions will oblige. Completeness is unattainable, and would probably be useless, but I have tried to err on the side of inclusion rather than exclusion. Even a note warning students off useless ground may be helpful.

APPENDIX A

OF BOOKS AND ARTICLES DEALING WITH QUANTITA-
TIVE VERSE AND PSEUDO-CLASSICAL POEMS.

*14th Century? Macaronic verse might be supposed to yield
' hexameters ' earlier than any I have cited. Thus, in Wright
and Halliwell's *Reliquiae Antiquae* (1841), Vol. I, p. 90, we find
condemnation of those who *mumble, skip,* or " *leap over* " part
of the Office :—

> Momylers, forscyppers, ovrelepers, non bene psallunt.

In the same book, p. 291, this line has grown into two, all English
but for *quoque* and *sic et* instead of *and.* Finally, in Wright's
edition of *Latin Poems attributed to Walter Mapes* (1841), p. 148,
note, comes this wholly English line on the same theme :—

> Momler, forscypper, stumler, scaterer, overhipper.

It is English, but is it quantitative ? I think Latin and English
were both read by accent, and hence the false quantities in both.
Other instances can doubtless be found ; probably the same rule
will always apply. The wonder is that such lines are not more
numerous. Usually, when Latin and English lines alternate, the
latter follow native measures ; compare, for example, the piece
at second reference above. When, however, such lines do occur,
I think they should be regarded as accentual, not quantitative.

The same argument applies to a supposed couplet by Chaucer
(see Skeat's edition, Vol. II, p. 419, and *cf.* Introduction to that
volume, p. xxiii, *note* ; also Saintsbury, *Hist. of Pros.,* Vol. I,
pp. 8, 10). If the words which conclude the first " Metre " of
Boethius are meant to form an ' elegiac ' couplet, as Prof. Saintsbury seems to hold, accent and not quantity is their basis.

J. Payne Collier (*Bibl. and Crit. Account,* Vol. I, p. xli) opined
that the words with which Chaucer " commences his prose version
of Boethius " were intended to form two hexameter lines, " as
correct as many of those " in Stanihurst. Few will agree with
him.

No truly quantitative verse, apparently, was produced in
England before the 16th Century, and Bishop Watson's lines
quoted by Ascham may be considered our earliest extant specimen
of such.

*16th Cent. I omitted to mention a line in which, according to Fuller, Queen Elizabeth addressed some grammar-school boys (see Walpole's *Royal and Noble Authors*, Vol. I, p. 31) :—

Pērsĭŭs, ā crāb-stăffe ; băwdў Mārtĭăl ; Ōvĭd, ă fĭne wāg.[1]

Her Majesty had been Ascham's pupil, and this is clearly meant to be quantitative. But if one of these boys had confused two Latin quantities as she confused *body* and *bawdy*, would he have 'scaped a whipping? She doubtless pronounced *Ovid* with a long *O*.

1545. ASCHAM (ROGER). *Toxophilus*, first edition. Well-known book (on archery), often reprinted ; Arber's English Reprints, 1868.[2] Contains incidental translations in quantitative verse.

The Scholemaster (1563–8 ?), first edition 1570 (posthumous). Also often reprinted ; Arber, 1870. A good edition in " Cambridge University Classics ".

1576. SANDFORD (JAMES). Mr. R. B. McKerrow directed attention in *Modern Language Quarterly* for December, 1902, to *Houres of Recreation . . . done first out of Italian into Englishe by James Sandford Gent.*, the second edition. At the end of this volume come " Certayne Poemes Dedicated to the Queenes moste excellente Maiestie ", which are on unpaged leaves, and did not appear in the first edition (1573).[3] One of these is in ' elegiac ' couplets, repeated in five different languages—Greek, Latin, Italian, French, and English. The last is specially interesting, because it antedates all our published quantitative lines except Ascham's, and is the first recorded attempt at writing ' pentameters' in English. I quote it entire, preserving the spelling, but adding symbols of quantity as seem necessitated by the metre.

Englānd wĭth thĭs vērse dŏth drēsse yŏu vĭrgĭn ăn āltār,
  Whŏm nŏt wātĕr, ŏr āyre, Ĭrŏn ŏr āge căn ănŏy,
Āge vŏlătĭve ēates nŏt sŭch vērse ās dĭd tŏ thē Grēekes būild
  Lāstĭng prāise, nŏr thāt Rōme ĕvĕr ēngrăvĕd ēarst.
Thēn rĕtĭrĭng Ĭ my stēppes, āftĕr thēir glŏrў wĭl ēnsūe,
  Mūrdrĭng ŏblĭvĭŏn, yŏur wĭll Ĭ glōrўe tŏ lĭve,
Ănd wĭth thĭs mĕsūred vērse yŏur hŏlўe nāme shăll ăbrŏde sprēade,
  Sĭth yŏur hŏllў făvŏur hēlpĕth ăn hŏlly fūrў.

---

[1] I add symbols in all cases of quantitative verse, to show quickly which syllables are accounted ' long ' and which ' short '. Foot-division my readers can supply for themselves. The last syllable of each line is marked *long* or *short* according to the general scheme of the metre, irrespective of actual [supposed] quantity.

[2] This admirable series, price one shilling and sixpence net per volume, is to be had in a new issue (A. Constable & Co., publishers). My references are to the original volumes, but I believe the paging of the new is uniform with the old.

[3] This had a different title : *The Garden of Pleasure . . . etc.*

It will be seen that quantity (" measured verse ") is attempted, with scant success, though *volatĭve* and *engrăvéd* may represent contemporary vocalisation. *Retĭring* evidently copies the French *retirant*. The sixth line is unintelligible as it stands, " your glory will I make to live " is what it should say. Was Sandford a pupil of Ascham, or did he follow Continental exemplars ? How little it profits to reproduce Elizabethan spelling is shown by " holy " being spelt first *holye* and then *holly*, without metrical reason so far as the first syllable is concerned. *Ing* is clearly reckoned ' long '. The lines are curious on account of both their date and their polyglot character.

[Several pieces that follow will be found in *Elizabethan Critical Essays* (Appendix B, 1904), *Critical Essays of the 17th Century* (*ibid.*, 1908–9), and *Cambridge University Classics*. This general mention may serve instead of particular reference.]

1580? SIDNEY (SIR PHILIP). *Apologie for Poetrie* (in later editions called *Defence of Poesie*). First published in 1595 (posthumous) ; often reprinted, *e. g.* Arber 1868, and Grosart (with Sidney's *Poems*) 1877. A few stray references to verse-structure.

Arcadia, written about same time, first published in 1590 (posthumous, imperfect ; first complete edition, 1598). Contains several pieces of quantitative verse.

Often reprinted, *e. g.* Arber as above ; J. Churton Collins, Oxford, 1907 ; and in the complete *Works*, ed. Feuillerat, Cambridge University Press, 1912.

1580. HARVEY (GABRIEL) and SPENSER (EDMUND). *Three proper, wittie, familiar letters, lately passed between two Universitie men. Two other very commendable letters, of the same men's writing* [these are of earlier date than the first three]. Both published in 1580 (separately).

This very interesting correspondence gives us the views of " Signior Immerito " [Spenser, *cf.* prefatory verses to *Shepherd's Calendar*, 1579] and Harvey about English accent and quantity. It seems to have been published by Harvey without Spenser's knowledge or permission, and the metrical experiments contained in it were never acknowledged or reprinted by Spenser. His two letters are printed in the *Globe Spenser* (Appendix, pp. 706–9), and all five in the *Oxford Poets Spenser*. Harvey's long letter about an earthquake (No. 2 of the first three) may be skipped ; his others are worth reading. His later *Four Letters* (1592) and his *Letter-book* (first published by Camden Society, 4to, 1884 ; afterwards by Grosart in his *Works of Harvey*, 3 vols., Huth Library series, 4to, 1884–5) contain several references to verse-structure and quantity, and must be studied by those desiring full acquaintance with the Elizabethan attempt at " reformed verse ".

Best reprint by Haslewood. Compare also *Gabriel Harvey's*

Marginalia, ed. G. C. Moore Smith (Shakespeare Head Press, 1913), which contains much new matter.

Gabriel's younger brother is mentioned in the third Letter as having written some quantitative lines, corrected by his senior. They follow Gabriel's quantities only too faithfully. I quote one couplet, as usual encomiastic of Queen Elizabeth :

> Nŏt thĕ līke Vīrgĭn ăgāine īn Āsĭa ŏr Āfrĭc ŏr Eūrōpe,
> Fŏr Rōyāll Vērtūes, fŏr Mājĕstĭĕ, Bōuntĭe, Bĕhāvĭoŭr.

Observe *like*, *in*, *Asi-[a* elided], *or* [as if *Oorope*], *Majestie*. It is interesting to see *behaviour* a trisyllable.

1582. STANIHURST or STANYHURST (RICHARD). *The first foure bookes of Virgil his Aeneis translated intoo English verse by Richard Stanyhurst, with oother Poetical Divises [devices] theretoo annexed. Imprinted at Leiden in Holland . . . 1582.*

Another issue by Bynneman, London, 1583, differs somewhat in spelling.

Reprint (of second edition) by James Maidment, Edinburgh, 4to, 1836 ; *ditto* (of first edition) in Arber's English Scholar's Library, 4to, 1880.

1583. GREENE (ROBERT). *Mamillia*, Part II (first published, 1593), contains hexameter lines. Reprint in Vol. II of Greene's *Works* edited by Grosart (15 vols. 4to, " Huth Library," 1881–6). See pp. 219–20.

Menaphon (1589 ?), with interesting preface by Nash in which he makes particular fun of Stanihurst ; Grosart, Vol. VI.

Mourning Garment (1590), first known edition, 1616 ; Grosart, Vol. IX. Contains hexameter lines " Alexis in laudem Rosamundae " (pp. 151–3), and " Rosamundae in dolorem amissi Alexis " (pp. 159–62).

Farewell to Folly (1591 ?), with introduction ; Grosart, Vol. IX. Some hexameter lines, translated from Guazzo (pp. 293–4).

1586. WEBBE (WILLIAM). *A Discourse of English Poetrie* (4to). Reprints by Haslewood, *ut ante* ; Arber, 1870.

Very rare till last Century. Little known of author. Written when he was private tutor in Essex.

1587. FRAUNCE (ABRAHAM). *The Lamentations of Amintas for the death of Phillis paraphrastically translated out of Latine into English hexameters.* Small 4to, rare.

Copy in Bodleian Library ; said to have been reprinted in 1588, 1589, 1596 ; copy of last in British Museum ; no modern reprint.

The Countess of Pembroke's Ivychurch, 1591, which contains nearly all Fraunce's verse, including *Phillis and Amintas, Corydon and Alexis*, a translation from Heliodorus, *Amintas Dale, Emanuel*, and some versions of *Psalms*.

Also *The Lawier's Logike*, 4to, 1588, and *The Arcadian Rhetorike*, 4to, 1588 ?.

Both very rare, latter in Bodleian Library, no copy in British Museum. The former brings in his own *Corydon and Alexis*; the latter quotes largely from Sidney's quantitative verse, and has a section dealing with *feet*, which is unfortunately imperfect in this copy.

*1588. HAKE (EDWARD). There are said to be some hexameters in *A Touch-stone of Wittes*, by this writer; but I believe no copy of the book is to be found. Warton (*Hist. of Poetry*, Hazlitt's edition, Vol. III, pp. 203-4) speaks as if he had seen it; his editor had " never met with it " (*ibid., note*). Schipper (*Engl. Metr.*, Vol. II, p. 11) and Gayley and Scott (*Lit. Crit.*, p. 498) briefly describe the book, I know not on what information. Warton says it is chiefly compiled, " with some slender additions," from Webbe's *Discourse*; the others make it derive from Fraunce.

*1588-9. Mr. McKerrow (*loc. cit.*) points out that ' hexameters ' were used in the " Martin Mar-prelate " controversy. In the original *Epistle* (1588; Arber's reprint, pp. 18, 19), two alternative lines are suggested for an epitaph on Dean Bridges, *viz.* :—

> Hēre līes Jōhn Brīdgēs, ā wōrthīe Prēsbȳtĕr hē wās;

and

> Hēre līes Jōhn Brīdgēs lāte Bīshōp, frīend tŏ thē Pāpā.

At the end of *Mar-Martine* (1589; anonymous tract, ascribed to Lyly, *cf.* Bond's *Lyly*, Vol. III, pp. 423-6) come six lines of reply, as follow :—

> Hēre hāngs knāve Mārtīne, ā trāitrōus Lībĕlĕr hē wās
> Ēnĕmīe prētēndĕd bŭt ĭn hārt ā frīend tŏ thē Pāpā.
> Nōw māde mēat tŏ thē bīrdes thăt ăbōut hĭs cārkăs ăre hāglīng.
> Lēarne bȳ hĭs ēxāmplē yēe rōute ŏf Prūrītăn āssēs,
> Nŏt tŏ rĕsīst thē dŏīngs ŏf ōur mōst grācīŏus Hēstĕr.
> Mārtĭn ĭs hāngd fŏr thē Māstĕr ŏf āll Hȳpŏcrītĭcăl hāngbīes.

The savage vigour of these lines makes one think Nash may have had a hand in them; he pretends to approve the spelling " pruritan " in *The Return of Pasquil* (1589). Grim comment is supplied by the fact that one author of the *Epistle* was actually hanged. In the British Museum copy of *Mar-Martine* [apparently unique], the last of the above lines is so much cut away as to be barely legible; Mr. Bond thinks " one or more " other lines may have followed.

It may here be noted that Mr. Bond (Vol. III, pp. 448-9) gives as Lyly's some ' hexameters ' which really belong to Sidney; *cf. Athenaeum*, April 4, 1903, p. 435.

1592. NASH (THOMAS). *Strange news of the intercepting certain letters, etc.* His first attack on Harvey. See *ante*, p. 22, foot-note. Reprint in Vol. II of *Works*, ed. Grosart (6 vols. 4to, " Huth Library," 1883-5). *Cf.* especially pp. 206 and 237.

Pierce Penniless, 1592.

Have with you to Saffron Walden, 1596. (Grosart, Vols. II and III ; some stray hits only.) *Cf.* preface to Greene's *Menaphon*, *ante*.

Best edition of Nash's *Works* by R. B. McKerrow (5 vols., 1904–10).

*1593. *The Phoenix Nest.*

Reprint in Thos. Parkes's *Heliconia*, Vol. II (4to, 1814). Prof. Saintsbury (*Hist. of Prosody*, Vol. II, pp. 132–3) speaks of this containing verses which are " Sapphics by intention at least ". I cannot see it, and in any case they are not quantitative.

1594. BARNFIELD (RICHARD). " Hellen's Rape : or, A light Lanthorne for light Ladies. Written in English Hexameters." Forms part of *The Affectionate Shepheard*, etc.

No name on title-page, but acknowledged by him later.

Reprint in No. 14 of *The English Scholar's Library*, by Arber (4to, 1883).

*1594. CHAPMAN (GEORGE), the well-known poet. The lines quoted are not in all editions of his poetical works.

*1595. PEELE (GEORGE). *The Old Wives Tale* (play). Reprint in *Works*, ed. Bullen (2 vols., 1885).

Some quasi-hexameter lines (latter, Vol. I, pp. 333–4), of which these two lines may serve as a specimen :

Jŭst bў thў sĭde shăll sĭt sūrnām'd grĕat Hŭănĕbāngō,
Sāfe ĭn mў ārms wĭll Ĭ kĕep thĕe, thrĕat Mārs, ōr blūndĕr Ŏlўmpūs.

[Can *blunder* be a misprint for *thunder* ?] Yes, see *Gayley's Representative English Comedies*, Vol. I, p. 373.

1595. SABIE (FRANCIS). *Pan's Pipe, Three Pastorall Eglogues in English Hexameter, with other poetical verses . . . etc.*

Small 4to, rare. Anonymous, but preface signed F.S. Some elegiacs and other verses come in. See *Dict. Nat. Biogr.*, but what it tells does not amount to much.

1596 ? DICKENSON (JOHN). *The Shephearde's Complaint. A passionate Eclogue, written in English Hexameters.* Other pieces follow.

Reprint in Grosart's " Occasional issues of unique or very rare books " (17 vols.), Vol. VI, 1878.

Despite title, the " Eclogue " and other pieces are in prose, with occasional verses interposed, some only of which are quantitative. *Cf.* pp. 10–13, 44, 57, 127.

1597. HALL (JOSEPH), afterwards Bishop. *Virgidemiarum* [satires in verse], first series 1597, second 1598. Often reprinted.

See Book I, Satires IV and VI, the second containing these lines :

Another scorns the homespun thread of rhymes
Matched with the lofty feet of elder times.
Give me the numbred [*sic*] verse that Virgil sung,
And Virgil's self shall speak the English tongue ;

> Manhood and garboils chaunt with changèd feet,
> And headstrong dactyls making music sweet.

Manhood and garboils " is quoted from Stanihurst.

1599. ANONYMOUS. *The First Book of the Preservation of King Henry the VII . . . compiled in English rythmicall hexameters.* Oblong 8ᵛᵒ ; rare.

" Epistle dedicatorie " fills 15 pages (lettered, not numbered), other introductory matter 9, the " First Book " 40 ; Second Book unfinished.

Reprint in Payne Collier's *Illustrations of Old English Literature,* Vol. II (3 vols., 4ᵗᵒ, 1866, privately printed).

1602. DAVIDSON (FRANCIS). Edited *Poetical Rhapsody . . . etc.* Enlarged in several later editions. Reprinted by Nicolas, 2 vols., Pickering, 1826, and Bullen, 2 vols., 1890.

Poems by many authors. In Vol. II some quantitative pieces, apparently by " A. W.", an extensive contributor (Davidson himself ?).

1602. CAMPION (THOMAS). *Observations in the Art of English Poesie.* Reprints by Haslewood, *ut ante* ; Bullen, *Works* of Campion, Chiswick Press, 1889 (new edition, 1903) ; Oxford Text Series edition of his *Works* (1909), ed. Vivian ; also in cheap editions of the two latter, Mr. Vivian's having an Appendix of doubtful poems. In this last is a piece which seems meant for " Asclepiads ", beginning :

> Whăt făir pŏmp hăve Ĭ spĭed ŏf glĭttĕrĭng lādĭes.

1603. " L. G." In *Sorrowe's Joy* (Cambridge) ; reprint in *Progresses of King James,* by John Nichols, F.S.A., 4 vols., 4ᵗᵒ, 1828.

Twelve hexameter lines, Vol. I, p. 13.

*1606. In *The Return from Parnassus,* Act II, Scene 2, are some quaint " echoing " hexameter lines which seem meant to be quantitative.

Reprinted in Arber's " English Scholar's Library of Old and Modern Books " (1895).

[The foregoing covers what I have been able to find of Elizabethan quantitative writings. It is much to be wished that students of this period would note any samples of pseudo-Classical verse they come across ; some may be still uncatalogued. During the next two centuries specimens will be found few and far between.]

1621. TAYLOR (JOHN), "Water-poet". *The Beggar,* a poem.

> A louse has six feet, from whose creeping sprawl'd
> The first Hexameters that ever crawl'd.

1638. CHAMBERLAIN (ROBERT). *Nocturnal Lucubrations . . . etc.,* 16ᵐᵒ, pp. 124 ; rare.

1640. JONSON (BEN), posthumous. *An English Grammar,*

made by Ben Johnson (*sic*). Copy in British Museum, thin folio, no place or publisher named ; has formed part of larger volume, and begins p. 34. It seems to have formed part of a projected Vol. II of his Works, another item being *Timber : or Discoveries* (Temple Classics edition, Note at end). This latter refers often to verse, not to metre.

*1653. WALLIS (JOHN), Oxford Professor. *Grammatica linguae Anglicanae*, first edition (the fifth, 1765, is best).

Introductory Section *De Sonis ; c.* 5, *de poesi*, short, treats of Classical attempts, *e.g.*

What shall I do ? shal I dy ? shall Amyntas murder Amyntas, and gives lines of his own, accentual rather than quantitative.

1657. HOCKENHULL (JOHN). Lines in *Barker's Delight, or the Art of Angling, the second edition much enlarged.* They are not in first edition (1851), nor in another (4to, 1653).

Reprint 12mo, 1820.

*1657 ? ANONYMOUS. *The English Parnassus*, by Joshua Poole, contains one line of doubtful authorship, addressing Ben Jonson as

Bĕnjămĭn ĭmmōrtāl, Jōhnsōn [*sic*] mōst hīghlў rĕnōwnĕd.

The book is a sort of *Gradus*, dealing mostly with terminations and rhymes.

Cf. Appendix B, same date.]

169– ? DRYDEN (JOHN). Preface to *Aeneas* (1697), as quoted.

Preface to *Juvenal* (1692), much about verse. " We have yet no English *Prosodia*, not so much as a tolerable Dictionary or a Grammar " ; he despairs of getting one, and thinks the language will decline, not advance (*c.* CXXXVI). Other references in Prefaces to *The Rival Ladies, Albion and Albanius, Fables Ancient and Modern.* The " Art of Poetry " and " Essay on Satire ", both in verse, have nothing to our purpose.

Compare *Essays of John Dryden*, ed. W. P. Ker (2 vols., 1900).

1710. WATTS (ISAAC). *Poems chiefly of the lyric kind. In three Books* (preface dated 1709). " The day of Judgment [*sic*]. An Ode. Attempted in English Sapphic." (About middle of Book I.)

1737. ANONYMOUS. *An Introduction of the Ancient Greek and Latin Measures into British Poetry.*

Preface, pp. i–xvii ; text, pp. 18–59. Rules of quantity in Preface, pp. xiii–xvii.

*1750 ? I did not mention Cowper's solitary piece of ' sapphics ', placed among his posthumously published " Early Poems ", therefore probably written about this date ; I cannot believe it was meant to be quantitative. If it was, it contains such dactyls as *dĕlăy ŏf execution, Judās mŏre ăbhorred, pĕnce sŏld hĭs.* But if Cowper read his lines—as most people do read English quasi-sapphic measure—by accent, giving four beats to the long lines and two to the short, these difficulties vanish. The first stanza would then divide thus :—

> Hatred and | vengeance, | my eternal | portion,
> Scarce can en- | dure de- | lay of exe- | cution,
> Wait with im- | patient | readiness to | seize my
>   Soul in a | moment.

So read, they differ from those of Dr. Watts, with which otherwise they might well be paralleled for loose quantity as for terrible subject ; Watts's lines are as faulty by accent as by quantity, Cowper's have a real and natural swing. If I am right, therefore, they should not be considered quantitative lines.

1763. GOLDSMITH (OLIVER). Essay on " Versification " in *British Magazine.* Now No. 18 in his " Miscellaneous Essays ". Compare also Essays 14 and 15.

[In *Essays and Criticisms by Dr. Goldsmith* (3 vols., 12mo, 1798) Essays 14 to 18 in most editions are numbered 15 to 19.]

*1760. MURRAY (JOHN). In *The Scots Magazine* for December (Vol. 22, pp. 629–32), paper on " The Rhythm of the Ancients ". Discussion in subsequent numbers (Vol. 23, pp. 70–2 ; 185–6).

Quoted here because he says no modern writer has handled the relation of syllables to time (p. 629, col. 1), and for the sake of this final sentence (in June 1761, p. 186) : " Every language must have a rhythmus peculiar to itself ; and which cannot be practised in another, unless they have been both, if I may so speak, originally cast in the same mould. The rhythmus of all modern tongues is very different from the musical rhythmus of Greek and Latin."

1773. TUCKER (ABRAHAM). *Vocal Sounds, by Edward Search, Esq.* [The pseudonym is transparent ; he refers to his *Light of Nature* (p. 3), and jokes about the Search family, *etc.*]

Sample hexameters, by himself, p. 69 *seq.*

1773. HERRIES (JOHN). *The Elements of Speech.* His misapprehension as to Classic quantity, and attempts to reproduce the supposed accentual structures of Latin metres, pp. 184–7.

*1793. SAYERS (FRANK). *Disquisitions.* Reprint in *Poetical Works* (1830).

Short paper on " English Metre ", advocating both rhymeless verse and quantity, but latter created by emphasis, not position.

*1798. LAMB (CHARLES). It is fairly obvious that Lamb was imitating the swing of " accentual sapphics ' in his well-known lines beginning

> I have had playmates, I have had companions.

1802. The metrical pieces in Odell's *Essay* [*cf.* text, 1806] pp. 178–86, written at or before this date, deserve notice. Such a ' sapphic ' line as—

> Gŏds ăbōve mĭght ēnvў thĕ fōnd ădōrĕr

would easily pass for quantitative. But Odell, who seems to have thought out his structure for himself, disregards positional length, and makes " emphasis " instead of duration of syllable his basis. *Hollow* is to him a trochee, and *essences* a dactyl. His lines are therefore really constituted by accent, but on a basis of strict feet ; the above line, for example, cannot be read like one of Cowper's. If verse of this type is to be written at all in English, Odell's is probably the best way to do it, avoiding at once the futility of supposed quantitative and the roughness of purely accentual metre. It is pretty much the way in which, to compare great things with small, Mr. Swinburne's " Sapphics " are written. Odell's first stanza runs thus :—

> Gods above might envy the fond adorer,
> Him who near thee sits, in a silent rapture,
> Thus to hear thee tenderly speak, and see thee
> Tenderly smiling.

It will be seen how near this comes to orthodox quantity ; the structural difference between " tenderly smiling " and " painfully silent " is as nought to an English ear. Other specimens follow, the longest being a translation from the *Iliad*, of which these are the first two lines :—

> Sing, O Muse, the destructive wrath of Pelead Achilles,
> Source of abundant toil and grief to the host of Achaeans.

1805 and 1842. DEAN WILLIAM HERBERT, who as a young man ' cut up ' Mitford in the *Edinburgh Review*, wrote quantitative verses more [*ex hypothesi*] correct than any predecessor. These, like his *Review* article, can be seen in his *Works* (1842), Vol. II. The ' sapphic ' stanza of which I quoted one line in my text reads thus (p. 70 in that volume) :—

> Ō līqūid strēamlĕts tŏ thĕ māin rĕtūrnĭng ;
> Mūrmŭrĭng wātĕrs, thăt ădōwn thĕ mōuntăin
> Rūsh ŭnōbstrūctĕd ; nĕvĕr ĭn thĕ ōcĕan
> Hōpe tŏ bĕ trānqŭil.

Rūsh is a false quantity, due doubtless to spelling ; *liquid, bĕ tran-*, perhaps *rĕturning*, seem questionable. But these are exceptional. Compare a set of ' alcaics ' (p. 214), of whose eight stanzas I give the last :—

> Ō hēar ălŏft, thŏu Quēen ŏ' thĕ bēautĭfŭl !
> Sĕrēne thĕ sŏft āirs trĕmblĕ ăt hĕr cŏmĭng ;
> Dēlīghtfŭl ēnchāntmēnt ăwākĕns
> Āll thĕ bŏsōm's trĕmŭlōus dĕvōtĭon.

Here *ăt hĕr* follows Latin precedent ; I notice nothing else to query. In another ' alcaic ' stanza (p. 155), *ŏf his* can be similarly explained ; *gentle movement*, first written, is altered in *Errata* to *gentle action*. Both Herbert's verses, and the pages in which they occur, should be read ; notice especially, on p. 71, the stanza contrasted with that first quoted above. His arguments do not convince me, either about Greek verse or about English ; the former are now out of date. But they are always interesting. [*Cf.* also Appendix B, 1805.]

*1812. DYER (GEORGE). *Poetics : or a series of poems, and disquisitions on poetry* (2 vols., 12ᵐᵒ).

Contents previously published in a magazine which I have not identified. Nothing to cite except a ' sapphic ' line beginning [the symbols are his] :

I've gŏt th' hēadāche ; gīve mĕ thĕn, bŏy, thĕ snūff-bŏx.

A friend of Charles Lamb.

*1817. DRAKE (NATHAN). *Shakespeare and his times* (2 vols.,4ᵗᵒ). Speaks of Sidney's " unfortunate attempt to introduce the Roman metres into modern poetry " (Vol. I, p. 550).

1824. FRERE (JOHN HOOKHAM). *Poems.* One in hexameters on " Malta ". *Cf.* translation of *Frogs* (1830), note at end. Accessible in *Works*, 3 vols., Pickering, 1874.

The poem on Malta professes to be " without false quantities " [? ?], and the *note* at end of *Frogs* justifies redundant initial syllable in hexameter.

1838. BLUNDELL (JAMES). *Hexametrical Experiments,* thin 4ᵗᵒ (Pickering) ; anonymous.

Translates four of Virgil's Eclogues (not the first four). Noteworthy Introduction.

1838. GUEST [see in Appendix B]. He (Skeat's ed., p. 550 *seq.*) seems to think that all " the experiments which have been made during the last three centuries " had an accentual basis ; in them, " instead of the accent representing the sharp tone, or the ictus, it has been considered as a substitute for the long quantity " (p. 551). Their rhythm was loose, and they " followed the triple rather than the common measure ", besides neglecting pauses (*ibid.*). " German hexameters " share this condemnation (p. 552). He thinks that by dividing centrally, and avoiding false accentuation, a satisfactory metre might be evolved ; and offers some lines of his own as a " test " (p. 553). Though these are not quantitative, I give three as a sample ; the *colon* indicates his " middle pause "

> Sing the wrath, O Goddess : Achilles' wrath the Pelides !
> Deadly it was, and whelm'd : with many a woe the Achaians,
> Many a soul it sent : of hero brave into Hades.

No doubt, lines of this length tend to break into halves, but I do not think this tendency should be exalted into a canon. Otherwise the lines read fairly well ; accentuation is clear, and there are no harsh masses of consonants. " The Pelides " comes in oddly ; the first syllable of " Pelides " had obviously no ' long ' sound to Guest. Such experiments, at their best, do but little toward naturalizing an unfamiliar metre. That, as a rule, can be done only by poets.

1843. O'BRIEN (WILLIAM). *The Ancient Rhythmical Art recovered* (Dublin; posthumous). " Isochronous bars ", p. 31 (*cf.* text).

*1843. BARHAM (THOMAS FOSTER). *The Enkheiridion of Hehfaistiown* [*sic*], besides prolegomena on " Rythm ", contains (pp. 218–28) imitations of Classic metre in English quantitative verse, but his rules of quantity are not given. *H* is evidently disregarded, elision allowed, and long vowels shortened before a following vowel. But even so can we justify such a hexameter line as

> Hĕrŏes, whŏ ūnbŭrïĕd tŏ dĕvŏurīng dŏgs wĕre ăbāndōn'd ?

1844. SHADWELL (LANCELOT). *The Iliad of Homer. Faithfully rendered in Homeric verse from the original Greek* (in parts, paper covers, Books I to IX, 371 only ; Pickering). See Note at end of Book II.

This writer's ' hexameters ' should be distinguished from the ruck of accentual verse, since they at least profess to follow quantity. The *Note*, or rather " Advertisement ", after Book II, indeed, declares that his is " the first specimen of real Hexameter verse that has appeared in the English language " ; also that " in this translation the rules of ancient art are strictly followed out, and never departed from ". It is difficult to know what this means, since the pledge given of further explanation was not redeemed. Ordinary rules of [supposed] quantity are not followed; the writer's position seems much like that of Odell or Guest. I quote the first four lines of Book II :—

> Soundly the rest of the gods, and the horseplume-helmeted heroes,
> Slept thro' the livelong night ; but, sleep staid not to Kroníon :
> Waking and thoughtful, he dwelt on his scheme, that the sons of Achaia
> Thickly should die at the ships, and Achilleus' name be exalted.

*1846. OXENFORD (JOHN). In *Classical Museum*, Vol. III, pp. 279–83, short paper on " The practice of writing English in Classic metres ".

This writer, like others of his time, abandons quantity as a basis, but tries to secure quantitative effect by great precision of " *ictus* ". He gives one specimen, in ' sapphics ', apologising for his unaccented syllables, but relying on the others. I give a sample stanza :—

> Wealthy Priam leaving his Troy—in safety
> Led by thee—avoided the proud Atrides [;]
> Pass'd Thessalian watchers, and pass'd encampments
> Hostile to Ilium.

1853. CLOUGH [*cf.* Appendix B, 1848]. Accentual hexameters of Clough and others are kept for my second Appendix, but here must be mentioned his quantitative attempts. The " Letters of Parepidemus " appeared first in *Putnam's Monthly Magazine of American Literature, Science, and Art* [which later became " Putnam's Magazine ", *tout court*], Vol. II (1853), pp. 72–4 and 138–40. The Second Letter touches on ' quantity '. Clough was then only feeling his way, and the sample lines there given are more accentual than quantitative. *Odoriferous* is still a spondee *plus* dactyl, and he has such contradictory scansions as *fŏllowed the yĕllow Menelaus.* By the early Sixties he had come nearer the position of Spedding [*cf.* below], but he never mastered the latter's rules. The " Essays in Classical Metres ", printed among his poems, show this. True, he now writes *ŏdōrĭfĕrous* and *sŏpōrĭfĕrous, ĕchoes, shĕpherd, căvern, ăttentive.* But he also writes *sŭnny, swĕlling, fŭrrow, cūrrent, hŏllow, radiănt, tō, ŏn, that, manў streamlets, watĕr overflowing.* It can be said only that he " essayed " to write quantitative verse, not that he succeeded in doing so. *Cf.* " Elegiacs ", " Alcaics ", and " Actaeon " in his minor poems, and some ' alcaic ' lines in *Amours de Voyage.*

1860. MUNRO (HUGH ANDREW JOHNSTONE). Paper in Cambridge Philosophical Society's *Transactions* (Vol. X, Part II) for February, with appendix dated July, 1861 ; "On a metrical inscription at Cirta."

[Other publications referring to this paper will be found in Appendix B, about this date.]

1861. SPEDDING (JAMES). Paper in *Fraser's Magazine* for June (Vol. 63, p. 703 *seq.*). Reprinted with corrections and additions in *Reviews and Discussions,* by James Spedding (1879).

The only lines, to my knowledge, in which Spedding exemplified his theory, are those in the *Fraser* article. He first gives as correct quantitative metre this line :—

Swēetlў cŏmēth slūmbēr, clōsīng th' ō'erwēariĕd ēyelīd ;

then says there would be two " shocking false quantities " if it ran—

Sweetly falleth slumber, closing the wearië̆d eyelid.

Later, he puts forth his *chef-d'œuvre,* eight lines, which are quoted by W. J. Stone. In them Stone had detected " two false quantities " when he first wrote ; in his revised edition the phrase is " two or three ". I recognise two in *procēssion* and *divīsion,* a third in *ĭs* followed by a vowel ; other syllables are dubious but legitimate. The elision in *quantity obeyeth* is of course monstrous. Spedding's practice certainly ill sets off his theory ; three blunders in eight lines is bad. It shows how little reality such ' quantities ' had to him.

Tennyson's lines to " J. S." will be remembered.

1861. CAYLEY (CHARLES BAGOT). Philological Society's *Transactions* (Berlin, 1861–2), Part I, pp. 67–85) ; " Remarks and experiments on English hexameters."

Ditto (1867), pp. 43–54, article on " The pedigree of English Heroic Verse ".
The Prometheus Bound of Aeschylus. Translated in the original metres (1867).
The Iliad of Homer, Homometrically translated (1877).
Rules in first paper and preface to Aeschylus. His *Iliad* has for preface seven lines beginning—

> Dōns, ŭndērgrădŭātes, ĕssăyĭsts, ānd pūblĭc, Ĭ āsk yōu,
> Āre thēse hēxămētērs trūe-tīm'd, ōr Klōpstŏckĭsh ūprōar ?

1864. TENNYSON (ALFRED). *Enoch Arden and other poems.* " Experiments."
Of these " Boädicea " is an imitation of a rare Latin metre ; in the " Alcaics " and " Hendecasyllabics " he tried to unite accent and long quantity on the same syllable, with not entire success. These latter two had appeared in the *Cornhill Magazine* for December, 1863, following six lines not reprinted in the *Enoch Arden* volume. All three were headed " Attempts at Classic Metres in Quantity ", and the six lines were entitled " Translations of Homer, *Hexameters and Pentameters,* and were followed lower by a Note saying : " Some, and among them one at least of our best and greatest, have endeavoured to give us the Iliad in English hexameters, and by what appears to me their failure have gone far to prove the impossibility of the task. I have long held by our blank verse in this matter, and now after having spoken so disrespectfully here [where ? in this Note or in the six lines ?] of these hexameters, I venture, or rather feel bound, to subjoin a specimen, however brief and with whatever demerits, of a blank-verse translation." Then comes the well-known rendering of lines from *Iliad,* Book VIII.
Neither these six lines nor the Note were in the *Enoch Arden* volume. The six lines soon reappeared in subsequent editions, but the Note not, I think,till the Eversley edition (9 vols., 1907–8). In ordinary editions the five pieces are usually placed together under the title " Experiments ", " Boädicea " coming first, then the six lines preceded by this heading :

In Quantity
On Translations of Homer
Hexameters and Pentameters,

the first words being probably meant to cover them and their two immediate successors.
The six lines form Tennyson's one published attempt in metre disjoining accent and long quantity, and the reference to " one of our best and greatest " is to Sir John Herschel the astronomer [*cf.* Appendix B, 1862], as certified in the Eversley edition of the *Poetical Works,* Vol. II, p. 379.
Except some juvenile " leonine elegiacs ", Tennyson published no other quasi-Classic verse, though " The Daisy ", " To F. D. "

Maurice," and other pieces are modelled after Classic types. His *Memoir*, by his son [often referred to by me as his *Life*], has many interesting references to verse-structure. Quantitative metres in English he ultimately regarded as "only fit for comic purposes".

*1866. BLACKIE (JOHN STUART). *Homer*, 4 vols. (Edinburgh). *Horae Hellenicae* (reprinted papers), Macmillan, 1874.

In former, see last Dissertation of Vol. I ; in latter are papers on " English Hexameters " and " Accent in Language ".

This lively but erratic writer contributed to magazines many articles on English verse. He held that ancient Greek accent was stress.

*1868. CALVERLEY (CHARLES STUART). *London Student* for October. Reprint in *Works* (Bell and Son, 1901).

An important paper for Classicists.

*1871. ELLIS (ROBINSON). The poems and fragments of Catullus, translated in the metres of the original (Murray).

In his interesting Preface (see especially p. xiv *seq.*) Prof. Ellis explains his rules, which are quite different from those advocated by later writers, or by Spedding and Cayley, of whose contemporary work he seems unaware. Entirely rejecting ' combative accent ', he tries (following Tennyson) to unite accent and quantity, allows a heavily accented syllable to count as ' long ', ignores initial *y* as well as *h*, but otherwise observes rules of ' position '. Thus, " *heavy level ever cometh any* " are usually trochees, sometimes pyrrhics; "*dolorous stratagem echoeth family*", usually dactyls, are sometimes tribrachs. As a " pure iambic line " he selects—

Thĕ pŭnў pīnnăce yŏndĕr yŏu, mў frĭends, dĭscērn ;

in which phonetic quantity is at least three times set aside. His rules therefore, as he sees himself (p. xvi), are almost wholly negative ; they merely prevent clumsy crowds of consonants, a result which might surely have been reached by simpler methods. Brilliantly wrought as the translations are, they strike me as being neither Classic verse nor English ; the "Attis", in particular, I find metrically unreadable. But both translations and preface repay study.

*1872. MONRO (CHARLES JAMES). *Journal of Philology* (Cambridge), Vol. IV, No. 8, pp. 223–30, " Latin metres in English."

Supports Spedding, finds false quantities in R. Ellis. Speaks of " the insidious fallacy, that quantity is a sort of legal fiction " (p. 228).

*1883. MEREDITH (GEORGE). *Poems and Lyrics of the Joy of Earth.* " Phoebus with Admetus ", and notes thereto. He scans by syllables only.

Cf. " Phaéthôn, attempted in the Galliambic measure ", and some " Fragments of the Iliad " in *A Reading of Life* (1901). Many editions.

In his Introduction to *Poems of Dora Sigerson Shorter* (1907) he says that " quantity is denied to the English tongue ".

*1886. TENNYSON (SECOND LORD). *Jack and the Bean-stalk. English Hexameters. By Hallam Tennyson. Illustrated by Randolph Caldecott.* 4to, Macmillan (London and New York).

This *jeu d'esprit* interests as reflecting the view of quantity held by its author's father. Aspirated *h* is ignored, and phonetic sound not always regarded, so that we find *widŏw, lŏoking, prŏtect, where an' Ŏ where, cursĭng hĭm hied to hĕr bed, ăn humble obeisance, etc.* Accent is not allowed to replace quantity, so far as I have noticed, and is sometimes contrasted with it, as in *ĕlĕphănt.* *Ng* is sometimes reckoned one sound, sometimes two.

This entry reminds me that I have nowhere referred to some burlesque quantitative scraps by the late Laureate, quoted in his son's *Memoir* (one-volume edition, pp. 425–6 ; *cf. note* [3] there). It will be remembered how Stone was " nearly reduced to tears " by a ' pentameter ' line ending in *grŭel !*

*1889. TISDALL (FITZGERALD). *Theory of Origin and Development of the Heroic Hexameter* (New York).

[Not seen. Not in British Museum Catalogue.]

*1892. ALLEN (GRANT). *Catullus : the Attis* (Nutt, Bibliothéque de Carabas).

Pp. 126–54, " On the Galliambic metre ". His translation is in ordinary English verse.

*1898. LEAF (WALTER). *Versions from Hafiz* (small 4to).

Here an accomplished scholar tries to represent Persian metre by quantitative English, symbols being placed by him over syllables for our guidance. Strict rules of quantity are not followed, unstressed syllables being regarded as " common ", while accent is allowed to create length [1] ; yet the general effect is quantitative, and unusual feet (*bacchius, epitritus, etc.*) are used. A favourable example is (Ode V)—

> Ăflāme wĭth blōom ĭs thĕ rĕd rōse,

which reads itself. So, without marks, would (Ode VI)—

> Wild of mien, chanting a love-song, cup in hand, locks disarrayed ;

but we are asked to believe that this should be read—

> Wīld ŏf mīen, chănt- | ĭng ă lŏve-sōng, | cŭp ĭn hānd, lŏcks | dĭsărrāyed‿ |.

So we are asked not to read as " bad anapaests " this line (Ode XIV)—

> Ăgāin see | mĕ vānqŭished | ănd lāid lōw | ŏf wĭnē‿ | ;

but how can we fail to parallel it with

> Behind shut the postern, the lights sank to rest ?

---

[1] " Both quantity and accent are in many cases what the English reader makes them " (p. 14). One would like to have heard Stone's criticism of this view.

Or how can we fail to read as an 'octosyllabic couplet' this other line (Ode IV)—

Ăn ĭf yŏn Tūrk | ŏf Shīrāz lānd | thĭs hēart wōuld tāke | tŏ hŏld īn fēe | ?

No, if quantity is to be a basis, it must be independent of accent ; combined with accent, it inevitably takes second place in English. These clever exercises prove this anew, while avoiding the worse error of supposing a purely quantitative basis of English metre to be tolerable.

1898. STONE (WILLIAM JOHNSON). *On the use of Classical metres in English.* (Paper covers, Oxford.) Revised edition (posthumous), with *Milton's Prosody by Robert Bridges,* in book form (Oxford, 1901).

This brilliant essay revived the quantitative heresy. His specimen verses do not appear in the posthumous edition. He died aged 26. His work has been carried on by Mr. Bridges (*infra,* 1903).

*1899. STONE (E. D.). W. J. Stone's trumpet-blast in favour of quantitative verse provoked illustration as well as comment. In the *Academy* for April 1, 1899, pp. 388–9, appeared some ' elegiacs ' by his father, Mr. E. D. Stone, beginning [the symbols are mine]—

> Hō ! jŏllў ŏld pārsŏns, whŏ smŏked lŏng pīpes ŏf ăn ēvenĭng,
> Smŏked lŏng chŭrchwārdĕns, sīpped ăt ă bēadў rŭmmĕr.

These lines should of course be read by " Will Stone's " rules, but there are a few divergencies, *e. g. stupĭdly, birĕtted, ŏf horseflesh, ĭs one, dĕckers ; rustical antiphones,* as the second half of a ' pentameter ', is perhaps one of the " two or three false quantities " to which the writer pleads guilty. Readers can judge for themselves the merit of such lines as—

> Rēd-tīled, smārtlў bănnĕred, māde tŏ ă tīdў pāttĕrn,

or

> Wŏndĕrs mĕn rĕckŏn ĭt sēemlў tŏ wēar pĕttĭcōats.

I cannot believe such verse capable of any but the comic effect happily created by it here.

*1899. CRAWLEY (A. E.). In *Literature* for May 13, 1899, is a letter containing " Sappho's Litany " in stanzas appropriate to the title. I quote the first and last of the seven.

> Thrŏn'd ŭpŏn līght, Thŏu vĕrў Gŏd, Lŏve ōur Quĕen,
> Dāughtĕr ŏf Gŏd, mўstĕrў-wŏrkĕr, hēar mĕ !
> Spāre frŏm āll lŏve's wēarĭnĕss ānd bĭttĕrnĕss
>   Mў spĭrĭt, Ŏ Quĕen !
>
> .   .   .   .
>
> Cŏme tŏ mĕ nŏw l ānd dĕlĭvĕr frŏm āll mў
> Hārd sŏrrŏws ; ānd ŏf thĕ lŏngĭng wĭthĭn mĕ
> Fūlfĭl āll ; ānd bē ĕvĕr, Ĭ bĕsēech Thĕe,
>   Mў sŭccŏur ānd shĭeld.

Except for the ignoring of *h* in *workĕr, hear*, these lines seem perfectly to carry out Stone's rules. They are followed by this rendering of an epigram ascribed to Plato :—

> Dāy Stār ōf thĕ līvīng wāst thōu ōnce shīnīng ămōng mēn,
> Nōw thōu'rt Ēv'nīng Stār ōf thĕ dĕad īn Părădīse.

Technically faultless, this couplet leaves me convinced of the unsuitability of such structure for serious English verse.

[Considerable discussion followed in the pages of the above journal at this time and elsewhere.]

*1900. HARFORD (F. K.). *A Note on the Scansion of the Pentameter and its use in English poetry* (pamphlet, Oxford).

Rightly claims that silence and sound are convertible, but seems unaware that this point of view has been taken by others, both in theory and practice.

*1900. CARPENTER (EDWARD). In *Cambridge Review* of 22nd and 1st March " On English hexameter verse ", reviewing Stone.

*1901. BAYNE (THOMAS). In *Notes and Queries* of 27th April, " English Hexameters and Elegiacs " ; very slight.

*1901. ANONYMOUS. In *Macmillan's Magazine* for October, same title as last, much same contents ; perhaps by same author.

1901–2. McKERROW (R[ONALD] B.). In *Modern Language Quarterly* (Vol. IV) for December, 1901 and April, 1902 (4to, Nutt), two papers on " The use of so-called Classical Metres in Elizabethan Verse ".

Good, thorough, independent. A brief reference is made at the end to Stone's pamphlet.

1903. BRIDGES (ROBERT SEYMOUR). [Compare also Appendix B, 1889.]

Now in wintry delights (4to, paper covers, Daniel Press, Oxford). Quantitative hexameters, with Note on their prosody at end.

This was its author's first substantial attempt in " quantity ". For reprints of this and following pieces see *Poetical Works of Robert Bridges, excluding the eight Dramas* (Oxford University Press, 1912), to which I refer. It contains additional pieces.

Monthly Review for June and July, ' alcaics ' and " Epistle to a Socialist ", with account of Stone's prosody.

Peace Ode (paper covers, Daniel Press, Oxford, 1902).

Demeter, a Mask (paper covers, Clarendon Press, Oxford, 1905). Several choruses in Classic metres, and " concealed " lines elsewhere ; alcaics and iambic ode at beginning of Act III. Notes at end.

New Quarterly for January, 1909. *Ibant Obscuri*, preceded by essay on prosody.

English Review for March, 1912. " Amiel ".., For this and other short pieces see *Works* as above.

Times Literary Supplement for 31st December, 1914. " Winter, 1914."

A new edition of *Ibant Obscuri*, with a translation from the *Iliad*, and comparative versions by other poets, and an Introduction on prosody (Clarendon Press, Oxford, 1917).

If any one can reconcile the English ear to quantitative verse, Mr. Bridges should do it. His lines are poetry as well as verse, his phonetic feeling sound. One would need to know his personal pronunciation, whether he sounds *wĕ* differently to *wēedy*, the first vowel of " Oriental " long or short, *etc., etc.*

I must not disguise my own convictions, but may give myself the pleasure of quoting the ' alcaics ' mentioned above.

> Lŏ, whēre thĕ vīrgĭn·vēilĕd [1] ĭn āirў bĕams
> Āll-hōlў Mŏrn, ĭn splēndŏr ăwākĕnĭng,
> Hēav'n's gāte hăth ūnbārrēd, thĕ gōldĕn
> Aĕrĭāl lăttĭcēs sĕt ōpĕn.

> Wĭth mūsĭc ēndēth nīght's prĭsŏnĭng tĕrrŏr,
> Wĭth flōw'rў īncēnse : Hāste tŏ sălūte thĕ sŭn,
> Thāt fŏr thĕ dāy's chāse, līke ă hŭntsmăn,
> Wĭth flăshĭng ārms cŏmĕth ō'er thĕ mōuntăin.

*1903. Reviews naturally discussed this attempt by Mr. Bridges. Particularly may be mentioned one in the *Times Literary Supplement* for 10th April. In the *Academy* of 18th July, and next year, amended, in a pamphlet of *Scattered Verses* (Pelton, Tunbridge Wells), were some satirical lines by myself, mentioned here only for completeness' sake.

1908. TREVELYAN (ROBERT CALVERLEY). *Sisyphus : an operatic fable* (4to).

In an earlier volume, *Mallow and Asphodel* (1898), " The Playmates " is in accentual elegiacs, with redundant syllables and resolved caesuras.

*1908. WARREN (THOMAS HERBERT). *Essays of poets and poetry.* Mentions hexameters (p. 119), but does not distinguish between accentual and quantitative.

[I have no record of later work in this field, though there have been short pieces. Nor of reviews, except a good one in the *Times Literary Supplement* of 8th March, 1917, and a singularly foolish one in the *Classical Review* for June of the same year, where a writer signing himself *Oxoniensis* criticised Mr. Bridges without understanding the meaning of his attempt, and was deservedly trounced by subsequent writers.

[1] It is shocking to find the *diaeresis* here used for an accent-mark, as printers are wickedly beginning to do, *e. g.* Brontë. Over the first two letters of " aerial " it would have been in place. This solecism is repeated in the *Works*.

An unsigned article of my own, by the way, in the *Academy* of 20th February, 1909, referred to in my text, requires mention here.

I shall be glad to receive references to any quantitative lines omitted in the foregoing list.   Accentual ones are not wanted ; their name is legion, and enumeration would be neither possible nor profitable.   A complete record of quantitative English verse is possible and desirable.   Few writers have attempted such metre ;   their work deserves note.   It forms a separate if not happy chapter in the history of our verse, which should be written in full.]

APPENDIX B

OF BOOKS AND ARTICLES DEALING WITH THE ANALYSIS OF ORDINARY ENGLISH VERSE

[Compare Notes prefixed to Appendix A.]

1575. GASCOIGNE (GEORGE).   *Certayne notes of instruction in English verse.*   Originally prefixed to his *Posies* (1575).   Reprinted in his *Works* (4to, 1587) ;   by Haslewood in *Ancient Critical Essays upon English Poets and Poesy*, Vol. II (4to, 1815) ; Arber, *English Reprints* (1868) ;   this volume contains other works of his, and is titled *The Steele Glas. Poetical Works*, re-edited by W. Carew Hazlitt (1868–9).

For complete *Works* see " Cambridge University Classics ".

1577.   BLENERHASSET (THOMAS).   In *Mirror for Magistrates*, Part II, " Induction " following poem called " The Complaint of Cadwallader ", our ordinary accentual verse is styled *iambic*. Reprints by Haslewood (3 vols., 4to, 1815), and in the above-mentioned " Classics "

*****1579.** GOSSON (STEPHEN)'s *School of Abuse* and *Apologie* for same (Arber, 1868) are mentioned here only because they provoked Sidney's treatise (Appendix A).

*****1579.** LODGE (THOMAS).   *A Defence of Poetry, Music, and Stage Plays* (privately printed ;   copy in Bodleian Library).   A reply to Gosson.   Reprint by Shakespeare Society, 1853 ;   also in his *Works*, ed. Gosse (Hunterian Club, Glasgow), 1872–82.

1585.   JAMES VI OF SCOTLAND.   *Essays of a Prentice in the divine art of poesie* (4to, Edinburgh) contains " Ane short treatise containing some rewlis and cautelis to be observit and eschewit in Scottis Poesie "

Rules reprinted by Haslewood (1815).   The whole book by Gillies (Edinburgh, 1814) and Arber (1869).

1589. PUTTENHAM (GEORGE). *The Art of English Poesie,* 4to. Published anonymously, and never acknowledged, but ascribed to the above, an officer of Queen Elizabeth's Court.

Reprints by Haslewood, *ut ante* (forms Vol. I of the *Essays*) ; Arber, 1869.

The first considerable treatise on English metric.

*1591. HARRINGTON or HARINGTON (SIR JOHN). " An Apologie of Poetrie," prefixed to his translation of *Orlando Furioso.* Reprint in Haslewood, Vol. II.

Nothing of importance, but refers to Puttenham's book as " by an unknown godfather ".

*1598. MERES (FRANCIS). *Palladis Tamia . . . being the second part of Wits' Commonwealth,* small thick 8vo, rare..

Compares English with Greek, Latin, and Italian poets (pp. 276–87), but has nothing on verse-structure.

1603 ? DANIEL (SAMUEL). *A Defence of Rhyme,* first known edition, 1607. Reprints in *Works,* 4to, 1623; 2 vols. 12mo, 1718; by Grosart, 5 vols. (Huth Library), 1885 and 1896. The *Defence* also in Haslewood, *ut ante.* In Grosart, Vol. V.

*1610–17. BOLTON (EDMUND). *Hypercritica.* Reprints by Hall (Oxford), 1722 ; Haslewood, *ut ante.* " Address IV, Section 3 " deals with verse, but not on its technical side.

*1619. DRAYTON (MICHAEL). " Epistle of Poets and Poetry " in *Poetical Works* (many editions).

In verse. Nothing about prosody, though much about other " brave translunary things ". Calls Gascoigne and Thomas Churchyard [author of *A Praise of Poetrie* (1595), not mentioned by me, because containing nothing *ad rem*] " great meterers ".

*1622. PEACHAM (HENRY). *The Compleat Gentleman . . . etc.,* 4to. Chap. X (pp. 78–96) is " Of Poetrie ", but nothing notable except list of poets at end.

*1637. SUCKLING (SIR JOHN). *A Sessions of the Poets.* Often reprinted in his *Works.*

Very weak triple-time verse.

*about 1640 ? BEAUMONT (SIR JOHN). Epistle " To his late Majesty, concerning the true form of English poetry ". [Seen only in *Chalmers' English Poets* (1810), Vol. VI, pp. 30–1.] Date uncertain.

76 lines, heroic couplets. Deals mostly with accentuation and rhymes, " closing sounds of some delightful bell ". In the next poem, " To the glorious memory of our late soveraigne lord, King James," that monarch is praised because

> He leads the lawless poets of our times
> To smoother cadence, to exacter rhymes.

Prof. Saintsbury thinks Beaumont's verse important historically, but his view of metre is merely the traditional one.

*1651. D'AVENANT (SIR WILLIAM). *Gondibert, an heroic poem.*

The preface, addressed to Hobbes, discusses mainly the subject-matter of verse, as does Hobbes's reply.

*1657 ? POOLE (JOSHUA) and J. D. [Cf. Appendix A, same date.]

The English [1] Parnassus : or a Helpe to English Poesie, contains a prefatory note by " J. D.", dealing merely with versification, though he does once make verse consist of " measure, proportion, and rhythm " [i. e. rhyme ?], and says that accent is " like right time in musicke ". A correspondent in Notes and Queries for 8th November, 1913 (11 S. VIII, p. 370) says in his copy the initials [sic] are Jⁿ Dⁿ, which suggests Dryden as author. But if, as I imagine, this merely means that the two small letters are added in ink to the printed ones, this may represent only the guess of some previous possessor.

*1667 and 1679. WOODFORD (SAMUEL), D.D. A Paraphrase upon the Psalms of David (1667) and A Paraphrase on the Canticles (1679) have prefaces referring slightly to structure. Trisyllabic feet are defended in the latter's, and a passage from Milton given in prose form. The date alone makes these worth naming.

*1668. MILTON (JOHN). Preface to Paradise Lost.
Speaks of " apt Numbers, fit quantity of Syllables ", etc.

*1669. HOLDER (WILLIAM). Elements of speech . . . .
An early work on phonetics. Accent and emphasis " now much confounded ".

*1678 ? RYMER (THOMAS). The Tragedies of the last Age considered . . . etc.
Second enlarged edition (1692–3) has in a new Part II some general remarks on verse, finding much fault with Shakespeare.

*1684. ROSCOMMON, EARL OF. An Essay on translated verse.
Second edition (1685) in British Museum.
In verse. Accent made supreme. Commendatory lines by Dryden speak of " pauses, cadence, and well-vowell'd words ".

*1690. TEMPLE (SIR WILLIAM). Miscellanea, The Second Part (third edition, only one seen). IVth Essay, " On Poetry."
Mainly talkee-talkee. Esteems Sir Philip Sidney " the Greatest Poet and the Noblest Genius of any that have left writings . . . in ours or in any other Modern Language " (p. 311).
Interesting for its well-known final sentence : " When all is said, Human Life is at the greatest and the best but like a froward Child, that must be play'd with and Humour'd a little to keep it quiet, till it falls asleep, and then the Care is over."

*1691. BUCKINGHAM, DUKE OF. An essay on poetry : by the Rt. Hon. the Earl of Mulgrave. Second edition same year. Another edition (1697) by the Marquis of Normanby.

[1] In former edition mistakenly called England's Parnassus, which title belongs to an earlier collection of quotations by Robert Allott (1600), reprinted in 1913 (Oxford Clarendon Press).

In verse. Often referred to at the time, but nothing of consequence.

*1693. DENNIS (JOHN). *The Impartial Critic . . . etc.* 4to. A
reply to Rymer's book, in dialogue form, upholding Shakespeare
as against Waller and later poets, but considers that Dryden's
" equal numbers in heroic verse " can never be surpassed till the
language alters.

*The Advancement and Reformation of Modern Poetry. A Critical
Discourse.* 1701.

Deals with matter, not form.

*1700. WESLEY (SAMUEL). *An epistle to a friend concerning
poetry.*

By the father of John and Charles Wesley. Speaks of " pauses
and accents ".

1702. BYSSHE (EDWARD). *The Art of English Poetry.* In
three parts : I. " Rules for making verses." II. A Rhyming
Dictionary (meagre). III. A collection of similes, *etc.*, separately
reprinted as *English Parnassus*, 2 vols., 1714 (*cf. ante*, 1657).
This last fills more than half the book. Many subsequent editions
of whole book, with substantial alterations. In the eighth edition
(2 vols., 20mo, 1737) the Rules are enlarged, the Dictionary of
Rhymes is put last, and by far the greater part of the two volumes
is occupied by the " Collection of the most Natural and Sublime
Thoughts ", *etc. etc.*, these being often long quotations.

1700-10 ? DYCHE (THOMAS). *A Guide to the English Tongue, in
two parts* . . . I cannot tell date of first edition ; the second is dated
1710. Often reprinted, *e. g.* 12mo, 1775 ; " new edition ", by Dean
and Munday, 12mo, 1830.

1700-10 ? DILWORTH (THOMAS). *A New Guide to the English
Tongue.* The earliest edition I have seen is the 13th (12mo, 1751).
Stereotype edition, 12mo, 1812.

*1709. COWARD (WILLIAM). *Licentia Poetica Discuss'd : or,
the true test of Poetry,* . . . [with] *Critical Observations on the Principal
Antient and Modern Poets, viz. Homer, Horace, Virgil, Milton,
Waller, Cowley, Dryden, &c., as frequently liable to Just Censure.
A Poem.* By W. Coward, Coll. Med. Lond. M.D.

Preface of some twenty-eight pages (unnumbered). The Poem
in two Books, many *notes*. Comments amusingly on the liberties
taken with syllables by poets. Favours trisyllabic feet.

1711. ADDISON (JOSEPH). Papers on Milton in *Spectator*
(collected, 1719 ; edited by Dodd, 1762).

Very little indeed about metre. *Cf.* No. 267, beginning ;
No. 285, on language.

1711. POPE (ALEXANDER). *Essay on Criticism* (in verse).
One famous passage, beginning—

> But most by numbers judge a poet's song.

Saintsbury (Hist. Pros., II, 471) quotes in full a letter of Pope's about versifying.

*1713. ANONYMOUS. *Essay on the Different Stiles of Poetry.*
In verse. Scorns the lower regions soared over by Pegasus, " Where Couplets jingling on their Accents run . . . Where lines by measure form'd in Hatchets lie " [whatever that phrase may mean]. The Preface says his " aim is instruction ".

1718. GILDON (CHARLES). *The Complete Art of Poetry. In Six Parts* . . . (2 vols., 12ᵐᵒ). Dedication to King George: preface: introduction addressed to Crites (i. e. Dennis). Text in five dialogues, pp. 1–303, followed by extracts from Shakespeare. Vol. II consists entirely of extracts from poets.
Vol. I, pp. 293–303, " Of English Numbers."
The Laws of Poetry . . . Explain'd and Illustrated. 8ᵛᵒ, 1721.

*1721. MALCOLM (ALEXANDER). *A Treatise of Musick, Speculative, Practical, and Historical* (Edinburgh). Text, pp. 1–608.
Often quoted, but I find no reference to verse-structure.

*1732. BENTLEY (RICHARD). Edition of Milton, with notes correcting metre as well as sense !

*1732. SWIFT (JONATHAN). *Milton restor'd and Bentley depos'd.*
Castigates the great critic's presumption.
Swift's *Proposal for correcting the English Tongue* (1711–12) should not be forgotten.

1738. PEMBERTON (H.). *Observations on Poetry, especially the Epic.*
Anonymous on title-page, but preface signed (a common habit at this time).
The first of several learned books, treating of accent and quantity, and incidentally of English verse.

*1739 or **1740.** ANONYMOUS. *The Quintessence of English Poetry* (3 vols., " sold by O. Payne ").
So states an advertisement in *Gentleman's Magazine* for April, 1740 (p. 208, b). No copy known ; not in the usual Catalogues. May be only a collection of passages from poems.

1739. BENSON (WILLIAM). *Letters concerning Poetical translations, and Virgil and Milton's Art of Verse.*
Anonymous, but ascribed as above. The Letters being dated September to December, 1736, how could there have been an edition in 1713, or even 1731 ?

1744. MANWARING (or MAINWARING) (EDWARD). *Of Harmony and Numbers, in Latin and English Prose, and in English Poetry.*
Chap. V is on English verse.
Earlier books by same author, e. g. *Stichology* (4ᵗᵒ, London, 1737), *An Account of Classic Authors* (8ᵛᵒ, London, 1737), refer very slightly to English verse.

1744. HARRIS (JAMES). *Three Treatises.* The first is on Art (pp. 1–45), the second on Music, Painting, and Poetry (pp. 49–103), the third on Happiness (107–247).

An early work by the author of *Hermes*. See his *Works*, edited by his son, the Earl of Malmesbury, 2 vols., 4to, London, 1801, where they are reprinted apparently without alteration.

1745. SAY (SAMUEL). *Poems, etc.* (posthumous, 4to). Two essays on " numbers ", the second having special reference to *Paradise Lost*.

Dedicated to " Mr. Richardson ". Say made up (from Chaucer and Spenser) two lines quoted by nearly every subsequent writer of the Century—

> And many an amorous, many a humourous lay,
> Which many a bard had chanted many a day.

*1748. FITZOSBORNE (SIR THOMAS). *Letters on several subjects* (2 vols.). " On numbers in prose writers " (Vol. I, p. 24). Some remarks on Pope's *Homer*, and skits on verbal critics. Unimportant.

[Some critics attribute these Letters to W. Melmoth, junior.]

1749. MASON (JOHN). Two *Essays* on the *Power of Numbers*. Published anonymously. Reprinted, with another paper, revised and altered, in 1761.

*1750 ? SMITH (ADAM). *Essays Philosophical and Literary* [by author of *Wealth of Nations*]. " On the Imitative Arts." See *Works*, ed. Dugald Stewart (Edinburgh, 1811–12).

Part [=Chapter] II speaks of " Rhythms, what we call Time or Measure ". *Cf.* fragment printed after Part III, time precedes tune, and is far simpler. One accent may be omitted in a line, never two together ; accent on odd syllable spoils heroic line. No distinction between grave and acute accent in English.

*1754. FORTESCUE (JAMES). *Pomery Hill. A Poem . . . With other poems*. Preface of 20 pages on Prosody, Latin and English. He takes " a liberty . . . perhaps unprecedented in English verse " by writing " to atone " instead of " t' atone ". Yet he prints " com'st ", *etc., etc.* Any foot used in our lyric verse may occur anywhere in heroic metre, even trochee in last foot.

Essays moral and miscellaneous [in verse], (Part I, 1752 ; Part II, 1754), contains nothing for us.

1755. JOHNSON (SAMUEL). *Dictionary*. Grammar at beginning has Section IV on " Prosody ".

Compare *Ramblers* Nos. 86, 88, 90, 94, 139, 140, dealing with Milton's verse ; also *Life* of Milton (in *Lives of the Poets*), near end, where he says blank verse too like prose.

*1757. ANONYMOUS. *Beauties of Poetry displayed, containing observations on the different species of poetry and the rules of English Versification* (2 vols., 12mo).

Preface, especially Section beginning p. xxiv. " Pure " Heroic

measure is when each alternate syllable is accented, which gives
" the most complete Harmony of which a single verse is capable ",
but soon becomes " tiresome and disgusting ". The only proper
pauses are after 4th and 6th syllables ; Milton's other ones are
condemned.

*1758. BAYLY (ANSELM). *An Introduction to Languages,
Literary and Philosophical . . in three parts.*

" Accent is in English the same as Quantity, making that
syllable long on which it is laid " (p. 181 ; but *cf.* below). Latin
hexameters given in musical notes, six bars of common time.

The Alliance of Musick, Poetry, and Oratory . . . (1789) ; especially pp. 79–114.

" Accent in modern acceptation is often confused with quantity
and emphasis " (p. 80). We shorten words in a barbarous way,
" knocking down the consonants " (pp. 90–1). Much about *feet.*
He rejects and derides elision by apostrophe.

1760 ? GRAY (THOMAS). *Observations on English Metre* (posthumously published). See *Works*, any complete edition, *e. g.*
ed. Gosse, 4 vols. (1884), pp. 323–409.

1762. SHERIDAN (THOMAS). See *infra*, 1775.

1762. FOSTER (JOHN). *Essay on different nature of accent and
quantity,* . . . first edition. Second edition, 1763 ; best edition,
1820, with dissertations by Gally (see below), and reply.

GALLY (as above) and PRIMATT (*Accentus Redivivi*, Cambridge,
1764) hardly require separate mention. The latter asserted that
accent invariably lengthened a syllable ! Gally had previously
published (anonymously) *A Dissertation against pronouncing the
Greek Language according to accents*, 1754.

1762. KAMES, HENRY HOME, LORD (of Session). *Elements of
Criticism*, 3 vols., no name on title-page, but dedication signed.
Vol. II, chap. 18 discusses " beauty of language ", § 4 being about
Versification. Reprint in one volume (1824).

1762. WEBB (DANIEL). *Remarks on the Beauties of Poetry.*
Reprinted, with other papers, in *Miscellanies, by the late Daniel
Webb, Esq.*, 4to, 1802. A later paper, *On the correspondence between
Poetry and Music* (1769), deals directly with verse-structure.

1763. BROWN (JOHN), Vicar of Newcastle-on-Tyne. *A Dissertation on the Rise, Union, and Power* . . . *of Poetry and Music* (12mo,
Dublin). Mainly about music.

1765. RICE (JOHN). *An Introduction to the Art of Reading
with Propriety and Elegance.*
Unpromising title, but *cf.* account in text.

*1766. HURD (RICHARD). In *A Dissertation on the Idea of
Universal Poetry* (folio) he proclaims " numbers " essential to
the highest form of poetry.

1771. HAWKINS (JOHN), SIR. *A general history of the Science
and practice of music* (5 vols., 4to). Later edition by Novello,
2 vols., 1853 [Brit. Mus. Cat. says 3 vols.].

Preliminary discourse, in Vol. I, often referred to by metrists of day.

1773 seq. MONBODDO, JAMES BURNETT, LORD (of Session). *Of the origin and progress of language* (6 vols., 1773–92). The second half of Vol. II deals with verse-structure.

1773. KENRICK (WILLIAM). *A New Dictionary of the English Language . . . to which is prefixed a Rhetorical Grammar* (4to).

1774 seq. WARTON (THOMAS). *History of English Poetry from the Twelfth to the close of the Sixteenth Century* (4 vols., 1774–81). New edition by W. Carew Hazlitt, 4 vols., 1871, with additions by Sweet and others.

1774. MITFORD (WILLIAM). *An Essay upon the Harmony of Language . . .* Anonymous. Second edition, much enlarged, appeared in 1804, as *An Inquiry into the principles of Harmony in Language, and of the mechanism of verse, modern and antient. By William Mitford, Esq.*

1775. SHERIDAN (THOMAS). *The Art of Reading, in two parts.* Part I, Lecture II, on Accent ; Part II, on verse-structure. An able discussion of principles less fully expounded in his *Dissertation* and *Lectures on Elocution* (1762), and in the " prosodical grammar " prefixed to his *Dictionary* (2 vols., 1780).

1775. STEELE (JOSHUA). *Prosodia rationalis : or, an essay towards establishing the melody and measure of speech. . . .* First (incomplete) edition ; *cf.* preface to second. Second edition, " amended and enlarged," 4to, 1779. Never reprinted.

1775. TYRWHITT (THOMAS). *The Canterbury Tales of Chaucer, with Essay, etc.* (4 vols. ; a fifth added later, 1778.) The Essay occupies Vol. IV. Reprint in one volume (4to), Moxon, 1843 ; Routledge, 1866.

1775. COCKIN (WILLIAM). [See description in text.] ? RAMSAY (ALLAN). [MS. only. See description in text.]

*****1775.** ANONYMOUS. *Sentimental Fables, translated from the French . . . to which is prefixed an Essay on English Versification. By a Country Curate* (Brentford). The " Essay " is merely part of the Preface (pp. iii–xx), and deals only with rhymes and caesural pauses.

1776. BEATTIE (JAMES). *Essays* (4to, Edinburgh). " An Essay on Poetry and Music as they affect the mind " (pp. 348–580). Written in 1762.

1776 seq. BURNEY (CHARLES), Mus. Doc. *General History of Music* (4 vols., 4to, 1776–89). Dissertation on Ancient Music fills most of Vol. I, but some references to verse.

1783. BLAIR (HUGH). *Lectures on Rhetoric and Belles Lettres,* 2 vols., 4to. Often reprinted. Vol. II, Lecture 38, on poetry. *Cf* Vol. I, Lecture 13, on " Structure of Sentences : Harmony ".

1784. NARES (ROBERT). *Elements of Orthoepy* . . . .
Good introductory remarks.

1785. SCOTT (JOHN), of Amwell. *Critical Essays on some of the Poems of several English Poets.*

***1786.** BARNES (THOMAS), D.D. *On the Nature and essential Characters of Poetry as distinguished from Prose* [*sic* in *Monthly Review* for second half of 1786, short notice, but no copy now known. The loss does not seem great].

1786. YOUNG (WALTER), REV. Royal Society of Edinburgh's *Transactions*, Vol. II, Part II, p. 55, paper " On Rythmical Measures ".

***1789.** DARWIN (ERASMUS). *The Botanic Garden* (4to). No name on title-page. I quote third edition (1794), which is fuller. Part II, " The Loves of the Plants," has " Interludes " in prose after each Canto. The first one asks " what is the essential difference between Poetry and Prose ", and the third discusses the relation of Poetry [verse] to Music. He thinks our " dactylic " verse has four crotchets to a bar, and gives Anstey's *Bath Guide* as an example [!], also that its time is slower than that of our " iambic " verse. He is sure the former's movement " much resembles " that of the Classic hexameter.

1791. WALKER (JOHN). *A Critical Pronouncing Dictionary* . . . *etc.* Introduction on " Principles of English Pronunciation ", sections on Accent and Quantity.
Cf. the same author's *Elements of Elocution* (2 vols., 1781) and *Key to Proper Names* (1798) ; also *Rhetorical Grammar* (1785). Other details in text.

1795. MURRAY (LINDLEY). *English Grammar.* Often reprinted ; good edition, 2 vols., York, 1808.
Part IV on Prosody.

1796. FOGG (PETER WALKDEN). *Dissertations, Grammatical and Philological* (Stockport). Forming part of his *Elementa Anglicana.*
Dissertation XI on Prosody ; XII on Versification.

1796. HORSLEY (SAMUEL), Bishop. *On the prosodies of the Greek and Latin languages.* Anonymous.

***1796.** TAYLOR (WILLIAM), of Norwich. *Monthly Magazine*, Vol. I (No. for June) contains Taylor's " transversion " from Macpherson's *Ossian*, in accentual hexameters, imitating Germans, who " scan by emphasis, not by position ". Short introduction ; mentions Klopstock, Bodmer, Goethe, Stolberg, Voss, Denis.
This marks the real beginning of such verses in English Literature, though Webb, Herries, and Beattie had had the idea.
Cf. Historic Survey of German Poetry (4 vols., 1828) by Taylor, when old. Much fuller ; many examples. Also *Memoir*, by J. W. Robberds (2 vols., 1843) for correspondence with Southey, in 1798–1800. Quotes Voss's *Luise* to him (August, '98). Southey

says, "Coleridge and I mean to march an army of hexameters into the country " (Sept. '99), and " A little practice has enabled me to hexametrize with facility " (Oct. '99). Taylor criticises sample of projected poem on " Mohammed ", by Southey and Coleridge (Dec. '99 ; Feb. 1800).

1797. WARNER (JOHN), afterwards D.D. *Metronariston : or a new pleasure recommended, in a Dissertation upon a part of Greek and Latin prosody.* Small 4to.

My previous ignorance of this amusing book's author was inexcusable. See *Dict. Nat. Biography*; also *Notes and Queries* for 14th December, 1861 (2nd Series, XII, 474) ; and W. P. Courtney's *Eight Friends of the Great* (1910), pp. 35–70. A notice of the book in *Monthly Review* for first quarter of 1798 (2nd Series, Vol. 25).

1797. CANNING (GEORGE) and others. The *Anti-Jacobin* (periodical), which ran from 20th November, 1797 to 9th July, 1798, contained parodies of Southey's early poems in Nos. 1, 2, 5, 6, and references to him in other numbers.

1798. WORDSWORTH (WILLIAM), COLERIDGE (SAMUEL TAYLOR), SOUTHEY (ROBERT). I bracket these together, in the year of *Lyrical Ballads'* publication, as practitioners of the " new verse " (new only to critics). The Taylor-inspired verses of Coleridge and Southey need not be further dwelt on (but *cf. infra*, 1821) ; Wordsworth, less of a scholar, held aloof from these.[1] Coleridge's chief prosodical pronouncement is of course the preface to *Christabel*, published in 1815, but talked over with Scott and others long before. Incidental references are frequent in *Biographia Literaria, Lectures on Shakespeare*, and *Table-Talk* (posthumous), of all which there are many editions. The Shakespeare Lectures (Routledge, 12mo [1908]) begin with the words " Poetry is not the proper antithesis to prose, but to science. Poetry is opposed to science, and prose to metre."

Of his *Poems* the best edition is that by E. H. Coleridge (Oxford, 1912), which contains several previously unpublished pieces. The first part of *Christabel* was written in 1797, the second in 1800 ; both were freely shown to friends.

***1798.** ANONYMOUS. In *Analytical Review* for January (Vol. 27, p. 102 *seq.*) article disclosing much dissatisfaction with Popian verse.

[1] Perhaps one should mention Coleridge's " Mahomet ", " Hymn to the Earth", and lines " written during a temporary blindness ", in hexameter ; and his ' Catullian Hendecasyllabics " (translated from German) ; as appearing in *Sibylline Leaves* (1817), though written earlier. " Metrical feet : lessons for a boy " is dated 1807. He seems to have followed rather than led Southey in this matter.

Southey's *Poems* of 1797 contained the pieces satirized by the *Anti-Jacobin*. There are four ' sapphic ' stanzas in *The Curse of Kehama* (4to, 1810), beginning of Section X.

1799. ROBERTSON (REV. JOSEPH). *An Essay on the Nature of the English Verse, with directions for reading poetry.*

1800. WORDSWORTH (WILLIAM). Preface to *Lyrical Ballads*, 2nd edition.

Important manifesto, dealing with matter more than form, but containing some profound remarks on the meaning and symbolic character of metre.

Much altered in later editions, but reprinted in Macmillan's one-volume edition of his *Works* (1888), which gives the poems in chronological order.

1801. ROE (RICHARD). *Cf. infra,* 1823.

*1804. SCOTT (WALTER). *Lay of the Last Minstrel.* Actually written this year (published Edinburgh, 4to, 1805), being thus the first important poem adopting Coleridge's principle of metre, and making it familiar ten years before *Christabel* was published.

In a note to *Sir Tristrem* (Fytte Second), Scott calls " the mode of slurring verse into prose, by reading it as such ", a modern fashion.

1805. KNIGHT (RICHARD PAYNE). *An analytical inquiry into the principles of taste.*

1805. MITFORD'S *Inquiry* (1804) is mentioned *ante,* 1774. The review of it by Herbert in the *Edinburgh Review* for July (Vol. VI), incidentally noticed in Appendix A, was reprinted, with additional Note at end, in *Works of the late Hon. and Very Rev. William Herbert, Dean of Manchester,* 3 vols., 1842 (Vol. II, pp. 31–78).

1806. ODELL (J.), M.A. [Cambridge]. *An Essay on the Elements, Accents, and Prosody, of the English Language.*

Written some years earlier, preface dated November, 1802.

1808. GREGORY (GEORGE). *Letters on Literature, Taste, and Composition* (2 vols., 12mo).

*1809. CAREY (JOHN). *Key to practical English prosody and versification.*

Old-fashioned analysis. Dislikes trisyllabic feet in heroic verse, but admits that they exist.

Author of *Gradus ad Parnassum, etc.*

[1812.] THELWALL (JOHN). *Illustrations of English Rhythmus.* N.D. Introduction, pp. vii–lxxii, analysing verse.

Cf. The poetical recreations of the Champion and his literary correspondents, . . . with . . . essays which have appeared in the Champion newspaper, 1822. " Sapphics," *etc.,* by Coleridge and himself (pp. 22, 29–31, 32, *etc.*). On p. 11 is Thelwall's " Song without a sibilant ".

1813. EDWARDS (RICHARD). (1) *Treatise on English Prosody* (12mo).

(2) *Specimens of English Accentuated Verse, wherein the Intensity of Pronunciation only is measured, and the length of the syllable is unnoticed* (12mo).

(3) *Specimens of Non-accentuated Verse, or Verse measured with a regard solely to the length of time required in the pronunciation of syllables, the accents and emphasis being entirely unnoticed* (12mo).

Mentioned in Watt, *Bibliotheca Britannica*. No copy known to exist [*query*, one book or three ?]. Guest tried in vain to find (3), see Skeat's edition, p. 108. They were small books, judging from prices in Watt.

See *Monthly Review*, Vol. 73 (first half of 1814). Places them 2, 3, 1. From (1) quotes : " As there were no poems in verse in the English language before those which I have recently written, no rules of English prosody were needed . . . there never has been a verse-writer in the language before " [! !]. Naturally, the Review quotes no more.

*1817. HAZLITT (WILLIAM), and HUNT (LEIGH). *The Round Table* (2 vols., Edinburgh).

Paper No. XI is on " The versification of Milton ", but contains nothing to quote.

1818. CHAPMAN (JAMES). *The Music, or Melody and Rhythmus, of Language* (Edinburgh).

The Original Rhythmical Grammar of the English Language (1821, Edinburgh).

1819. CAMPBELL (THOMAS). *Specimens of the British Poets* (7 vols.). " Essay on English Poetry ". The whole work reprinted in one volume (1841) ; the Essay and his " notices " of poets (16mo, 1848).

1819. BRYANT (WILLIAM CULLEN). *North American Review* for September, article " On trisyllabic feet in iambic measure ". Reprint, with additions, in Vol. I of his *Works* (6 vols., New York, 1884), as the third of three " Literary Essays ", all concerned with poetry.

*1820. " J. D." *Blackwood's Magazine* for September (Vol. VII, No. 42), article on " Sweetness of Versification ", signed " J. D." " The recurrence . . . of accents in certain places . . . constitutes rhythm " (p. 642). No clue to authorship.

1821. SOUTHEY (ROBERT). *A Vision of Judgment* (4to).

Accentual hexameters, with preface. Placed here separately because it introduced the metre to the British public.

1821. *Edinburgh Review* for July. Vol. XXXV, pp. 422–36. Review of Southey's poem.

1822. TILLBROOK (SAMUEL). *Historical and Critical Remarks upon the modern Hexametrists, and upon Mr. Southey's Vision of Judgment* (Cambridge).

1822. DOUGLAS (SYLVESTER), LORD GLENBERVIE. Translation of *Ricciardotto* (by Forteguerri), Canto I.

Note 95 (pp. 158–85) goes into questions of versification, being " an extract from an essay I have in part composed " on the subject. [This never published. He died next year.]

The book had been privately published in 1821.

1823. ROE (RICHARD BAILLIE). *The Principles of Rhythm both in speech and music ; especially as exhibited in the mechanism of English verse* (4to, Dublin).

The Elements of English Metre (small 4to, 1801).

I have recently been given a copy of the latter book, which was not in any public library (now in British Museum). It is simpler, but less developed, than the later work. The parts of metre, he says, "are those solely of time or duration" (p. 1). Feet are distinguished by accent and quantity (p. 6), and the whole fabric of English metre rests upon equidistance of accents (p. 7). All feet, whether consisting of few syllables or many, are equal (*ibid.*). His notation is merely a *scale*, with upright lines denoting the syllables. Accented syllables may be short, and unaccented long (p. 13). He lays great stress on what he calls "retarded syllables", without much apparent result. While parts of lines differ as to number of syllables, "the mind, by a natural propensity to order, always considers them as equidistant" (p. 20). Most of the book is occupied with scansions, of no great novelty, nearly all being taken from Milton as the supreme authority (pp. 55–6), Cowper being also praised. A brief account of the difference between verse and prose (pp. 73–8) contains nothing of consequence. On the whole, this book adds little to our knowledge of Roe's teaching, but isochrony is strongly insisted on.

1827. CROWE (WILLIAM). *A Treatise on English Versification* (Oxford).

1827. RUSH (JAMES). *The Philosophy of the Human Voice* (Philadelphia, U.S.A.). Best edition the third (*ibid.*, 1845).

1828. WILSON (JOHN). In *Blackwood's Magazine* for November (Vol. XXIV, No. 145), "Noctes Ambrosianae No. 39."

*1830. BARBER (JONATHAN) *A Grammar of Elocution ; containing the principles of the arts of reading and speaking ...* (Newhaven, Connecticut, 12mo).

By a London M.R.C.S. Follows Rush entirely. In Section on "Measure of speech" (pp. 125–43) uses Steele's symbols, and reproduces much of his teaching.

*about 1830 ? DE QUINCEY (THOMAS). Of many scattered sentences by this discursive writer I quote two, from his Essays on "Rhetoric" and "Style" respectively. These were published, I think, in magazines, but I quote the Edinburgh edition of his *Works* (15 vols., 1862–3, and supplementary volume, added 1871), Vol. X.

"Metre is open to any form of composition, provided it will aid in the expression of the thoughts" (p. 40).

"Rhythmus is both a cause of impassioned feeling, an ally of such feeling, and a natural effect of it" (p. 204).

*1831. FORDE (WILLIAM). *The true spirit of Milton's Versi-*

*fication developed in a new and systematic arrangement of the First
Book of Paradise Lost. With an introductory essay* . . . (thin 4to,
pp. lxviii and 36, London and Cork).

Divides by sense. Thinks Shakespeare and his contemporaries
abandoned decasyllabic metre, and Milton followed suit.

" The relative lengths of the syllables are as well ascertained
and felt in English, as they were in Greek or Latin " (p. xvi, foot-
note). Our verse might use them, but does not. " The least
deviation from Quantity is as offensive in a Parliamentary
speaker as it would have been to an Athenian from the lips of
Demosthenes " *(ibid.).*

1832. GARDINER (WILLIAM). *The Music of Nature.* Last two
chapters, on " Rhythm " and " Quantity ".

1836 ? BROWN (GOOLD). *A Grammar of English Grammars* . . .
(New York).

Introduction dated " New York, 1836 ". Greatly enlarged in
subsequent editions, *e.g.* the tenth (1875). Not in British Museum
Catalogue, but Advocates' Library, Edinburgh, has a copy dated
1851. Of another book by him, *Institutes of English Grammar,*
I have not seen a copy.

1837 *seq.* HALLAM (HENRY). *Introduction to European Literature in the 15th, 16th, and 17th Centuries* (4 vols., 1837–9).

1838. *Eclectic Review* for April (" New Series " [the third],
Vol. III, p. 395 *seq.*).

1838. GUEST (EDWIN). *History of English Rhythms* (2 vols.).
New edition by Prof. Skeat in one volume (1882), which adds
some valuable notes and other matter.

1841. LATHAM (ROBERT GORDON). *The English Language.*
Section on " Prosody ". Much enlarged and altered in later
editions, *e.g.* 4th (1855) and 5th (1862), where it is Section VI.

*1841. HORNE (RICHARD HENGIST). *The Poems of Geoffrey
Chaucer ; modernized.* Introduction, pp. v–cxxxviii, nearly all
about verse.

1841. LONGFELLOW (HENRY WADSWORTH). *The Children of
the Lord's Supper,* from the Swedish of Tegner. In accentual
hexameters ; short preface.

Cf. Evangeline (1847), *Miles Standish* (1858), and several pieces
among his minor poems.

*1842. *North American Review,* July, Vol. LV. Review of
Longfellow's poems. Learned discussion. Rather contemptuous
of Longfellow's hexameters.

1844. HUNT (JAMES HENRY LEIGH). *Imagination and Fancy.*
Introductory essay, " What is poetry ? ", pp. 1–70.

*1844. " PHILHELLEN ETONENSIS." *Iliad,* Book I, tract, no
preface.

Scholarly, but slight. Accentual hexameters ; many weak
beginnings.

*1845. *Westminster Review* (April–June), Vol. 43. Article on "Homer's Iliad", reviewing Shadwell and others. Signed "M. C."

*1845. *Fraser's Magazine* for December (Vol. 36, p. 665). Dialogue on English Hexameters, probably by Whewell (see below, also 1847, 1849, and 1862).

Cf. later articles, Vol. 39 (pp. 103 and 342) on Clough, the second being again a dialogue.

*1846. LOCKHART (JOHN GIBSON). *Blackwood's Magazine*, Vols. 59 and 60.

In *March* number, hexameter translation from Iliad XXIV, by "N. N. T." (last letters of his three names), with short preface. And in *May* number ditto. Book I, with note mentioning Shadwell's version, just received.

Between these, in *April* number, some specimens of "rhymed hexameters and pentameters", and letter signed "M. L." (last letters of William Whewell), criticising, and giving specimens of his own.

*1847. LOWELL (JAMES RUSSELL). *A Fable for Critics* (New York).

—" talk of *iambs* and pentameters
Is apt to make people of common-sense damn metres."

*1847. *English Hexameter Translations, from Schiller, Göthe, Homer, Callinus, and Meleager* (oblong 8vo, Murray).

This is the only edition I have traced. Yet the book is referred to in *Fraser's Magazine* for December, 1845 (*cf.* above).

Verses by Whewell, Herschel, Hawtrey, Hare, and Lockhart (initials only given). Short preface signed "The Editor" [Whewell?]. Often quoted as "Cambridge hexameters". Purely accentual; inspiration German; Whewell and Herschel far largest contributors, but contains Hawtrey's often quoted lines beginning

"Clearly the rest I behold . . .".

*1847. MALDEN (HENRY). In *Proceedings of the Philological Society* (Vol. III, p. 95 *seq.*) paper "On Greek and English Versification".

Time is made synonymous with syllabic quantity.

*1847. HUMPHREY (ASA). *English Prosody* [not seen ; referred to by Goold Brown].

1848. CLOUGH (ARTHUR HUGH). *The Bothie of Toper-na-Fuosich* [*sic*], first edition, now *Tober-na-vuolich*. *Amours de Voyage*, 1849.

[Compare Appendix A, 1853.]

1848. ELLIS (ALEXANDER JAMES). *Essentials of phonetics*. Section 25 gives three degrees of quantity, *long, brief, stopt*. See also pp. 75–7.

An early work. Author afterwards President of Philological Society, and our highest authority on phonetics. *Cf.* his translation of Helmholz, and work on *Early English Pronunciation*. Also the following :
Speech in Song (Novello), N.D.
Pronunciation for Singers (Curwen), N.D.
" On the physical constituents of accent and emphasis ", in Philological Society's *Transactions* (1873–4, 8th paper). Presidential addresses in same volume. *Encyclopaedia Britannica* article " Speech-sounds " (1887).

1848. POE (EDGAR ALLEN). In *Southern Literary Messenger* for October and November (Vol. XIV), papers entitled " The Rationale of Verse ".
Reprints in *Works*, ed. Ingram (4 vols., Edinburgh, 1875), Vol. III; in *Poe's Best Poems and Essays*, ed. Cody (Chicago, 1903); and elsewhere.

1848. EVERETT (ERASTUS). *A System of English Versification* . . . (New York).

1848. WHELPLEY (JAMES DWIGHT). In *American Review* for May, pp. 484–92, paper on " The art of measuring verses ".

*1849. *Athenaeum* (April to July).
Letters about hexameters, notably those by M. Philarète-Chasles and W. W[hewell].

*1850. LANDOR (WALTER SAVAGE). *Fraser's Magazine* for June (Vol. 42, pp. 62–3), mock-Southeyan lines.

Germans may flounder at will over consonant, vowel, and liquid.

Heroic Idylls (1863), No. 132 of " Additional Poems ", burlesque lines " On English Hexameters ".

*1850. RITSO (F. H. I.) ? *The first three cantos of Homer : a metrical version most conformable* [*sic*], *though not identical in construction with, the original Greek hexameter.* (Rivington's) anonymous.
Short preface, not about metre. Quasi-anapaestic lines, poor. Republished 1861.

*1851. SMITH (ALBERT). In his periodical *The Month* (September), pp. 192–6.
" Syringaline : by Professor Long-and-short-fellow." Burlesque hexameters, showing how an English ear naturally treats the measure. Redundant syllables, no caesura, *etc., etc.*

1852. EVANS (R. W.). *A Treatise on Versification* (Rivington's).

*1852. KINGSLEY (CHARLES). *Andromeda :* a poem.
Perhaps our best piece of accentual hexameters, natural quantity being studied instinctively. No preface, but *cf.* his *Letters and Memories, edited by his wife,* Vol. I, Chap. XI, where his views are fully given, and some important rules suggested (pp. 347–9) for latter.

Cf. also one piece of accentual "Elegiacs" among his minor poems.

1852. DALLAS (ENEAS SWEETLAND). *Poetics.* Book III, chap. 2, on " Verse ".

*1853. *North British Review* for May (Vol. XIX, No. 37).

Review of Longfellow, Clough, and other hexametrists. Good historical remarks, little real criticism.

*1854. *Tait's Edinburgh Magazine,* Vol. XXI, p. 219.

Review of *Evangeline* and other hexameter pieces. Sensible article ; some good quotations. Scholars oppose, ordinary people like, such verse.

*1854. WALKER (WILLIAM SIDNEY). *Shakespeare's Versification* . . . Verbal matters mainly.

*1854. *Dublin University Magazine* for July (Vol. 44, No. 259). Article on "German Epics and English Hexameters ". Disappointing paper, no definite conclusions.

(*Cf.* in No. 260, some accentual hexameters by MORTIMER COLLINS.)

*1855. SPIERS (A. A.). *Study of English Poetry,* preceded by a treatise on English Versification.

In Preface he " attaches much importance " to his treatise, since " nothing satisfactory has . . . been yet given on the subject ". Yet his own view merely postulates absolute regularity of syllabic order.

1855. WHITMAN (WALT). *Leaves of grass,* first issue.

Cf. " author's copyright edition " (London, 1881), and others.

*1855. ANDERSON (JAMES R.). *The rationale of poetry.* By *Aliquis* (Kirkwall).

A slight tract. In Bodleian Library.

1856. MASSON (DAVID). *Essays Biographical and Critical : chiefly on English Poets.*

No. IX, " Theories of Poetry ", on Dallas, deals with origin of metre (p. 443 *seq.*).

No. X, " Prose and Verse," also suggestive.

Cf. edition of *Milton* (3 vols., 1882), essay or Milton's Versification (Vol. III, pp. 206–32).

*1857. BATHURST (CHARLES). *The difference in Shakespeare's Versification at different periods of his life.*

This and Sidney Walker's book (*ante*) began a long controversy.

1857. PATMORE (COVENTRY). In *North British Review* for August (Vol. 27, No. 53, pp. 127–61), article on " English Metrical Critics " [chiefly Guest and O'Brien].

Reprinted, with slight changes, as preface to his poem *Amelia* (1878) ; then as appendix to *Poems* (2 vols., 1900), and entitled " Essay on English Metrical Law " ; and now in the " Collective edition " of his *Works.*

*1857. CRAIK (GEORGE LILLIE). *The English of Shakespeare illustrated by a philological commentary on his Julius Caesar.*

Prolegomena, Section VI, the first few pages of which are on
" the mechanism of English verse ", more original than many
such, but not wholly trustworthy.

My reference is to the sixth edition (1878).

1859. MITFORD (J. T. F.), 2ND LORD REDESDALE (nephew of
William Mitford, *ante*). *Thoughts on English Prosody* . . . (tract,
Parker, Oxford and London). *Further thoughts* . . . (the same).

Slight ; by-thoughts of a man active in other fields. Wants
Universities to settle rules of quantity.

*1859. "OWEN MEREDITH" (2ND LORD LYTTON). *The
Wanderer.* See two pieces, " Sea-side Elegiacs " and " The
Shore ". The former is in ordinary pseudo-Classic metre, the
latter treats the same metre with great freedom. (Reprint in
" Canterbury poets ", pp. 47 and 49.)

*1860. BARHAM (THOMAS FOSTER). In Philological Society's
Translations (Berlin, 1860–1), Part I, pp. 45–62, " On Metrical
Time, and the Rhythm of Verse, ancient and modern."

A remarkable paper. Too many people think " numbers "
means number of syllables. Feet should be " uttered in successive equal periods of time " (p. 46), thus enabling us to " correct
the defects or excesses of natural quantity " (p. 53). Some sample
lines, but rules not stated.

[*Cf.* also Appendix A, 1843.]

*1861. ARNOLD (MATTHEW). *Lectures on translating Homer.*
Also postscript to same. " Last Words," dated 1862. Reprint of
both in " popular edition " (1896), and ed. Rouse (1905).

Amusing, suggestive, on literary points valuable, but not on
metrical matters. His own attempts at accentual hexameter
verse very poor.

*1861. NEWMAN (FRANCIS WILLIAM). *Homeric translation in
theory and practice. A reply to Matthew Arnold, Esq.* (Williams
and Norgate).

A scathing rejoinder to Arnold's persiflage. One or two remarks
on English verse.[1]

*1861. ALFORD (HENRY). *The Odyssey of Homer, in English
Hendecasyllable Verse.* Books I–XII. (Longmans.)

Short preface, praises hexameter, " but the merely English
reader can make nothing of it."

*1861–2. WORSLEY (PHILIP STANHOPE). *The Odyssey of
Homer translated into English verse in the Spens rian Stanza.* See
prefaces.

---

[1] *Cf. Miscellanies* (1869), now forming first vol. of same (Trübner).
Lecture II on "forms of poetry" has a few sentences about metre
(pp. 82–4). Our so-called anapaestic and dactylic metres are really in
"minuet or dancing time", and come very near to prose, *e.g.* "if
parallel rays come contrary ways, and fall upon opposite sides".

Preface to Vol. I deals with Pope's couplet, that to Vol. II with hexameter. Both slight.

*1861–2. *Modern Metre*, a monthly magazine.

Contains not a word about the technique of verse.

*1862. ANGUS (JOSEPH). *Handbook of the English Tongue*, Chap. VII on " punctuation and prosody ", the latter being pp. 343–65.

Metre is " the recurrence within certain limits of similarly affected syllables " (this from Latham). Classic names of feet are misleading [but he uses them].

Cf. The Handbook of English Literature [N.D.], pp. 274–83, for a similar " Note on English Versification ".

1862. ARNOLD (THOMAS). *A Manual of English Literature, historical and critical. With an appendix on English metres.*

See text. 7th edition revised (1897). The appendix is pp. 403–15 in former, pp. 633–44 in latter, edition.

1862. WHEWELL (WILLIAM). In *Macmillan's Magazine* for April and August (Vols. V, p. 487, and VI, p. 297) two papers on recent hexameter translations.

Whewell had been one of the first adopters, and continued a chief critic, of accentual hexameters on German models. Much good doctrine in these papers. The books reviewed are mostly those which follow in next entry.

1862 (and after). Various translations, viz. :

COCHRANE (JAMES INGLIS). *Iliad*, Book I, first, then rest (1867). Had translated much from German before.

DART (JOSEPH HENRY). The same ; whole *Iliad* (1866).

MURRAY (JOHN), Commander R.N. The same, combining quantity with accent.

LANDON (J. T. B.), Oxford. The same, and part of Book II later.

GRIST (W.). *Aeneid*, Book I, with preface.

SIMCOX (EDWIN W.). *Iliad* (whole), 1865.

HERSCHEL (SIR J. F. W.). *Iliad* (whole), 1866. (Book I in *Cornhill Magazine* for May, 1862.)

The above are grouped together, to give some faint idea of the mass of hexameters published during the " Sixties " of last Century. Cochrane and Herschel were assiduous cultivators of this metre. Most of them have prefaces about prosody. With them may be mentioned a pamphlet on the other side, *Homer and English Metre* (1862), by W. G. T. BARTER. All are interesting to students only.

*1862. LINDSAY (ALEXANDER WILLIAM CRAWFORD), Lord. *On the theory of the English Hexameter . . . A letter to William John Hamilton* (tract, 31 pages ; Murray).

Interesting references to unpublished criticisms by Frere, Morritt, and others. Neither his theory nor his practice is good. Much of it had been privately printed years before.

1862. MARSH (GEO. P.). *Lectures on the English Language* (Murray), ed. W. Smith, LL.D., and headed " The Student's Manual of the English Language ". The *Lectures* had previously appeared in America. A subsequent English edition, in 1868, is called the fifth edition.

1863–4. TENNYSON (ALFRED). [See Appendix A, 1864.]

*1864. DERBY (EDWARD), EARL OF. *The Iliad of Homer.* 2 vols. (Murray).

Translation in blank verse. Preface denounces the " pestilent heresy " of so-called hexameters.

*1866. SWINBURNE (ALGERNON CHARLES). *Poems and Ballads.* Accentual " Hendecasyllabics " (p. 233), " Sapphics " (p. 235). *Ditto, second series* (1878). " Choriambics " (p. 141).

It need hardly be said that all Swinburne's metrical work is full of suggestions to the student.

*1866. *Christian Remembrancer* Magazine for January (Vol. 51, No. 131, pp. 190–213).

Review of Dart's *Iliad.* Very amusing paper, claiming naturalness of " hexameter " in English.

*1866. LYTTON (EDWARD BULWER), First Lord. *Lost Tales of Miletus.*

Preface about metre : slight.

1869. HOOD (TOM), the younger. *The Rules of Rhyme.* (Hogg) [N.D.].

Unpretentious summary of common rules. Based on " Young poet's guide ", by whom I know not.

*1869. BREWER (R. F.). *A Manual of English Prosody.* [*Cf. infra,* 1893.]

1869. WADHAM (E.). *English Versification ; a complete practical guide to the whole subject.*

1869. ABBOTT (EVELYN A.). *Shakespearian Grammar.* Third edition (1870), " revised and enlarged ".

*1870 ? HARTE (BRET). *Parodies.* " The lost tails of Miletus." Reprint in *Poetical Works,* Routledge's pocket library, 1886. Shows a casual reader's notion of " hexameters ".

1870. SYLVESTER (JAMES JOSEPH). *The Laws of Verse, or principles of versification exemplified in metrical translations.* Tract (Longmans).

Spring's Début : a Town Idyll. See text, 1870 (foot-note).

*1871. FORMAN (HARRY BUXTON). *Our living poets : an essay in criticism.* On *feet,* pp. 46 and 66–7.

A few lines from Tennyson symbolled, and corrections suggested.

1871. EARLE (JOHN). *The Philology of the English Tongue.* Best edition (third), Clarendon Press, 1880.

Last chapter on " Prosody, or the Musical Element in Speech ".

1871. ABBOTT (E. A.) and SEELEY (J. R.). *English Lessons* *for English People*. Section on " Prosody ". Several later editions.

*1873. ASHE (THOMAS). *Edith, or Love and Life in Cheshire* (H. S. King, paper covers). In accentual hexameters, very ' trochaic '. No preface or notes.

Cf. Poems, complete edition (Bell, 1886), pp. 288–302, 322, *etc.* Several metrically interesting pieces ; one version of Horace, Odes I, 14, in an approximately imitative metre.

*1873–4. PHILOLOGICAL SOCIETY'S *Transactions*. (Berlin and London.)

Many very interesting papers, including first drafts of work by Mayor and Sweet (see 1886 and 1888), and the paper on " Accent and Emphasis " by A. J. Ellis (*cf. ante*, 1848).

1874. SYMONDS (JOHN ADDINGTON). Paper on " Blank Verse ", in *Fortnightly Review* for December. Reprinted in *Sketches and Studies in Italy* (1879), and separately (1880 and 1895).

1878. CONWAY (GILBERT). *A Treatise on Versification.*

*1879. MYERS (FREDERIC WILLIAM HENRY). *Essays, Classical and Modern* (2 vols., 1883) ; Essay on " Virgil ".

This eminent poet and scholar says, among other things : " Poetry . . . appeals to that mysterious power by which mere arrangements of sounds can convey an emotion which . . . no known laws can explain." " In poetry of the first order, almost every word . . . is raised to a higher power. It continues to be an articulate sound and a logical step in the argument ; but it becomes also a musical sound and a centre of emotional force " (p. 114).

1880. RUSKIN (JOHN). *Elements of English Prosody, for use in St. George's Schools.* Pamphlet (Allen).

1880. GURNEY (EDMUND). *The Power of Sound* (4to). Chapter XIX on " The sound-element in verse ".

Tertium Quid (2 vols., 1887). Vol. II, Chapter VII, on " the factors of melodic form ". As an instance of how prose can be metrical, quotes

> And so no force, however great,
> Can strain a cord, however fine,
> Into a horizontal line
> That shall be absolutely straight.

1880. LANIER (SIDNEY). *The Science of English Verse.* Boston, U.S.A. New edition (1898 ; Scribner, New York).

Cf. Shakespeare and his Forerunners (4to, New York).

*1880. MUNBY (ARTHUR JOSEPH). *Dorothy, a country story in elegiac verse. With a preface.* Anonymous.

The last paragraph alone of preface mentions metre.

Cf. Poems, chiefly lyric and elegiac (4to, 1901) ; several other pieces of " elegiacs ".

*1881. MOORE (GEORGE). *Pagan Poems.* Several pieces in accentual metres.

1881. HODGSON (SHADWORTH). *Outcast Essays and Verse Translations* (Longmans). Pp. 207–360 on " English Verse ".
Specimen verses in accentual hexameter and other metres.

*1881. BAYNE (PETER). *Two great Englishwomen, Mrs. Browning and Charlotte Bronte ; with an Essay on Poetry* . . . .
The Essay touches slightly on metrical forms, naming lyric as the oldest type of verse (pp. xxxiii–iv).

*1883. BROWNING (ROBERT). *Jocoseria,* poem of " Ixion ". In ordinary accentual elegiacs, treated with his usual roughness and power.

1883. JENKIN (FLEEMING). Papers in *Saturday Review* during February and March. Reprinted in *Memoir* by R. L. Stevenson, Vol. I, p. 149 *seq.*

1883. HOLMES (OLIVER WENDELL). *Pages from an Old Volume of Life* (Boston). A collection of essays, written 1857–81. Essay IX is on " The physiology of versification ".

*1884. BROWNE (GEORGE H.). *Notes on Shakespeare's Versification* (tract, Boston, U.S.A.).
For pupils, curt but full, phonetics insisted on. Says diphthongs often resolved.

1884. WITCOMB (C.). *On the structure of English verse.*

1884. LECKY (JAMES). Paper read before Philological Society, 19th December. See *Transactions* for 1885–7, " Proceedings," pp. ii–vi, where heads only given.

1885. WATTS-DUNTON (THEODORE). *Encyclopaedia Britannica,* Vol. XIX, pp. 256–73, article on " Poetry ". Separately published (1914).

1885. GUMMERE (FRANCIS B.). *A handbook of poetics for students of English verse* (Boston, U.S.A.). Part III, on " Metre ".
The beginnings of poetry (New York, 1901). Chap. II on "Rhythm as the essential fact of poetry ".
In *American Journal of Philology,* Vol. VII (1886), No. 25, pp. 46–78, article on " The translation of Beowulf, and the relations of Ancient and Modern English verse ".
In *Modern Language Notes* (Baltimore), Vol. I (1886), pp. 35–6 and 83–4, replies to a critic. In the same, Vol. II (1887), No. 6, pp. 159–62, a review of Prof. Mayor.
In *Child Memorial Volume* (Boston, 1897), essay on " The Ballad and communal poetry " [not seen].

1885. STEVENSON (ROBERT LOUIS). In *Contemporary Review* for April, "On some technical elements of style in literature." Reprinted in *Essays in the Art of Writing* (1905).

1885. GOODELL (THOMAS DWIGHT). In American Philological Association's *Transactions* for 1885–7 (Vol. XVI, pp. 78–103), on ' Quantity in English Verse ".

Cf. Chapters on Greek Metric (New York and London, 1901), and American *Nation* newspaper for October, 1911, where letters followed a review by him.

1885. RAYMOND (GEORGE LANSING). *Poetry as a representative Art* (New York and London). Fifth edition, 1903 (*ibid.*).

Rhythm and Harmony in Poetry and Music (*ibid.*, 1895).

Two volumes in a long series by same author.

1886. MAYOR (JOSEPH B.). *Chapters on English Metre.* London and Cambridge. Second edition, enlarged, 1901.

The new edition adds criticism of Skeat and Bridges (Chap. VI), Shelley (Chap. XIV), and " The English Hexameter " (Chap. XV).

A Handbook of English Metre (1903) repeats the teaching of the above in a condensed form for students.

1886. HALL (G. STANLEY) and JASTROW (JOSEPH). In *Mind* (Vol. XI, pp. 55–62).

Experiments in sound. The authors write from Johns Hopkins University, Baltimore.

1887. SAINTSBURY (GEORGE EDWARD BATEMAN). *History of Elizabethan Literature.*

Nearly all this writer's *Histories* contain remarks on metre, but all, and even his " Introduction " to a *Rhymers' Lexicon* (1905), are superseded for our purpose by his great *History of English Prosody* (3 vols., 1906–10), his *Historical Manual of English Prosody* (1910), and his *History of English Prose Rhythm* (1912). To these may be added *History of Criticism* (3 vols., 1900–4), *Loci Critici* (1903), and *Recent Studies in English Prosody* (tract, British Academy, Vol. IX, 1919).

1887. BRIDGES (ROBERT SEYMOUR). [*Cf.* Appendix A, 1903.]

Milton's Prosody, in Clarendon Press *Milton.* Separately published (tract, Oxford, 1889), and often since, in continually enlarged editions. With Stone's treatise (Oxford, 1901). A " final revised " edition now in press.

The Feast of Bacchus (poem, N.D.). Note at end on " stress-rhythm ".

Nero (*ditto*), Note to Part II.

Purcell Ode (1896), Preface.

Keats, in " The Muses' Library " edition, Introduction.

In the *Athenaeum* for January, 1904, three papers on " Miltonic Elision ".

In the *Musical Antiquary* for October, 1909, " A Letter to a Musician on English Prosody ".

The theories and practice of this writer have had much influence on younger poets.

*1887. MORRIS (LEWIS), SIR. *Songs of Britain.* " The Physicians of Myddfai."

In *Vox Clamantium* (1894), " Meliora."

Harvest-tide (1901). " The March of Man."

Accentual elegiacs, written freely.

*1887. BOWEN (CHARLES), RIGHT HON. SIR. *Virgil in English verse, Eclogues and Aeneid I–VI.*
Preface on hexameter, might succeed in hands of Tennyson or Swinburne, but he has adopted modified form.

1887. TOLMAN (ALBERT H.). In *Andover Review* (Boston, U.S.A.), Vol. VII, pp. 326–37, " The laws of tone-color in the English Language ". Reprinted, with next entry and other papers, in *Hamlet and other essays* (*ibid.*, 1906).
In *The 46th birthday of Sidney Lanier* (Baltimore, 1888), pp. 37–45, " Lanier's Science of English Verse."
In *Modern Language Notes* for April, 1891 (Vol. VI, p. 124), " The Dactylic Hexameter in English Prose."

1888. DAVIDSON (JAMES WOOD). *The Poetry of the Future* (New York).

1888. SWEET (HENRY). *History of English Sounds* (Oxford). Greatly enlarged from earlier edition (1874).
For analysis of English verse-structure, based on phonetic principles, see especially §§ 356–8, 609, 616, 939, 942 ; and *passim*.

1888. BLAKE (J. W.). *Accent and rhythm explained by the law of monopressures.* (Anonymous, Edinburgh.)

*1889. GARNETT (RICHARD). In *Universal Review*, paper " On translating Homer ". Reprinted in *Essays of an ex-librarian* (1901).
Chiefly disagrees with Matthew Arnold.

*1889. MEAD (WILLIAM E.). *The Versification of Pope in its relation to the Seventeenth Century* (Leipzig). [Not seen.]

1890. BROWNE (WILLIAM HAND). In *Modern Language Notes* (Baltimore), paper on " Certain considerations touching the structure of English Verse ".

*1890. SCHELLING (FELIX E.). In same as last entry, paper on " The inventor of the English hexameter " [Gabriel Harvey].
In *Publications of the Modern Language Association of America* (Vol. XIII, No. 2), " Ben Jonson and the Classical School ".
Poetic and Verse Criticism of the reign of Elizabeth (Philadelphia). [Two latter not seen.]

1890. WOOD (HENRY). In *American Journal of Philology* (Vol. XI), paper on " The Beginnings of the Classical Heroic Couplet in England ".

*1890. PALMER (GEORGE HERBERT). In *Atlantic Monthly* (Vol. 66, pp. 526–34), paper on " Hexameters and Rhythmic Prose ".
' Hexameters ' please because " less rigidly metrical " than other lines, but as "the prevalent movement of English verse is iambic ", a sort of " iambic recitative " might be better, though it is difficult to make accents sufficiently obvious without rhythm (pp. 526–8). A sample version of *Odyssey*, Book XXIII, occupies remainder of paper.

*1891. PARSONS (JAMES C.). *English Versification for the use of Students* (Boston, U.S.A.) ; second edition (1894).

*1891–5. *Versification ; a monthly magazine of measure and metre* ; later called " Poetry and prose ". In first number (p. 79), and in last number (p. 58), prosody referred to. Otherwise *nil.*

1892. CORSON (HIRAM), LL.D. *A Primer of English Verse, chiefly in its aesthetic and organic character* (Ginn & Co., Boston).

1892. STEDMAN (EDMUND CLARENCE). *The Nature and Elements of Poetry* (Houghton & Co., Boston and New York ; Cassell & Co., London). A " revised and extended " form of lectures delivered in Johns Hopkins University, and printed in the *Century Magazine* for 1892 (Vols. 43 and 44).

*1892. BELJAME (ALEXANDRE). *Enoch Arden* (Paris), with Introduction and Notes. The former has a good deal about metre.

*1892. HUMFREYS (MILTON W.). In American Philological Association's *Transactions* (Vol. 23, pp. 155–77), paper " On the Equivalence of Rhythmical Bars and Metrical Feet ".

A valuable paper. Mostly about Greek metre, but first five pages more general. Ridicules the idea that " a collection of accents " can make verse ; what does so is " quantity, *i.e.* time ". Rhythm founded on equal divisions ; the limit of enjoyed variations differ in different persons, but the wider they are the more difficult is rhythm to follow.

1893. BREWER (ROBERT FREDERICK). *Orthometry.* This is a greatly enlarged edition of a book mentioned before (1869). Pp. 280–96 give the fullest list of English writers on prosody that I have met with.

1893 *seq. Literary World.* Articles and discussions on metre ; *cf.* references in same paper of dates 5th and 26th June, 1903.

*1893. GAYLEY (CHARLES MILLS). *Classic Myths in English Literature* (Boston, U.S.A.). Original hexameter translations, pp. 261–6 and 278–81.

Representative English Comedies (1903), No. VIII, by R. Greene. Appendix on Greene's verse (pp. 503–11).

[*Cf. infra,* 1899 and 1908.]

1894. DIXON (WILLIAM MACNEILE). *English Poetry from Blake to Browning.*

1894. LARMINIE (WILLIAM). In *Contemporary Review* for November (Vol. 66, pp. 717–36), article on " The development of English metres ".

*1894. HALLARD (J. H.). *The Idylls of Theocritus* translated. (Longmans.) Second edition (Rivington, 1901).

Some excellent remarks on metre in preface.

1894. BOLTON (THADDEUS L.). In the *American Journal of Psychology* for January (Vol. VI, pp. 145–238), paper on " Rhythm ", experimentally investigated.

First part historical, after p. 178 experimental. Subsequent pages in same volume (310–11 and 488) hardly add anything of consequence.

*1895. WATSON (WILLIAM). *The Father of the Forest, and other poems.* Contains his fine " Hymn to the Sea ", in accentual elegiacs.

1895–1910. COURTHOPE (WILLIAM JOHN). *A History of English Poetry* (6 vols.).
Life in Poetry : Law in Taste (1901).

1895. WALLASCHEK (RICHARD). In *Mind* (New Series, Vol.IV, pp. 28–35), paper on " The difference of [*i. e.* between] time and rhythm in music.
Primitive Music (1893).

1896. BATESON (HAROLD DINGWALL). *An introduction to the study of English rhythms, with an essay on the metre of Coleridge's Christabel.* Tract (24 pages), reprinted from *Manchester Quarterly Review.* No name or date. Separately published (Manchester, 1904), with new Preface, and short list of writers on prosody.

*1896. SEAMAN (OWEN). *The Battle of the Bays* (Lane).
" Elegi Musarum ", parodying Mr. Watson.

1897. ROBERTSON (JOHN MACKINNON). *New Essays towards a Critical Method* (John Lane). Its predecessor (Fisher Unwin, 1889) bore the same title *minus* the word " New ".
[*Cf. infra,* 1911.]

*1897. MORGAN (GEORGE OSBORNE, SIR). *The Eclogues of Virgil. Translated into English hexameter verse* (4to).
Ordinary accentual lines. He fancied no one had preceded him in translating any of the Eclogues into this measure.

*1897. BEATTIE (A.). *Browning's Verse-form, its organic character.*
[American ? Not seen ; not in British Museum Catalogue.]

*1897–9. Much discussion of metre in papers like the *Spectator, Athenaeum, Literature, Saturday Review, Guardian, Bookman,* and even daily journals.

1898. SKEAT (WALTER WILLIAM). Paper on the " Scansion of English poetry ", read before Philological Society on January 14th, see *Transactions* for 1895–8, pp. 484–503. (This paper recasts and expands the argument contained in his *Chaucer,* Vol. VI, Introduction pp. lxxxii–xcvii).

*1898. MASSON (ROSALINE). *Use and Abuse of English* (small handbook, thin, Edinburgh), Chapters V and VI.
[These rules are probably based on the teaching of her father ; *cf. ante,* 1856.]

*1898. TARELLI (CHARLES CAMP). *Persephone and other poems.* (Macmillan).
" Persephone " is in accentual hexameters ; two other pieces, " Catullus " and " Juventus Anni ", in accentual elegiacs.

*1898. HARDY (THOMAS). *Wessex poems.* Harper (London and New York).

The first piece, " The Temporary and the All," seems intended for sapphic metre.

1898. KER (W. P.). In Philological Society's *Transactions* for 1899–1901, Part I, pp. 113–28, paper read December 2, 1898, on " Analogies between English and Spanish verse (Arte Mayor) ".

1898. LEWIS (CHARLTON M.). *The Foreign Sources of English Versification, with especial reference to the so-called iambic lines of eight or ten syllables* (Halle, paper covers).

The Principles of English Verse (New York and London, 1906).

*1898. TAMSON (GEORGE J.). *Word-stress in English. A short treatise on the accentuation of words in Middle-English as compared with the stress in Old and Modern English* (Halle, paper covers).

Mainly a collection of instances.

*1898. LANGBRIDGE (FREDERICK). In *The Girl's Own Paper* for May to September, " How to write verse."

Easy lessons by a critic who is himself a poet.

*1898. LAWTON (WILLIAM CRANSTON). *The Successors of Homer* (Innes & Co.).

Numerous accentual hexameters throughout the book.

In American Philological Association's *Proceedings* (Vol. 26, pp. 1–7), paper on " A national form of verse the natural unit for the thought ".

1899. BRIGHT (JAMES WILSON). In *Athenaeum* of 8th July, condensed report of paper " Concerning English Rhythm " read before our Philological Society.

In *Publications of the Modern Language Association of America* (Baltimore, 1899), Vol. XIV, pp. 347–68, article on " Proper names in Old English verse ".

In *An English Miscellany presented to Dr. Furnivall in honour of his 75th birthday* (Clarendon Press, 1901), paper " Concerning grammatical ictus in English verse ".

Cf. review in *Athenaeum* of 1st June, 1901. [See also *infra,* 1910.]

In *University of Texas Bulletin* of 1st January, 1917, paper on " Rhythmic Elements in English, with illustrations from Shakespeare."

1899. SPINGARN (JOEL ELIAS). *A History of Literary Criticism in the Renaissance, with special reference to the influence of Italy in the formation and development of modern classicism* (New York and London ; Macmillan).

Part III deals with English authors, see especially pp. 298–304 on " Classic Metres ".

Critical Essays of the Seventeenth Century (3 vols., 1908–9).

1899. HURST (A. S.) and MᶜKAY (JOHN). In *University of Toronto Studies,* psychological series (No. 3, pp. 57–75), article entitled " Experiments on time relations of poetical metres "

1899. SCRIPTURE (EDWARD WHEELER). In *Studies from the Yale Psychological Laboratory* (New Haven, Connecticut), Vol. VII, two papers by him as Director, viz. " Researches in experimental phonetics " (pp. 1–101), and " Observations on rhythmic action " (pp. 102–8).
Elements of Experimental Phonetics (1902). *Researches in Ditto* (Washington, 1906).

1899. GAYLEY (CHARLES MILLS) and SCOTT (FRED NEWTON). *An introduction to the methods and materials of literary criticism. The bases in aesthetics and poetics* (Boston, U.S.A.).
Invaluable handbook. Chap. VII deals with our subject.
[As these pages go to press, I see advertised, after twenty-one years, a second volume of the above, entitled *Methods and materials of literary criticism. Lyric, Epic, and Allied forms of Poetry.* By Charles Mills Gayley and Benjamin Putnam Kurtz (Ginn & Co., New York). It contains a " Bibliography of the History of Poetry " in 66 pages, and an Index of 64 pages.]

***1900.** YEATS (WILLIAM BUTLER). *The Shadowy Waters* (Play : 4to).
A sample of the " new " blank verse, based on the stress-rhythm theory, *e.g.*

> The mountain of the gods, the unappeasable gods.

Are such lines metrical ? Not an alexandrine.
In *Monthly Review* for May, 1902, paper on " Speaking to the psaltery " ; *cf. Academy* during May and June.
In *Contemporary Review* for October, 1906, " Literature and the Living Voice ".

***1900.** RITCHIE (FRANK). In *Longman's Magazine* for December, pp. 114–24, article on " Rhyme ".

1900. VAN DAM and STOFFEL. *William Shakespeare. Prosody and text. An Essay in Criticism. Being an introduction to a better editing and a more adequate appreciation of the works of the Elizabethan poets. By B. A. P. van Dam, with the assistance of C. Stoffel* (Williams & Norgate, N.D.).
Cf., by same authors, *Chapters on English Printing, Prosody, and Pronunciation (1550–1700). By Bastian A. P. van Dam and Cornelis Stoffel* (Heidelberg, paper covers, 1902, in series of *Anglitische Forschungen*).

***1901.** BEECHING (HENRY CHARLES). In the Furnivall Miscellany mentioned *ante* 1899, " A note upon Waller's distich " (pp. 4–9). Canon Beeching queries some popular ideas, and asserts that Marlowe always placed a strong syllable immediately before or after a weak one metrically accented, *e.g.*—

> Who builds a palace and *rams* up the gate.
> To whom you offer, and *whose* nun you are.
> Her mind *pure* and her tongue . . .

Cf. also in *Athenaeum* of 1st June, review of Prof. Bright [*ante*, 1899].

*1901. TEN BRINK (BERNHARD). *The Language and Metre of Chaucer* (translated). First edition of original, 1884.

Technical and professorial ; deals only with syllables.

1901. DABNEY (JULIA P.). *The Musical Basis of Verse* (New York).

*1901. BROWN (GEORGE DOBBIN). *Syllabification and Accent in the Paradise Lost* (John Murphy Co., Baltimore). Mentioned in text immediately after Prof. Bright, of whom he was a follower.

*1901. HUGUENIN (JULIAN). *Secondary Stress in Anglo-Saxon. Determined by metrical criteria* (John Murphy Co., Baltimore). Author was also a pupil of Prof. Bright.

1901. WALLIN (J. E. WALLACE). In *Studies from the Yale Psychological Laboratory*, Vol. VII, pp. 1–142 [the entire volume], " Researches on the rhythm of speech."

1901. TRIPLETT (NORMAN) and SANFORD (EDMUND C.). In *The American Journal of Psychology*, Vol. XII, No. 3, pp. 361–87, " Studies of rhythm and meter."

1901. SQUIRE (C. R.). In the same, No. 4, pp. 492–589, " A genetic study of rhythm."

*1902. ARCHER (WILLIAM). *Poets of the Younger Generation* (Lane).

Much about metre. Criticises Newbolt and Phillips (Stephen), also Milton's initial double trochees. Mentions discussion in *Star* newspaper from 16th August to 3rd September, 1898, between James Douglas and Phillips.

1902. WOODS (MARGARET LOUISA). *The Princess of Hanover.* Play (Duckworth). Short Preface on metre.

Cf. by same author, " The Builders," poem in *Cornhill Magazine* for December, 1902 ; and " The May morning, &c." in ditto for May, 1907, showing use of " stress-rhythms ".

1902. COTTERILL (H. B.). *Milton's Lycidas* (Blackie & Son). Appendix I (pp. 97–105) is " On rhythm in English verse ".

Homer's Odyssey : a line-for-line translation in the metre of the original (4to, illustrated, Harrap, 1911).

Good accentual hexameters, but these are not " the metre of the original ". Interesting preface (pp. vii–xviii).

An Introduction to the Study of Poetry (1882). Too vague to be of much use.

*1902. TODHUNTER (JOHN). In *Fortnightly Review* for February (pp. 346–60), article entitled " Blank verse on the stage ". Mainly about elocution.

1902. LIDDELL (MARK H.). *An Introduction to the scientific study of English Poetry. Being Prolegomena to a science of English Prosody.* New York (Doubleday, Page & Co.).

1902. MILLER (C. W. E.). *The Relation of the Rhythm of Poetry to that of the Spoken Language* (Baltimore). [Not seen.]

*1903. VICTORY (LOUIS H.). *Imaginations in the dust*, 2 vols. (Gay & Bird).

Essay in Vol. II on " elementary metres ".

1903. NEWMAN (ERNEST). In *The Weekly Critical Review* (Paris) for 3rd, 10th, 17th, and 24th September, a series of articles on " The rationale of English verse-rhythm ".

1903. OMOND (THOMAS STEWART). *A Study of Metre* (Grant Richards, now Moring). Earlier publications such as *English Hexameters* and *English Verse-structure* (both Edinburgh, 1897, now out of print), and " English Prosody " in *Gentleman's Magazine* for February, 1898, are superseded by the above, while later papers like "A hint on the reading of verse " (*Journal of Education* for June, 1908), *etc., etc.*, are hardly worth chronicling.

English Metrists [Part I] (Pelton, 1903), and [Part II], 18th and 19th Centuries (Oxford Univ. Press, 1907), are now recast into the present volume.

In *Essays and Studies by members of the English Association* (Clarendon Press, Oxford, 1912), paper on " Arnold and Homer ".

*1903. *American Quarterly, The.* Formerly called " Poetlore".

The title might cover discussion of metre, but such numbers as I have seen did not include this.

*1903. VAN DYKE (HENRY). In *Atlantic Monthly* for October (pp. 469–75), " Some remarks on the study of English verse."

*1904. COLLINS (JOHN CHURTON). *Studies in Shakespeare* (Arch. Constable & Co.).

1904. SMITH (G. GREGORY). *Elizabethan Critical Essays, edited with an Introduction by* (2 vols., Clarendon Press).

Referred to in Appendix A. This contains reprints of many treatises mentioned in my list, *e. g.* those of Gascoigne, Webbe, Puttenham, James VI, Campion, Daniel, *etc.*, besides several others ; it may be said to replace " Haslewood ". For some remarks on prosody, see Introduction, pp. xlvi–liv.

*1904. NORTHCROFT (GEO. J. H.). *How to write Verse : being studies in the principles and practice of the art of English verse-structure* (Smith's Publishing Co.).

1904. THOMSON (WILLIAM). *The Basis of English Rhythm* (paper covers, Holmes, Dunlop St., Glasgow). 2nd edition, 1906.

The Rôle of Number in the Rhythm of Ancient and Modern Languages, Notes for (1907).

Rhythm and Scansion (1911).

Scansion and Rhythm (1913).

Laws of Speech-rhythm (1914).

[The last four are slender tracts.]

*1904. POPE (GEORGE UGLOW). *Browning's ' Death in the Desert ' with Introduction and Notes* (12mo).

Appendix III (pp. 128–32), " Hints on the metre." Conven-

tional scansion. If metrical beat falls on an insignificant syllable
" it is a defect ".

1904. MILLER (RAYMOND DURBIN). *Secondary Accent in
Modern English Verse (Chaucer to Dryden)* (J. H. Furst & Co.,
Baltimore).

This, like the pamphlets of Brown and Huguenin *ante*, 1901],
is written by a pupil of Prof. Bright, and adopts his view without
question. [*Cf. infra*, 1910.]

*1904. SETZLER (EDWIN B.). *On Anglo-Saxon Versification,
from the standpoint of Modern-English Versification* (stiff paper-
boards, Furst & Co., Baltimore).

*1904. JOHNSON (CHARLES F.). *Forms of English Poetry*
(American Publishing Co.; and Sidney Appleton, London), [N.D.]

1904. ALDEN (RAYMOND MACDONALD). *English Verse . Specimens illustrating its principles and history* (New York).

An Introduction to Poetry, for students of English literature (ibid.,
1909).

The Development of the use of prose in the English Drama
(pamphlet, 4to, University of Chicago, 1909).

In the *Modern Language Review* for July, 1914 (pp. 298–308),
paper on " The mental side of metrical form ".

1904. SCOTT (FRED NEWTON). In *Publications of the Modern
Language Association of America* for June (Vol. XIX, which is
also XII of " new series ", No. 2, pp. 250–69), paper on " The
most fundamental differentia of poetry and prose ".

In *Publications . . . etc.*, as above (1905), Vol. XX (" new series ",
XIII), No. 4, pp. 707–28, paper on " The scansion of prose
rhythm ".

In *Modern Language Notes* for December, 1915, paper on " Vowel
Alliteration in modern poetry ".

In *Publications . . . etc.*, as above (1908), Vol. XXIII, No. 4,
" The Genesis of Speech."

[The above are all reprinted in pamphlet form.]

1905. RUDMOSE-BROWN (THOMAS B.). *Étude comparée de la
versification française et de la versification anglaise : l'alexandrin
et le blank verse* (privately printed, Grenoble ; paper covers).

*1 05. DIXON (RICHARD WATSON). *Last Poems* (Frowde).
" The silent heavens " (pp. 30–1).

Elegiacs by a capable poet, with redundant initial syllables and
resolved caesuras.

*1905. C. E. D. In *Cornhill Magazine* for November, lines
" On the Oxford Circuit ".

Poor, but free use of redundant initial syllables.

1906. SAINTSBURY (G. E. B.). *History of English Prosody*,
Vol. I. [*Cf. ante*, 1887.]

*1906. DAVIDSON (JOHN). *Holiday and Other Poems* (E.Grant
Richards). See Note at end, " On poetry."

*1906. BOURNE (GEORGE). In *Macmillan's Magazine* for June, pp. 541–9, article on " Rhythm and rhyme ".
*1906. KEARY (C. F.). In *Fortnightly Review* for November, pp. 811–26, " Some thoughts on the technique of poetry."
Suggestive, but too dogmatic, opinions taken for facts.
*1906. SCHOFIELD (PERCY). *The Triumph of Man. A Dramatic Poem* (Elliot Stock).
Contains some curious quasi-elegiac pieces on pp. 39–40.
*1906. MELTON (W. F.). *The Rhetoric of John Donne's Verse* (Baltimore).
Says ditto to the views of Prof. J. W. Bright (*ante*, 1899).
1907 *seq.* *Cambridge History of English Literature* (14 vols., 1907–16).
1907–8. THOMAS (WALTER). In *Modern Language Review* (Vols. II, pp. 289–315 ; III, pp. 16–39 and 232–56), papers on " Milton's heroic line viewed from an historical standpoint ".
Cf. Vols. IV, pp. 93–101 ; V, pp. 107–12.
*1908. ANDERSEN (JOHANNES C.). From *Transactions of the New Zealand Institute* the following (paper covers, Wellington, N.Z.) :
Metre (1908).
A Natural Classification of English Poetry (1909).
Classification of Verse (1910).
The Verse-unit (1911).
And Letters in the *Academy* between September 1908 and 1909, chiefly on the natural limit of line-length.
[During the same period there was much discussion about " inverted feet ".]
1908. BROWN (WARNER). *Time in English Verse Rhythm : an empirical study of typical verses by the graphic method* (New York).
In *Psychological Review* (University of California, Vol. XVIII, No. 5) for October, 1911, paper on " Temporal and Accentual Rhythm ".
1908. GAYLEY (CHARLES MILLS) and YOUNG (C. C.). *English Poetry : its principles and progress* (Macmillan Company).
I regret to have missed seeing this book. " Poetry " here probably = verse, as so often in U.S.A.
1909. WOODRAW (HERBERT). *A quantitative study of rhythm* (Columbia University, U.S.A.).
[Not seen, but said to state that a longer sound appears louder.]
1910. MORTON (EDWARD PAYSON). *The technique of English non-dramatic Blank verse* (Chicago).
In *Modern Philology* for April, 1907 (Vol. IV, No. 4), paper on " The Spenserian Stanza before 1700 " (*ibid.*).
In the same for January, 1913 (Vol. X, No. 3), paper on " The Spenserian Stanza in the Eighteenth Century " (*ibid.*).

And in *Modern Language Notes* for April, 1900 (Vol. XV, pp. 97–101), short paper on " A method of teaching Metrics ".

*1910. MAXIM (HIRAM STEVENS), SIR. *The science of poetry and the philosophy of language* (large 8ᵛᵒ).
Very dogmatic. Definitions of poetry in Chap. IV. " The periodical recurrence of any phenomenon constitutes rhythm " (p. 137). Thinks he can improve Shakespeare's and Milton's verse.

*1910. WOODBERRY (GEORGE EDWARD). *The Inspiration of Poetry* (Macmillan).
In first Chapter gives popular account of tribal origin of verse.

1910. SCHIPPER (JAKOB). *A History of English Versification* (Clarendon Press, Oxford).

1910. VAN DRAAT (P. FIJN). *Rhythm in English Prose* (Heidelberg), in series *Anglistische Forschungen*.

*1910. BRIGHT (J. W.) and MILLER (R. D.). [*Cf. ante*, 1899 and 1904.]
The elements of English Versification (Boston, U.S.A., and London, Ginn & Co.).
Professes to avoid controversy. Scans wholly by accents.

*1910. HUDSON (WILLIAM HENRY). *An Introduction to the study of literature* (Harrup).
Some definitions of poetry on pp. 82–4.

*1911. JACK (ADOLPHUS ALFRED). *Poetry and Prose : being Essays on modern English poetry* (Constable).
Speaks of " Byron's maddening habit of stressing the metre as if his readers were metrically deaf " (p. 124), and of " omitted accents " (p. 212).

1911. HALL (W. WINSLOW). *English Poesy : an Induction* (Dent & Sons).
The contents of this volume had appeared in a little periodical called *Brotherhood*.

1911. GOSSE (EDMUND). In *Encyclopædia Britannica*, article entitled " Verse ".

1911. *Edinburgh Review* for January, anonymous article, " English Prosody."

1911. ROBERTSON (JOHN MACKINNON). In *English Review* for June, paper on " Form in Poetry ". [*Cf. ante*, 1897.]

1911. *Quarterly Review* for July, anonymous article, " English Prosody."

*1911. RANSOME (ARTHUR). In *Oxford and Cambridge Review* for October (pp. 135–44), " Kinetic and potential speech."
Prose such as we all use is " purely kinetic speech " ; music is " purely potential speech " ; poetry is always a combination of both. The Symbolists tried to write poetry that should be purely potential.

1911. KALUZA (MAX). *A short history of English Versification from the earliest times to the present day* (George Allen & Co.).

1911. MATTHEWS (BRANDER). *A Study of Versification* (Boston, New York, and Chicago).

1912. NEWBOLT (HENRY). In the *English Review* for January, March, June, and August, articles entitled " A New Study of English Poetry ". Reprint as volume (Constable, 1920).

*1912. " T. D. R." In *Cornhill Magazine* for September, " Prosaic views on poetry."

Ignores the difference between verse and prose.

1912. VERRIER (PAUL). In the *Modern Language Review* for October (Vol. VII, pp. 522–35), remarks on " English Metric ".

Originating in a review (Vol. VI, pp. 230–40) by Prof. Rudmose-Brown of M. Verrier's great *Essai sur les principes de la metrique Anglaise* (3 vols., Paris, tallest 8ᵛᵒ), discussion was carried on at intervals till January, 1915.

I regret that confinement to writings in English prevents my noticing either the above great work, or numerous essays on English and French verse published by M. Verrier since 1895.

*1912. FITZHUGH (THOMAS). *Indo-European Rhythm* (Charlottesville).

The Indo-European Superstress and the Evolution of Verse (*ibid.*, 1917).

The Old-Latin and Old-Irish Monuments of Verse (*ibid.*, 1919).

The above are Nos. 7, 9, and 10 of " Bulletins of the School of Latin ", a list of others being given in the last-named (p. 38). My quotation in *ditto* (p. 16).

*1912. SHELLY (JOHN). In *Church Quarterly Review* for April (pp. 81–98), paper on " Rhythmical Prose in Latin and English ".

With this scholars should compare, in addition to Saintsbury's *History of English Prose Rhythm*, the following :

The Cursus in Mediaeval and Vulgar Latin (1910) and *Prose Rhythm in English* (1913), by Albert C. Clark (both Clarendon Press, Oxford).

In *Studies in Philology* (University of North Carolina) for January, 1912, " The Cadence of English Oratorical Prose," by Morris W. Crole.

Two papers in *Essays and Studies by members of the English Association* (*cf. infra*, 1913 and 1914).

The discussion is hardly for English readers. More to the purpose, because dealing more broadly with the subjective differences in our sense of rhythm, is the following book :

The Rhythm of Prose, by William Morrison Patterson (Columbia University Press, 1916).

1913. MACDONAGH (THOMAS). *Thomas Campion and the art of English Poetry* (Dublin).

1913. HARDIE (WILLIAM ROSS). In the *Proceedings* of the Classical Association of Scotland (small 4ᵗᵒ), paper entitled " What is Metre and how should it be taught ? " [Copies of the paper sold separately ?]

Res Metrica (Oxford University Press, 1920).

*1913. ELTON (OLIVER). In *Essays and Studies by members of the English Association* (Clarendon Press, Oxford, Vol. IV), paper on " English Prose Numbers ".

1914. MacCOLL (DUGALD SUTHERLAND). In same as the last (Vol. V), paper on " Rhythm in English Verse, Prose, and Speech".

1914. COWL (RICHARD POPE). *The Theory of Poetry in England, its development in doctrines and ideas from the Sixteenth Century to the Nineteenth Century* (Macmillan).

1915. COUTTS (FRANCIS), now LORD LATYMER. *Ventures in Thought* (Lane).

1916. ODLING (WILLIAM). *The Technic of Versification* (Parker, Oxford). [Died since this went to press.]

*1916. MILLER (DAYTON CLARENCE). *The Science of Musical Sounds* (Macmillan Company). [Not seen.]

*1917. LAMBORN (E. A. GREENING). *The Rudiments of Criticism* (Clarendon Press, Oxford).

An excellent little book where it treats of verse, by a writer who seems curiously unaware how much has been written upon his subjects by others.

1918. HOPKINS (GERARD MANLEY). *Poems of Gerard Manley Hopkins, now first published. Edited with notes by Robert Bridges, Poet Laureate* (H. Milford).

1918. JACOB (CARY F.). *The Foundations and Nature of Verse* (New York and Milford, London).

1918. CRAPSEY (ADELAIDE). *A Study in English Metrics* (Alfred A. Knopf, New York).

1918. SNELL (ADA L. F.). *Pause : A Study of its Nature and its Rhythmical Function in Verse, especially Blank Verse* (Ann Arbor, paper covers).

One of " contributions to rhetorical theory ", edited by Prof. F. N. Scott [*ante*, 1904].

1919. MONCRIEFF (CHARLES K. SCOTT). *The Song of Roland done into English in the original measure* (Chapman and Hall).

1919–20. BAYFIELD (MATTHEW ALBERT). *The Measures of the Poets* (Cambridge University Press, 1919).

A Study of Shakespeare's Versification (*ibid.*, 1920).

In *Modern Language Review* for April, 1918, paper on " Our traditional prosody and its alternative " ; also letters in *Times Literary Supplement* of 30th January and 13th February, 1919. There had been discussion of the subject in that newspaper during May and June, 1918.

See also *Educational Times* for June and July, 1920.

1920. FLINT (F. S.). *Otherworld Cadences* (Poetry Bookshop).

See discussion in *Athenaeum* during July, and compare *Cadences* (*ibid.*, 1916).

Three Critical Essays on Modern English Poetry (*ibid.*, 1920).

1920. ANDREWS (CLARENCE EDWARD). *The writing and reading of verse* (Appleton, New York and London).

This author has also compiled *A Collection of Trench Verse* (Appleton, New York).

1920. LOWELL (AMY). In *The Musical Quarterly* (U.S.A.) for January, paper on " Some Musical Analogies in Modern Poetry ".

[Not seen, but sharply criticised in next entry, apparently with reason.]

1920. JONES (LLEWELLYN). *Free Verse and its propaganda* , reprinted from *The Sewanee Review* of July and September.

1920. HICKEY (EMILY). In *Nineteenth Century and after* for December, paper on " The making of English Blank Verse "

A good account of the origin and early development of our heroic metre.

INDEX

[Where references are numerous, the more important are italicized. Bracketed figures refer to pages where the thing or person is not actually named.

It will be obvious that figures posterior to 270 denote pages in the Appendices.]

THE END